V&R

WERNER KAHL

New Testament Miracle Stories in their Religious-Historical Stetting

A Religionsgeschichtliche Comparison from a Structural Perspective

VANDENHOECK & RUPRECHT
IN GÖTTINGEN

Forschungen zur Religion und Literatur
des Alten und Neuen Testaments

Herausgegeben von
Wolfgang Schrage und Rudolf Smend

163. Heft der ganzen Reihe

Die Deutsche Bibliothek – CIP-Einheitsaufnahme

Kahl, Werner:
New Testament miracle stories in their religious-historical
setting: a religionsgeschichtliche comparison
from a structural perspective / Werner Kahl. –
Göttingen: Vandenhoeck und Ruprecht, 1994
(Forschungen zur Religion und Literatur des Alten und
Neuen Testaments; H. 163)
Zugl.: Diss.
ISBN 3-525-53845-6
NE: GT

Gedruckt mit Unterstützung des Forschungs- und Beihilfe-
fonds Wissenschaft der VG Wort

Acknowledgements

It is a pleasure to express my indebtedness to all those who contributed, in one way or the other, to the completion of this dissertation.

I am grateful to the following professors for various helpful suggestions at different stages of the thesis: Dr. Thomas Schmeller, Dr. Carl R. Holladay, Dr. John H. Hayes, Dr. Carol A. Newsom, Dr. Fred B. Craddock, and Dr. Gail O'Day. From among the staff of the marvelous Pitts Theology Library I would like to thank Mrs. Ida Boers for her efforts in locating and quickly ordering rare publications from far places. I am also indebted to Dr. M. Patrick Graham who read through the final draft and corrected many orthographic and stylistic errors. I also want to thank Mrs. Dorcas Doward whose computer I was allowed to use and who always patiently helped me solve my problems with the program.

My very special thanks go to two persons who have had a real impact on my life beyond their involvement in the production of the thesis. Professor Dr. Hendrikus Boers, my *Doktorvater*, not only introduced me to the field of text-linguistics but also into computer-work. His interest in the topic of the dissertation, his critical and sharp mind, the constant eagerness and openness to discuss any issue related to the topic as well as his *Gastfreundschaft* provided an atmosphere of cooperation which was both intellectually challenging and deeply satisfying. That our contact necessarily will be less intensive now is the only regrettable effect of the completion of the thesis.

Naila Khairallah, *ḥabibati*, helped me enormously through creative discussions of various issues and with typing the manuscript in her free time. Without her tireless support, the production of the thesis would have taken much longer.

I also would like to express my thanks to the Graduate Division of Religion at Emory University, the *Kirchenkreis Essen-Nord* (Superintendent H. Gehring), *Kirchenkreis Essen-Süd* (Superintendent K. Gillert) and the *VG Wort* for financial assistance.

Thanks also go to professors Dr. W. Schrage and Dr. R. Smend for including this work in the FRLANT series. I dedicate this study *in Dankbarkeit* to my parents, Mr. and Mrs. Friedrich and Marlies Kahl.

Table of Contents

List of Symbols

AS	active subject
BNP	bearer of numinous power
D	demonstration
DLL	demonstration of lack liquidated
FGL	formgeschichtlich
FGS	Formgeschichtliche Schule
InvBNP	invocation of the bearer of numinous power
iNP	instrumental narrative program
L	lack
LL	lack liquidated
MNP	mediator of numinous power
NAP	narrative anti-program
NP	narrative program
P	performance
PNP	petitioner of numinous power
Prep	preparedness
PrepBNP	preparedness of the bearer of numinous power
RGL	religionsgeschichtlich
RGS	Religionsgeschichtliche Schule
RSC	representative of subject of circumstance
S	sanction
SC	subject of circumstance
→	indicator of the direction of narrative development

I. Nature and Significance of the Topic

This thesis intends to illumine the *structure* and *function* of the NT miracle traditions by assessing them in their religionsgeschichtliche (RGL)[1] context. The focus will be on miracle narratives preserved in the synoptic tradition. A *textwissenschaftlich* sound method provides the means for the RGL comparison to be undertaken. Even though it will be possible to relate to scattered insights of traditional RGL approaches, the usual way of RGL comparison will be challenged. While German biblical scholarship especially, standing in the enlightened tradition set forth by J. S. Semler and J. Ph. Gabler, claims to be both critical and "wissenschaftlich" (scientific), an overview on the history of the interpretation of the synoptic miracle narratives shows that this claim has barely been taken seriously. In fact, research on the synoptic miracle tradition has seldom met the standards of being either critical or "wissenschaftlich." "Critical" scholarship implies, first of all, the notion of critique and reflection upon one's own motivations, beliefs, unquestioned presuppositions, and prejudices. Scholarly work on the synoptic miracle narratives has been deeply shaped by dogmatically motivated preliminary decisions. A most alarming example is the unfortunate racist, anti-Jewish remarks by G. Delling in his *Jesu Wunder in der Predigt* (1940).[2] Other scholars disqualify their contributions by religious biases: only Jesus Christ performed miracles, while the other ancient miracle workers were magicians or charlatans. Still others tend to impose too quickly their modern world views onto the material in deciding what was and was not possible for Jesus. I will refrain from passing judgments of this kind. Nevertheless, I presuppose that the synoptic miracle stories as narratives reflect the cultural environment and belief-systems of the narrators more accurately than they provide reliable historical information about the

---

[1] RGL does not refer specifically to the *religionsgeschichtliche Schule*, but to every interpretation which depends on the religious background of the NT texts.

[2] (Dresden/Leipzig: Verlag C. L. Ungelenk). Cf., e. g., concerning miracles ascribed to rabbi Eliezer, 13: "Unglaublich sind die Märchen, die den Rabbinen in den Mund gelegt werden, jedes Sinnes bar; sie können nur als krankhafte Phantastereien beurteilt werden ... An diesen Geschichten, die mit Religion gar nichts mehr zu tun haben, kann die Keuschheit der neutestamentlichen Wunderberichte deutlich werden. Die der Rabbinen sind vielfach nur Ausgeburten von Wunschträumen ... Die Wunderberichte der jüdischen Überlieferung werden bezeichnenderweise immer phantastischer, rachsüchtiger, lächerlicher."

activities of Jesus of Nazareth.[3] The narrators of miraculous performances by Jesus consciously or unconsciously made use of a certain language, certain motifs and forms which were familiar to other miracle traditions of the ancient world.[4]

Structural analysis, by guaranteeing methodologically neutral investigative procedures, allows the intercultural comparison of narratives on a fundamentally *textwissenschaftliche* foundation.[5] The most important insight from a structural perspective concerns the distinction between a morphic and a phenomic level. With *morphic* I refer to the underlying structure of a narrative, whereas *phenomic* denotes motifs on the surface of texts. On the basis of morphological analysis it will, for example, be possible to answer as accurately as possible – and without arbitrarily dissecting given texts – the question of origin and acculturation ("ecotypification") of miracle traditions within the synoptic gospels.

RGL comparison (in particular of the synoptic miracle-tradition) has often been marked by a kind of "parallelomania," the punctual juxtaposition of motifs, in which the non-NT material is considered only as quarry without taking the functions of those motifs in their respective contexts into account. The result of such a fundamentally "unwissenschaftliche" method has been a distorted presentation of the synoptic material against its RGL background. Only after having established the characteristics of each tradition comprehensively can one pursue the question whether the style, vocabulary, motifs, etc., in short, the *narrative performance* of a synoptic miracle tradition, more closely resembles an ancient *pagan* or *Jewish* tradition. Only through an unbiased comparison with other miracle traditions will it be possible to identify the *specifics* of the synoptic miracle narratives.

The *focus* of this thesis will be on the elaboration of the surface structure and the functions of those narratives which relate a miraculous restoration to health in the broadest sense and the raising of dead persons.

---

[3] Cf. J.B. Pritchard, "Motifs of Old Testament Miracles," in *Crozer Quarterly* 27 (1950), 109: "When miracles do appear, little is added to our knowledge of the person about whom the story is told, but much is implied about the character and beliefs of the folk audience for whom the miraculous stories were devised."

[4] Ibid., 109: "The miracle story is a mirror in which is reflected the life of those who tell or hear it."

[5] To be sure, by stressing the "Wissenschaftlichkeit" of the applied method, I do not claim to engage in an "objective" investigation. Any claim of objectivity is an illusion. Nevertheless, *within* the limits that I set concerning the selection of the material, structural analysis seems to reduce the possibility that personal preferences of the investigator distort the historical evidence.

II. Survey of the History of Research

1. Introductory remarks: the prelude of the Religionsgeschichtliche approach

The following survey of the history of research is a selective presentation of scholarly contributions that tried to arrive at a more accurate understanding of the synoptic miracle stories by assessing them against their Jewish and pagan backgrounds. Certain periods in the history of research concerning this issue can be distinguished, although clear-cut delineations would result in a distorted picture of the historical facts, since one development merges into another.

The initial stages of a RGL approach to the NT date back to the seventeenth century.[1] Thus, Wettstein's collection of parallels to the NT from the Jewish and pagan Greco-Roman world for his critical edition of the NT (1751/52)[2] does not mark a totally new beginning. The scholarly tradition which began to take seriously the claim that the NT could only be understood against the background of its environment had preceded Wettstein by about a century. But it was only towards the end of the eighteenth century, after J. S. Semler[3] distinguished the Word of God from "Holy Scripture" and "Theologie" as "Wissenschaft" from "Religion" as "Gottvertrauen" (trust in God), and after J.Ph. Gabler[4] distingu-

---

[1] Cf. W.G. Kümmel, *Das Neue Testament. Geschichte der Erforschung seiner Probleme* (Freiburg/München: Verlag Karl Alber, 1958), 37, who refers to *Anmerkungen zum Neuen Testament* by H. Grotius (1583–1645) and to *Horae Hebraicae et Talmudicae* by J. Lightfoot (1602–1675). The comparison of Jesus' miracles with those of other figures of the ancient world is manifest already for the second century. It had its function in the apologetic-polemic confrontation between Christians and heathen. Cf. Justin Martyr, *Apol.* I 22:6; 54:10.

[2] J. Wettstein, Novum Testamentum Graecum (Graz: Akademische Druck- und Verlagsanstalt, 1962), Vol. I/II. Cf. the information on the cover-page: "Nec non commentario pleniore ex scriptoribus veteribus Hebraeis, Graecis et Latinis Historiam et vim verborum illustrante."

[3] J.S. Semler, *Abhandlung von freier Untersuchung des Canon; nebst Antwort auf die tübingische Vertheidigung der Apocalypsis* (Halle 1771), reprinted in H. Scheible (ed.), *Texte zur Kirchen- und Theologiegeschichte*, Heft 5 (Gütersloh: Gütersloher Verlagshaus Gerd Mohn, 1967). Cf. G. Hornig, *Die Anfänge der historisch-kritischen Theologie. Johann Salomo Semlers Schriftverständnis und seine Stellung zu Luther* (Göttingen: Vandenhoeck & Ruprecht, 1961).

[4] J.Ph. Gabler, "De iusto discrimine theologiae biblicae et dogmaticae redundisque recte utrisque finibus," in Th.A. and J.G. Gabler, *Jo. Phil. Gableri Opuscula Academica*, Vol. II

ished biblical from dogmatic theology and differentiated between pure and true biblical theology, that a historical-critical exegesis of biblical writings – (supposedly) free of dogmatic preliminary decisions – could be established. With regard to research on the biblical writings the Enlightenment led to the rejection of the orthodox presupposition, "scriptura sacra est verbum dei."[5] The way was paved for an investigation of the "sensus litteralis historicus."[6]

2. D. Fr. Strauss:
Das Leben Jesu, kritisch bearbeitet (1835/36)

D.Fr. Strauss took the demand for an undogmatic and historical-critical investigation of the biblical writings seriously and, for the nineteenth century, to an extreme. His mythic critique – as opposed to the rationalistic and the supranaturalistic interpretations of the NT – is an attempt to get at the "eternal truth" *behind* the mythically-shaped stories of the gospels. The early Christians, according to Strauss, lived in a cultural environment full of myth and thus shared the mythical expressions of the ancient world. Although he was familiar with miracle accounts of the pagan Greco-Roman tradition which provide detailed similarities to the miracle stories of the gospels,[7] Strauss claimed that it was the OT which had the determining influence on the shaping of the gospel accounts in general, and the miracle stories in particular. The reason for this assumption was that Judaism of the first century C.E. expected miraculous performances by the messiah who, in so doing, would resemble Moses and the prophets, who also performed such miracles. Furthermore, Strauss maintained that the demonology in the synoptics represents an "unvermischt jüdische Denkweise," whereas the writings of Josephus, Justin, and the later rabbis were "Produkt nun der Ausgleichung jener jüdischen Vorstellungen ... mit diesen griechisch-römischen."[8] Consequently, for the narration of the resuscitation of the young man at Nain (Lk 7:11–16), the OT (1 Kings 17:17–24; 2 Kings 4:18–37) provides "die geeignetsten Vorbilder."[9] The account of the resuscitation

---

(Ulm 1831), 179–198. Cf. H. Boers, *What is New Testament Theology? The Rise of Criticism and the Problem of a Theology of the New Testament*, Guides to Biblical Scholarship, New Testament Series (Philadelphia: Fortress Press, 1979), 23–38.

[5] Semler, *Abhandlung*, vol. II, 598.
[6] Hornig, *Anfänge*, 80.
[7] Cf., e.g., Strauss, *Leben Jesu*, Vol. II, 12–13, 29, 38, 173, 191.
[8] Ibid., 13.
[9] Ibid., 172.

of a young bride by Apollonius from Tyana,[10] on the other hand, is interpreted as a linear "Nachbildung der evangelischen [Erzählung]."[11] This assessment of Philostratus' life of Apollonius rests upon the thesis elaborated by Strauss' teacher *F.Ch. Baur* in *Apollonius von Tyana und Christus. Ein Beitrag zur Religionsgeschichte der ersten Jahrhunderte nach Christus* (1832),[12] namely, that Philostratus had used the gospel accounts deliberately for his biography of Apollonios.[13] Notwithstanding Strauss' assumption that the OT was prevalent in the shaping of the synoptic miracle accounts, and in some tension with his general view of the late and syncretistic character of Josephus, he does occasionally point to motifs incorporated in the works of Josephus and also pagan writers in order to illuminate the *Jewish-Palestinian* "Zeitmeinung" concerning demons.[14] This inconsistency becomes evident in his discussion of the RGL background of the "Walking on the Water" pericope (Mk 6:45–52 parr): Strauss refers here to OT passages (2 Kings 2:14; 6:6) as well as to pagan writers of the Greco-Roman environment (the lives of Pythagoras by Porphyrios and Jamblichos, and Lucian's Philopseudes). He concludes, "... der gemeine Volksglaube lieh manchen Thaumaturgen die Fähigkeit, auf dem Wasser zu gehen (reference to Lucian, Philopseudes 13): und es erscheint so die Möglichkeit, daß sich aus allen diesen Elementen und Veranlassungen eine gleiche Sage auch über Jesum bilden konnte ..."[15]

3. The Religionsgeschichtliche approach

During the decade before World War I, about seventy years after Strauss' *Leben Jesu*, the scholarly opinion on the RGL background of the synoptic miracle-stories was reversed: the OT was rejected as a source of influence. The new focus was on the assessment of the NT against its *Hellenistic* background, pagan as well as Jewish. The scholars of the Religionsgeschichtliche Schule (RGS) were preoccupied with the endeavor to grasp what Strauss called the "gemeine Volksglaube" during the time of Jesus. Terms like "Volkstümlichkeit," "volksmässig," "Volkssprache," "Kleinliteratur," etc., found throughout the publications of the RGS, manifest the new interest in the cultural environment of the NT.

---

[10] Philostratus, Vita Apol. IV 45.
[11] Strauss, *Leben Jesu*, Vol. II, 173, fn. 57.
[12] [2]1876.
[13] Cf. Strauss, *Leben Jesu*, vol. II, 29.
[14] Ibid., 38 with respect to Mk 5:1–20 parr.
[15] Ibid., 191.

This fresh approach was stimulated by sensational discoveries of papyri and archaeological sites.

With regard to miracle stories, contributions of classical philologists played an important role in the evaluation of Greco-Roman miracle traditions, while excluding the synoptic-material from their analyses. *R. Reitzenstein*'s introductory remarks to his *Hellenistische Wundererzählungen* (1906)[16] are characteristic of the *Zeitgeist* among the RGL scholars: while studying two miracle-embracing hymns incorporated in the Acts of Thomas, he comes to the "surprising conclusion" that his material was derived from pagan sources. Thus, he commits himself to the task of describing "die hellenistische Wundererzählung in ihrer Entwicklung" before engaging in an interpretation of the Acts of Thomas.[17] After having generally shown the *dependence* of Christian apostle-acts on pagan aretalogies as their models, Reitzenstein draws the following conclusion:

> In den drei großen Epochen frühchristlicher Wundererzählung, der Evangelienliteratur, an die sich als Spätling die kanonische Apostelgeschichte reiht, den apokryphen Apostelakten, endlich der Mönchsliteratur treffen wir die gleichen literarischen Zusammenhänge mit der hellenistischen Literatur. Sie gibt den literarischen Grundcharakter, sie gibt die Art der Polemik ..., sie gibt endlich einzelne Vorbilder, welche direkt übernommen werden. Freilich verlangt jeder dieser Fälle eingehendste Untersuchung, ob nur gleiche Grundanschauung, volksmässige d. h. legendarische ... Nachbildung oder planmässiges schriftstellerisches Schaffen vorliegt.[18]

This quotation has been given in extenso because the reasoning demonstrated here is symptomatic for the RGL as well as for the slightly later formgeschichtliche (FGL) approach to the synoptic miracle stories: the conclusion based on analogy.

Reitzenstein's warning that the nature of similarity needs to be investigated carefully for each individual case would often be neglected due to the broad lines of historical development as drawn by NT scholars of the RGS and the Formgeschichtliche Schule (FGS). This is not true for the philologist *O. Weinreich* who, in 1909, published a careful study, *Antike Heilungswunder. Untersuchungen zum Wunderglauben der Griechen und Römer*.[19] Although he does not cover the NT miracle tradition,[20] his study is still of great importance for NT scholarship. First of all, Weinreich is hesitant about establishing *literary* dependencies. He rather

---

[16] (Stuttgart: B. G. Teubner Verlagsgesellschaft).
[17] Reitzenstein, *Wundererzählungen*, 1.
[18] Ibid., 82–83.
[19] GVV (Giessen: Verlag A. Töpelmann).
[20] Ibid., V.

assumes that *similar forms* of miracle accounts arise "spontan, auf Grund gemeinsam gegebener Voraussetzungen menschlichen Denkens."[21] A certain "Gesetzmässigkeit der Mirakel"[22] is established through the identification of recurring topoi[23] that are shared by three main groups of healing miracle stories, namely healings by means of the hand, through dreams or by means of statues and pictures. Consequently, he rejects Baur's (and Strauss') claim that Philostratus made use of the gospel accounts for his life of Apollonios. From his RGL perspective, he goes so far as stating that "nicht einmal wörtliche Anklänge zu [der] Annahme [literarischer Abhängigkeit] führen [sollten], denn Loci communes sind gerade in der Wundererzählung häufig."[24]

A. Deissmann's programmatic publication *Licht vom Osten. Das Neue Testament und die neuentdeckten Texte der hellenistisch-römischen Zeit* (1908)[25] makes extensive use of newly found inscriptions, ostraca, and papyri to illuminate the "volkstümliche" environment of early Christianity. Quoting the Epistle to Diognetus, he argues that "concerning land, language, and customs, the Christians are not different from other people"[26] and defines as the future task for NT scholarship: "Die Typen des volkstümlichen Erzählstils müßen durch die antiken Kulturen hindurch verfolgt werden, insbesondere die Wundererzählung, der Rettungs- und der Heilbericht ..."[27] In this regard Deissmann also emphasizes the importance of ancient Judaism.[28]

P. Fiebig devoted himself to the evaluation of rabbinic material for a better understanding of Jesus and the synoptics.[29] In 1911 he made three major contributions concerning the RGL background of the synoptic miracle tradition: two collections of rabbinic and "ancient" (Greek and

---

[21] Ibid., VI.

[22] Ibid., VIII.

[23] Ibid., 195–201: Failure of physicians, the sudden and paradox character of the miracle, and the notion that more miracles could be told.

[24] Ibid., 171–72, fn. 2.

[25] (Tübingen: J.C.B. Mohr [P. Siebeck], [2/3]1909).

[26] Epistle to Diognetus, 5.

[27] Ibid., 303–04.

[28] Ibid., 304; cf. 302, fn. 4.

[29] Cf. P. Fiebig, *Aufgaben der neutestamentlichen Forschung in der Gegenwart* (Leipzig: Hinrichs, 1909); idem, *Rabbinische Formgeschichte und Geschichtlichkeit Jesu* (Leipzig: Hinrichs, 1931), 44, fn. 1. Cf. also his numerous publications on that topic: e.g., "Die Wunder Jesu und die Wunder der Rabbinen," in *ZWTh* 54 (1912), 158–79, *Der Erzählungsstil der Evangelien im Lichte des rabbinischen Erzählungsstils untersucht, zugleich ein Beitrag zum Streit um die "Christusmythe"* (Leipzig: Hinrichs, 1925); *Die Umwelt des Neuen Testamentes. Religionsgeschichtliche und geschichtliche Texte, in deutscher Übersetzung und mit Anmerkungen versehen, zum Verständnis des Neuen Testamentes* (Göttingen: Vandenhoeck & Ruprecht, 1926), cf. also the following footnotes.

Latin) miracle stories in their original languages[30] and a comparative
study on the rabbinic material.[31] Although he acknowledges the importance of an investigation of the pagan Greco-Roman miracle tradition –
since Palestine in the time of Jesus had in part been "hellenistisch-grie-
chisch-römisch bestimmt" – his focus is on "das Nächstliegende,"[32] the
Jewish-rabbinic milieu as it can be established from the rabbinic material.
Fiebig stresses that a comparative study first of all requires a comparison
of *form*, and only secondarily an analysis of content.[33] Furthermore, a
sound comparison presupposes a study of texts as units (and not in terms
of motifs) in their original languages. In his own analysis and comparison
of the material, Fiebig is in particular concerned with proving the existence of Jesus.[34] He arrives at the following seven conclusions: 1) it was
a common practice for Jews in Palestine of the first century C.E. to tell
miracle stories about their rabbis; 2) the previous point gives proof, "daß
es falsch ist, die Wunder Jesu allein oder vorzugsweise aus seiner Messia-
nität abzuleiten;"[35] 3) one characteristic feature of the rabbinic material
is that the miracles appear to be "Gebetserhörungen," and as such are
deeds of God rather than of humans. With regard to the gospels, he
points out that in Joh 11 (the Feeding-stories and the story of the Stilling
of the Tempest) there were traces of prayer performed by Jesus in connection with miracles, which is not evident in Mk 6:30–44 parr and
6:45–52! Nevertheless, in an attempt to minimize this obvious difference
between the NT and rabbinic sources, he distorts the evidence when he
writes: "Dieser Sachverhalt [miracles as God's answer to prayers] ist
auch im N.T. lebendig, hier begegnen jedoch *auch* Wundergeschichten,
in denen von einem Gebet Jesu *nicht ausdrücklich* gesprochen wird;"[36]
4) the OT is only *one* source for the gospel miracle tradition but not
in the sense of literary dependency; 5) the tannaitic as well as the NT
miracle stories were originally orally transmitted; 6) concerning the narrative style, Fiebig detects numerous similarities: shortness of expressions, direct speech, OT quotations, neglect of date and localization,

---

[30] *Rabbinische Wundergeschichten des neutestamentlichen Zeitalters in vokalisiertem Text*,
Kleine Texte für Vorlesungen und Übungen 78 (Bonn: A. Marcus und E. Webers Verlag,
1911); *Antike Wundergeschichten zum Studium der Wunder des Neuen Testamentes*, Kleine
Texte für Vorlesungen und Übungen 79 (Bonn: A. Marcus und E. Webers Verlag, 1911).
[31] *Jüdische Wundergeschichten des neutestamentlichen Zeitalters unter besonderer Berücksichtigung ihres Verhältnisses zum Neuen Testament bearbeitet. Ein Beitrag zum Streit um die
"Christusmythe"* (Tübingen: J.C.B. Mohr [P. Siebeck], 1911).
[32] Ibid., 71–72.
[33] Ibid., 6.
[34] Ibid., 75–77.
[35] Ibid., 72.
[36] Ibid., 72–73, fn. 4 (italics are mine). Cf. idem, "Wunder Jesu," 173.

etc.; 7) in a comparison of different "types" (Arten) among rabbinic miracle stories by means of the *content criterion*, Fiebig distinguishes miracles of punishments, for rain, etc. He observes that the NT does not contain rain-miracles. For stories of exorcism, healing of the lame or the blind, and the use of spittle, Fiebig refers to non-rabbinic Hellenistic literature.

A. Schlatter, who was also engaged in the assessment of the gospels from the perspective of rabbinic literature, disputes in *Das Wunder in der Synagoge*[37] the results of Fiebig's research. He claims 1) that Judaism of the first century C.E. does not provide models for the miraculous activity ascribed to Jesus, and 2) that the absence of prayer in the synoptic miracle accounts illustrates the superiority of Jesus over the rabbis, "Von Jesus wurde das Wunderbare getan, nicht nur empfangen."[38] Only by means of a definition of miracles that *excludes* exorcisms, healings through conjuration, or prayer, can Schlatter uphold his judgment that neither Josephus nor the Mishna contain *any* miracle story which dates back to the first century C.E. The miracles that are told in the Mishna, according to Schlatter, are solely a means of proving Scripture. Only after 200 C.E., the rabbinic corpora tend to include more and more miracle stories about rabbis. Furthermore, he distinguishes the Palestinian from the Babylonian Talmud with regard to historical value: although the Babylonian Talmud contains plenty of material about Palestinian miracle workers, it needs to be kept in mind that it was completed only around 500 C.E. in Babylon. While Fiebig presupposes that the Talmudic stories ascribed to different rabbis date back to the time of the respective rabbis, Schlatter radically disputes all evidence of rabbinic miracle stories for the first century C.E.

Neither Fiebig's nor Schlatter's approach does justice to the rabbinic material. Their work serves to sustain two different preliminary decisions: in the case of Fiebig[39] the closeness of Jesus to the rabbis, and in the

---

[37] (Gütersloh: Bertelsmann, 1912).

[38] Schlatter, *Wunder*, 53.

[39] Cf. also the dispute beteen Fiebig and Dibelius on the importance of the rabbinic material for an assessment of the synoptic miracle stories: e.g., very drastically in [2]*RGG* 5 (1931), article "Wunder," 2040–2041, where Fiebig ("II. B. Im Judentum") expresses his conviction that the Jewish miracle narratives of the NT era, as preserved in rabbinic literature, were of great importance for the understanding of the NT, and where Dibelius declares in the immediatly following paragraph ("III. Im NT"): "Dabei liefert das rabbinische Judentum der ersten christlichen Jahrhunderte nicht sehr viel gleichartiges Material." For their different opinions concerning this subject, cf. also Fiebig and Dibelius' public dispute "Rabbinische und evangelische Erzählungen. Eine Diskussion," in *ThB* 11 (1932), 1–12.
Concerning an accurate assessment of the rabbinic material cf. J. Neusner, "Current Events in the Study of Rabbinic Sources," in idem, *Invitation to the Talmud. A Teaching Book* (New York: Harper & Row, [2]1984), 329–50.

case of Schlatter, the superiority of Jesus Christ over the rabbis. Schlatter's faith in Jesus the Christ distorts the historical evidence. This becomes obvious, e. g., in his arbitrary statement that not Jesus but the rabbis made use of magical devices.

4. Religionsgeschichte from the perspective of the Formgeschichtliche Schule

RGS and FGS merge into each other.[40] From the beginning RGL scholars occasionally made use of formal criteria in comparing literature (e. g., Weinreich and Fiebig). A difference of focus emerges with the FGS, which is a distinguishable development within the RGS. The recognition of the originally oral and dispersed character of the synoptic material[41] leads to the analysis of simple units (pericopes) and their distinct forms. From there the FGS moves to RGL comparison with the intention of establishing "Sitze im Leben" of different "Gattungen" (genres) at the preliterary stages of the synoptic tradition.[42] The two fundamental works of the FGS by Dibelius and Bultmann are presented and discussed here only with regard to their treatment of the miracle stories.[43]

It is *Bultmann*'s intention in *Die Geschichte der synoptischen Tradition* of 1921[44] to trace the *history* of the "Einzelstücke der Tradition."[45] Since "Sitz im Leben" is "ein soziologischer Begriff, nicht ein ästhetischer" (and one should add "und auch nicht ein historischer," as it subsequently becomes), he declares categorically, "daß die formgeschichtliche Arbeit weder in einem ästhetischen Betrachten, noch in einem deskribierenden und klassifizierenden Verfahren besteht ..."[46] With regard to the synoptic miracle narratives, Bultmann allots the material to two different genres: *Apophthegmata* and *Wundergeschichten*. Apophthegms are "Stücke, deren Pointe ein in einem kurzen Rahmen gefasstes Jesuswort

---

[40] Cf. Kümmel, *Geschichte*, 259–414.

[41] Cf. K. L. Schmidt, *Der Rahmen der Geschichte Jesu. Literarkritische Untersuchungen zur ältesten Jesusüberlieferung* (Berlin: Trowitzsch & Sohn, 1919).

[42] Cf. Dibelius, "Diskussion," 1.

[43] Even though Dibelius' *Die Formgeschichte des Evangeliums* (Tübingen: J. C. B. Mohr [P. Siebeck], 1919/²1933/⁶1971) appeared earlier than Bultmann's *Die Geschichte der synoptischen Tradition*, FRLANT, N. F. 12 (Göttingen: Vandenhoeck & Ruprecht, 1921/⁹1979), I will first discuss Bultmann's work, since Dibelius' contribution is considered here in its significantly enlarged, second edition.

[44] ²1931: revision. Bultmann's *Geschichte* is accompanied by an *Ergänzungsheft* (Göttingen: Vandenhoeck & Ruprecht, 1958. ⁵1979 is prepared by G. Theißen and Ph. Vielhauer).

[45] Bultmann, *Geschichte*, 4.

[46] Ibid., 4.

bildet."[47] This genre is subdivided into "Streit- und Schulgespräche" and "Biographische Apophthegmata." The former group includes five pericopes in which a healing is the cause for a dialogue or saying of Jesus (Mk 3:1–6 parr; Lk 14:1–6; 13:10–17; Mt 12:22–37 parr; Mk 2:1–12), whereas only one miracle narrative (Lk 17:11–19) is included in the latter. In addition, two stories (Mk 7:24–31 par; Lk 7:1–10 par) are treated separately and taken as variants due to the following common features: the Syro-phoenician woman and the centurion from Caphernaum are both heathen; both ask for Jesus' help for a sick child; and, in both cases, Jesus is persuaded by a clever comment from the parents. Furthermore, these are the only *healings at a distance* narrated in the synoptics. In a similar way, Bultmann interprets the three Sabbath-healing stories (Mk 3:1–6 parr; Lk 13:10–17; 14:1–6) as variants of the same motif (Sabbath-healing). For Lk 17:11–19, he claims dependence on Mk 1:40–45. With regard to the apophthegms he observes that the saying-material is generally older than the respective "frames." All other pericopes which narrate a miracle are gathered as narratives under the heading "Wundergeschichten," a genre that is subdivided into "healing-miracles" and "nature-miracles."

Concerning the "style" of the synoptic miracle stories, Bultmann presents a collection of motifs, which is enriched by parallels from ancient Jewish and pagan as well as modern sources (folktales from all over the world). These motifs are organized according to their appearance either in the exposition, the performance, or the recognition of the success of the miracle. The RGL parallels illustrate the milieu which shaped the development of the synoptic miracle tradition. Due to the oral tradition process, "volkstümliche Wundergeschichten und Wundermotive" found their way into the synoptic material.[48] OT miracle stories are almost totally rejected as a source for the NT miracle narratives.[49]

Bultmann is primarilly interested in the oral and "volkstümliche" process that lies behind the actual texts as collected in the synoptics. In reaction to a common overestimation of the OT as literary source for the NT, Bultmann moves to the other extreme when he considers RGL parallels from a pagan Hellenistic environment and even includes material beyond that era from all over the world, while disregarding very close OT analogies, as is the case for 1 Kings 17:10–16; 2 Kings 4:1–7, and 4:42–44. In so doing, Bultmann does not take into account that also

---

[47] Ibid., 8.

[48] Ibid., 246. Bultmann relies here on the observations of W. Bousset, *Kyrios Christos. Geschichte des Christusglaubens von den Anfängen des Christentums bis Irenäus* (Göttingen: Vandenhoeck & Ruprecht, 1913. ²1926), 60–62.

[49] Bultmann, *Geschichte*, 245–246.

OT stories that were regularly read and translated in synagoges must have had some impact on the shaping of the minds of a Jewish audience.[50]

M. Dibelius' approach in *Die Formgeschichte des Evangeliums* is deliberately "constructive."[51] The synoptic material which contains miracle narratives is allotted either to *Paradigmen* (short, self-contained units with the focus on the *word* of Jesus for usage in sermons) or to *Novellen* (novelettes, detailed narratives with the focus on the miraculous performances of Jesus, which share many features with non-Christian miracle stories and were used for purposes of propaganda and missionary activity). The paradigms are more historically reliable and older than the novelettes. Although this distinction between paradigmatic and novellistic miracle stories corresponds to Bultmann's two genres "Apophthegmata" and "Wundergeschichten," the two scholars disagree sharply with regard to the distribution of the material among the two groups. Dibelius criticizes Bultmann's category "Wundergeschichte" as solely based on "das inhaltliche Kriterium, daß hier wie dort ein Heilungswunder geschieht,"[52] whereas his own approach takes style-critical observations seriously. Especially for the novelettes, Dibelius points out a detailed list of topics which the NT miracle stories have in common with other ancient material. He notes a certain "Artverwandtschaft zwischen den evangelischen Novellen und nichtchristlichen Wunder-Erzählungen"[53] and arrives at the following conclusion: "Die Novellisten haben fremde Züge oder Handlungen übernommen, aber sie haben sie christianisiert."[54] Dibelius investigates this relationship between Christian and non-Christian material more closely in a chapter devoted to "Analogien." For the rabbinic material, he distinguishes "Theodizee-Legenden" (focus is not on the miracle as such, but the "*Verkündigung eines göttlichen Rechts, nach dem der Mensch leben soll*"[55]) from "Personallegenden" (which honor certain rabbis). For the latter group it is characteristic that the miracle-rabbis are not "große Könner, sondern große Beter."[56] Dibelius

---

[50] Cf., concerning the public discussion of the OT in Palestine of the first century C.E., D. Ben-Amos, "Narrative Forms in the Haggadah: Structural Analysis" (Ph.D. diss, Indiana University, 1967), 26–28.

[51] Cf. only Dibelius, *Formgeschichte*, 77 where he takes Mk 7:36–37; 6:52; and 8:26 as secondary, since they could not function as "der stilgerechte Abschluß einer Novelle." Cf. also the critique of E. Fascher, *Die formgeschichtliche Methode. Eine Darstellung und Kritik. Zugleich ein Beitrag zur Geschichte des synoptischen Problems*, BZNW 2 (Gießen: A. Töpelmann, 1924), 78: "Dibelius bietet demnach nicht Formgeschichte, sondern Stilkritik mit einer Geschichtskonstruktion."

[52] Dibelius, *Formgeschichte*, 52.

[53] Ibid., 90.

[54] Ibid., 99.

[55] Ibid., 144.

[56] Ibid., 146.

further observes that only the less known among the rabbis are depicted as miracle-workers in rabbinic literature (reference to Chanina ben Dosa). Although the rabbinic and the NT novelettes occasionally share the same topic, there is a major difference: the NT novelette basically narrates a divine epiphany, whereas the rabbinic legends illustrate the power of a pious, praying rabbi from a human perspective.

In a comparison with ancient pagan miracle-stories, Dibelius discusses healing-miracles by Asclepios. His analysis of stelai from Epidauros leads to the following reconstruction of the generation of these miracle-collections: the stereotypical form of part of the material is due to a redaction by cultic officials, who basically processed inscriptions on presents for the divine healer.[57] However, the stelai also contain healing-stories which are bare of stereotypical form. Here Dibelius shows the probability that these accounts represent folkloric miracle-narratives that had only secondarily been connected to the Asclepios-cult in Epidauros.[58] Every group originally had a different "Sitz im Leben." The oldest material as represented in the inscriptions on presents of consecration had the intention of expressing the gratitude of the healed and, at the same time, to honor the divine healer. The folkloric novelettes, on the other hand, have their origin in the "Lust am Mirakel."[59] The final redaction of the fourth century B.C.E., which stereotypically shaped the inscriptions of consecration and added folkloric miracle stories to the stelai, was motivated by the intention to propagate the Asclepios cult. Dibelius discovers an analogous tradition process to the synoptic material. For both the Asclepios and the synoptic traditions, the stereotypical accounts or paradigms contain material which only later had been reshaped for a new purpose. Furthermore, both traditions then added folkloric miracle stories which share the same topic as miracle novelettes.

Different from Bultmann's motif-focused collections, Dibelius discusses the rabbinic parallels, as well as the Epidauros material, against their respective backgrounds and within their respective contexts. In his comparison, Dibelius is more interested in the recognition of analogous developments within different traditions and in different functions or "Sitze im Leben" of pericopes than in the juxtaposition of motifs. This approach makes it possible for him to point out similarities as well as differences in various miracle traditions and prevents a distortion of the non-synoptic material. Nevertheless, his analysis of the synoptic miracle stories is problematic, especially his categorization of the material in paradigms

---

[57] This is obvious for no. 1 on stele A.
[58] Examples: no. 25, 46, and 47 on stele B.
[59] Dibelius, *Formgeschichte*, 171.

of a pure and a "minder reinen" type, and in novelettes,[60] which is based
on questionable "stilkritische" observations (e. g., length, pious or world-
ly character, etc.).

E. Fascher, in his presentation and critique of the "formgeschichtliche
Methode" (1924),[61] criticizes Dibelius for confusing style with form and
calls for a strict distinction between the two: "Es muß bei jeder Stoff-
gruppe das Konstitutive als Form, das Ornamentale als Stil bezeichnet
werden, doch so, daß durchgehends die Form dem Stil übergeordnet
ist."[62] Fascher's demand which already anticipates observations made by
structuralist inspired NT scholars some fifty years later, is taken seriously
by O. Perels in Die Wunderüberlieferung der Synoptiker in ihrem Verhältnis
zur Wortüberlieferung.[63] It is Perels' intention to prove that the "Aus-
spruchsgeschichten" (Apophthegmata) had a common history of tradition with the narratives (including the miracle stories) rather than with
the sayings material. He thus challenges Bultmann's allotment of apophthegms to the tradition of the words of Jesus. His basic criticism of
both Bultmann and Dibelius is that their categories are determined by
subjective observations (Dibelius) or are oriented to criteria concerning
content (Bultmann). Both lack an objective, purely formal approach.

Perels argues that from a formal perspective the structure of miracle
and pronouncement stories is basically the same. It is only a secondary
question "ob ein Anliegen oder eine Erwiderung durch direkte Rede,
indirekte Rede oder Handlung ausgedrückt ist."[64] The following observations account for the structural similarity of these two narrative types:
"Menschen kommen zu Jesus und wollen etwas von ihm."[65] Jesus reacts
by healing the sick and answers the questioners. His enemies are sometimes demons but at other times tempting questioners. It is the powerful
word of Jesus that effects healing and provides answers.

Perels then goes on to investigate the influence of non-synoptic miracle
traditions on the synoptic accounts in order to illuminate the tradition
process of the synoptic material. He does not present a detailed or
systematic analysis but makes some general observations: the closest parallels to the NT miracle narratives are to be found in the OT Elijah/Eli-
sha-cycles. He observes an identical structure and also identical themes
of miracle narratives for both traditions: resuscitation, healing of a leper,
and feeding-miracles. As to differences, he points out that the OT mi-

---

[60] Ibid., 40.

[61] For the full title see fn. 56.

[62] Fascher, Methode, 211. Fascher defines style as "subjektive Ausdrucksweise" (209)
and distinguishes "ornamentale" from "konstitutive Motive" (210).

[63] (Stuttgart: Kohlhammer, 1934).

[64] Perels, Wortüberlieferung, 59.

[65] Ibid., 67.

racles are effected by prayer (and thus are performed by God), lack a word of power, and include miracles of punishment. The topic "removal of the audience," which the synoptics share with the OT, is a typical Jewish feature. With regard to rabbinic material, Perels points out a similar structure to the synoptics concerning accounts of exorcisms but emphasizes as a major difference that the rabbinic miracle stories tend to sustain a certain doctrine.[66] With Schlatter he rejects Jewish-rabbinic influences on the synoptic material. However, he does not take into account that the NT pronouncement stories which include miracles also focus on teaching. With regard to the Hellenistic-pagan world he observes that Mark and Luke share more common motifs with pagan miracle accounts than does Matthew. As a useful rule Perels states that only when a synoptic miracle story shares more than a single common feature with the pagan (and other) material, is it sound to allot that story to the same milieu.[67] In applying this rule, he finds only *five* synoptic miracle accounts as of pagan origin[68] (in contrast to the impression left by Bultmann's catalogue of motifs!). Perels concludes that brief miracle narratives of a dialogue form mark the beginning of the synoptic miracle tradition on Palestinian soil. Under Hellenistic influence the miracle stories subsequently became more and more detailed.[69]

While Fascher and Perels accepted the basic presuppositions of the FGL approach and present modifications on that basis, *L. J. McGinley* in his critique of Dibelius and Bultmann in *Form-Criticism of the Synoptic Healing Narratives. A Study in the Theories of Martin Dibelius and Rudolf Bultmann*[70] declares from the beginning that the "Gospel accounts form a separate class in the history of literature,"[71] which prohibits conclusions of analogy based on comparative studies in the area of popular traditions. According to him, it was the dominant intention of the early Christian

---

[66] Cf., for a much more detailed and differentiated analysis, Dibelius, *Formgeschichte*, [2]1933.

[67] Cf. O. Weinreich, "Gebet und Wunder. Zwei Abhandlungen zur Religions- und Literaturgeschichte," in *TBA*, 5. Heft (Stuttgart: Kohlhammer Verlag, 1929), 169–464, reprinted in idem, *Religionsgeschichtliche Studien* (Darmstadt: Wissenschaftliche Buchgesellschaft, 1968), 1–298, who concludes on the basis of motif-accumulations and lexographical studies that the "door-opening miracles" in Acta belong to the pagan Hellenistic world. Cf. also G. Delling, "Botchaft und Wunder im Wirken Jesu," in H. Ristow, K. Matthiae (ed.), *Der historische Jesus und der kerygmatische Christus. Beiträge zum Christusverständnis in Forschung und Verkündigung* (Berlin: Evangelische Verlagsanstalt, [3]1964), 389–402, esp. 400.

[68] Mk 5:1–20: The Gerasene Demoniac; 7:31–37: Healing of a Deaf Mute; 8:22–26: Blind Man of Bethsaida; 9:14–29: Healing of an Epileptic Child; and Lk 7:11–17: The Widow's Son at Nain.

[69] But cf. V. Taylor, *The Transformation of the Gospel Tradition. Eight Lectures* (London: MacMillian and Co., 1933. [2]1935) 202–09, according to whom the reverse is true.

[70] (Woodstock,Maryland: Woodstock College Press, 1944).

[71] Ibid., 5.

community to preserve historical facts about Jesus. Furthermore, the "Jewish and Greek converts to the primitive Christian community did not introduce into the synoptic tradition the motifs of the rabbinic and Hellenistic traditions they knew so well."[72] Consequently, McGinley's comparison of the synoptic healing stories with those of rabbinic, and pagan traditions focuses on the *differences* between them. His "truly Christian"[73] exegesis leads him to declare the superiority of the gospel healing accounts over against the non-Christian parallels. Even though he provides a detailed survey of synoptic, rabbinic and "Hellenistic" healing traditions by means of lists, his conclusions distort the historical evidence due to his value judgments: the rabbinic and Hellenistic healing stories are determined by superstition and exaggeration whereas the synoptic "style is real, sober."[74] From this perspective, McGinley is able to interpret a single phenomenon differently for the three traditions under investigation: he observes, for example, that spittle occurs in connection with healing not only in the synoptics but also in rabbinic and "Hellenistic" sources, but for Jesus spittle is not a magical means of healing but "definitely symbolic," since Jesus heals "because He wills the cure,"[75] even though the accounts in Mk 7:31–37 and 8:22–26 do not contain words of Jesus which refer explicitly to his will. McGinley's approach is a deliberate retreat to a pre-critical view.[76] However, his systematic juxtaposition of the three traditions according to content, style, and the three topics: exposition, miracle, and conclusion, could provide a limited, but nevertheless useful means of RGL comparison.

5. Recent developments

The FGL approach, especially with respect to the conclusions drawn from RGL parallels, quickly provoked reactions from scholars who vehemently refused to accept the method and results of the FGS. Particularly disturbing to these scholars were the conclusions, if one followed the FGS,[77] that, due to the presupposition of the generative creativity

---

[72] Ibid., 153.

[73] Ibid., 154.

[74] Ibid., 152.

[75] Ibid., 150.

[76] Concerning this assessment of means in the healing activity of Jesus, cf. already Arnobius, *Adv. gent.* 1:48–49, from ca. 300 C.E.

[77] E.g., G. Petzke, "Die historische Frage nach den Wundertaten Jesu dargestellt am Beispiel des Exorzismus Mark. IX. 14–29 par," in *NTS* 22 (1975/76), 202, who determines as "Sitz im Leben" for the synoptic miracle story the missionary activity of the early Christian communities "in der religiösen Auseinandersetzung der hellenistischen Welt."

of early Christian communities, hardly any information about the activity of Jesus seemed to be reliable, or, alternatively, if one took seriously the RGL parallels,[78] that Jesus was a magician like so many among his contemporaries. Apologetic voices called for a different assessment of the RGL parallels. Following McGinley, *H. van der Loos'* voluminous publication on *The Miracles of Jesus*[79] is another retreat to pre-critical exegesis. For example, although he recognizes that spittle, touch by hand, spellings, and "looking up into heaven" are magical devices widely employed as miracle-techniques in the ancient world, he is of the opinion that Jesus did not use these devices in a magical but rather in an accommodative sense.[80]

O. *Böcher* intends to illumine the RGL background of the Christian baptismal sacrament from a purely demonological and magical perspective. His focus is on ancient exorcist practices with respect to healings, which allows a discussion of his contributions in the context of this study. In *Dämonenfurcht und Dämonenabwehr. Ein Beitrag zur Vorgeschichte der christlichen Taufe*,[81] Böcher gives a comprehensive collection of ancient Jewish (OT until Rabbinic times) and pagan Greco-Roman references for exorcist practices. His investigation is shaped by the hypothesis that ancients believed that the world was pervaded by demons. With respect to sickness and healing, this means: "Ganz allgemein ... gilt für die Antike, daß man keine natürliche Ätiologie der Krankheiten gekannt hat, sondern alle Krankheiten auf die Einwirkungen von Dämonen zurückführte. Deshalb sind die Heilmethoden der antiken Medizin *durchweg* exorzistisch-apotropäischer Natur."[82] This statement is too general to be true. The so-called empirical-scientific medicine which was still more or less interwoven with a magical or astrological worldview in antiquity, but nevertheless rejected demonology,[83] can be traced back at least to Hippocrates in the fifth century B.C.E.[84] The Hellenistic pathologists Herophilos from Chalcedon[85] and Erasistratos from Iulis[86] developed human anatomy[87] in the third century B.C.E. Thus the foun-

---

[78] E.g., M. Smith, *Jesus the Magician* (San Francisco: Harper & Row, 1978).

[79] SNT 9 (Leiden: E.J. Brill, 1965). Also following McGinley concerning the assessment of the synoptic miracle stories is L. Sabourin, "Hellenistic and Rabbinic 'Miracles'," in *BThB* 2 (1972), 281–307.

[80] Van der Loos, *Miracles*, 305–36.

[81] BWANT 5. Folge, Heft 10 (Stuttgart, etc: Verlag W. Kohlhammer, 1970).

[82] Ibid., 152; italics are mine.

[83] Cf. H.C. Kee, *Medicine, Miracle and Magic in New Testament Times* (Cambridge: Cambridge University Press, 1986), 27–64.

[84] Cf. F. Kudlien, article "Hippocrates aus Kos," in *Der Kleine Pauly*, 1975, Vol. II, 1169–72.

[85] Cf. idem, article "Herophilos. 1," in ibid., 1109.

[86] Cf. idem, article "Erasistratos," in ibid., 343–44.

[87] Cf. idem, article "Anatomie," in *Der Kleine Pauly*, 1975, Vol. 1, 335–36.

dation was laid for the development of surgery which reached its climax in the first century C. E.[88] Böcher disregards this interest in the natural and causal, explitly non-demonological, understanding of sickness in antiquity. A non-demonological understanding of sickness, and consequently non-exorcist methods of healing, are also evident in the miraculous healings of Asclepios as testified in the inscriptions from Epidauros, dating from the fifth to the third century B. C. E. The healing-dreams at Epidauros describe *surgery* of a kind, which was not possible for human physicians of that time.

Böcher's onesidedness leads to a distortion of the historical evidence. One example may suffice to demonstrate that he does not take the ancient material seriously, but makes it fit his preconceived opinion. In an effort to show the responsibility of demons for *all* kinds of sickness in antiquity, Böcher suggests that the blindness of Tobit[89] is fundamentally caused by demonic influence, in spite of the textual evidence which clearly describes his predicament as the result of an accident. From Böcher's perspective, even accidents cannot be understood without the involvement of the demonic.

Böcher devotes a second volume, *Christus Exorcistica. Dämonismus und Taufe im Neuen Testament,*[90] to the localization and interpretation of demons and exorcism in the NT. Following his procedure for the collection of the respective RGL material, Böcher presupposes, "Da auch Jesus und seine Apostel in den Krankheiten das Werk schädlicher Dämonen sahen, kann Heilung *nur* die Vertreibung von Dämonen bedeuten."[91] In order to reduce this argument to absurdity it suffices to point to his interpretation of Lk 22:51. Since he interprets *all* sickness and especially the "laying on of hands" or "touching" in the context of an allegedly all pervasive ancient demonology and exorcism, he lists Lk 22:51 as evidence for "exorzistische Heilung durch Berührung."[92] Again, the predicament of the δοῦλος τοῦ ἀρχιερέως is clearly not caused by any demonic force, but is the result of fight. Consequently, Jesus does not exorcize any demon when ἁψάμενος τοῦ ὠτίου ἰάσατο αὐτόν.

A more differentiated investigation of healing and exorcism narratives is necessary in order to do justice to the ancient material. That Böcher distinguishes *Heilungswort*[93] from *Exorzismuswort*[94] indicates an incon-

---

[88] Cf. idem, article "Chirurgie," in ibid., 1150.
[89] Tobit (LXX) 2:1–10.
[90] BWANT, 5. Folge, Heft 16 (Stuttgart, etc.: Verlag W. Kohlhammer, 1972).
[91] Ibid., 77, italics are mine.
[92] Ibid., 81.
[93] Ibid., 86.
[94] Ibid., 87–88.

sistency in his system, but does point in the right direction. Another methodological weakness, typical for many RGL investigations, is that Böcher does not distinguish between classical Greek and late Hellenistic periods. Thus he is unable to recognize that for the Greco-Roman world outside "of Jewish circles there is no clear account of exorcism until the third [second? (Lucian!), W. K.] century C. E. when Lucian and Philostratus appear on the literary scene."[95]

A new approach towards a FGL investigation of the synoptic miracle tradition is G. *Theißen's Urchristliche Wundergeschichten* (1974).[96] Theißen investigates the synoptic miracle tradition from a synchronic, a diachronic, and a functional perspective. For the synchronic investigation, Theißen makes use of a structuralist method as it had been proposed for NT scholarship by *E. Güttgemanns*,[97] by applying Saussure's linguistic distinction between "langue" and "parole" in the analysis of texts. With regard to individual features he distinguishes between "Motiven" and "Motivvarianten,"[98] and with regard to genre (Gattung) between "überindividuellen Gattungsnormen" and "Gattungsexemplar."[99] I will concern myself here only with the former. For these methodological considerations[100] Theißen explicitly refers to observations of V. Propp[101] and A. Dundes.[102] Unfortunately, he does not adopt the clear terminology of either of them to differentiate unambiguously between structural features and their more contingent realizations.[103] He labels the structural features as "Motive" – the term Dundes reserved for the level of realization – and their realizations as "Motivvarianten." In this way a confusion of terms is predetermined.

---

[95] E. A. Leeper, "Exorcism in Early Christianity," (Ph. D. diss., Duke University, 1991), 85.

[96] G. Theißen, *Urchristliche Wundergeschichten. Ein Beitrag zur formgeschichtlichen Erforschung der synoptischen Evangelien* (Gütersloh: Verlagshaus G. Mohn, 1974. [5]1987).

[97] Cf. E. Güttgemanns, *Offene Fragen zur Formgeschichte des Evangeliums. Eine methodologische Skizze der Grundlagenproblematik der Form- und Redaktionsgeschichte.* BEvTh 54 (München: Chr. Kaiser Verlag, 1970), and idem, "Einleitende Bemerkungen zur strukturalen Erzählforschung," in *LingBibl* 23/24 (1973), 20–21, who recognizes the importance of *structural analysis* for synoptic miracle stories.

[98] Theißen, *Wundergeschichten*, 17.

[99] Ibid., 25, fn. 21.

[100] Ibid., 13–27.

[101] *The Morphology of the Folktale* (Austin and London: University of Texas, [5]1975).

[102] "From Etic to Emic Units in the Structural Study of Folktales," in JAF 75 (1962), 95–105; cf. also idem, *The Morphology of North American Indian Folktales*, FF Communications 195 (Helsinki: Academia Scientiarum Fennica, 1964) which had not been considered by Theißen.

[103] Cf. the critique of Frankemölle, "Exegese und Linguistik – Methodenprobleme neuerer exegetischer Veröffentlichungen," in *ThR* 71 (1975), 1–12, esp. 12.

Furthermore, although Theißen claims that his definition of "Motiv"[104] was close to the meaning of *function* in Propp's work,[105] his "Inventar der Motive" is certainly not an allotment of 33 *structural* features of miracle stories. From a structural perspective, this list rather presents a *mixture* of structural features and their realizations. For example, Theißen's "Motive" 9–12 (Erschwernis der Annäherung, Niederfallen, Hilferufe, Bitten, und Vertrauensäußerung) can all function as realizations of a single structural feature,[106] the Proppian function *mediation*. The "Auftreten" of different characters ("Motive" 1–6) cannot be isolated from their respective *actions* and can thus only be defined by their functional significance for the development of the plot. "Motive" 3–5 (Auftreten des Hilfsbedürftigen, von Stellvertretern, und von Gesandtschaften) represent different realizations of a subject that is somehow associated with a lack (e.g., sickness as a lack of health), which can motivate ("Motive" 9–12) another subject who is able to reverse this initial lack into its opposite. Another example of a misinterpretation of structural analysis is the identification of "Berührung," "heilende Mittel," and "wunderwirkendes Wort" as different "Motive" (22–24). From a structural perspective, these are all different manifestations of a single structural feature: they represent different *means* of a *performance* which reverses the initial lack into its opposite.[107] "Motive" 30–32 (Admiration, Akklamation, and Ablehnende Reaktion) describe different expressions of the structural feature "sanction,"[108] either in a positive or a negative sense.

From these observations it becomes clear that Theißen remains at the level of Bultmann's list of "Motive" in his treatment of "Motive" and "Motivvarianten."[109] In this regard he does not move beyond Bultmann.

---

[104] "Kleinste unselbständige Erzähleinheiten" (16), or: "erzählerisch relevante(n) kleinste(n) Einheiten" (16, fn. 8); cf. Güttgemanns' critique in "Bemerkungen," 20, fn. 120.

[105] Propp, *Morphology*, 21, defines function "as an act of a character [="tale role," cf. H. Jason, "The Problem of 'Tale Role' and 'Character' in Propp's Work," in idem, D. Segal (eds.), *Patterns in Oral Literature* (The Hague/Paris: Mouton & Co., 1977), appendix I, 313–20] defined from the point of view of its significance for the course of the action."

[106] Cf. X. Léon-Dufour, "Structure et Fonction du Récit de Miracle," in idem (ed.), *Les Miracles des Jésus selon le Nouveau Testament* (Paris: Éditions du Seuil, 1977), 289–353, who – inspired "des travaux remarquable de Gerd Theißen" (290) – lists these as different "motifs" (297) but shortly afterwards describes (correctly) "prosternement," "cris d'appel," and "demande confiante" as manifestations of the same function: mediation of a lack (302).

[107] Cf. again X. Léon-Dufour, "Structure," whose "motif" no. 23 embraces both Theißen's no. 22 and 23 under the heading: "Moyens gestuels de guérison" (299).

[108] Cf. Propp's function no. XXVII: "The Hero is recognized."

[109] Cf. Frankemölle, "Methodenprobleme," who attests Theißen that his synchronic approach is determined "inhaltlich, nicht aufgrund linguistischer Textstrukturen," (9) which is true especially for "seine Inventarisierung der Motive ... nach *inhaltlichen* Kriterien" (10).

While there is validity in Bultmann's approach, since he was concerned only with the *phenomenological* analysis and comparison of miracle stories, Theißen's list contributes to a distortion of the morphological approach, since he claims to engage in structural analysis. This critique also holds true in an inverse sense for his notion of different "Haftpunkte eines Motivs." He observes, for example, that the "Motiv Niederfallen" (10) can appear either *before* or *after* the miracle performance. This shows that he is not familiar with C. Bremond's evaluation of the double function of motifs,[110] which would have enabled him to account fully for this phenomenon. Structurally considered, "bowing down at the feet" realizes two different functions, either as (part of) an act of manipulation which aims at the motivation of an able subject to overcome an initial need or as (part of) an act that expresses gratefulness and recognition of the hero-subject after the successful fulfillment of the initial need.

Theißen's work, in spite of its shortcomings,[111] marks the beginning of a promising new approach for the assessment of the synoptic miracle stories, but it also shows that a clearer methodological foundation is needed which takes the results of the non-theological *Textwissenschaft* seriously. Otherwise an "imperfect union"[112] would remain which is not satisfying in any respect.[113]

---

[110] Theißen's bibliography does not mention any work by Bremond. Of invaluable importance concerning this issue, the double function of motifs, is Bremond's critique of Dundes, *Morphology*: "Postérité américaine de Propp," in *Communications* 11 (1968), 148–64.

[111] Cf. the critiques of Güttgemanns, "Bemerkungen," Frankemölle, "Methodenprobleme," H. Boers, "Sisyphus and His Rock, Concerning Gerd Theissen, *Urchristliche Wundererzählungen*," in *Semeia* 11 (1978), 1–48, and P.J. Achtemeier, "An Imperfect Union: Reflections on Gerd Theissen, *Urchristliche Wundererzählungen*," in *Semeia* 11 (1978), 49–68.

[112] Cf. the title of Achtemeier's critique.

[113] In Germany no comprehensive and systematic investigation of the synoptic miracle tradition has been published *after* Theißen's Habilitationsschrift from 1972. The two volumes on miracle stories in the work-book series *So liest man synoptisch. Anleitung und Kommentar zum Studium der synoptischen Evangelien*, Vol. II: "Exorzismen-Heilungen-Totenerweckungen," Vol. III: "Rettungswunder-Geschenkwunder-Normenwunder-Fernheilungen" (Frankfurt am Main: Josef Knecht, 1976) by R. Pesch and R. Kratz deliberately follow Theißen's approach. Their "Motivrepertoire" embraces 45 "Motive" and is marked by the same problem Theißen's list revealed. Their subdivision of miracle stories in seven groups according to *themes* is even more problematic than Theißen's six thematic groups. From a structural point of view, Propp is correct in stating, "Just as the subject of seizure does not determine the structure of the tale, neither does the object which is lacking" (*Morphology*, 36). Accordingly, a subdivision into exorcisms, healings, resurrections, "Rettungs-," "Geschenk-," and "Normenwunder," as well as "Fernheilungen," certainly does not contribute to clarification. The five first groups are defined from the perspective of a certain need which is caused by an initial lack (being freed from a demon, being healed from sickness, being resurrected from the dead, being saved from a storm, being given

After Theißen, there have been a few attempts to apply structural methods to the analysis of NT miracle stories.[114] One of these is *R. W. Funk's* "The Form of the NT Healing Miracle Story."[115] Funk intends "to lay a new formal basis for the form-critical analysis of healing miracle stories in late antiquity,"[116] an analysis that would guarantee "formal, especially linguistic controls"[117] with regard to classification which had been determined by criteria resting on content and subjective-intuitive decisions. Funk claims for his study, both to stand in the form-critical tradition and to move beyond it by means of a structuralist approach inspired by Propp's work. He tackles a threefold task: uncovering of the "Rudiments of a Narrative Grammar,"[118] development of a "New Typology of Healing Stories"[119] based on an analysis of the *narrative structure*, and finally, investigation of the "Structure of the Dialogue."[120] Even though Funk refers explicitly to Propp, and in spite of the fact that he occasionally makes use of a structuralist terminology, his approach is explicitly "purely formal,"[121] and not at all morphological in the structuralist sense. This difference to a function-oriented structuralist

---

food), whereas the two latter categories are defined by means of other criteria. The strength of this contribution is certainly *that* RGL parallels are systematically compared with the synoptic material by means of the same criteria (motifrepertoire and themes) even though the applied criteria prove to be insufficiant. Because morphic and phenomic levels are not distinguished, their RGL comparison remains dissatisfying and the results confusing.

The publication *Wesen und Wirklichkeit der Wunder Jesu. Heilungen-Rettungen-Zeichen-Aufleuchtungen*, ANTI 2 (Frankfurt am Main: Peter Lang GmbH, 1977) by O. Betz and W. Grimm offers many important insights into the relationship between the Gospel and OT miracle stories. *Forschungsgeschichtlich*, however, their approach represents a precritical understanding of the Gospel material when the OT is considered the sole and only source which influenced the generation of the synoptic miracle tradition. *Other* RGL material is not taken into consideration at all. The problematic of the oral history of at least some of the NT material is disregarded.

[114] Cf. Groupe d'Entrevernes, *Signes et paraboles: sémiotique et texte évangélique* (Paris: Éditions du Seuil, 1977; ET: 1978); J. Calloud, G. Combet, J. Delorme, "Essai d'Analyse Sémiotique," in X. Leon-Dufour (ed.), *Les miracles*, 151–81, CADIR, "Recits de Miracles et Recit Évangélique. Remarques de grammaires narratives," in *SB* 10 (1978), 27–44; R.W. Funk, "The Form of the NT Healing Miracle Story," in *Semeia* 12 (1978), 57–96. For an exception cf. D. Zeller, "Wunder und Bekenntnis. Zum Sitz im Leben urchristlicher Wundergeschichten," in *BZ* 25 (1981), 204–22, who analyses the final moments of miracle stories (phase "recognition") in comparison with OT and other RGL material in order to illuminate the question of whether some miracle stories had their original Sitz im Leben in the grateful proclamation of the healed.

[115] Cf. previous fn.

[116] Funk, "Form," 57.

[117] Ibid., 58.

[118] Ibid., 61.

[119] Ibid., 70.

[120] Ibid., 74.

[121] Ibid., 61.

approach becomes evident in his analysis of the "narrative structure" of healing stories: Funk classifies all stories by means of the criterion "dialogue." First of all, he differentiates dialogue and healing as the two main components of the nucleus of these stories. Then he goes on to distinguish four different types according to who is the dialogue partner of Jesus. While in the "B" (patient) and "R" (representative of patient) type stories a *request* is made to overcome an initial disequilibrium, the "D" (demon) type stories are delineated in the following way: "The demon does not make a request so much as a protest in the form of a recognition of A" (the exorcist).[122] The fourth group is made up of stories where the partner is represented by "a group of opponents" ("O" type stories). An additional group, called "r" (reduced) type, is marked by the lack of any dialogue.

This classification is problematic, and not only from a structuralist perspective. The differentiation between dialogue and healing is not a helpful means for comparing healing stories because, first of all, the dialogues in these narratives can have different *functions*. The dialogue in the B and R stories often has the function of motivating somebody to overcome an initial disequilibrium. Thus, concerning the request, B and R type stories are identical. It does not matter, functionally, *who* expresses the need. This is a secondary question. The "request" of the demon in D type stories is of quite a different quality. The demon does not want an initial equilibrium to be overcome. On the contrary, an equilibrium is sought to be maintained (the demon's remaining in a body: the very act that causes the disequilibrium of the sick person).[123] While this functional difference is not accounted for in Funk's description of the R type, the function of the dialogue in the O type is not discussed at all. It is sufficient at this point to note that the dialogue of the O type has yet another function than in either the B, R or D type. Furthermore, the formal distinction between dialogue and healing becomes once more dubious when the r type stories are taken into consideration. Even though these are stories that lack a dialogue before the healing, they may well contain actions other than oral communication mediating the need to overcome an initial disequilibrium. A most vivid example is Mk 2:1-10 where the overcoming of an obstacle ("And when they could not bring him to Jesus, because of the crowd, they removed the roof above him; and after having dug through it, they let down the mat on which the paralytic lay;" v. 4) substitutes for a dialogue. In other words, the non-verbal action performed by the characters associated with the person in need has the *same function* as an oral statement of faith in

---

[122] Ibid., 72.
[123] Cf. Mk 1:24; 5:7-12; Mt 12:43-45.

other miracle stories.[124] While Funk's classification is misleading and predetermined to lead to confusion, his observation "that the introduction to a narrative is devoted to the focalizing process which involves participants, place, time, and other descriptions,"[125] while "the conclusion as defocalizer expands, shifts, or blurs these same elements"[126] is helpful for taking into account the function of these descriptive elements surrounding the nucleus (or nuclei) of a story.

H.C. Kee, in *Medicine, Miracle and Magic in New Testament Times*,[127] presents a balanced, comprehensive overview and interpretation of ancient RGL material concerning miracle stories. Different from the predominantly a-historical investigations of the older FGL school, Kee sharply distinguishes between documents from before and after 100 C.E. Furthermore, even though he thoroughly evaluates the pagan material, he does not fail to recognize the importance of assessing Jewish sources of a pre-Christian or contemporary origin. The material under survey is organized according to its character as either medical, miraculous or magical. The following helpful definitions of medicine, miracle, and magic are given from a strictly ancient perspective: "*Medicine* is a method of diagnosis of human ailments and prescription for them based on a combination of theory about and observation of the body, its functions and malfunctions. *Miracle* embodies the claim that healing can be accomplished through appeal to, and subsequent action by the gods, either directly or through a chosen intermediary agent."[128] *Magic* involves "the expectation that they (the gods) can be coerced if the proper formulae are used,"[129] to achieve a desired end regardless of *who* uses the magical technique. These definitions are, of course, abstractions: "... in practice the lines are not always so sharply drawn."[130] Especially for the medical traditions from Hippocrates down to Galen, the author points out underlying astrological and magical aspects.[131] Based on his evaluation of the RGL material, Kee is convinced that the phenomenon of healing "was a major feature of the Jesus tradition from the outset," which had then "been embellished in the process of transmission."[132] For this assessment, he can point to Jewish sources such as Josephus, Tobit, and

---

[124] This is sustained by Jesus' reaction who (according to Mk 2:5) is motivated ἰδὼν δέ ... τὴν πίστιν αὐτῶν.

[125] Funk, "Form," 65.

[126] Ibid., 67.

[127] (Cambridge: Cambridge University Press, 1986).

[128] Ibid., 3.

[129] Ibid., 105; cf. 3.

[130] Ibid., 124.

[131] Cf. ibid., 27–66.

[132] Ibid., 124.

the Qumran material. The Palestinian, Early Christian depiction of Jesus as miraculous healer is seen in continuity with OT eschatological expectations: "Jesus is pictured in the gospel tradition as pre-eminently the agent of Yahweh the Healer."[133] For the Gospel of John, Kee observes that miracles function as *symbols*, "conveying the significance of Jesus for human participation in eternal life, and for membership in the new people of God."[134] In the rabbinic tradition miracle stories have yet another function, "confirmation of authority in the interpretation of the law."[135] On the basis of RGL comparison, Kee concludes that the healing tradition in the NT "stands on the whole in sharp contrast to magic"[136] and, in general, cannot be associated with medical practices of antiquity. It remains unclear, however, how the usage of spittle in Mk 7:33; 8:22 and Joh 9:6 and the often attested "laying on of hands" are to be understood. Are these not magical, medical, or miraculous devices?[137] Or, what is the function of those acts of the OT prophets Elijah and Elisha which accompany their prayer to God in behalf of ill persons?

6. Conclusions

The recognition of the importance of RGL comparison for an accurate assessment of the NT, going back to the very beginnings of critical scholarship, shaped NT exegesis concerning the synoptic miracle tradition since the time of the RGS. Initially, RGL comparison with respect to NT miracle stories was undertaken basically on the level of *motifs* without taking into account the context and function of the same motifs found in different miracle traditions of the ancient world (but note, with respect to the rabbinic and Epidauric material, the careful considerations by Dibelius!).[138] Bultmann groups the material according to formal cri-

---

[133] Ibid., 125; cf. 72–73.

[134] Ibid., 90. A correction: in the Gospel of John there are not *two* signs which depict healing (5:1–18; 9:1–41; cf. page 88) but three. Joh 4:46–54 has been forgotten.

[135] Ibid., 125; cf. 82.

[136] Ibid., 126.

[137] Even though Kee identifies spittle as magical device in the context of his discussion of Plinius' *Natural History*, he interprets Jesus' use of clay and spittle in Joh 9:6 in the light of *medical* prescriptions of that time (cf. 89).

[138] Cf. the criticism of S. Sandmel, "Parallelomania," in *JBL* 81 (1962), 1–13, and also the apt comment of K. Berger, "Hellenistische Gattungen im Neuen Testament," in W. Haase (ed.), *ANRW* II. 25/2 (Berlin/New York 1984), 1031–432: "Grundsätzliche Zweifel an der motivgeschichtlichen Arbeitsweise, die in diesem Fall der älteren religionsgeschichtlichen Schule entspricht, legen sich … nahe. Trotz des wertvollen und interessanten Ma-

teria (apophthegmata, miracle stories) and content (healing and nature miracles). The shortcomings of such a phenomenological approach were soon to be realized, and first attempts were made to compare non-canonical with synoptic material on the basis of *underlying structures* (especially Perels, but cf. also Fiebig and Fascher). Perels' concern was to account for morphic similarities between apophthegmata and miracle stories, taking direct and indirect speech and "Handlung" as expressions of the same structural feature. He was, however, not yet able to apply methodologically sound criteria which would allow for a systematic analysis that could account for the underlying structure of miracle stories. These early attempts to move from a purely phenomenological to a morphological investigation of miracle stories were taken up almost half a century later by Theißen who, however, did not succeed in consistently separating the levels of structure and realization. After Theißen, structural analysis was occasionally applied to miracle stories, especially among French scholars, but the usefulness of a structural approach for a *RGL comparison* of miracle stories has not yet been recognized.

---

terials führte die Orientierung an Einzelmotiven häufig zu einer Überinterpretation der Texte" (1214). Cf. also F. Martin, *Narrative Parallels to the New Testament*, SBL Resources for Biblical Study 22 (Atlanta: Scholars Press, 1988), 5, and C. Westermann, "Sinn und Grenze religionsgeschichtlicher Parallelen," in *ThLZ* 60 (1965), 489–96.

III. Methodology

1. Structuralism as a means
for the comparison of narratives

The problem of RGL comparison is methodological. It should go without saying that serious treatment of this question has to be informed by results of the discipline of *Textwissenschaft*, the scientific investigation of texts. The overview of the history of research suggests that a move away from a purely phenomenological to a strictly morphological approach is necessary for the analysis and comparison of ancient miracle stories. The basic rule is that only comparable entities should be compared with each other.[1]

With regard to RGL comparison of tales, *V. Propp* declares, "If we are incapable of breaking the tale into its components, we will not be able to make correct comparison."[2] Propp, while rejecting classification of folktales according to motifs and themes, distinguishes *constant functions* from *variable means of realization* of those functions.[3] This

---

[1] Cf. A. Dundes, "The Anthropologist and the Comparative Method in Folklore," in idem (ed.), *Folklore Matters* (Knoxville,TN: University of Tennessee, 1989), 57–82, esp. 69–70: "The word 'compare' literally refers to bringing together 'equal' or 'similar' elements. The idea is that one should compare only 'comparable' items." This is of course a truism. Nevertheless, the principle has often been disregarded.

[2] Propp, *Morphology*, 15.

[3] This insight into the difference between *functions* as morphic slots and *motifs* as phenomic fillers, which is shared today by the different structuralist schools, had occasionally already been sensed by scholars involved in RGL comparison of religious texts in the thirties of this century. L. Bieler, in a comparison of 2 Kings 4:18–37 with medieval types of legends concerning resuscitation by means of συνανάχρωσις, explicitly distinguishes "Einzelmotive" from their respective "Funktionen." Consequently, he can demonstrate that the "Wunderakt selbst" can be realized by "bald bloßes Gebet oder Machtspruch, bald in Verbindung mit äußeren Handlungen. ... " ("Totenerweckung durch Συνανάχρωσις. Ein mittelalterlicher Legendentypus und das Wunder des Elisa," in *ARW* 32 [1935], 228–45, esp. 237). In ΘΕΙΟΣ ANHP. *Das Bild des "göttlichen Menschen" in Spätantike und Frühchristentum*, (Darmstadt: Wissenschaftliche Buchgesellschaft, 1976) Vol. I, of the same year, Bieler – in anticipation of observations made by structuralistic inspired Textwissenschaftler in the western world some thirty years later – declares, "Parallelen liegen nur vor, wenn auch die Funktion der Motive die gleiche ist" (146). The closeness of these insights to those manifest in Propp's *Morphology of the Folktale*, first published in Russian in 1928, is striking. A dependence, however, does not need to be assumed here. Güttgemanns

distinction is based on the observation "that the names of the dramatis personae as well as their attributions changed but ... the actions or functions of the dramatis personae did not change."[4] Propp defines function as, "an act of a character, defined from the point of view of its significance for the course of the action."[5] The functional components underlying structural features are *abstractions* derived from the level of realization. Thus, narratives have to be compared first of all according to their morphic structure, and not according to their realizations. Propp established a list of thirty-one functions as constituent parts underlying every Russian magical folktale in a chainlike manner. While the sequence of these functions is stable, it is not necessary that all functions be present in a given tale. Then he collected the numerous motifs employed as realizations or fillers of these underlying functions. Furthermore, he described as a *major narrative move* a development from some sort of initial lack (it is often narrated how this lack came about)[6] towards the liquidation of that lack.

Propp's methodology was completed in 1928, but it was not until 1964, due to the late English translation of his *Morphology* (1958), that the method presented by him was adopted and modified for the analysis and comparison of quite a different kind of folktale by *A. Dundes* in *The Morphology of North American Indian Folktales*, which coincided with efforts of French semioticians to develop a narrative grammar of texts.[7] It marks a new beginning for the systematic analysis and comparison of narratives, especially folktales, from a strictly structural perspective.[8] The method for this comparative study had, in part, already

---

("Strukturale Erzählforschung und Ideologie," *LingBibl* 53 [1983], 9–44), mentions that various Russian Textwissenschaftler (before and parallel with Propp) were working on a structural and functional analysis of narratives (20–22).

[4] A. Dundes, "Emic Units," 100.

[5] Propp, *Morphology*, 21. Cf. H. Jason, "Problem," 316, who translates "tale role" instead of "character."

[6] It has often been correctly observed that "lack" denotes a state, not an action. Thus, it does not fit the Proppian definition of function. Nevertheless, "lack" is a morphic feature (motifeme).

[7] Cf. only Bremond, "Le message narratif," in: *Communications* 4 (1964), 4–32; idem, "La logique des possibles narratifs," in *Communications* 8 (1966), 60–76.

[8] It had already been observed by C. W. von Sydow, "Popular Prose Traditions and Their Classification," in L. Bødker (ed.), *C. W. von Sydow, Selected Papers on Folklore* (Copenhagen: Rosenkilde and Bagger, 1948), 127–45, that the common classification of folktales according to motifs does not fulfill the requirements of "a natural scientific system for the classification of folktales" (127), because that classification pays "no regard to the action or composition of fables" (131). The following objections would perfectly fit also much of the RGL and FGL work done during the first three decades of this century: "An inherent weakness of the principle of differentiation worked out by Aarne lies in the fact that different variants of quite the same action types must be placed in different groups if

been developed and presented by Dundes as early as 1962.[9] Most important for Dundes is the distinction between the analysis of *structural* features on the one hand, and of *phenomic* features (the actual textual phenomena) on the other. This distinction had already been drawn independently of Propp by *K. L. Pike* for his linguistic-anthropological research.[10] On this basis Dundes replaces the terminology of Propp with the more unambiguous terms coined by Pike: *Motifeme* takes the place of "function" and refers to a minimum structural feature. *Allomotif* is used for Propp's "motif" whenever different motifs function as "fillers," that is, representatives of one and the same motifeme. *Motif* now denotes all phenomic units without referring to any specific motifeme.[11] Pike designates features on the very surface of a text *etic* units (derived from the linguistic term "phonetic"), while he regards those features constituting the structure of a text as *emic* units (derived from the linguistic term "morphemic").[12] The *etic units (motifs or allomotifs)* function as fillers for "functional slots" which are situated on the emic level of the motifemes.[13] By means of this new terminology, Dundes is able to avoid certain terminological inconsistencies that pervade Propp's work. For example, Propp's *function* no. 8a (lack) which denotes a state and not an action,[14] belongs to the structural level. It functions as slot and is thus termed "motifeme." The motifeme "lack" could serve an unlimited variety of motifs (allomotifs) functioning as fillers for the specific slot. Dundes, versed in comparative literature and mythology, emphasizes that the "emic unit replaces the etic unit as a structural unit to be used as the basis for comparative studies,"[15] without disregarding the importance of a secondary analysis and comparison of etic units.[16] Hence Dundes, following Propp,[17] rejects any analysis and comparison of folklore on the basis of performance level features: "emic slots in texts can

---

the system is exactly followed" (131). "Such difficulties throw light on the weakness of an artificially made system which is based on purely occasional incidents without regard to the chief idea in the fable, and which just therefore can vary greatly" (132).

[9] Cf. Dundes, "Emic Units."

[10] K. L. Pike, *Language in Relation to a Unified Theory of Human Behavior,* Vol. I-III, (The Hague: Mouton & Co, [2]1967, orig. 1954-60).

[11] Cf. Dundes, "Emic Units," 101; idem, *Morphology*, 58-59.; Bremond, "Postérité," 149-150; Güttgemanns, "Bemerkungen," 17.

[12] Cf. Pike, *Language*, 57.

[13] For the terminology of "filler" and "functional slot," cf. Pike, *Language*, 30-31, and Dundes, "Texture, Text, and Context," in *SFQ* 28 (1964), 251-65, esp. 264.

[14] Contrary to Propp's own definition of "function," cf. above.

[15] Dundes, *Morphology*, 61.

[16] Cf. Dundes, *Morphology*, 264; idem, "Emic Units," 102.

[17] Cf. Propp, *Morphology*, 3-5.

be filled by different etic units, that is, different motifs (allomotifs) may be used in a given motifeme."[18]

Dundes analyzes, compares, and classifies North American Indian Folktales by means of purely morphologico-functional criteria. Instead of Propp's stable sequence of thirty-one motifemes ("functions"), Dundes reduces the list of motifemes to ten, which he organizes in coupled groups. The motifeme sequence Lack/Lack Liquidated (L → LL), describing a move from a state of disequilibrium to a state of equilibrium, is present in most of these folktales. It is termed "nuclear two motifeme sequence." Only the simplest folktales are structurally determined by this motifeme sequence alone. More complex folktales exhibit structures that consist of combinations of the motifeme pairs L → LL, Interdiction/Violation (Int → Viol), Deceit/Deception (Dct → Dcpn), Consequence/Attempted Escape (Conseq → AE), and Task/Task Accomplished (T → TA).

In a constructive critique of the method employed by Dundes for a description of the morphology of folktales of a specific culture, the French structuralist C. *Bremond* affirms the principles set forth by Dundes, but observes that this approach "s'ârrete á mi-chemin des résultats [que la tentative] laisse espérer."[19] Bremond's own critical reception of Propp for the analysis of narratives leads him to two corrections of Dundes' method. First, he points out that most of the coupled motifemes designate *states*, although they are supposed to denote "functions," that is, *actions* in the Proppian sense. Presupposing that "la fonction" is "l'unité de base, l'atome narratif ... appliquée comme chez Propp, aux actions et aux évenements,"[20] Bremond proposes that the functions be "groupées en triades."[21] Thus, an action develops in three steps: "état de départ, processus proprement dit, résultat."[22] For example, between L and LL an action takes place describing "la phase de realisation du processus." Second, and more significant, Bremond takes seriously the insight that actions often have more than just one function. With regard to a so called "exorcism-story," for example, it can be shown that one action effects the liquidation of a "lack" for the possessed subject while, at the same time, it establishes a "lack" for the possessor. This insight into the *multiple-function* of actions can also serve as an important tool for the analysis of the so-called "apophthegmata," where, for example,

---

[18] Dundes, "Texture," 264; cf. idem, "Emic Units," 102, and already Propp, *Morphology*, 66.

[19] Bremond, "Postérité," 151.

[20] Idem, "Logique," 60.

[21] Idem, "Message," 31.

[22] Idem, "Postérité," 152.

an action brings about the healing of a sick person and, at the same time, functions as a persuasive means. In this way a single motif renders two distinct motifemes.

2. Narrative programs

Another French structuralist, the semiotician *A. J. Greimas*[23] and his school[24] developed a comprehensive semiotic system. The results of structuralists like Propp, Dundes, Bremond, and others who focus on the syntagmatic analysis of folklore have been taken into consideration and are integrated into the semiotic system represented by Greimas' school. Greimas' semiotic theory is captivating due to very refined and clear terminology by means of which he is able to describe with great accuracy the meaning-generating-process of texts. Greimas' system makes provision for a strictly *wissenschaftliche* analysis of texts, "wissenschaftlich" in the sense that the results can be verified by anyone who makes use of the same or a similar analytic method.

It is the intention of this study to apply strictly a method for the RGL comparison of texts which allows for a verifiable distinction of morphic and phenomic levels in order to compare morphic structures with each other, on the one hand, and phenomic realizations of these underlying structures, on the other. Basically following the examples of Propp, Dundes, Bremond, and others who successfully employed this method in the field of comparative literature, this study is a *syntagmatic*[25] analysis of texts with the overall objective of *comparing literature*. Furthermore, the method proposed here is informed by the insights and

---

[23] Cf. A.J. Greimas, "Eléments pour une théorie de l'interprétation du récit mythique," in *Communications* 8 (1966), 28–59; idem, "Elemente einer narrativen Grammatik," in H. Blumensath (ed.), *Strukturalismus in der Literaturwissenschaft* (Köln: Kiepenheuer & Witsch, 1972), 47–67; idem, *Structural Semantics. An Attempt at a Method* (Lincoln: University of Nebraska Press, 1983; Frz. orig. 1966); idem, *Maupassant. The Semiotics of Text. Practical Exercises* (Philadelphia: John Benjamins Publ. Comp., 1988; Fr. orig. 1976); idem, J. Courtés, *Sémiotique. dictionnaire raisonné de la théorie du langage*, LLC (Paris: Hachette, 1979) [ET: *Semiotics and Language. An Analytical Dictionary* (Bloomington,Indiana: University Press, 1982)].

[24] Cf. the Groupe d'Entrevernes, *Signes*; idem, *Analyse sémiotique des textes. Introduction. Théorie-Pratique* (Lyon: Press Universitaires, 1979); J. Calloud, *Structural Analysis of Narrative* (Philadelphia: Fortress Press 1976; Fr. orig. 1973); D. Patte, *The Religious Dimensions of Biblical Texts. Greimas' Structural Semiotics and Biblical Exegesis*, SBL Semeia Studies (Atlanta: Scholars Press 1990).

[25] "Syntagms" are "chain-like series of actions that form a narrative development" according to Patte, *Dimensions*, 54.

clear terminology presented and elaborated by Greimas. His method
provides the means for the syntagmatic analysis of narratives to be
undertaken in this thesis.

Syntagmatic analysis of narratives is concerned with the identification
of elementary narrative units and their relations. Narrative units denote
actions as transformations of circumstances. Thus they are, for the most
part,[26] identical with Propp's functions. Following Propp, Dundes, Bremond, and others in this regard, Greimas recognizes a move from an
initial lack to the liquidation of that lack as pivotal for narrative development.[27] This *basic* narrative move is embedded in a sequence of other
narrative moves. Greimas' semiotic system is an attempt to describe the
complexity of narrative development. A narrative move representing the
transformation of a situation can be described as a *Narrative Program*
(NP).[28] The NP consists of two utterances: it is "constitué d'un énoncé
de faire regisant un énoncé d'etat."[29] It is essential for syntagmatic analysis to deconstruct a text "en énoncés d'état (être ou avoir) et en énoncés
du faire"[30] and to identify their interrelations. Only then would it be
possible to account for the structural complexity of narratives. While
Dundes was correct in identifying a move L → LL as a "nuclear two
motifeme sequence" of a given narrative, he neglected those narrative
transformations which necessarily *precede* and *follow* the main NP. Re-
grouping Propp's thirty-one functions, Greimas is concerned with the
establishment of an organizing principle for all narrative discourse. He
proposes a *Narrative Schema* which helps to identify the respective
functions of narrative transformations.

The basic move of a narrative, its "main NP," which is the junction
of an object and a subject (conjunction with or disjunction from), con-
stitutes the phase of the *performance*[31] in the Narrative Schema. The
object which is communicated between two subjects (active subject, subject of circumstance) is called "object of value."[32] For example, if the
subject of circumstance were in need of health, and the NP were concerned with the liquidation of this lack, the active subject would, in a

---

[26] But cf. Propp's "function," *Lack* and *Lack Liquidated*.

[27] Cf. Greimas, Courtés, *Sémiotique*, 222; ET, 169.

[28] Cf. Greimas,Courtés, *Sémiotique*, 297-298; ET, 245-246.

[29] Ibid., 297; ET, 245.

[30] Cf. Groupe d'Entrevernes, *Analyse*, 19.

[31] Cf. Patte, *Dimensions*, 256: "The narrative program is thus the overall transformation
accomplished throughout a narrative, the transformation of a 'situation of lack' into a
'situation of lack fulfilled'."

[32] Groupe d'Entrevernes, *Analyse*, 22: "*transformation* d'états est égalment un *transfert*
de l'objet valeur, une communication d'objet entre deux actants."

performance, fulfill this need by conjoining the subject of circumstance with the desired object of value, health.

However, this NP, describing the main performance, requires another phase which *prepares* the active subject for the performance. NPs leading to the preparation of the active subject are, from the perspective of the main NP, *instrumental NPs* (iNP). The phase of *preparation* is concerned with the attribution of *modal objects* to the active subject (AS). Different stages can be distinguished.

First, the active subject must be bestowed with qualities and/or means which are necessary for the success of the main performance. This stage provides for the *competence* of the active subject. The NPs belonging to this stage describe the conjunction of the active subject with a modal object in order that this subject has the *know how* (*savoir-faire*) and *is able* (*pouvoir-faire*) to engage successfully in the main performance. Often the modal object attributed to the subject requires additional iNPs which provide the active subject with some kind of helper (e. g., a magical agent).

Second, the active subject must be motivated and thus activated to carry out a given program. A "destinator subject" *causes* the active subject *to will* (*faire-vouloir*) to do something. This action of the "destinator subject" has the function a "'mise en route' d'un program narratif."[33] This fundamentally manipulative activity can either appeal to the *will* of an active subject (*vouloir-faire*) or consist of an *obligation*, forcing the active subject to engage in a certain performance (*devoir-faire*). Thus, the "faire-persuasif" is concerned with the establishment of a *contract* between a "destinator subject" and the active subject. This contract determines the specific value-object sought for, or to be disposed of, and must be regarded as "une des composantes essentielles du schéma narratif canonique,"[34] which, in turn, appears "comme la projection syntagmatique de la structure contractuelle."[35]

The phase following the performance of the main NP is called *sanction*. Narrative transformations belonging to this phase describe a judgment on either the performance of the active subject or its preparedness. First, with regard to the performance: *positive* sanction signals the success of the performance, whereas *negative* sanction means that the carrying out of the proposed program resulted in a failure. Second, sanction with regard to preparedness is a positive or negative judgment on the preparedness of an active subject, assessed from the point of view

---

[33] Groupe d'Entrevernes, *Analyse*, 53.
[34] Greimas, Courtés, *Sémiotique*, 221; ET, 185.
[35] Ibid., 70; ET, 60.

of the proposed program of action, and could signal by implication the success or failure of the performance.

By means of these distinctions Greimas is able to account for the functions of all NPs involved in transforming a certain circumstance of lack into a circumstance of lack fulfilled.

3. Application of structural insights to the RGL comparison of miracle stories

In the preface to his edition of the LXX Genesis, A. Rahlfs wrote, "Aber wenn wir weiterkommen wollen, müssen wir uns nicht von vorgefaßten Theorien, sondern lediglich von dem gegebenen Material leiten lassen."[36] The quotation from Rahlfs, coined in the context of LXX studies, serves well also as a warning and reminder not to superimpose arbitrarily any text theory onto the material under investigation, and not to make the miracle narratives fit a narrative schema.[37] Rather, any text theory should be regarded solely as a *means* for analysis. With these warnings in mind I apply the method of syntagmatic analysis to the RGL comparison of

---

[36] This passage is from A. Rahlfs' preface to his edition of the LXX Genesis, here quoted from D. Fraenkel, U. Quast, J.W. Wevers, "Geleitwort," in idem (eds.), *Studien zur Septuaginta – Robert Hanhart zu Ehren. Aus Anlaß seines 65. Geburtstages* (Göttingen: Vandenhoeck & Ruprecht, 1990), 9–18, 12.

[37] Scholars in the tradition of the FGS too often tend to measure the function as well as the age of a text or its component parts by means of dubious ideal-typical patterns, thus forcefully superimposing an alien concept onto the material. For a single example, cf. D.-A. Koch, *Die Bedeutung der Wundererzählungen für die Christologie des Markusevangeliums*, BZNW 42 (Berlin: de Gruyter, 1975), 96, concerning Mk 4:38. He does not recognize the accusing question of the disciples (οὐ μέλλει σοι ὅτι ἀπολλύμεθα;) as a "legitimate" and verifiable (cf. 1 Kings 17:18; 2 Kings 4:28, 30!) narrative possibility to realize the motifeme "activation of the active subject." The question of the disciples, the SCs, is an appeal to the *vouloir-faire* of the bearer of numinous power, Jesus. Koch's redaction-critical reasoning unfolds as follows: "eine *echte* Bitte um Hilfe (ist) *stilgemäßer Bestandteil* in Wundergeschichten. … Deshalb ist anzunehmen, daß in der Formulierung von V. 38c eine sekundäre Umformung und Zuspitzung eines vorgegebenen Erzählmotivs vorliegt" (italics are mine). It appears as if there were "natural laws" for the redaction process of ancient narratives which caused them to move from some sort of pure form to inferior derivations! Koch does not recognize that the disciples' question is also an "echte Bitte um Hilfe" which bears, in this case, accusing overtones. There exists an unlimited number of possibilites in miracle stories to fill the emic slot of the "activation of the active subject," as will be demonstrated in this study. The FGL view represented by Koch credits the scholar with more phantasy than the early Christian narrator, a misjudgment which results in the distortion of the NT texts, as well as their and their narrators' history.

miracle stories. This method distinguishes itself for a critical comparison of narratives insofar as all material can be analyzed by means of the same criterion.[38] Furthermore, since this method was developed on the basis of analyses which paid special attention to the specific nature of *narratives*, recognizing that sequences of transformations determine this sort of text, it promises to do justice to precisely that nature of narratives, namely, their *dynamic character*. It is common knowledge among structuralists that any narrative development is triggered by some sort of disequilibrium which is then turned into a corresponding equilibrium.[39] This insight is especially valuable for miracle narratives. It has correctly been observed by Güttgemanns that "im Neuen Testament speziell die Textsorte der 'Wundergeschichten' aus dem 'Kern' der Motifem-Sequenz L → LL generiert werden kann."[40] The synoptic miracle stories are "geradezu die Mustersorte ... , auf die sich – mit gewissen Varianten – sogar die Syntagmatik der 'Funktionen' Propps für das Zaubermärchen mit seiner gewissen Spannung und Bewegung zwischen dem 'Mangel' und der 'Beseitigung des Mangels' ... ohne Schwierigkeiten anwenden läßt."[41] As reference model for the systematic analysis and comparison of miracle narratives I propose Greimas' Narrative Schema as presented by H. Boers:[42]

I. Lack	*II. Preparedness*	*III. Performance*	*IV. Sanction*
A subject of a circumstance, disjoined from a desirable object, or conjoined with an undesirable object	An active subject, willing or obliged, and able (having the power), to overcome the initial lack by a performance	The active subject attempts, by means of a performance, to reverse the initial situation	Judgement on the preparedness or recognition of the outcome of the performance

[38] Groupe d'Entrevernes, *Analyse*, 22: "Elle se présente comme l'unité de mesure' pour mesurer les récits."

[39] Cf. Propp, *Morphology*, who states concerning his function VIII (villainy), 31: "This function is exceptionally important, since by means of it the actual movement of the tale is created," and also Greimas, Courtés, *Sémiotique*, 222: "Dans le schéma narratif canonique, dérivé de Propp, le manque est l'expression figurative de la disjonction initiale entre le sujet et l'objet de la quête: la transformation qui opère leur conjonction (ou la réalization) joue un rôle de pivot narratif (permettant de passer d'un état de manque á sa liquidation). ... " (ET, 169).

[40] Güttgemanns, "Bemerkungen," 20.

[41] Ibid., 21.

[42] Cf. Boers, *Neither on This Mountain Nor in Jerusalem. A Study of John 4*. SBL Monograph Series 35 (Atlanta: Scholars Press, 1988) 9. Cf. also van Dijk, *Some Aspects of Text Grammars. A Study in Theoretical Linguistics and Poetics* (The Hague: Mouton, 1972), 293, who distinguishes five "basic universal functions" for narratives.

It is possible to distribute Propp's 31 functions among these few phases.[43] It would, however, not be appropriate to try simply to recognize
Propp's functions – derived from Russian folktales – in ancient miracle
narratives. The "functions" (motifemes) of miracle narratives need to be
derived from miracle stories. The Narrative Schema helps to *identify* the
phases in the flow of the narrative by locating them in an overall
structure. It should be noted that only one of these phases represents
the statement of an action (performance), and all the others are, strictly
speaking, statements of a circumstance (lack, preparedness, and
sanction). For that reason it is inappropriate to refer to all of these
phases as functions. In actual narratives, however, those other three
phases may be represented by actions (performances), either as separate
programs, for example, a prior program which brings about a need, or
as instrumental programs (iNP) which result in the preparedness of the
active subject of the performance, or demonstrate the sanction rather
than merely stating it. Once the syntagmatic sequences of various narratives have been established it will be possible to compare those miracle
narratives accurately with each other. The examples that follow will serve
to clarify this further.

Examples for narrative analysis by means of the Narrative Schema

1. Epidauros A 20

Functions of NPs	Lack	Preparedness	Performance	Sanction
NP: Performance of miracle	Λύσων Ἑρμιόνευς παῖς ἀϊδής.		οὗτος ὕπαρ ὑπὸ κυνὸς κατὰ τὸ ἱερὸν θεραπευόμενος τοὺς ὀπτίλλους	ὑγιὴς ἀπῆλθε.

In this miracle story only three statements in the single main NP are
represented: the statement of the need, the performance of the miracle,
and a demonstration of its success (sanction). The sanction can be recognized as an iNP.

Functions of NPs	Lack	Preparedness	Performance	Sanction
iNP: Demonstration of results (sanction)			ὑγιὴς ἀπῆλθε.	

---

[43] Cf. Jobling, *The Sense of Biblical Narrative II: Structural Analysis in the Hebrew Bible*,
JSOTSS 39 (Sheffield: JSOT Press, 1986), 65, who distinguishes four phases and distributes
Propp's functions among them.

Most narratives, however, have a more complex structure involving a larger number of narrative programs. The main NP is often preceded by a number of iNPs, which prepare the active subject (AS) (*faire-persuasif [vouloir faire, devoir faire]*, *savoir faire, pouvoir faire*) for the main performance, which aims at the liquidation of a particular need. Other narrative moves can be identified as narrative anti-programs (NAP) which create the need and stand in opposition to the main NP. The term narrative *anti*-program is purely formal; it does not introduce a value judgment. It is a question of *perspective* which narrative trajectory one identifies as NP and which as NAP. From the point of view of the performance which brings about the need (illness, demon possession, etc.) the performance of the miracle is the anti-program. For the sake of a uniformity which is necessary for the analysis of the miracle stories all narrative programs in this investigation will be viewed from the perspective of the performance of the miracle, which is why the programs which include that performance are identified as the main narrative programs (NP).

The following story is far more complex, even though it is still a single narrative program. The three statements in the phase of preparedness and the sanctioning statement can be distinguished as iNPs, but we will not illustrate that here.

2. Mark 1:29-31

Functions of NPs	Lack	Preparedness	Performance	Sanction
Arrival of the miracle worker			29 Καὶ εὐθὺς ἐκ τῆς συναγωγῆς ἐξελθόντες ἦλθον εἰς τὴν οἰκίαν Σίμωνος καὶ Ἀνδρέου μετὰ Ἰακώβου καὶ Ἰωάννου.	
Statement of the need and of providing the miracle worker with *savoir-faire*	30 ἡ δὲ πενθερὰ Σίμωνος κατέκειτο πυρέσσουσα,	καὶ εὐθὺς λέγουσιν αὐτῷ περὶ αὐτῆς.		
The miracle worker acquiring *pouvoir-faire*, performance of the miracle, and sanction		31 καὶ προσελθὼν ἤγειρεν αὐτὴν κρατήσας τῆς χειρός·	καὶ ἀφῆκεν αὐτὴν ὁ πυρετός,	καὶ διηκόνει αὐτοῖς.

An important difference between the stories is that in the Epidauros miracle the miracle worker, a dog, is the active subject of the performance, whereas in Mark the active subject is the fever whose will has been subjected by the miracle worker as the means of performing the miracle. In that regard this miracle resembles an exorcism as in Mark 9:14–29, discussed below. What has been established through this analysis about the fever as active subject is confirmed by the Lukan version of the story, where ἐπετίμησεν, the word for the driving out of demons, is used (καὶ ἐπιστὰς ἐπάνω αὐτῆς ἐπετίμησεν τῷ πυρετῷ καὶ ἀφῆκεν αὐτήν; Lk 4:39). Thus, in a preliminary way we can already distinguish two types of miracle stories, those in which the miracle worker is the active subject and those in which the miracle worker subjects the will of an active subject to perform the miracle.

3. Mark 9:14–29

This story is highly complex, and in order to clarify this complexity more than one NP, a NAP, and a number of iNPs must be differentiated. Note that certain statements represent different phases in more than one narrative sequence.

Functions of NPs	Lack	Preparedness	Performance	Sanction
iNP1a Arrival of the miracle worker		14 Καὶ ἐλθόντες πρὸς τοὺς μαθητὰς	14 εἶδον ὄχλον πολὺν περὶ αὐτοὺς καὶ γραμματεῖς συζητοῦντας πρὸς αὐτούς.	
iNP1b Acclamation of the miracle worker		[14 Καὶ ἐλθόντες πρὸς τοὺς μαθητὰς …]		15 καὶ εὐθὺς πᾶς ὁ ὄχλος ἰδόντες αὐτὸν ἐξεθαμβήθησαν, καὶ προστρέχοντες ἠσπάζοντο αὐτόν.

Functions of NPs	Lack	Preparedness	Performance	Sanction
iNP2a Establishment of the need	[14 ... εἶδον ὄχλον πολὺν περὶ αὐτοὺς καὶ γραμματεῖς συζητοῦντας πρὸς αὐτούς.]	16 καὶ ἐπηρώτησεν αὐτούς, Τί συζητεῖτε πρὸς αὐτούς;	17 καὶ ἀπεκρίθη αὐτῷ εἷς ἐκ τοῦ ὄχλου, Διδάσκαλε, ἤνεγκα τὸν υἱόν μου πρὸς σέ, ἔχοντα πνεῦμα ἄλαλον· 18 καὶ ὅπου ἐὰν αὐτὸν καταλάβῃ ῥήσσει αὐτόν, καὶ ἀφρίζει καὶ τρίζει τοὺς ὀδόντας καὶ ξηραίνεται· καὶ εἶπα τοῖς μαθηταῖς σου ἵνα αὐτὸ ἐκβάλωσιν, καὶ οὐκ ἴσχυσαν.	
NP1a Peformance of the miracle (failure)	[17 καὶ ἀπεκρίθη αὐτῷ εἷς ἐκ τοῦ ὄχλου, Διδάσκαλε, ἤνεγκα τὸν υἱόν μου πρὸς σέ, ἔχοντα πνεῦμα ἄλαλον· 18 καὶ ὅπου ἐὰν αὐτὸν καταλάβῃ ῥήσσει αὐτόν, καὶ ἀφρίζει καὶ τρίζει τοὺς ὀδόντας καὶ ξηραίνεται·]	[καὶ εἶπα τοῖς μαθηταῖς σου ἵνα αὐτὸ ἐκβάλωσιν,]		[καὶ οὐκ ἴσχυσαν.]

Functions of NPs	Lack	Preparedness	Performance	Sanction
NP1b Performance of the miracle (negative sanction)				19 ὁ δὲ ἀποκριθεὶς αὐτοῖς λέγει, Ὦ γενεὰ ἄπιστος, ἕως πότε πρὸς ὑμᾶς ἔσομαι; ἕως πότε ἀνέξομαι ὑμῶν;
iNP3a Preparation of the performance		φέρετε αὐτὸν πρός με.	20 καὶ ἤνεγκαν αὐτὸν πρὸς αὐτόν.	
NAP Creation (reassertion) of the need		καὶ ἰδὼν αὐτὸν	τὸ πνεῦμα εὐθὺς συνεσπάραξεν αὐτόν, καὶ πεσὼν ἐπὶ τῆς γῆς ἐκυλίετο ἀφρίζων.	
iNP2b Establishment of the need		21 καὶ ἐπηρώτησεν τὸν πατέρα αὐτοῦ, Πόσος χρόνος ἐστὶν ὡς τοῦτο γέγονεν αὐτῷ;	ὁ δὲ εἶπεν, Ἐκ παιδιόθεν· 22 καὶ πολλάκις καὶ εἰς πῦρ αὐτὸν ἔβαλεν καὶ εἰς ὕδατα ἵνα ἀπολέσῃ αὐτόν·	
iNP3b Preparation: activation of the miracle worker		ἀλλ' εἴ τι δύνῃ, βοήθησον ἡμῖν σπλαγχνισθεὶς ἐφ' ἡμᾶς.		23 ὁ δὲ Ἰησοῦς εἶπεν αὐτῷ, Τὸ εἰ δύνῃ – πάντα δυνατὰ τῷ πιστεύοντι.

Functions of NPs	Lack	Preparedness	Performance	Sanction
iNP3c Preparation: activation of the miracle worker		24 εὐθὺς κράξας ὁ πατὴρ τοῦ παιδίου ἔλεγεν, Πιστεύω· βοήθει μου τῇ ἀπιστίᾳ.		
iNP3d Preparation: activation of the miracle worker		25 ἰδὼν δὲ ὁ ᾿Ιησοῦς ὅτι ἐπισυντρέχει ὄχλος		
NP1 Performance of the miracle (*devoir faire of demon*)		ἐπετίμησεν τῷ πνεύματι τῷ ἀκαθάρτῳ λέγων αὐτῷ, Τὸ ἄλαλον καὶ κωφὸν πνεῦμα, ἐγὼ ἐπιτάσσω σοι, ἔξελθε ἐξ αὐτοῦ καὶ μηκέτι εἰσέλθῃς εἰς αὐτόν.	26 καὶ κράξας καὶ πολλὰ σπαράξας ἐξῆλθεν·	
NP2 Demonstration of results (failure)			καὶ ἐγένετο ὡσεὶ νεκρός,	ὥστε τοὺς πολλοὺς λέγειν ὅτι ἀπέθανεν.
NP3a Demonstration of results (success)			27 ὁ δὲ ᾿Ιησοῦς κρατήσας τῆς χειρὸς αὐτοῦ ἤγειρεν αὐτόν,	
NP3b Demonstration of results (success)			καὶ ἀνέστη.	
NP2a Request of information concerning failed miracle		28 καὶ εἰσελθόντος αὐτοῦ εἰς οἶκον	οἱ μαθηταὶ αὐτοῦ κατ᾿ ἰδίαν ἐπηρώτων αὐτόν, Ὅτι ἡμεῖς οὐκ ἠδυνήθημεν ἐκβαλεῖν αὐτό;	

Functions of NPs	Lack	Preparedness	Performance	Sanction
P2b Sanction of preparedness				29 καὶ εἶπεν αὐτοῖς, Τοῦτο τὸ γένος ἐν οὐδενὶ δύναται ἐξελθεῖν εἰ μὴ ἐν προσευχῇ.

This miracle story has an even more complex structure. The successful performance of the NP is preceded by a number of iNPs, a failed NP, and an NAP. Furthermore, the NP is followed by a narrative move which links it back to the failed NP. The additional functions represented by these NPs occur predominantly in the phase of preparedness; they concern primarily the activation of the miracle worker (iNP3b, c, and d) and concern his *vouloir faire* and *devoir faire*. Another act of preparation takes place in iNP3a, where the miracle worker prepares the performance of the miracle. This iNP manifests the miracle worker's *savoir faire*. How the miracle worker was bestowed with the ability to engage in the proposed NP is not narrated. His *pouvoir faire* is presupposed. The variety of ways in which the performance is prepared in the miracle story is a mark of its particular style. Other functions are also manifest more than once. The need is established twice (iNP2a and 2b), and the success of the performance demonstrated by two distinct actions (NP3a and 3b).

The following functions (in Propp's sense) of this miracle story have been established: arrival of the miracle worker, acclamation of the miracle worker, establishment of the need, preparation for the performance of the miracle, performance of the miracle, demonstration of the results, and a NAP, creation or reassertion of the need for the miracle. A number of these can be recognized as allomotifs representing single motifemes, for example, the motifeme preparedness can be realized by different *allomotifs*: iNPs concerned with the activation of the miracle worker (*vouloir faire, devoir faire*) or with the acquiring of competence (*pouvoir faire, savoir faire*). It will be further the task of this investigation to identify the motifemes and the respective allomotifs as their realizations. In order to do so more miracle stories will have to be analyzed until a point of redundancy is reached where no more allomotifs are found for which a motifeme has not yet been established. The task would also include determination if there is a fixed sequence of the motifemes. The motifemes established in this way would make it possible to reduce Propp's thirty-one functions substantially.

In a preliminary way it was possible to establish two distinct kinds of miracles: those in which the miracle worker is the active subject in the performance of the miracle (the Epidauros miracle), and those in which the miracle worker subjects the will of an active subject to carry out the performance (the two gospel miracles). Another variant would be where the so-called miracle worker prays to the deity to perform the miracle which is a characteristic feature in Jewish miracle stories (cf. OT, Qumran, Rabbinic literature). A question would be whether performances in which the will of the active subject is subjected (*devoir faire*), as in an exorcism, and those in which an appeal is made to the will of the active subject (*vouloir faire*), as in a miracle which relies on a deity, represent allomotifs of a single motifeme, or are to be considered different motifemes.

The task to be undertaken in this investigation consists primarily of the identification of motifemes and allomotifs. The distinction between motifemes and allomotifs, between the morphic and phenomic levels of the narratives is important, because it proved to be – in particular in NT scholarship – insufficient and misleading to compare motifs without taking into account their respective motifemic functions. After the morphological analysis has been completed it will be possible to evaluate the miracle stories from *different perspectives.*

a. The *structure* of miracle stories

Here the question will be if there exists one "universal" morphological structure for all miracle stories or if different structures can be identified for different traditions. If there is only a single structure, the question becomes what features there are to account for differences between the various miracle traditions?

b. The *types* of miracle stories

As has been indicated above, a classification of miracle stories according to theme has to be rejected due to its inaccuracies and arbitrariness. According to Propp, a typology of narratives has to be based on structural observations. Here the question is whether it is possible to establish different categories of miracle stories.

c. The *function* of miracle narratives

In this case the question is: are there structural features which indicate the function of a miracle narrative?

d. Ecotypes and the question of *origin* with regard to the synoptic miracle stories

Von Sydow introduced the term *oicotype* (=ecotype) into the field of comparative literature.[44] By means of this concept he tried to account for different realizations of the "same story" in different cultures. Determining factors for ecotypification are the attitudes of the narrator and audience "towards their ancient ethno-cultural heritage and towards changing socio-cultural conditions (acculturation)."[45] Dundes extended the concept of ecotype to the structural level.[46] For some North American Indian folktales, Dundes was able to point out the process of "acculturation" with respect to the *nature* and *sequence* of emic units. *Structural* variants serve as the strongest indicators of a certain narrative belonging to a specific culture.[47] A second step – at the phenomic level – undertakes a comparison of the *fillers* of motifemic slots: "If one does examine a group of tales ... all of which are based upon a certain motifemic sequence ... one may see at a glance which motifs are culturally preferred."[48] Only after having established ecotypes for different miracle traditions, considering both the morphic and the phenomic levels, can one proceed to draw conclusions concerning the relationship of the synoptic miracle stories to other traditions.

---

[44] Von Sydow, "Geography and Folk-Tale Oicotypes," in L. Bødker (ed.), *C. W. von Sydow, Selected Papers on Folklore* (Copenhagen: Rosenkilde and Bagger, 1948), 44–55. This term is borrowed from the field of natural science: "In the science of botany *oicotype* is a term used to denote a hereditary plant-variety adapted to a certain *milieu* (sea-shore, mountain-land, etc.) through natural selection amongst hereditarily dissimilar entities of the same species. When then in the field of traditions a widely spread tradition, such as a tale or legend [i.e. sagn], forms special types through isolation inside and suitability for certain cultural districts, the term oicotype can also be used in the science of ethnology and folklore" (243, fn. 15).

[45] D. Noy, "The Jewish Versions of the 'Animal Languages' Folktale (AT 670). A Typological-Structural Study," in J. Heinemann and D. Noy (eds.), *Studies in Aggadah and Folk-Literature* (Jerusalem: At the Magnes Press, 1971), 207. Cf. Dundes, *Morphology*, 99: "It is virtually a platitude among folklorists that borrowed tales may often be adapted to fit the borrower's local patterns." Cf. also P. Wendland, *Die hellenistisch-römische Kultur in ihren Beziehungen zu Judentum und Christentum.* HNT I/2 (Tübingen: J.C.B. Mohn [Paul Siebeck], ²/³1912), 220: "Der Eintritt des Christentums in die griechisch redende Welt, die Beteiligung von Heidenchristen, die ihren früheren geistigen Besitz nicht wie ein Gewand ablegen konnten, sondern einen Teil desselben in die Kirche hinübernahmen, bringt notwendig das Einströmen hellenistischer Kulturelemente mit sich. Das Maß dieses Einflusses ist durch die Notwendigkeit, durch die höhere oder niedrigere Bildung des einzelnen bedingt."

[46] Cf. Dundes, "Preface," XIII-XIV.

[47] Cf. T. Cochrane, "The Concept of Ecotypes in American Folklore," in *JFR* 24 (1987), 33–55, esp. 44, where the author gives the folloing schema concerning features which are affected by ecotypification:
"... Most Adaptable .... Most Conservative ...
        Style + Content   Form   Function Structure."

[48] Dundes, "Emic Units," 100; cf. idem, "Structural Typology," 211.

This investigation has its focus on those narratives which include an episode with the following features: a protagonist incorporates or has access to some sort of *divine power*, which brings about the *restoration* of humans who are either ill (from a modern perspective: physically or mentally) or who have died prematurely. Most of the synoptic narratives traditionally referred to as miracle stories belong to this type.[49]

The comparable RGL material to be considered includes all those traditions of the ancient world that could have been familiar to or reflect a Palestinian, Asia Minor, or Greco-Roman milieu of the Hellenistic world. These spatio-temporal limitations cover the area in which the spreading of Early Christianity took place.

---

[49] Traditionally, these stories would be called: healing miracles, exorcisms, and resuscitations, respectively, but also "healings at a distance" and "Apophthegmata" or "Normenwunder" need to be considered here.

IV. Morphological Analysis: Motifemes and their Realizations

1. Introduction

This chapter is devoted to the identification and description of motifemes in ancient miracle stories. The motifemes are listed in a sequence relative to their occurrence in miracle narratives. Thus, the sequence begins with the motifeme *initial lack* and ends with *sanction*, the motifeme following the *performance of the miracle*. This chapter represents the results of the analysis of all the relevant material from antiquity by means of the Narrative Schema. The motifemes are derived from a broad RGL basis. Texts from pagan Greco-Roman, Jewish, and Christian milieus have been analyzed and compared indiscriminately.

2. List of narratives considered

This investigation is primarily concerned with *"restoration* miracle narratives."* These are stories which narrate a miraculous restoration to health in the broadest sense including the raising of dead persons. I sought near-comprehensiveness concerning the selection of texts for the time *prior* to the final redaction of the synoptic gospels, around 100 C. E. For the time *after* 100 C. E., texts have been considered only sporadically, and Christian miracle stories from that period have been disregarded altogether. A number of non-Christian miracle narratives are considered here for the first time in connection with a RGL assessment of the Christian texts.

Each narrative is given a title. The titles are assigned for reasons of identification only. They do *not* try to render the pivotal point of each narrative. Whenever possible, the titles introduce the *subject of a circumstance* (the ill person, etc.), the *circumstance* (conjunction with illness, etc.), and the *active subject* (the healer, etc.). In those cases where a confusion of miracle worker and *destinator subject* is possible, the mediating activity of a destinator subject is indicated by verbs like *intervene, assist,* or *help.*

The sequence of the texts listed corresponds to their age, moving from older to younger sources. A broken line in the Jewish and pagan lists roughly indicates material from before and after the final redaction of the synoptics.

2.1. The Jewish milieu[1]

Old Testament
Gen 20:1-18: Abraham intervenes with the result that God heals Abimelech
Ex 4:1-9: God heals the leprous hand of Moses
Num 12:1-16: Moses intervenes with the result that God heals Miriam's leprosy
Num 21:4-9: Moses intervenes with the result that God saves the Israelites from snakebites
1 Sam (LXX: 1 Kings) 16:14-23: David gives Saul relief from an evil spirit
1 Kings (LXX: 3 Kings) 13:1-10: A Man of God assists in restoring Jeroboam's withered hand
1 Kings (LXX: 3 Kings) 17:17-24: Elijah assists in reviving a widow's son
2 Kings (LXX: 4 Kings) 4:18-37: Elisha assists in reviving the Shunammite's son
2 Kings (LXX: 4 Kings) 5:1-19: Elisha assists in healing Naaman from leprosy
2 Kings (LXX: 4 Kings) 13:20-21: Elisha causes the revival of a man
2 Kings (LXX: 4 Kings) 20:1-11: Hezekiah is healed by God from a serious illness
Isa 38:1-22: cf. 2 Kings 20:1-11

Between 200 B.C.E. and 100 C.E.
Artapanus, Frg. 3:24-25: Moses revives the Egyptian king
Aristeas the Exegete, Frg. 1: God tests Job's faith and relieves him of his sores
Tobit (LXX): God lets Raphael have Tobias drive out an evil demon from Sarah, and have him heal his father's blindness
1QapGen 19:10-20:32: Abram helps to expel an evil spirit from the Pharao[2]

---

[1] It is informative for the question of acculturation to consider the OT in its Hebrew and Greek traditions and also to compare parallel accounts in Josephus. This Jewish author who spent the first thirty years of his life in Palestine lived in Rome after 70 C.E. There he published in 93/94 C.E. the Ιουδαϊκὴ ἀρχαιολογία. By means of this work, Josephus intended to present the essence of Judaism to a Roman-hellenistic audience. The way in which he recast biblical miracle stories might reflect Greco-Roman modes to narrate miracles. Cf. G. Delling, "Josephus und das Wunderbare," in idem, *Studien zum Neuen Testament und zum hellenistischen Judentum. Gesammelte Aufsätze 1950-68*. Ed. by F. Hahn, T. Holtz, and N. Walter (Göttingen: Vandenhoeck & Ruprecht, 1970 [orig. of essay: 1958]), 130-45, who observes the tendency of Josephus to *rationalize* OT miracle stories (esp. 139-40).

[2] The other Qumranic text narrating a miraculous healing, 4QorNab, *The Prayer of Nabonid*, has to be disregarded for the identification of motifemes and allomotifs. This is due to the fragmentary quality of the extant text which was probably originally part of a much longer narrative as has been suggested by R. Meyer ("Das Gebet des Nabonid. Eine in den Qumran-Handschriften wiederentdeckte Weisheitserzählung," in *Zur Ge-*

Philo, De Vita Mosis:
I 79–80: cf. Ex 4:1–9
I 126–129: Moses intervenes on behalf of Egyptians suffering from ulcers
Josephus, Antiquitates:
VI 166–169: cf. 1 Sam 16:14–23
VIII 45–50: Eleazar casts out a demon
VIII 325–327: cf. 1 Kings 17:17–24
IX 182–183: cf. 2 Kings 13:20–21
X 24–29: cf. 2 Kings 20:1–11
Pseudo-Philo, Antt. Biblicae LX 1–3: cf. 1 Sam 16:14–23

– – – –

Rabbinic literature
b.Berachot 5b: R Hanina assists in raising R Yohanan from the sickbed
b.Berachot 34b: R Hanina b Dosa assists in healing the son of Gamaliel
b.Berachot 34b: R Hanina b Dosa assists in healing the son of Yochanan bZakkai
b.ʿErubim 29b: Rabbis assist in healing R Hanina b Dosa from sickness due to a poisonous onion
b.Pesahim 112b: R Hanina b Dosa limits the reign of the demon Agrath bat Mahlat[3]
b.Meʿila 17a-b: R Simeon b Yochai exorcizes a demon from the emperor's daughter
b.ʿAboda Zara 10b: A disciple of Rabbi assists in raising a servant of Antonius
b.Hagiga 3a: Rabbi assists in healing two mute men
y.Berachot 9d: R Hanina b Dosa assists in healing the son of Gamaliel

2.2. The pagan milieu

Homer, The Iliad:
4:192–219: Machaon treats wounded Menelaus
14:402–15:299: Zeus revives wounded Hector
Odyssey: 5:394–398: The gods free a father from a sickness-demon
19:448–468: The sons of Autolycos still the blood of Odysseus
Pindar, Pythian Odes 3:47–53: Asclepios heals people with various sicknesses

---

schichte und Theologie des Judentums in hellenistisch-römischer Zeit. Ausgewählte Abhandlungen von Rudolf Meyer. Ed. by W. Bernhardt. Neukirchen: Neukirchener Verlag, 1991, pp. 71–129, orig.: Berlin 1962). The fragmentary character of 4QorNab makes it impossible to determine the *functions* of actions, since the *relationship* between actions too often remains dubious. For example, it is unclear whether the sins were forgiven by God or by the גזר. Was Nabonid punished by God באיפא for his idolatry? What caused the Jewish seer to intervene on behalf of the Babylonian king? The text poses too many unanswerable questions to be structurally analyzed in a responsible manner.

[3] This narrative is not a restoration miracle story. Even though, it is listed here for two reasons: 1. it is at least *related* to the theme of restoration miracle stories in so far as it describes a *preventive* act with regard to the possession of demons, and 2. this story illustrates the common motif "granting a concession to a demon" for a normative Jewish tradition.

Bacchylides, Epinicia 11:40–112: Artemis assists in healing the mad daughters of Proitos

Pherecydes, FGrHist 3 F114: Melampous assists in healing the mad daughters of Proitos

Herodotos, Historia 2:111: Pheros' blindness is healed due to an oracle

Inscriptions from Epidauros:

A1: Asclepios heals Kleo from a five-year pregnancy
A2: Asclepios heals Isathmonike from a three-year pregnancy
A3: Asclepios heals a man with paralyzed fingers
A4: Asclepios heals the blind eye of Ambrosia of Athens
A5: Asclepios heals a mute boy
A6: Asclepios heals the Thessalian Pandaros' forehead from marks
A7: Asclepios refuses to heal Echedoros' marks
A8: Asclepios heals Euphanes, a boy of Epidauros, from a stone
A9: Asclepios heals a blind man
A11: Asclepios heals blind Aeschines
A12: Asclepios heals Euhippos wounded by a spear
A13: Asclepios heals a man of Torone from leeches
A14: Asclepios heals a man with a stone in his membrum
A15: Asclepios heals the paralyzed Hermodicos of Lampsacos
A16: Asclepios heals lame Nicanor
A17: A serpent heals the toe of a man
A18: Asclepios heals blind Alcetas of Halieis
A20: A dog heals the blind boy Lyson of Hermione
B21: Asclepios heals dropsical Arata of Lacedaemon
B22: Asclepios heals blind Hermon of Thasus
B23: Asclepios heals Aristagora of Troezon from a tapeworm
B25: Asclepios heals Sostrata of Pherae from worms
B26: A dog heals a boy of Aegina from a growth on the neck
B27: Asclepios heals a man from an abscess in the abdomen
B29: Asclepios heals Hagestratos from headaches and insomnia
B30: Asclepios heals Georgias of Heracleia wounded by an arrow
B32: Asclepios heals blind Anticrates of Cnidos
B33: A serpent heals Thersandros of Halieis from consumption

Antiphanes: Metagyrtes, Frg. 154: The Mother of Gods provides for the healing of a lame man

Aristophanes, Plutos 633–747: Two serpents heal Plutos' blindness

Bentresh-Stela 4–28: The God Chonsus exorcizes a demon from Bintresh[4]

---

[4] This *Egyptian* text from late Persian or early Hellenistic times has been included here because its structure and some of its motifs closely resemble some traditions under consideration in this investigation. Cf. the assessment of K. Thraede, "Exorzismus," in *RAC* 7 (1969), 44–117: "Als Vorklang späterer E.[xorzismus]erzählungen bedeutsam ist schließlich die E.legende der Bentresch-Stele ... Dieses Modell, Unterwerfungsbekenntnis und Konzessionsgewährung im Rahmen eines Gesprächs, ist später in die hellenistische Wundererzählung eingegangen" (48). The implied claim of a genealogical development and historical connection, however, is problematic.

Inscriptiones Graecae IV² 1:125: Asclepios heals Hermodicos from an abscess in his chest and from paralysis in his hands

Inscriptiones Creticae I 17:9: Asclepios heals Demandros of Gortyn from sciatica

Diodorus of Sicily, Bibliotheca Historica XVII 103:4–8: Alexander heals wounded Ptolemy

Inscriptiones Creticae I 17:

17: Asclepios heals Poplius Granius Rufus from a constant cough

18: Asclepios heals Poplius Granius Rufus from a pain in his shoulders

19: Asclepios heals a woman from a maligment sore on her little finger

Livius, Ab urbe conditia libri 2:36: Jupiter heals Titus Latinius

Ovid, Fasti VI 743–762: Asclepios revives Hippolytos

Metamorphoses 15:504–540: Asclepios revives Hippolytus

15:618–745: Asclepios heals the inhabitants of Rome from pestilence

Apollodoros, Bibliotheca:

II 2: Melampous heals the mad daughters of Proitos

III 3: Polyidos revives Glaukos

– – – –

Petronius, Satyricon 131: An old woman heals Encolpius' impotence

Plutarch, Life of Pericles 13:7–8: Athena gives Pericles advice for healing one of his workers

Tacitus, Historiae 4:81: Vespasian heals a blind man and a man with a lame hand

Suetonius, Vespasianus 7:2–8: Vespasian heals a blind man and a lame man

Galen, Subfiguratio Empirica X: Asclepios heals a man from elephantiasis and leprosy

Lucian of Samosata, Philopseudes:

11: A Babylonian heals poisoned Midas

[16: A Syrian exorcizes a demon]⁵

Inscriptiones Graecae IV² 1:126: Asclepios heals M. Julius Apellas from indigestion

Inscriptiones Graecae XIV 966:

a. Asclepios heals blind Gaius

b. Asclepios heals Lucius suffering from pleurisy

c. Asclepios heals Julian suffering from spitting blood

d. Asclepios heals blind Valerius Aper

Oxyrhynchos Papyrus 11:1381: Imouthes-Asclepios heals a man and his mother⁶

Pausanias, Descriptio Graecae X 38:13: Asclepios heals blind Phalysios

Apuleius, Metamorphoses II 27–30: The Egyptian prophet Zatchlas intervenes to raise a young man from the dead

Aelianus, De natura animalium:

IX 33: cf. Epidauros B 23

---

⁵ This text is more a summary of the miraculous activities of the Babylonian than a miracle narrative. It is nevertheless included here since it shares various motifs with regular exorcism narratives.

⁶ This extensive narrative from the second century C.E. is listed here as an example of a Hellenistic *Egyptian* miracle story.

XI 32: Serapis heals an insane husbandman
XI 34: Serapis heals poisoned Cissus
Flavius Philostratus, Vita Apollonii:
[III 38: A wise man provides for the security of a demoniac boy][7]
III 39: Indians heal a lame man
IV 20: Apollonios heals a demoniac boy
IV 45: Apollonios raises a girl from the dead
VI 43: Apollonios heals a boy bitten by a mad dog
Dio Cassius, Roman History 65:8: Vespasian heals a blind man and a man with a lame hand
Marinos, Vita Procli 29: Proclus assists to heal Asclepigenia[8]

2.3. First century Christian texts

Mk 1:21–28/Lk 4:31–37: Jesus heals a man with an unclean spirit
Mk 1:29–31/Lk 4:38–39/Mt 8:14–15: Jesus heals Peter's mother-in-law from fever
Mk 1:40–45/Lk 5:12–16/Mt 8:1–4: Jesus heals a leper
Mk 2:1–12/Lk 5:17–26/Mt 9:1–8: Jesus heals a paralyzed man
Mk 3:1–6/Lk 6:6–11/12:9–14: Jesus heals a man with a withered hand
Mk 5:1–20/Lk 8:26–39/Mt 8:28–34: Jesus heals a Gerasene demoniac
Mk 5:21–43/Lk 8:40–56/Mt 9:18–26: Jesus heals a bleeding women, and he raises the daughter of Jairus
Mk 7:24–30/Mt 15:21–28: Jesus heals a Syro-phoenician woman's demoniac child
Mk 7:31–37/Mt 15:29–31: Jesus heals a deaf mute
Mk 8:22–26: Jesus heals a blind man of Bethsaida
Mk 9:14–29/Lk 9:37–43a/Mt 17:14–20: Jesus heals a demoniac boy
Mk 10:46–52/Lk 18:35–43/Mt 20:29–34/9:27–31: Jesus heals blind Bartimaeus/two blind men
Q: Mt 8:5–13/Lk 7:1–10: Jesus heals the servant of a centurion
Q: Mt 9:32–34/12:22–36/Lk 11:14–23: Jesus heals a demoniac deaf (and blind) man
Mt 21:14–17: Jesus heals the blind and lame
Lk 1:5–25,57–65: Zechariah is restored from muteness

---

[7] This is not really a restoration miracle narrative since no miracle is narrated, even though it may well be *expected* to happen (the narrative ends with the transfer of a helper-agent: ἐπιστολὴ πρὸς τὸ εἴδωλον ξὺν ἀπειλῇ καὶ ἐκπλήξει). In addition, the magical helper-agent seems to aim not at the disjunction from the δαίμων-εἴδωλον but is rather supposed to avert the danger that the demon threatens to afflict on the possessed boy, ἀποκτενεῖν ... τὸν υἱόν· "θάρσει," ἔφη ὁ σοφός, "οὐ γὰρ ἀποκτενεῖ αὐτὸν ἀναγνοὺς ταῦτα," καί τινα ἐπιστολὴν ἀνασπάσας τοῦ κόλπου ἔδωκε τῇ γυναικί, ...

[8] This late text, stemming from the fifth century C.E., has been incorporated here as a *pagan* example for the so-called "miracles at a distance" (cf. Mt 8:5–13; Lk 7:1–10; Joh 4:46–53; b. Berachot 34b; y. Berachot 9d; and Mk 7:24–30; Mt 15:21–28). The term "miracle at a distance," however, is not unambiguous as will be demonstrated later. Cf. here only Lk 17:11–19. For another pagan example cf. Epidauros B21.

Lk 7:11-17: Jesus raises a widow's son at Nain
Lk 13:10-17: Jesus heals a woman with a spirit of weakness
Lk 14:1-6: Jesus heals a man with dropsy
Lk 17:11-19: Jesus heals ten lepers
Lk 22:47-53: Jesus heals the servant of the High Priest with a severed ear
Joh 4:46-54: cf. Mt 8:5-13/Lk 7:1-10
Joh 5:1-18: Jesus heals a paralyzed man
Joh 9:1-41: Jesus heals a blind man
Joh 11:1-54: Jesus raises Lazarus
Acts 3:1-10: Peter assists in healing a lame beggar
Acts 9:1-19a: God heals blind Saul through Ananias
Acts 9:32-35: Peter assists in healing paralyzed Aeneas
Acts 9:36-43: Peter assists in raising Tabitha
Acts 14:8-18: Paul heals a lame man
Acts 16:16-24: Paul exorcizes a spirit of divination from a slave girl
[Acts 20:7-12: Paul raises Euthychos][9]
Acts 22:6-16: Ananias heals blind Saul
Acts 28:7-10: Paul assists in healing Poplios' father from fever

3. Motifemes and their realizations

Each narrative describes at least the liquidation of one principal lack. Healing miracle stories describe the liquidation of a lack of *health* by means of a miraculous power. However, it cannot be presupposed that the motif *restoration to health* necessarily represents the liquidation of the *principal* lack in every narrative containing a healing miracle. It may well be, as will be shown in Chapter V. in detail, that in some cases restoration to health functions as an iNP in fulfillment of another main NP. This is the case in some of the so-called apophthegmata. Here, the miracle might function as a means to demonstrate the validity of a certain norm or the authority of a miracle worker to those attacking him. In these cases, the *miraculous deed* has a double function: it brings about restoration of health and, as such, functions as persuasive means. In

---

[9] It is unclear whether Paul's performance (καταβὰς ... ἐπέπεσεν αὐτῷ καὶ συμπεριλαβὼν αὐτῷ) is to be understood as having a restorative function (cf., among others, E. Haenchen, *Die Apostelgeschichte*, Kritisch-exegetischer Kommentar zum Neuen Testament, Abt. 3. [Göttingen: Vandenhoeck & Ruprecht, [5] 1965], 518-19, who refers to 1 Kings 17:21-22 and 2 Kings 4:34 as "Vorbild(er)" for this story. The observation that Paul does not say "Seine Seele ist *noch* in ihm.," which Haenchen takes as evidence for his argument, is useless: ἡ γὰρ ψυχὴ αὐτοῦ ἐν αὐτῷ ἐστιν is neither to be rendered "denn seine Seele ist *wieder* in ihm!") or if it simply describes how he checked the boy for any signs of life (cf., e.g., L. Bieler, "Totenauferweckung," 238, fn. 1, and O. Weinreich, "Zum Wundertypus der συναναχρωσις," in *ARW* 32 [1935], 246-64, 259, fn. 1).

fact, it might be that the healing miracle itself is subordinate to a main NP aimed at, for example, the persuasion of an enemy. These observations already indicate the probability that a variety of structures exists with respect to narratives involving restoration miracles.

It becomes clear that "miraculous restoration to health" is a category on the level of *motifs*. To classify all those stories containing a restoration miracle under the thematic label "healing miracle story" is therefore, from a structural perspective, problematic and misleading.[10] For this investigation, the motif "miraculous healing" serves as a heuristic device for the collection of narratives from antiquity which employ this motif. The analysis of these narratives will lead to a more differentiated classification, on the basis of which a more accurate comparison will be possible. The task is to break down all these narratives into their component parts, the motifemes, and to describe the interrelatedness of the motifemes. It is the sequence of and relation between the motifemes which account for the structure and thus for the type of a given narrative. The next step is then to compare the realizations of the motifemes on the level of motifs (allomotifs). This *narrower* RGL investigation, compared with the prior establishment of structural patterns, pays attention to the distribution of allomotifs among the different traditions under scrutiny.

All miracle narratives considered here describe the liquidation of a lack belonging to a health category by an active subject with the necessary preparation to carry out a miraculous performance. The corresponding motifemic slots present in narratives of this sort are at least: $L \rightarrow Prep \rightarrow P \rightarrow LL$. L describes the initial circumstance marked by a lack, Prep the preparedness of the AS, and P is a *performance* which liquidates the lack. LL stands for the result of that performance (the *lack* has been *liquidated*). The subject formerly conjoined with an undesirable object or disjoined from a desirable object,[11] defined from the point of view of the main NP, is now disjoined from the undesirable object or conjoined with a desirable object.

A distinctive feature of miracle stories, including healing miracle stories is the intervention of a subject representing a numinous power. The reversal of the initial circumstance depends on the involvement of some numinous power, since, from the perspective of normal human ability, the initial lack is irreversible. Consequently, the involvement of a *bearer of numinous power* (BNP) in the narrative process, its activation for and

---

[10] Cf. Propp, *Morphology*, 7: "… the division according to theme leads to total chaos."

[11] So, for example, that a subject is blind, conjoined with blindness, can also be expressed as lacking sight, disjoined from the ability to see.

engagement in a NP aimed at the reversal of the initial circumstance, plays a crucial role in miracle stories. If the BNP does not activate itself on its own initiative (*intransitive* activation), instrumental NPs are employed the function of which is to activate the BNP *transitively*. This transitive activation of the BNP presupposes a certain competence and motivation on part of the activating subject, usually the S(ubject of) C(ircumstance) itself or its representative(s) (RSC). Distinct iNPs can be identified concerning the bestowal of the SC or RSC with this competence and motivation required for the transitive activation of a BNP.

In some cases, however, the activation of the BNP presupposes a specific competence which the common SC or RSC does not possess. In those cases, the SC or its representative(s) directs its efforts towards the activation of a subject who is bestowed with the competence needed for the activation of the BNP, a *petitioner of numinous power* (PNP). From this it becomes clear that numerous iNPs can fill the phase preparedness of the BNP. However, the achievement of the activation of the BNP does not necessarily lead immediately to the main performance.

An immediate engagement of the BNP in this performance presupposes that the BNP is identical with the AS, though this is not always the case. In those instances where the AS is different from the BNP, it is not the BNP's function to bring about the liquidation of the initial lack *directly*, but to *prepare* an AS for the main performance. The AS might be an anti-subject (for example, a demon), whose will the BNP is able to subject (*devoir-faire*) through its numinous power. But the BNP might not even come into direct contact with the AS. It might, for example, bestow the SC itself temporarily with a numinous knowledge or power enabling it to prepare an AS sufficiently for the main performance. Alternatively, it may accomplish this through a subject specially prepared to act as a mediator (of the BNP's) numinous power (MNP). Numinous power is always present in a miracle story, even if, as has been indicated, its function may vary. In miracle stories, this numinous power is always involved in a narrative development *before* the LL.

The motifemic slot *following* the performance, sanction of the successful outcome of the healing performance could be expressed explicitly, either verbally, for example, by an acclamation of the BNP, sanctioning its preparedness, or by a performance in an iNP, demonstrating the success of the healing performance. Such performances may be prepared in a variety of ways, for example, through a command by the AS. This motifeme, the *sanction*, expressing the recognition of the preparedness of the BNP or its representative to liquidate the lack, or the successful outcome of the main performance, liquidating the lack, usually concludes a miracle story.

The following analysis of roughly 150 ancient Mediterranean miracle stories aims at the identification and description of all underlying motifemes and gives examples of the various allomotifs employed to fill respective motifemic slots.

3.1. The initial lack

3.1.1. The initial circumstance

A restoration miracle narrative presupposes a subject of a circumstance marked by the absence of health or life, or conjoined with an undesirable object.[12] The circumstance of this subject is the result of a previous NAP, defined as an anti-program from the perspective of the main miracle NP.[13] This is true even though the undesired circumstance of the subject is often *simply stated* without reference to a prior performance from which it resulted, for example,

- a great man of power, suffering from *leprosy* (מצרע והאיש היה גבור חיל; 2 Kings 5:1 = καὶ ὁ ἀνὴρ ἦν δυνατὸς ἰσχύι λελεπρωμένος; 4 Kings 5:1 [LXX]),
- a *sick* son (חלה בנו; bBer 5b/34b/yBer 9d),
- a man whose fingers, with the exception of one, were *paralyzed* (ἀνὴρ τοὺς τᾶς χηρὸς δακτύλους ἀκρατεῖς ἔχων πλὰν ἑνός; Epidauros A3),
- a *mute* boy (παῖς ἄφωνος; A5),
- a *blind* man (τυφλὸς ἐών; A18),
- one of the common people of Alexandria, well known for his *loss of sight* ... another, whose *hand was useless* (e plebe Alexandrinae quidam oculorum tabe notus ... alius manum aeger; Tacitus, hist. 4:81),
- a woman with a *tapeworm* (γυνὴ εἶχεν ἕλμινθα; Aelian, De nat. animal. IX 33),
- a man with *a spirit of an unclean demon* (ἄνθρωπος ἔχων πνεῦμα δαιμονίου ἀκαθάρτου; Lk 4:33),
- a man with *a withered hand* (ἄνθρωπος ἐξηραμμένην ἔχων τὴν χεῖρα; Mk 3:1),
- a man with *an unclean spirit* (ἄνθρωπος ἐν πνεύματι ἀκαθάρτῳ; Mk 5:2),
- a woman suffering from *hemorrhages* for twelve years (καὶ γυνὴ οὖσα ἐν ῥύσει αἵματος δώδεκα ἔτη; Mk 5:25),
- a *deaf* man with an *impediment in his speech* (καὶ φέρουσιν αὐτῷ κωφὸν καὶ μογιλάλον; Mk 7:32),

---

[12] Objects are here defined as "undesirable" or "desirable" always from the perspective of the base-NP bringing about the restoration of a subject in need of health.

[13] Cf. Wendland, *Kultur*, 217–18: "Die Hypostasierung der Krankheiten und ihre Herleitung von Geistern teilt das Christentum mit seiner Zeit. Wie die Krankheiten überhaupt, so wurden von den Griechen schon seit ältesten Zeiten besonders epileptische Zufälle, Aeußerungen von Geistesstörung und Tobsucht aus der Besessenheit durch eine Gottheit oder durch einen Dämon erklärt." It should be noted, however, that not every single illness is deduced from the influence of gods or demons in antiquity.

- a servant lying at home, *paralyzed* in terrible distress (ὁ παῖς μου βέβληται ἐν τῇ οἰκίᾳ παραλυτικός, δεινῶς βασανιζόμενος; Mt 8:6),
- a man *blind* from birth (εἶδεν ἄνθρωπον τυφλὸν ἐκ γενετῆς; Joh 9:1),
- a man in Lystra who could not use his feet and never walked, for he had been *crippled* from birth (καί τις ἀνὴρ ἀδύνατος ἐν Λύστροις τοῖς ποσὶν ἐκάθητο, χωλὸς ἐκ κοιλίας μητρὸς αὐτοῦ; Acts 14:8), ... etc.

In these statements, the subject's connection with an undesirable object is expressed by means of verbs indicating "being" (εἶναι) or "having" (ἔχειν), or by other intransitive verbs indicating a circumstance. The circumstance is often simply indicated by attributive adjectives, by adjectival nouns, by participles, or simply by prepositions like ἐν or μετά indicating conjunction. These grammatical constructions are used to describe circumstances and not the events that lead to them.

Frequently, additional NPs and motifs are employed to illustrate the *seriousness* of a subject's condition, or to describe it more closely, indicating its gravity, persistence, symptoms, worsening, and the human inability to heal.

3.1.1.1. Circumstantial information

The seriousness of an illness can be emphasized by means of *adjectives* in an attributive or adverbial position, as in the following examples:

- a *grievous* illness (νόσῳ χαλεπῇ; Jos. Ant. X 25; Marinos, Vita Procli 29),
- suffering *dreadfully* (δεινῶς διακείμενος; Epidauros A17),
- being in *a very bad* way (ἐμ παντὶ ἐοῦσα; Epidauros B25),
- being *so badly* (οὕτω σφοδρῶς; Epidauros B30),
- a *violent* attack of illness (ingens vis morbi; Livy, Ab urbe II 36:5),
- lying in a *sorry* plight (διέκειτο μοχθηρῶς; Plutarch, Life of Pericles 13:8),
- having a *violent* fever (με σφοδρὸς ἔφλεγε πυρετός; Oxyr. 1381:96),
- a person who was *almost blind* (οὐ πολὺ ἀποδέον τυφλῷ· Pausanias, Descr. Graec. X 38:13),
- a man *full* of leprosy (ἀνὴρ πλήρης λέπρας; Lk 5:12).

3.1.1.2. Temporal information

Temporal indicators are often specific. Numbers make explicit the persistence of a predicament.[14] Sometimes, the temporal indicators are of a more general nature, as in the following examples:

- the affliction had *lasted for some time* (ἡ νόσος πόρρω τοῦ χρόνου ἦν; Aelian, De nat. animal. XI 32),
- from *childhood* (ἐκ παιδιόθεν; Mk 9:21),
- from *birth* (ἐκ γενετῆς; Joh 9:1, ἐκ κοιλίας μητρὸς αὐτοῦ; Acts 3:2; 14:8).

---

[14] Cf. Tobit 2:10 (א = Sinaiticus); 1QapGen 20:18; Bacchylides, Epinicia 11:92; Pherekydes, Frg. 3; Epidauros A1,2,12,B30; Phil., Vita Apol. III 38, IV 43; Mk 5:25; Lk 13:11; Joh 5:5; 11:39; Acts 9:9,33.

3.1.1.3. Symptoms

With regard to illness, the lack is often manifest in descriptions of *symptoms*, for instance, by means of *comparison*: "leprous as white as snow" (מצרעת כשלג; Ex 4:6; Num 12:10). Most commonly, however, NPs with the subject of circumstance *as* active subject describing the lack *demonstrate* the successful performance of a previous NAP which brought about the lack addressed in the main NP, for example,

- king Jeroboam whose hand withered "could not draw it back to himself" (לא יכל להשיבה אליו/οὐκ ἠδυνήθη ἐπιστρέψαι αὐτὴν πρὸς ἑαυτόν; 1 Kings 13:4b). Here it is the *inability* of the subject of circumstance to engage successfully in a performance.
- after having been wounded by an arrow [NAP], Gorgias Heracleiotas had suppurated so badly "that he filled sixty-seven basins with pus" (ὥστε ἑπτὰ καὶ ἑξήκοντα λεκάνας ἐνέπλησε πύους (Epidauros B30). Gorgias is the active subject of this performance.[15]
- a man vomits blood (αἷμα ἀναφέροντι; Inscr. Graecae XIV 966c). Here it becomes explicit that the vomiting of blood is a performance of the subject of circumstance demonstrating the circumstance.[16]

The descriptions of symptoms can be very detailed, as in Diodorus of Sicily, Bibl. Hist. XVII 103:5. This is especially true for cases of madness and "demonic possession" where the *strange conduct* of the ill person is depicted:

- mad young women flee into the *wilderness* and utter *terrible cries* (Bacchylides, Epinicia 11:55–56; cf vv. 92–95),
- the mad women run *indecently* (μετ' ἀκοσμίας ἁπάσης) through the *desert* (Apollodoros, Bibliotheca II 2),
- a Syrian takes care of possessed persons, "those who fall down in the light of the moon and roll their eyes and fill their mouths with foam" (καταπίπτοντας πρὸς τὴν σελήνην καὶ τὼ ὀφθαλμὼ διαστρέφοντας καὶ ἀφροῦ πιμπλαμένους τὸ στόμα; Lucian, Philops. 16; cf. 11),
- the character of a demon (ἦθος τοῦ δαίμονος) is determined as mocker and liar (εἴρωνα καὶ ψεύστην) which results in the possessed boy being without reason (νοῦν). He refuses to attend school and archery, does not remain at home, "but (the demon) drives him out into the *desert places*. And the boy does not even retain his own voice, but speaks in a deep hollow tone, as men do; and he looks at you with other eyes rather than his own ...; he does not recognize me" (ἀλλ' ἐς τὰ ἔρημα τῶν χωρίων ἐκτρέπει, καὶ οὐδὲ τὴν φωνὴν ὁ παῖς τὴν ἑαυτοῦ ἔχει, ἀλλὰ βαρὺ φθέγγεται καὶ κοῖλον, ὥσπερ οἱ ἄνδρες, βλέπει δὲ ἑτέροις ὀφθαλμοῖς μᾶλλον ἢ τοῖς ἑαυτοῦ ... ὁ οὐκ οἶδέ με; Philostratus, Vita Apol. III 38),

---

[15] Cf. the effect of the blow against Hector in Homer's Iliad 14:435–439 and 15:10–11: ὁ δ ἀργαλέῳ ἔχετ' ἄσθματι κῆρ ἀπινύσσων, αἷμ' ἐμέων.

[16] For additional examples, cf. Aelian, De nat. animal. XI 32; Oxyr. 1381:96–102.

- after having been bitten by a mad dog, a boy behaves exactly like a dog (ἐς τὰ τῶν κυνῶν πάντα; Philostratus, Vita Apol. VI 43).

It should be noted that often, and especially in the case of demonic possession, the ἦθος of the anti-subject determines, and becomes identical with, the behavior of the subject of circumstance. For NT examples of this phenomenon, see,

- a possessed man lives in graves, screams day and night, and hits himself with stones (Mk 5:3,5),
- as a consequence of demonic possession, a boy foams, grinds his teeth, becomes rigid, and falls to the ground (ἀφρίζει καὶ τρίζει τοὺς ὀδόντας καὶ ξηραίνεται ... καὶ πεσὼν ἐπὶ τῆς γῆς ἐκυλίετο ἀφρίζων; Mk 9:18,20),
- a woman who has a spirit of divination cries out and reveals the identity of the apostles (Acts 16:17).

While in all these instances the successful outcome of the performance of an anti-program is demonstrated by means of a *performance of the subject of circumstance*, descriptions of the lack of *preparedness* of that subject with regard to another NP function in the same way:

- after an evil spirit (רוח באישא) had afflicted the king and everyone in his family [NAP], the king could not approach Sarai and did not sleep with her (לו יכל למקבר בהא ואף לא ירעהא; 1QapGen 20:17). The king's negative *pouvoir-faire* is a direct consequence of his being attacked by an evil spirit.
- he could not talk with them (οὐκ ἐδύνατο λαλῆσαι αὐτοῖς; Lk 1:22),
- she was bent over and could not stand upright (καὶ ἦν συγκύπτουσα καὶ μὴ δυναμένη ἀνακύψαι εἰς τὸ παντελές; Lk 13:11).

3.1.1.4. Aggravation of illness
This motif describes the worsening of a predicament. The aggravating force may be inherent in the initial condition and may not be explicitly motivated:

- And after two years the plagues [of the evil spirit] against him [the king] and all other people of his household grew stronger and worse (1QapGen 20:18),
- Hanina ben Dosa, after having eaten a poisonous onion, became sick and was close to death (חלה ונטה למות; b. 'Erub. 29b).

In other cases, the aggravation appears to be the result of a NP which stands in between the original lack and its aggravated state, for example, in Tobit 2:10 (codex Sinaiticus, which expands here on the versions presented by codices B and A) the transition from the original to the aggravated condition, from Tobit's conjunction with "white spots" (λευκώματα) on his eyes to his being blind (ἀδύνατος τοῖς ὀφθαλμοῖς), is brought about by a NP describing a failed performance by physicians attempting to heal him. For other examples of this kind, aggravation of a condition as a consequence of a failed main performance, cf. Epidauros B23; Aelian, De nat. animal. IX 33; and Mk 5:26b: "she grew worse" (ἀλλὰ μᾶλλον εἰς τὸ χεῖρον ἐλθοῦσα; this motif is dropped in Lk 8:43). Apollodoros describes how the madness of some young women grows worse after the representative of the subjects of circumstance fails to agree upon a contract proposed by the bearer of miraculous power. Not only is the condition of the subjects of circumstance aggravated, but their madness spreads to other women as well (Bibliotheca II 2).[17] Sometimes, however, the aggravation might be effected by other causes. As an example, cf. Jos., Ant. X 25: "and the illness was aggravated by the dreadful despair of the king when he considered his childlessness …"[18]

3.1.1.5. Failed NPs and other expressions of human inabilities

As has been indicated under 3.1.1.4., the initial lack can be intensified by failed NPs describing an attempt by physicians or other active subjects to heal. These attempts result in failure and may even effect an aggravation of the original condition. In most cases, however, the failure is explicitly attributed to the absense of *pouvoir-* and/or *savoir-faire* with regard to respective active subjects. These active subjects are *not able* to carry out a proposed NP. A most vivid example is Epidauros B23: a woman with a tapeworm dreams that "the sons of the god" (τοὺς υἱοὺς τοῦ θεοῦ [who himself is not present at that time]) cut off her head but were not able to put it back again (τὰγ κεφαλὰν ἀποταμεῖν, οὐ δυναμένους δ' ἐπιθέμεν πάλιν). The parallel account in Aelian, De nat. animal. IX 33, *adds* a variation of this motif: "and the cleverest of the physicians failed to cure her" (καὶ ἰάσασθαι αὐτὴν ἀπεῖπον οἱ τῶν ἰατρῶν δεινοί).[19] Mk 9: 14–29 exhibits a similar structure: Jesus' successful performance is preceded by a failed NP of his disciples who "were not able" (οὐκ ἴσχυσαν) to exorcize the demon.[20]

---

[17] οὐκ ἐπιτρέποντος δὲ Προίτου θεραπεύειν ἐπὶ μισθοῖς τηλικούτοις, ἔτι μᾶλλον ἐμαίνοντο αἱ παρθένοι καὶ προσέτι μετὰ τούτων αἱ λοιπαὶ γυναῖκες …

[18] τῇ δὲ νόσῳ προσετίθετο καὶ ἀθυμία δεινὴ ὑπὸ τοῦ βασιλέως αὐτοῦ (Hezekiah), τὴν ἀπαιδίαν λογιζομένου …

[19] Against the background of the inabilities of both the ἰατροί and the ζάκοροι (who οὐκ ἐδύναντο οὐκέτι to attach the head to its original joint since they engaged in an ἔργῳ δυνατωτέρῳ τῆς ἑαυτῶν σοφίας), Aelian points out the ability and preparedness of the god Asclepios who performs with ἀμάχῳ τινὶ θείᾳ δυνάμει in his σοφίᾳ.

[20] Similar to the Aelian passage, Mk 9:14–29 focuses on the *preparedness* of the *disciples* of the miracle worker, especially on their pouvoir-faire. With regard to the miracle worker's helpers, cf. verses 18 and 28–29, with regard to the miracle worker himself, verse 22b: ἀλλ᾽ εἴ τι δύνῃ, and, finally, with regard to the preparedness of the petitioner, cf. verse 23b: πάντα δυνατὰ τῷ πιστεύοντι. In this pericope, the availability of δύναμις is described as solely dependent on πίστις. This relation between δύναμις and πίστις is explicitly stressed three times, always as sanctions of Jesus (subjective genitive): Ω γενεὰ ἄπιστος (v. 19a), verses 23b and 29: Τοῦτο τὸ γένος ἐν οὐδενὶ δύναται ἐξελθεῖν εἰ μὴ ἐν προσευχῇ. As an

In this context another motif which describes *the lack* should be mentioned. While the above examples imply the hopelessness of a certain condition as a result of failed NPs, the same motif can be formulated in *expressions of despair* sanctioning the existence of the undesirable circumstance:

– friends of the subject of circumstance do not expect any change for the better (χρηστὸν δὲ περὶ αὐτοῦ οὐδὲν προσεδόκων οὐδ' οἱ φίλοι; Jos., Ant. X 25);
– being *despaired of* by everyone (ἀφελπισμένῳ ὑπὸ παντὸς ἀνθρώπου; Inscr. Graecae XIV 966 b.c).

3.1.2. The creation of the initial circumstance

Sometimes *how* a condition came about is explicitly indicated or extensively narrated, presenting the NPs which resulted in the attribution of a certain object to a subject who then becomes in need of being disjoined from that particular object. Distinct thematic NAPs representing allomotifs for the motifeme *creation of a need* can be distinguished. The cause of a certain predicament might be divine punishment, independent attacks of demons or illnesses, accidents, fights, attempts at murder, etc.

3.1.2.1. Divine punishment

The lack to be liquidated in the main NP can be the consequence of divine punishment. The punishment, however, presupposes an act of disobedience on the part of the subject of circumstance: either a prohibition was transgressed or a command disregarded. The motifeme sequence *divine order* (negative or positive)-*disobedience-punishment resulting in lack* accounts for the structure of punishment-stories, which often result in irreversible death or handicap for the disobedient subject.[21] All motifemes need not be manifest in a given narrative; the *divine order*, for example, can be silent and simply implied or presupposed. A punishment-narrative preceding a healing miracle story can effect different ty-

---

example for prayer in the context of exorcism, cf. 1QapGen 20, as examples for prayer in the context of non-demonic healings, cf. Acts 9:11 and 28:8.

For additional examples of failed NPs, cf. 1 Kings 17:21aα; 2 Kings 4:29-31; Tobit (BA - א) 2:10; 1QapGen 20:19-20; Jos., Ant. VI 166; X 25; Plutarch, Live of Pericles 13:8; Aelian, De nat. animal. IX 33; Marinos, Vita Procli 29; Mk 5:26/Lk 8:43.

With regard to 1 Kings 17:21aα, it seems as if Elijah's unsuccessful performance *before* he asks God for help, needs to be considered as failed NP. This motif is dropped in Josephus' account of this story (Antt. VIII 326). For 2 Kings 4:29-31, note that the following successful NP of Elisha is introduced by a *prayer* to God, a motif missing in the failed NP of his disciple. A. Oepke, Art. "ἰάομαι etc.," in ThWNT III (1938), 194-215, correctly observes that the "Totenerweckungen 1 Kö 17, 20ff und 2 Kö 4, 33ff ... auf Gebet hin [geschehen]" (202).

[21] Cf., e.g., Gen 19:17-26; 2 Kings 2:23-25; Epidauros A7; Acta 5:1-11.

pes of illness, inflicted either directly or mediated by agents, such as, animals or demons.[22]

In cases where the punishment is direct, without a mediator, the god can appear explicitly as the active subject of a performance which brings about the predicament of a subject of circumstance, for example

- *Yahweh* closed fast all the wombs of the house of Abimelech because of Sarah (כי עצר עצר יהוה בעד כל־רחם לבית אבימלך על דבר שרה) = ὅτι συγκλείων συνέκλεισεν κύριος ἔξωθεν πᾶσαν μήτραν ἐν τῷ οἴκῳ τοῦ Αβιμελεχ ἕνεκεν Σαρρας; Gen 20:18),
- a man fails to bring thanks-offerings which has the effect that *Asclepios* makes him blind again (μετὰ δὲ τοῦτο τὰ ἴατρα οὐκ ἀπάγοντα ὁ θεός νιν ἐπόησε τυφλὸν αὖθις; Epidauros B22).
- because of their blasphemy, the goddess *Hera* frightens away the daughters from their father's house while bestowing them with madness (τὰς ἐξ ἐρατῶν ἐφόβησε παγκρατὴς Ἥρα μελάθρων Προίτου, παραπλῆγι φρένας καρτερᾶι ζεύξασ' ἀνάγκαι; Bacchylides, Epinicia 11:43–46).

If a mediating agent is engaged, a god's activity consists of the *preparation* of that agent: for instance, the god *sends* a demon. Such preparatory activity by a god is manifest in 1QapGen 20:16–17: "In that night God Most High sent him a spirit of affliction to afflict him and everyone in his household, an evil spirit" בליליא דן שלח לה אל עליון רוח מכתש למכתשה ולכויל) אנש ביתה רוח באישא). In cases where a god prepares an agent to inflict a certain plague, the agent, be it a demon (evil spirit), an angel, or a personified sickness, functions as active subject of a performance which effects the liquidation of a lack in the present NAP, the need of punishment, and, at the same time, produces a lack for the subject of a circumstance to be liquidated in the main miracle NP:

- an evil spirit from Yahweh torments Saul (ובעתתו רוח־רעה מאת יהוה; 1 Sam 16:14),[23]
- an evil spirit afflicts the king (והואת כתשא לה; 1QapGen 20:17),
- a violent attack of illness suddenly lays a man low (ingens vis morbi adorta est debilitate subita; Livy, Ab urbe 2:36.

Kings 13:4b describes the consequence of an improper intention of the king Jeroboam: he stretches out his hand from the altar saying

Seize him [the direct object is the Man of God who proclaimed the devastating judgment of Yahweh concerning the altar], but the hand that he had stretched

---

[22] Cf. Gen 20:1–18; Num 12:1–15; 21:4–9; Artapanus, Frg. 3:24–25; 1QapGen 19:10–20:32; Bacchylides, Epinicia 11:43–46, 53–54; Pherecydes, Frg. 3; Epidauros B22; Livius, Ab urbe 2:36; Lk 1:5–25.

[23] Cf. LXX: καὶ ἔπνιγεν αὐτὸν πνεῦμα πονηρὸν παρὰ κυρίου, and Jos., Ant. VI 166: τὸν Σαοῦλον δὲ περιήρχετο πάθη τινὰ καὶ δαιμόνια πνιγμοὺς αὐτῷ καὶ στραγγάλας ἐπιφέροντα.

out against him withered, so that he could not draw it back to himself (וַתִּיבַשׁ ידו/καί ἰδοὺ ἐξηράνθη ἡ χεὶρ αὐτοῦ, ἣν ἐξέτεινεν ἐπ᾽ αὐτόν, καὶ οὐκ ἠδυνήθη ἐπιστρέψαι αὐτὴν πρὸς ἑαυτόν).

In yet other cases, neither the act of disobedience nor the performance of the punishment may be manifest in a narrative. Instead, they may be only implied or presupposed, cf. Artapanus, Frg. 3:24–25: here only the *act of disobedience* is narrated and the success of a silent performance demonstrated: "but when the king heard it (ἀκούσαντα δὲ τὸν βασιλέα [what is forbidden to be heard]) he fell over speechless (πεσεῖν ἄφωνον)."

3.1.2.2. Independent attacks by demons or illness

As has been shown under 3.1.2.1., attacks by demons or illness can function as means to carry out punishment. Nevertheless, demons or various kinds of illnesses commonly appear as forces attacking a subject independently, without any connotation of punishment. The NPs in this category simply focus on the attack by the anti-subjects: a performance creating a lack (from the perspective of the following main NP) is carried out. The following phrases describe some ways in which active subjects attack respective victims:[24]

- Ben-Tamaljon went ahead and *entered* the daughter of the emperor (קדים בן תמליון] הוא על בברתיה דקיסר;[25] Meʿila 17a-b),
- sickness has *pervaded* her (Bintresh's) body (Bentresh Stela 5–9),
- my mother was distracted by an ungodly quartan ague, which had *seized* her ... and a fever *burned* me exceedingly (τῇ μητρὶ ἐπισκήψασα ἄθεος τεταρταία, ἡ φρείκη αὐτὴν ἐστρόβει ..., καί με σφοδρὸς ἔφλεγε πυρετός, ... (Oxyr. 1381:67–69,95–96),
- the demon who *drives you on* (ὁ δαίμων, ὃς ἐκλαύνει σε; Phil., Vita Apol IV 20),
- she *was stricken* with a grievous illness (N.N. ... νόσῳ χαλεπῇ κατείχετο; Marinos, Vita Procli 29),
- the mother-in-law ... *was suffering* from a severe fever (πενθερά ... ἦν συνεχομένη πυρετῷ μεγάλῳ; Lk 4:38),
- and whenever it *seizes* him, it *dashes him down* ..., the spirit immediatly *convulsed* him (καὶ ὅπου ἐὰν αὐτὸν καταλάβῃ ῥήσσει αὐτόν ... τὸ πνεῦμα εὐθὺς συνεσπάραξεν αὐτόν; Mk 9:18,20; cf. Lk 9:39,42),
- it happened that the father of Poplios lay sick in bed *suffering* from fever and dysentery (ἐγένετο δὲ τὸν πατέρα τοῦ Ποπλίου πυρετοῖς καὶ δυσεντερίῳ συνεχόμενον; Acts 28:8).[26]

---

[24] Cf. also the examples given under 3.1.2.1. concerning the performances of agents sent by a god.

[25] Nominal phrases are the exception for the description of this kind of performance. These performances are usually illustrated by verbal clauses.

[26] πυρετοῖς and δυσεντερίῳ function as dativus auctoris and signify the *agens* of the passive συνεχόμενον.

3.1.2.3. Accidents (including attacks by animals)

Often the predicament of a subject, marked by a lack of health, is caused by an unpredictable accident, for example:

- and since my eyes were open, the sparrows *defecated* their hot stuff *into my eyes* (καὶ τῶν ὀφθαλμῶν μου ἀνεῳγότων ἀφώδευσαν τὰ στρουθία θερμὸν [Sinaiticus: ἐκάθισεν τὸ ἀφόδευμα αὐτῶν] εἰς τοὺς ὀφθαλμούς μου; Tobit 2:10),
- and it happened that rabbi Hanina *ate* half an onion and half of the *poison* in it (ומעשה ברבי חנינא שאכל חצי בצל וחצי נחש שבו; 'Erub. 29a-b),
- but he *fell from the tree* onto some fencing (καταπετὼν οὖν ἀπὸ τοῦ δένδρεος περὶ σκόλοπάς τινας; Epidauros A11),
- the child Glaukos, in chasing a mouse, fell into a jar of honey and died (Γλαῦκος δὲ ἔτι νήπιος ὑπάρχων, μῦν διώκων εἰς μέλιτος πίθον πεσὼν ἀπέθανεν; Apollodoros, Bibliotheca III 3),
- for the most active and zealous one of the artificiers lost his footing and *fell from a great height* (ὁ γὰρ ἐνεργότατος καὶ προθυμότατος τῶν τεχνιτῶν ἀποσφαλεὶς ἐξ ὕψους ἔπεσε; Plutarch, Pericles 8),
- Midas ... had been *bitten by a viper* ..., the creature had crawled up and *bitten* him on the great toe (Μίδαν ... ὑπὸ ἐχίδνης δηχθέντα ... προσερπύσαν τὸ θηρίον δακεῖν κατὰ τὸν μέγαν δάκτυλον; Lucian, Philops. 11),
- a mad dog had *attacked* a young man (κύων ἐνεπεπτώκει ἐφήβῳ λυττῶν; Philostratos, Vita Apol. VI 43, cf. III 39),
- Eutychos ..., overcome by sleep, *fell* to the ground three floors below (Εὔτυχος ... κατενεχθεὶς ἀπὸ τοῦ ὕπνου ἔπεσεν ἀπὸ τοῦ τριστέγου κάτω; Acts 20:9).

The active subject in these performances can be identical with the subject of circumstance (cf. the subjects of אכל and πίπτειν). In instances where the two subjects are not identical, various animals are the active subjects.

3.1.2.4. Fights

The lack to be liquidated is often the result of a fight. This motif, in the context of miracle narratives, is numerous in the *pagan* Greco-Roman world, but missing in Jewish miracle narratives. The earliest evidence goes back to Homer's Iliad:

- Menelaos ... , whom some man well skilled in archery has smitten with an arrow (Μενέλαον ..., ὅν τις ὀϊστεύσας ἔβαλεν, τόξων εὖ εἰδώς; IV 195-196),
- great Ajax hoisted one of the stones and heaved it at Hector's chest and struck him over the shield-rim, close to the throat (τῶν [χερμαδίων] ἐν ἀείρας στῆθος [Τελαμώνιος Αἴας] βεβλήκει ὑπὲρ ἄντυγος ἀγχόθι δειρῆς; XIV 411-412, in the context of Hector's restoration XV 220-299).[27]

---

[27] Cf. also the Epidauros inscriptions: N.N. ἐμ μάχαι τινὶ τρωθεὶς εἰς τὸμ πλεύμονα τοξεύματι ... (B30), N.N. ἔν τινι μάχαι ὑπὸ δόρατος πλαγεὶς δι' ἀμφοτέρων τῶν ὀφθαλμῶν ... (B32), as well as Diodoros of Sicily, Bibl. Hist. XVII 103:4-6.

The NT only knows of one such incident in the context of a healing miracle. In the episode where Jesus is taken captive, Luke mentions a miraculous healing after "one of them (his followers) struck the slave of the high priest and cut off his right ear" (ἐπάταξεν εἷς τις ἐξ αὐτῶν τοῦ ἀρχιερέως τὸν δοῦλον καὶ ἀφεῖλεν τὸ οὖς αὐτοῦ τὸ δεξιόν; 22:50).

All these examples narrate how a wound, resulting from a fight, was miraculously healed. The active subjects of these NAPs are, in most cases, enemy soldiers.

3.1.2.5. Murder and attempted murder

Sometimes, the initial lack is the result of murder or an attempted murder. The active subject in the performance which brings about the initial lack is a (potential) murderer or a subject of circumstance *prepared* by the murderer):

- the Roman emperor Antonius kills one of his slaves at the door of Rabbi and another at the door of his palace (חד קטליה אבבא דבי רבי וחד קטליה אבבא דביתיה; ʿAboda Zara 10a-b),
- I was murdered by the evil arts of my new bride and sacrificed to her poisoned cup . . . (Malis novae nuptae peremptus artibus et addictus noxio poculo, ...; Apuleius, Metam. II 29).

These two performances are successful and result in the deaths of the victims. Aelian (De nat. animal. XI 34) presents an *almost* successful murderous act: "Cissos ... was the victim of a plot on the part of a woman whom he had once loved and later married: he ate some eggs of a snake, which caused him pain; he was in a grievous state and in danger of death."[28] It should be noted here, which is also true for the previous example, that the subject of circumstance is explicitly involved in the performance: *he* eats the poisonous snake eggs.

3.1.2.6. Additional allomotifs concerning the creation of the lack

In addition to the above identified five recurrent thematic NPs bringing about an initial lack, there are a few miracle narratives which ascribe an initial lack to other causes: Aristeas the Exegete (Frg. 1:3) mentions illness (τὸ σῶμα ἑλκῶσαι) as one of the misfortunes by means of which God *tested* Job's faith. In Ex 4: 1–9 God *prepares* Moses by subjecting his will (εἰσένεγκε τὴν χεῖρά σου εἰς τὸν κόλπον σου) to engage in a performance which brings about a lack in order to *teach* Moses an act to be used in the confrontation with his people. In Acts 9:1–9 and

---

[28] Κίσσος ... ἐπιβουλευθεὶς ὑπὸ τῆς πρότερον μὲν ἐρωμένης ὕστερον δὲ γαμετῆς, καὶ ᾠὰ ὄφεως φαγών, ὠδυνᾶτο καὶ ἑαυτοῦ κακῶς εἶχε, καὶ ἐπίδοξος τεθνήξεσθαι ἦν.

22:6–11, the loss of sight is attributed to the *circumstances* of Paul's vision: ὡς δὲ οὐκ ἐνέβλεπον ἀπὸ τῆς δόξης τοῦ φωτὸς ἐκείνου ... (Acts 22:11).

3.1.3. Summary: The interrelatedness of the motifeme lack with other motifemic slots

The initial lack of a NP describing a healing has been described as the result of a NAP which creates this lack. The NAP does not necessarily need to be *manifest* in a miracle narrative. Most miracle narratives, especially those of the NT, start off with the establishment, sanctioning, of the initial lack, and not with its creation.

1QapGen 19:10–20:32 is a good example of a narrative which describes extensively the creation of a lack. Various narrative moves from Abram's trip to Egypt because of a famine in Hebron to the king's seizing of Sarai lead to the performance of the NAP which brings about a circumstance of illness, the lack of health, which is transformed into a lack of illness by the performance in the main miracle NP. In the NAP, Abram, through prayer accompanied by tears, implores God to *punish* the king because of the crime committed and to *take precaution* that Sarai not be "defiled." Abram *prepares* his god through invocation for a performance to liquidate a dual lack: punishment of the king for the transgression of divine law concerning adultery[29] and *protection* of Sarai who is about to be sexually approached by another man. In the NAP "the most high god" reacts and *prepares* an active subject for the performance by sending out an evil spirit to scourge the king and all his household. The evil spirit carries out the proposed NAP performance: "and it scourged him and all his household". Different motifs demonstrate the *success* of the evil spirit's performance, which fulfills the *two* expressed needs *in one action*: the king is unable to approach Sarai; he is sick for two years; after two years the seriousness of the illness grows worse; and the attempts of Egyptian physicians, magicians, and sages to heal him fail. Only now do we come to the main miracle story program. The circumstance of the king, his being conjoined with a scourging evil spirit, is the *lack* in the main NP which is reversed by the performance, which is described as an exorcism.

---

[29] This motif is, of course, problematic in this context since the king did not know about the marital status of Sarai which had been concealed by a lie of Sarai and Abram by means of which he wanted to save his life. This problematic is, however, not a topic in 1QapGen, even though it had already been recognized by the Elohist, cf. Gen 20:1–18, esp. verses 4–6.

3.2. Allomotifs leading to the preparation of the active subject

The phase preparedness aims at the bestowal of an active subject with motivation (*vouloir-/devoir-faire*) and *ability* (*savoir-/pouvoir-faire*) to engage successfully in a performance. "Active subject" (AS) refers to the subject which engages in the actual performance aimed at the reversal of a circumstance of a lack or need. In miraculous healing stories the AS is *not necessarily* the "miracle worker." The designation "miracle worker" is used in such a wide range of meanings that a definition is difficult, if not impossible. Figures, such as, Yahweh, Abraham, Moses, Elijah, Elisha, Tobit, Eleazar, Hanina ben Dosa, Jesus of Nazareth, Peter, Ananias, Paul, Asclepios, Vespasian, Alexander, Apollonios of Tyana, and others, are indiscriminately referred to as "miracle workers," regardless of clearly distinguishable *functions* which they fulfill in miracle stories: Moses, Elijah, Elijah, Hanina, Peter, and Paul are usually depicted as men who are able to activate their god by means of *prayer* (appeal to *vouloir-faire*),[30] whereas Yahweh, Jesus, Asclepios, and Apollonios *incorporate* a divine power in themselves, which enables them either to function as active subjects (AS) in a main NP or activate (*devoir-faire*) another AS by means of *divine authority*. Finally, there are Abraham (the Abram of 1QapGen), Moses, Tobit, Vespasian, and Alexander, themselves not bearers of numinous power, but who are sometimes, in addition to their ability to invoke their god, allowed by the bearers of numinous power to *mediate* that power in the performance of a miracle. Because of this diversity I will refrain from using the term "miracle worker" in my analysis, and introduce instead the terms "bearer of numinous power" (BNP) for subjects who *incorporate* healing power in themselves, "petitioner of numinous power" (PNP) for those whose function is to activate their gods through prayer, and "mediator of numinous power" (MNP) for those subjects who mediate a BNP's numinous power for the performance of a miracle. The BNP plays a crucial role in miracle stories. Even though it may be overshadowed by the actions of other subjects, and thus allowed to recede into the background of the narrative development, an aspect of its power must *always* be present. In miracle stories *everything* ultimately depends on the activation and involvement of a BNP endowed with the ability to ensure the success of the miracle performance. However, the BNP itself does not always engage *directly* in the performance. Its function may be to *prepare* another active subject for the purpose.

A healing miracle narrative consists of at least two contrary circumstances of a subject, marked by L and LL, in between which a perform-

---

[30] For a detailed description of this category, cf. below, 3.2.1.2.2.4.

ance (P) of an active subject takes place. In what follows, motifemes which express what happens between L and LL will be investigated: first, those narrative moves which aim at the *preparation* of the BNP, and then, those which lead from there to the preparedness of the AS, who could be, but does not have to be the BNP, for the main *performance*. Finally, the motifeme which follows the main performance, *sanctioning* the liquidation of the lack and/or the preparedness of the AS, BNP, PNP, or MNP, will be investigated.

3.2.1. The preparedness of the bearer of numinous power (BNP)

3.2.1.1. The ability (savoir-/pouvoir-faire) of the BNP

In miracle stories, the ability of a BNP, its *savoir-* and *vouloir-faire*, is always presupposed. It is never narrated *in* a miracle story how the BNP was bestowed with this ability. If it were narrated, this subject would depend on another subject, which would then represent the BNP. *Savoir-faire* refers to the BNP's *knowledge* of how to engage successfully in a performance reversing the initial circumstance. *Pouvoir-faire* refers to the *power* necessary for the carrying out of an envisioned NP which the BNP incorporates. The competence of the BNP amalgamates *savoir-* and *pouvoir-faire*. This holds true for the case of *gods* as BNPs and can easily be demonstrated from the OT.

According to Jer 10, which describes the might of the Hebrew god over against the powerlessness of pagan idols, Yahweh is the one "who made the earth by his power (בכחו/ἐν τῇ ἰσχύι αὐτοῦ), who established the world by his wisdom (בחכמתו/ἐν τῇ σοφίᾳ αὐτοῦ), and by his understanding (בתבונתו/τῇ φρονήσει αὐτοῦ) stretched out the heavens" (v. 12 = 51:15). Yahweh has all *pouvoir-faire* (כח וגבורה/ἰσχὺς καὶ δυναστεία, cf. 1 Chr 29:12) as well as *savoir-faire (חכמה//σοφία and תבונה/φρόνησις) and is thus able to act powerfully and wisely. But the OT goes even further: Yahweh *is* power (עז: cf. Ex 15:2; Isa 12:2; Jer 16:19; Ps 118:14) and has, according to Sirach, created σοφία before the creation of the world (1:4, 9: προτέρα πάντων ἔκτισται σοφία ..., κύριος αὐτὸς ἔκτισεν αὐτήν, cf. 24:9). "With God are wisdom and strength; he has counsel and understanding ...; with him are strength and wisdom" (Job 12:13, 16a).[31] Therefore, all knowledge and power on earth are derived from God: "Yahweh gave wisdom and understanding" (נתן יהוה חכמה ותבונה) to the artists involved in the construction of the sanctuary (Ex 36:1), Yahweh bestows Solomon with חכמה ותבונה (1 Kings 5:9; et al.) and is expected to give "power and strength to his people" (עז ותעצמות לעם/δύναμιν

---

[31] עמו חכמה וגבורה לו עצה ותבונה עמו עז ותושיה/παρ' αὐτῷ σοφία καὶ δύναμις, αὐτῷ βουλὴ καὶ σύνεσις. παρ' αὐτῷ κράτος καὶ ἰσχύς.

καὶ κραταίωσιν τῷ λαῷ αὐτοῦ; Ps 68[LXX: 67]:36). Also the surname of Yahweh,[32] צבאות, even though it embraces a wide range of meanings and so cannot be defined concretely, clearly indicates power and might.[33] This interpretation is supported by the LXX's usual rendering, κύριος τῶν δυναμένων or κύριος παντοκράτωρ. In this context it is also significant that אל, the term for deity, even though its etymology has not yet been fully clarified, appears closely related to איל as designation for power, might. Both seem to be derived from a hypothetical אול = to be ahead, to be strong.[34]

This conception of the Hebrew god is attested by Judaism of "biblical," as well as rabbinic times,[35] and is shared by the NT writers. The only new development around the turn of the eras is that the tetragrammaton became more and more substituted by גבורה/δύναμις, and Yahweh thus completely identified with power and might. The best-known example for this development is Mk 14:62/Mt 26:64 (different Lk 22:69), where Jesus uses δύναμις as substitute for God.[36] Yahweh's *pouvoir-* and *savoir-faire* enable him to function as the exclusive power over life:

> I kill and I make alive, I wound and I heal; and no one can deliver from my hand (אני אמית ואחיה מחצתי ואני ארפא ואין מידי מציל/ἐγὼ ἀποκτενῶ καὶ ζῆν ποιήσω, πατάξω κἀγὼ ἰάσομαι, καὶ οὐκ ἔστιν ὃς ἐξελεῖται ἐκ τῶν χειρῶν μου; Dtn 32:39b; cf. 1 Sam 2:6; Ex 15:26; Job 5:18; Hos 6:1-2).

---

[32] Cf., e.g., Jer 10:16: יהוה צבאות שמו.

[33] Cf. article "צבא" in Koehler, Baumgarten, *Hebräisches und Aramäisches Lexikon*, 933–35.

[34] Cf. ibid., articles "אל IV/V," 47–48 and "איל II," 21 as well as the discussion in K. Scholtissek, *die Vollmacht Jesu. Traditions- und redaktionsgeschichtliche Analysen zu einem Leitmotiv markinischer Christologie*. Neutestamentliche Abhandlungen, N.F. 25 (Münster: Aschendorffsche Verlagsbuchhandlung, 1992), 36–37.

[35] For references, cf. H. Kosmala, article "גבר etc.," in ThWAT I 901-19, esp. 906. For the conception of God in Philo, cf. G. Delling, "Wunder – Allegorie – Mythus bei Philon von Alexandreia," in idem, *Studien*, 72-129: "Gott ist der μόνος πάντα δυνατός, ... ᾧ δυνατὰ τὰ παρ' ἡμῖν ἀδύνατα" (128). Philo presupposes the "Allmacht Gottes im strengen Sinn" (128). Correspondingly, in the punishment and deliverance miracle stories in Exodus, Moses is "überhaupt nicht als der Handelnde, sondern nur als der Weissagende und Weisung Gebende beschrieben" (76), "... in erster Linie erscheint auch bei Philon (wie bei Josephus) *Gott als der Wundertäter*" (76-77; italics are mine). Philo's work does not contain many miracle healing narratives. The passage All. III 177-178 makes it plain that Philo ascribed healing to the power of God; cf. again the description of Delling: "Das Gesundsein schenkt Gott δ' ἑαυτοῦ μόνον, die Genesung aus einer Krankheit auch durch die Heilkunst, indem er der Wissenschaft und dem Kunstfertigen (dem Arzt) den Schein des Heilens zuschreibt, in Wahrheit aber selbst sowohl durch diese wie auch ohne sie heilt ..." (127). Cf. Sirach 38:1-15 where God is depicted as creator of the physician (v. 1: καὶ γὰρ αὐτὸν [ἰατρὸν] ἔκτισεν κύριος) as well as of medicine (v. 4: κύριος ἔκτισεν ἐκ γῆς φάρμακα) with the consequence that God is not only the BNP but also the AS of every healing: ἐν [τοῖς θαυμασίοις αὐτοῦ] ἐθεράπευσεν καὶ ἦρεν τὸν πόνον αὐτοῦ (v. 7; cf. v. 9: εὖξαι κυρίῳ, καὶ αὐτὸς ἰάσεταί σε).

[36] Cf. Kosmala, "גבר," 906.

What has been specified for the Jewish and Christian god is also valid for the gods of pagan Greco-Roman mythology. The only difference is that these gods have *specific* abilities, whereas Yahweh, as the one and only god, is identified with all power.[37] Asclepios has a specific ability which makes him the *god of healing.*[38] *Divine* power of healing is at his disposal. This competence is attributed to his being the son of the god Apollo with Coronis, his mother. As a result, Asclepios is characterized by divine σοφία and δύναμις which provide him with specific competence for the healing of the sick.[39] The bestowal of divine ability through the divinity of one parent is a common motif in Greco-Roman antiquity. A *variation* of this motif is attested with regard to Apollonios of Tyana.[40] Just before Apollonios' birth, Proteus, ὁ Αἰγύπτιος θεός, appears to his mother in a φάσμα and annunciates to her that the child she bears is the god's own *incarnation* (Philostratus, Vita Apol. I 4).[41] Consequently, Apollonios is bestowed with divine σοφία and δύναμις.[42] Philostratus makes clear that Apollonios is a BNP, and not a PNP. Damis, the disciple of Apollonios, witnesses how his master frees himself of chains-Apollonios is the AS of this performance – "without sacrificing ... and without praying at all, without even saying anything" (μὴ γὰρ θύσαντα ... μηδ' εὐξάμενόν τι, μηδὲ εἰπόντα). Apollonios does not invoke the gods for help. Therefore, Damis for the first time really understands his master's nature (φύσις), "that it was divine and superhuman" (ὅτι θεία τε εἴη καὶ κρείττων ἀνθρώπου; VII 38).

Also Jesus generally appears as a BNP in the gospels. Unlike the OT prophets, the rabbis, and the apostles in Acts, he does not need to come before his god as a suppliant, or refer to a BNP mightier than himself whenever he wants to effect healing. In Mark 1:10–11 (cf. 9:7) Jesus is publicly *declared* son of a heavenly being at his baptism. The πνεῦμα descends on him from heaven and a heavenly voice proclaims: σὺ εἶ ὁ υἱός μου ὁ ἀγαπητός, ἐν σοὶ εὐδόκησα. The narrative moves following this moment demonstrate Jesus' divine competence: for forty days he is

---

[37] Cf. Josephus, Contra Apionem II 190–92 and 239–49, who ridicules the variety and characters of the Greek gods.

[38] Cf. E.J. and L. Edelstein, *Asclepius. A Collection and Interpretation of the Testimonies* (New York: Arno Press, 1975 [orig.: 1945]), Vol. II, 73–74.

[39] Cf. Aelian, De nat. animal. IX 33.

[40] Cf. G. Petzke, *Die Traditionen über Apollonius von Tyana und das Neue Testament.* Studia ad corpus Hellenisticum Novi Testamenti 1 (Leiden: E.J. Brill, 1970), 162–64.

[41] Against Petzke, *Traditionen*, 162, who interprets this passage as an indication that Proteus announces himself as *father*. The text, however, clearly states that Apollonius had a *human* πατὴρ who carried the same name as his son. There is no indication that Proteus claims the parenthood of Apollonius.

[42] Cf. idem, 172–82.

tempted, in vain, by Satan in the desert (1:12–13), he begins to preach τὸ εὐαγγέλιον τοῦ θεοῦ (1:14–15), calls his first disciples with authority (1:16–20), teaches in synagogues, drives out demons and helps people with various kinds of illness (1:21–39) with the result that the people marvel at his διδαχὴ καινὴ κατ' ἐξουσίαν and his superhuman ability to subject the wills of demons (1:27). Jesus is ἰσχυρότερος than John the Baptist (1:7) and teaches ὡς ἐξουσίαν ἔχων καὶ οὐχ ὡς οἱ γραμματεῖς (1:22). A numinous δύναμις (5:30) dwells in him and he is bestowed with marvelous σοφία (6:2). Thus, he is able to act as a self-sufficiant BNP in miracle stories and does not need to activate the power of a mightier BNP for a successful performance.

In both Matthew and Luke, the infancy narratives are in tension with the *declaration* of sonship following Jesus' baptism. Matthew's infancy narrative has Mary conceive Jesus ἐκ πνεύματος ἁγίου (1:18) and also has, parallel to Mk 1:9–11, the account of the descent of the πνεῦμα τοῦ θεοῦ on Jesus in conjunction with the public declaration of divine sonship (Mt 3:16–17).

Luke attributes the superhuman ability of Jesus to his conception through the πνεῦμα ἅγιον, the δύναμις ὑψίστου (1:35), for which reason he will be called υἱὸς θεοῦ (1:36). The expression in the baptism story, ἐγὼ σήμερον γεγέννηκά σε (3:22), taken as the original reading,[43] is clearly in tension with Luke's infancy narrative, which stresses a divine conception of Jesus. Neverthless, on another level both statements serve Luke's intention to emphasize that Jesus is less independent and self-sufficient than appears in Mark. This is indicated by his frequent references to God as the originator of Jesus's power. Luke portrays Jesus as *(super-)prophet*,[44] a feature only alluded to in his Markan *Vorlage*,[45] cf.

- a prophet mighty in deed and word before God and all the people (ἀνὴρ προφήτης δυνατὸς ἐν ἔργῳ καὶ λόγῳ ἐναντίον τοῦ θεοῦ καὶ παντὸς τοῦ λαοῦ; Lk 24:19),
- a great prophet has arisen among us (λέγοντες ὅτι Προφήτης μέγας ἠγέρθη ἐν ἡμῖν; 7:16).

Jesus is more powerful than his OT predecessors (cf. δυνατὸς and μέγας προφήτης). Due to his genealogical connection with God (cf. besides 1:35–36 and 3:22 also 3:38), he is bestowed with knowledge (cf.

---

[43] This is suggested by H. Greeven, *Synpose der drei ersten Evangelien mit Beigabe der johanneischen Parallelstellen* (Tübingen: J.C.B. Mohr, [13]1981).

[44] Cf. similarly J.A. Fitzmyer, *The Gospel According to Luke I-IX. Introduction, Translation, and Notes*, AB 28 (New York: Doubleday, 1981), 213–15, who concludes that "Jesus is thus considered to be an eschatological prophet" (214).

[45] Cf. Mk 6:4; 6:15 and 8:28 represent assessments by those who still wonder who Jesus is.

2:40,52), wanders ἐν τῇ δυνάμει τοῦ πνεύματος (4:14), and drives out demons ἐν ἐξουσίᾳ καὶ δυνάμει (4:36). The OT prophets did not have available their own numinous healing power, but rather the specific, miraculous ability to *invoke* their god for help.[46]

A feature which Luke's miracle healing narratives share with some of those in the OT is that *God*, and not Jesus (or the prophets in the OT), is praised for a successful performance. For Luke, Jesus' miraculous deeds always point towards God as the originator and aim of Jesus' competence and mission.[47] Thus Luke, clearly expanding on his Markan *Vorlage*,[48] has *God* usually sanctioned instead of Jesus. So, in 5:25, Luke *adds* to his Markan *Vorlage* that the healed person δοξάζων τὸν θεόν, and in 8:39a he *replaces* Mark's ambiguous ὁ κύριος (referring either to God or to Jesus) with ὁ θεὸς as the BNP behind the miracle performance: Jesus instructs the healed Gerasene to proclaim "what God had done" (ὅσα ... ἐποίησεν ὁ θεός). In verse 39b, however, he returns to the formulation in Mark that the healed SC preached "what *Jesus* did for him" (ὅσα ἐποίησεν αὐτῷ ὁ Ἰησοῦς). So also in 9:43, where Luke *adds* the motif that "all were astounded at the *greatness of God*" (ἐξεπλήσσοντο δὲ πάντες ἐπὶ τῇ μεγαλειότητι τοῦ θεοῦ).

The motif of the glorification of God is especially prominent in the miracle narratives from Luke's *Sondergut*:

- in 7:11-17, *The Widow's Son at Nain*, Luke has the people sanction Jesus' competence in the following way: Fear seized all of them; and they praised *God*, saying, "A great prophet has risen among us!" and "God has looked favorable on his people." (ἔλαβεν δὲ φόβος πάντας, καὶ ἐδόξαζον τὸν θεὸν λέγοντες ὅτι Προφήτης μέγας ἠγέρθη ἐν ἡμῖν, καὶ ὅτι Ἐπεσκέψατο ὁ θεὸς τὸν λαὸν αὐτοῦ; 7:16),
- in 13:10-17, *The Healing of the Woman with a Spirit of Infirmity*, the woman, after having been healed by Jesus, praised *God* (ἐδόξαζεν τὸν θεόν),

---

[46] Cf. below 3.2.1.2.2.4.

[47] This fact, the praise of God instead of Jesus in Luke, has also been observed by P. Achtemeier, "The Lucan Perspective on the Miracles of Jesus: A Preliminary Sketch," in *JBL* 94 (1975), 547-62: "Formal analysis also indicates Luke's predilection for adding a reaction of the crowd, usually to praise God ..." 549-50). Achtemeier, in his assessment of this evidence, comes to the same conclusion: "That validating power is also indicated in the typically Lucan response to a miracle of Jesus, viz., praising God, indicating the source of Jesus' power" (552), and: "Thus in Luke, the reaction to miracles is to see God behind the activity of Jesus, thus acknowledging Jesus to be the one whom God has chosen to do his work" (554).

[48] In Mark, God is only sanctioned once for a miraculous performance of Jesus: ὥστε ἐξίστασθαι πάντας καὶ δοξάζειν τὸν θεὸν λέγοντας ὅτι Οὕτως οὐδέποτε εἴδομεν (2:12). Usually Jesus' competence as BNP or his performance is sanctioned, cf. 1:27-28, 45-46; 3:6; 5:15-20, 42b; 7:37: ἐξεπλήσσοντο λέγοντες, Καλῶς πάντα πεποίηκεν; 10:51: καὶ ἠκολούθει αὐτῷ ἐν τῇ ὁδῷ.

- in 17:11–19, *The Healing of Ten Lepers*, the Samaritan *thanked Jesus* but "was praising *God* with a loud voice" (μετὰ φωνῆς μεγάλης δοξάζων τὸν θεόν; v. 15).
- in 18:35–43, *The Healing of Bartimaeus*, Luke *adds* to his Markan Vorlage that the healed Bartimaeus was "praising *God*" (ἐδόξαζεν τὸν θεόν) while following Jesus, and that the whole people glorified *God* (πᾶς ὁ λαὸς ἐδὼν ἰδωκεν αἰνον τῷ θεῷ; 18:43).

This tension between Jesus' principal importance in healing miracle stories and the following sanction of God in the form of praise and glorification can nevertheless not disguise that *Jesus* is presented as a BNP, and not as a MNP in Luke's actual miracle stories, *except for the sanctions*. The addition of the motif *glorification of God* following the successful performance of Jesus, however, is a manifestation of Luke's portrayal of Jesus as the *means* of God's plan with the world.[49] Even though Jesus *acts* as independent BNP in the miracle stories themselves, Luke's *interpretation* of this activity determines *God* as the originator of the miraculous deeds. This theological understanding of Jesus' miracles is expressed in the speech Peter delivers to the Jews in Acts 2:22. Addressing the Israelites, Peter accuses them of having killed

> Jesus of Nazareth, a man attested to you by God with deeds of power, wonders, and signs that God did through him among us ('Ιησοῦν τὸν Ναζωραῖον, ἄνδρα ἀποδεδειγμένον ἀπὸ τοῦ θεοῦ εἰς ὑμᾶς δυνάμεσι καὶ τέρασι καὶ σημείοις οἷς ἐποίησεν δι' αὐτοῦ ὁ θεὸς ἐν μέσῳ ὑμῶν).

According to this interpretation, *God* performed the various miracles *through* Jesus (δ' αὐτοῦ). For Luke's theology, the function of Jesus with regard to miracles is close to the function of the wonder-working apostles, whose miraculous deeds are also interpreted as acts originating from God: "And God did extraordinary miracles *through* Paul" (δυνάμεις τε οὐ τὰς τυχούσας ὁ θεὸς ἐποίει διὰ τῶν χειρῶν Παύλου; Acts 19:11).[50] Διὰ τῶν χειρῶν is a prepositional phrase meaning "through" (cf. Hebr. ביד/LXX: διὰ χειρός). The statement in Acts 2:22, quoted above, provides the key for an accurate interpretation of Jesus' function in Luke's miracle stories.

---

[49] Cf. Delling, "Botschaft," 389–402: "Nach alledem ist nicht zu übersehen, daß die Heilungen Jesu in den Synoptikern weithin als Taten Gottes verstanden werden" (396). However, besides Mk 2:12 parr, Mt 15:31 (καὶ ἐδόξασαν τὸν θεὸν Ισραηλ), and Mt 12:28 par (εἰ δὲ ἐν πνεύματι θεοῦ ἐγὼ ἐκβάλλω τὰ δαιμόνια, ἄρα ἔφθασεν ἐφ' ὑμᾶς ἡ βασιλεία τοῦ θεοῦ), Jesus, in Mark and Matthew, is always depicted as *independent* BNP. Delling's statement is, however, accurate with respect to the gospel of Luke.

[50] Cf. 14:3 and 5:12: Διὰ δὲ τῶν χειρῶν τῶν ἀποστόλων ἐγίνετο σημεῖα καὶ τέρατα πολλὰ ἐν τῷ λαῷ.

Throughout his gospel, Luke stresses the motif of Jesus' *subordination* to God. This motif has been recognized as a characteristic feature of Luke's Christology. H. Braun argued that the terminology of Jesus' resurrection in Acts is a manifestation of a subordinate Christology in Luke.[51] Jesus is depicted as an *"eschatological* prophet"[52] or "prophetic *messiah."*[53] For the depiction of Jesus, Luke borrows from the OT, especially from the accounts of the prophets Elijah and Elisha. Jesus, however, supersedes his OT predecessors. He is the *final* prophet. The subordination of Jesus to God is also manifest in the motif of him praying to God, a characteristic feature of Luke's gospel.[54] It is, however, remarkable that Luke never depicts Jesus praying to God *in miracle stories*, a motif common in OT miracle healing stories as well as in the gospel outside of miracle stories. Luke, in borrowing from the OT, does not go so far as to present Jesus as a PNP in miracle stories. He leaves Jesus as a BNP in the miracle stories themselves, thus allowing Jesus to appear as superior to the OT figures. Jesus does not need to invoke God in every situation where a miraculous healing is about to take place.

This distinction is even more pronounced in comparison with the apostles in Acts. Peter and Paul have to invoke the ascended Jesus or refer to his name in *every* case of a healing miracle: Jesus incorporates the healing power personally, functioning as the *means* of God's healing activity. The apostles function as PNPs and MNPs who channel the divine power to the SC. An important feature of Luke's conception of Jesus is that through his ascension he *becomes* a transcendent BNP. While walking on earth, Jesus "was bound to suffer and *enter into his glory"* (ἔδει παθεῖν τὸν Χριστὸν καὶ εἰσελθεῖν εἰς τὴν δόξαν αὐτοῦ; Lk 24:26). As a terrestrial being Jesus was, according to Luke, the *Messias designatus*[55] who acquired his *full power and glory* through his ascension:[56] "God has made him both Lord and Messiah, this Jesus whom you crucicied" (κύριον αὐτὸν καὶ Χριστὸν ἐποίησεν ὁ θεός, τοῦτον τὸν Ἰησοῦν ὃν ὑμεῖς ἐσταυρώσατε, Acts 2:36).[57] In his risen status, sharing

---

[51] H. Braun, "Zur Terminologie der Acta von der Auferstehung Jesus," in ThLZ 77 (1952), 533-36.

[52] For the term, cf. Fitzmyer, *Luke*, 215.

[53] Cf. L. T. Johnson, *The Writings of the New Testament. An Interpretation* (Philadelphia: Fortress Press, [3]1988), 214-17.

[54] Cf. 6:12; 9:18, 28-29; 10:21; 11:1; 22:32, 41-46; 23:46.

[55] Cf. W. Wiefel, *Das Evangelium nach Lukas.* ThHKNT 3 (Berlin: Evangelische Verlagsanstalt, 1988).

[56] Cf. Johnson, *Writings*, 222-23: "The ascension, therefore, does not signal a removal of Jesus from the story, but symbolizes his presence in a new mode ... The period of the church is a period not of Jesus' absence but of his presence in a *new and more powerful way"* (italics are mine).

[57] Cf. Fitzmyer, *Luke*, 202-03.

directly in God's "Holy Spirit," Jesus "pours out" the "Holy Spirit" on his followers (Acts 2:33). The apostles not only receive that spirit but also, through invocation, the power of healing. They invoke or refer to the *risen and ascended* Jesus Christ as BNP in restoration miracles.

In John, Jesus is more than a miracle working BNP. Recognizing him as such misses the point of his miracles as signs, σημεῖα, which point beyond themselves to him as the one sent by God. The relationship between Jesus and his father in the Gospel of John is marked by *identity*, as in 10:30: ἐγὼ καὶ ὁ πατὴρ ἕν ἐσμεν (cf. also 10:38; 14:10, 20; 17:11, 20–23). This is not contradicted by his prayer in 11:41–43, which is not a prayer of supplication, but a *prayer of thanks* to his divine father in order that the people surrounding him might πιστεύσωσιν ὅτι σύ με ἀπέστειλας.[58] Bultmann observes that Jesus "does not need to make prayer requests like others, who have to rouse themselves out of their attitude of prayerlessness and therefore godlessness, for he *continually* stands before God as the asker and *therefore* as the receiver."[59] According to the Gospel of John, Jesus stands in such a close relationship to his father that he *constantly* partakes in God's power.

As with Asclepios and Apollonios, Jesus' superhuman ability is due to divine descent, to his quality as divine son, but in this case his ability as BNP has a subservient function. In the Fourth Gospel Jesus is more than a miracle working BNP. To recognize him only as such is to miss his true meaning, equivalent to a lack of faith, formulated as a sharp rebuke in 6:26, "Very truly, I tell you, you are looking for me, not because you saw signs, but because you ate from the loaves and were filled." In John, the power of Jesus as BNP has been elevated beyond the boundaries of the miracle story.

The distinct mediators, PNPs *and* MNPs, are characteristic of the OT-Jewish tradition, but almost non-existent in the pagan Greco-Roman world, and there not verifiable before the second century C.E. (cf. Apuleius, who describes how an Egyptian prophet invokes the sun and places a certain herb on the SC [Metam. II 28]; Marinos, who describes how the philosopher Proclos invokes the BNP Asclepios on behalf of a SC [Vita Procli 29]). Abraham, Moses, Elijah, Elisha, Hanina ben Dosa,

---

[58] So already P. Wendland, *Die urchristlichen Literaturformen*. HNT I/3. (Tübingen: Verlag von J.C.B. Mohr [Paul Siebeck], 2/31912), 306: "Das Gebet Jesu ist keine Bitte um Auferweckung, sondern Dank für die Erhörung, und er versichert noch, daß er nur zum Zeugnis für die umstehende Menge bete und es eigentlich gar nicht nötig habe."

[59] *The Gospel of John. A Commentary* (Philadelphia: Westminster Press, 1971), 408; italics are mine. Cf. also Grundmann, article "δύναμαι, δύναμις," in ThWNT 2 (1935), 286–318: "Seine Kraft ist die Kraft Gottes, die ihm in der Gemeinschaft, die der Vater mit ihm hat, geschenkt ist" (304).

and others, are not endowed with the ability to heal those who are, from a human perspective, incurable. They have a different kind of numinous competence; as PNPs they have the ability to *activate* Yahweh for a performance by means of *prayer*. The function of these individuals is, however, not always limited to the activation of God; they often also function as MNPs, channeling the divine healing power to the SCs. The apostles Peter and Paul function in the same way in Acts.[60] L. Bieler points out "daß das Judentum [as manifest in the OT and in contrast with Hellenism] keine Heroisierung des Menschen im antiken Sinne und keinen Heroenkult kennt ...: die Theokratie zieht eine strenge Scheidelinie zwischen Gott und Mensch."[61]

This conclusion is correct as a *general rule* for the assessment of the Jewish material. However, there are a few instances in Jewish literature, from OT to rabbinic times, where some of the above PNPs are *presented* as BNPs. A dead man is thrown into Elisha's grave, "touches the bones of Elisha" (ויגע נאיש בעצמות אלישע), and is restored to life (2 Kings 13:20-21). For Josephus, this proves that Elisha had divine power even after his death (μετὰ τὴν τελευτὴν ἔτι δύναμιν εἶχε θείαν; Ant. IX 183). The "divine power" is depicted here as a force independent of the *will* of its carrier.[62] Artapanus, Frg. 3:25, relates how the Egyptian king, after having collapsed speechless (ἄφωνον), was "picked up by Moses and came back to life again" (διακρατηθέντα ὑπὸ τοῦ Μωΰσου πάλιν ἀναβιῶσαι). In this case, Moses does not appeal to God for help; he seems to incorporate a numinous power in himself.[63] For examples from rabbinic literature, see b.Pesahim 112b (Hanina ben Dosa) and b.Me'ila 17a-b (rabbi Simeon ben Yochai).

The only instance where an apostle engages as a BNP in a miraculous healing is Acts 14:8-18,[64] where Paul himself has the power to reverse the condition of a SC directly. The miraculous restoration of a lame

---

[60] For a detailed analysis of the functions of these numinous mediators, cf. below, 3.3.2.

[61] Θεῖος Ἀνήρ, II, 24.

[62] A similar case in the NT is Mk 5:25-34, where the healing δύναμις is transmitted from Jesus, the BNP, to the sick woman by means of a touch (ἄπτεσθαι, cf. נגע) without the involvement of Jesus' knowledge or will. Cf. Mk 6:56; 3:10; Acts 5:15; 19:12. For a more detailed analysis of Mk 5:25-34, cf. below.

[63] This has also been observed by G. Vermes, *Jesus the Jew. A Historian's Reading of the Gospels* (Philadelphia: Fortress Press, 1981), 66-67. Cf. Eusebius, Frg. 3:23, where the doors of the prison open *mysteriously* (αὐτομάτως) so that Moses escapes. The version in Eusebius leaves open *who* the AS of this performance was. The parallel account in Clement, however, is specific and attributes this door opening miracle to the βούλησις τοῦ θεοῦ.

[64] Acts 20:7-12 is not to be considered as additional evidence since it does not seem to present a *miracle* story.

man is due to Paul's saying "in a loud voice, Stand straight up on your feet!" (μεγάλη φωνῇ· ἀνάστηθι ἐπὶ τοὺς πόδας σου ὀρθός). Unlike the other instances of miraculous healing in Acts, all of which involve in one way or another, *divine* participation,[65] Paul is portrayed here as a BNP. The subsequent reaction of the pagan people who witness what Paul did (ἰδόντες ὃ ἐποίησεν Παῦλος) is to identify Paul and Barnabas with their gods Hermes and Zeus, who are thought to have taken on the shape of humans and descended to them, and to sacrifice for them (14:11–13).[66] Luke then makes use of this conception to present it himself as a misinterpretation to take Paul as a BNP. Paul makes it clear that he and Barnabas are mere MNPs, and that his miraculous act should lead them to recognize God as the sole BNP, Ἄνδρες, τί ταῦτα ποιεῖτε; καὶ ἡμεῖς ὁμοιοπαθεῖς ἐσμεν ὑμῖν ἄνθρωποι, εὐαγγελιζόμενοι ὑμᾶς ἀπὸ τούτων τῶν ματαίων ἐπιστρέφειν ἐπὶ θεὸν ζῶντα ὃς ἐποίησεν τὸν οὐρανὸν καὶ τὴν γῆν καὶ τὴν θάλασσαν καὶ πάντα τὰ ἐν αὐτοῖς (14: 15).

It should be noted in this context that there are other traces in Acts which suggest a conception of Peter and Paul as BNPs. In Acts 5:15–16, Peter *incorporates* and *radiates* numinous healing power, so that even his shadow heals. The same is true for Paul (19:12), whose healing power can be transmitted to the SCs through cloths that touched his skin. Both passages are introduced by the same formula (ὥστε καί ...). More remarkable, however, are the identical headings of these two texts. In 5:12 and 19:11, the author of Acts makes clear that the apostles were, in contrast to the impression left by their depiction as BNPs, *means* of God's healing activity: δυνάμεις τε οὐ τὰς τυχούσας ὁ θεὸς ἐποίει διὰ τῶν χειρῶν Παύλου (19:11; cf. 5:12: διὰ δὲ τῶν χειρῶν ἀποστόλων ...). Obviously Luke interprets and corrects, as in 14:8–18, a distinct view of the miracle-effecting activity of the apostles. He changes their image from immanent BNPs to PNPs and MNPs. In so doing, he applies to the apostles a conception pointed out earlier in his narrative with respect to Jesus: in the final analysis, he also was not an independent BNP but the *mediator* of God's healing power.

---

[65] Acts 3:1–10; 9:1–19a, 32–35, 36–43; 16:16–24; 22:6–16; 28:7–10. Cf. the detailed analysis below (3.3.2.). It is instructive that manuscripts C, D, and others *add* as first part of the command, σοι λέγω ἐν τῷ ὀνόματι τοῦ κυρίου Ἰησοῦ Χριστοῦ, and thus try to bring this passage into line with the miracle healings listed above.

[66] J. Roloff, *Das Kerygma und der irdische Jesus. Historische Motive in den Jesus-Erzählungen der Evangelien*, (Göttingen: Vandenhoeck & Ruprecht, 1970), observes "daß die Apostel sich ... durch das Wunder als göttlich zu verehrende θεῖοι ἄνδρες vor den Leuten von Lystra legitimieren" and that "das Wunder in sich zweideutig ist" (189). His critique of Bultmann, however, who assumes that the belief in the miraculous ability of Jesus was, in the post-Eastern missionary activity of the early Christian church, *replaced* by the belief "an die Kraft des Apostels zum Wunder (Ag 14, 9)" [ThWNT 6, 206], is only partly valid.

3.2.1.2. Activation of the BNP

Miracle stories are characterized by the involvement of a numinous power. Usually, this numinous power is invested in a BNP. The question
is *how* the BNP gets *involved* in the narrative process. In the miracle
material of antiquity it is possible to distinguish two types of activation:
the BNP either *activates itself* (self-activation) or is *transitively* activated
by a SC, its representatives, or a PNP. This distinction is important,
because it will demand attention in iNPs depicting the activities of other
subjects involved in the activation of a BNP.

3.2.1.2.1. Self-activation.
In those cases in which a BNP is not acti-
vated by other subjects to engage in a performance, but activates itself,
the BNP nevertheless needs to have a special *preparedness* to do so, viz.,
it needs to have *information* about the predicament of a SC or needs to
identify the condition of a SC as marked by a lack. The BNP, incorporating *savoir-* and *pouvoir-faire*, is moved by its own *vouloir-faire*.
The BNP envisions, proposes to itself, and thus *initiates* the NP.

The iNPs which prepare the BNP by transfering information about a
lack are not always manifest in a miracle story. In such cases the BNP
is presented as *omniscient*. However, the BNP's self-engagement is prepared by the fact of a circumstance of lack and the BNP's unmediated,
mysterious knowledge of it. In Gen 20:3–8, God, without having been
invoked to do so, contacts Abimelech in a dream (ויבא אלהים אל־אבימלך
בחלום הלילה/καὶ εἰσῆλθεν ... ἐν ὕπνῳ τὴν νύκτα). The function of this
performance by the BNP is to bestow the SC with numinous *savoir-faire*
concerning the activation of a PNP (Abraham) who, in turn, has the
numinous capacity to *prepare* the same BNP (God) for the performance.
In this case the BNP is the AS of the main performance which leads to
the liquidation of the lack (LL). The entire movement of the narrative
development in Gen 20:1–17 can be depicted in the following schematic
way: BNP → SC → PNP → BNP/AS → P → LL.

Other examples of a BNP's self-activation to provide numinous *savoir-faire* to another subject, and thus proposing a NP, are

- 1QapGen 20:22a; (the subject transmitting the numinous *savoir-faire* בחלם to
  a representative of the SC is, however, not explicitly identified),
- Diodorus, Bibl. Hist. XVII 103:7 (a snake appears to the RSC Alexander
  κατὰ τὸν ὕπνον and shows him τὴν δύναμιν καὶ τὸν τόπον of a plant to be
  used for the healing of wounded Ptolemy),
- Insc. Graecae XIV 966a-d (the god Asclepios ἐχρημάτισεν the SCs what to
  do. Similar to Gen 20:1–17, the god prepares the SC to be able to prepare
  the god=BNP by coming to the temple and προσκυνῆσαι),
- Livius, Ab urbe 2:36 (Jupiter appears to the SC in a "somnium" and commu-
  nicates to him how the predicament can be changed by the SC himself),

- Tacitus, Hist. IV 81/Suetonius, Vespasianus 7:2–3/Dio, Roman Hist. 65:8 (while Tacitus and Suetonius simply relate *that* Serapis instructed the SCs about a cure without going into detail about the means of the divine revelation, Dio adds ἐξ ὄψεως ὀνειράτων).

At times, a BNP which activates itself functions not only as a transmitter of *savoir-faire* but also prepares the subject by subjecting its will (*devoir-faire*). In these cases, the subjects bestowed with *savoir-* and *devoir-faire* function solely as means for the BNPs to achieve their purpose:

- Insc. Creticae I 17:9 (the god Asclepios προσέταξε the CS to come to the temple ὅτι θεραπεύσειν),
- Galen, Sub. Emp. X (a dream drives a SC to the Asclepios temple at Pergamum where Asclepios, appearing in a dream, prescribes to him a cure: τοῦ θεοῦ προστάξαντος ὄναρ αὐτοῦ ...),
- Plutarch, Life of Pericles 13:7 (ἡ θεὸς ὄναρ φανεῖσα συνέταξε θεραπείαν and thus prepares a RSC as AS),
- Pausanias, Descr. Graecae 38:13 (Asclepios, by means of a vision, gets into contact with and πέμπει a mediator to the SC),
- Acts 9:10–17 (God instructs and subjects the will of Ananias ἐν ὁράματι to heal Paul from his blindness; cf. 22:12–13, where this motif is dropped).

In the above cases, the BNPs are depicted as transcendent and self-activating gods which do not need to be prepared in any way. They bestow human beings with *savoir-* and/or *devoir-faire* and get into contact with them by means of dream appearances. In some cases of self-activation, BNPs might be prepared through iNPs depicting the transfer of knowledge about a lack. *Spatial focalizers*[67] account for the *contact* between the sphere of the SC and the sphere of the numinous. The establishment of spatial contact, in these instances, is usually *coincidental*: the BNP happens to be where a SC is located, or verbs like ἀπ/ὑπαντᾶν or εὑρίσκειν indicate the establishment of a contact.[68] This contact enables the BNP to become *aware* of a circumstance of a lack. The BNP itself can *perceive* the lack by means of βλέπειν.[69]

In other cases, the BNP is present when the lack is *created*. This is a motif especially common in exorcism stories.[70] In Artapanus, Frg. 3:24–25, Moses is present when the king collapses. In these instances, the BNP has to *identify* the circumstance as marked by a lack. So also in Philostratus, Vita Apol. IV 20, where Apollonios correctly diagnoses the

---

[67] Cf. Funk, "Form," 63–65.

[68] Mk 3:1 parr; 5:1–7 parr; Lk 7:11–12; 13:10–11; 14:1–2; 22:5; Epidaurus B25; Philostratus, Vita Apol. 4:44; 6:43; etc.

[69] Homer, Iliad XV 9–12; Mt 8:14; Lk 7:13a; 13:12; Joh.5:6–7; 9:1; 11:33.

[70] Mk 1:23–24 par; 5:7 parr; Acts 16:17; Philostratus, Vita Apol. IV 20.

cause of a young man's misconduct. After looking at him Apollonios says, "it is not yourself that perpetrates this insult, but the demon, who drives you on without your knowing it" (οὐ σύ ... ταῦτα ὑβρίζεις, ἀλλ' ὁ δαίμων ὃς ἐλαύνει σε οὐκ εἰδότα), and then he proceeds with the preparation for the exorcism.

Sometimes, the lack has already been identified by others who can transfer (λέγειν) information about it to the BNP *without* proposing a NP (Mk 1:30b; 9:17b-18a parr). 2 Kings 5:1-19a needs to be considered here among those narratives whose main NP is initiated by a quasi-BNP or MNP (Elisha is depicted as bearer of miraculous *savoir-faire*), even though Naaman, the SC, tries to prepare an AS, the king of Isarael. His efforts, however, are not successful since he tries to activate an *unprepared* subject, who negatively sanctions the attempt of the SC by tearing up his clothes and by proclaiming his own incompetence and affirming *Yahweh's* authority over life and death. Elisha, upon hearing about this incident (כשמע), sends for the SC and bestows him with numinous *savoir-faire*, thus preparing his healing. There is some internal tension in this narrative: a Jewish girl, in the beginning of the story, informs the wife of the SC about the "prophet in Samaria, who can free him from his leprosy" (v. 3; transfer of *savoir-faire* to the SC). Naaman, however, after having passed on this information to the Syrian king, is sent to the king of Israel and not to the prophet, in order that the king of Isarael might free him from his leprosy (v. 6).

The information-transferring activity itself can be prepared by a request of the BNP. In Mk 9:29a, Jesus asks for background information about the lack, represented by the boy's epilepsy, and, in so doing, *prepares* the father's performance, an iNP which bestows the BNP with the information requested (vv. 21b-22). A similar case is Epidauros B25, where a SC with companions, on the way home from an unsuccessful trip to Epidauros, meets Asclepios who inquires about its bad luck (ὃς πυθόμενος παρ' αὐτῶν τὰς δυσπραξίας τὰς αὐτῶν).

At times, the BNP envisions and carries out a program of healing as a *means* to fulfill a *different* need. In Mk 2:6-7 parr and 3:2-4 parr, Jesus, the BNP, is confronted by those who doubt his *authority* (2:7: τίς δύναται ἀφιέναι ἁμαρτίας εἰ μὴ εἷς ὁ θεός;) to engage in a healing. Here, the miracle healing functions as an *iNP* for a main NP concerned with the *demonstration* of Jesus' authority and his victory over his enemies. But healing can also be chosen by a BNP as a means of positive retribution. In Aristeas the Exegete, Frg. 1:4, God is moved by Job's fortitude (εὐψυχία) in the face his severe predicament and so rewards him with health and goods.

Other motifs associated with the recognition of a need can specify the BNP's *motivation* to engage in a NP of healing: the BNP *marvels* about the fortitude of the SC (τὸν δὲ θεὸν ἀγασθέντα τὴν εὐψυχίαν αὐτοῦ; Aristeas the Exegete, Frg. 1:4), or is moved by the SC's *faith*: "Paul, looking at him intently and seeing that he had faith to be healed" (ἰδὼν ὅτι ἔχει πίστιν τοῦ σωθῆναι) engages in a main performance (Acts 14:9). For an *emotional* involvement of the BNP, cf. Joh 11:33, 35, 38:

– Jesus was greatly disturbed in spirit and deeply moved ...; he began to weep ...; Jesus was greatly disturbed (ἐνεβριμήσατο τῷ πνεύματι καὶ ἐτάραξεν ἑαυτόν ... ἐδάκρυσεν ὁ ᾿Ιησοῦς ... ᾿Ιησοῦς οὖν πάλιν ἐμβριμώμενος ἐν ἑαυτῷ).

3.2.1.2.2. Transitive activation. Whereas in the preceding descriptions the BNP itself "*se fait vouloir* opérer la transformation,"[71] representing "la forme réfléchie" of the activating process, *transitive* activation refers to the *intentional* attempt of a subject other than the BNP to appeal to the BNP's *vouloir-faire* to engage in a NP: "... il s'agit de constituer en Jésus [the BNP] un sujet opérateur compétant du vouloir-faire pour la performance pragmatique (le pouvoir-faire étant toujours déjà acquis)."[72] This transitive activation presupposes a specific knowledge on the part of the activating subject: "dans la requête, la demande faite ... suppose chez celui qui demande ... un savoir sur la compétence de Jésus [the BNP] (savoir sur le pouvoir-faire ...)."[73] One will have to ask *how* the activating subject is bestowed with this knowledge. The question concerns the *preparedness* of the activating subject in an iNP. At the same time, the activating subject has the ability to "prévoir un programme narratif (virtuel)."[74] This envisioned, virtual NP is communicated to the BNP in order for it to identify with the program and to transform it into a *realized* NP by means of a performance: "la performance pragmatique [of the BNP] dans le miracle nous apparaîtra comme la *réalisation* de la fiction anticipatrice mise en place par le bénéficiaire," the subject of circumstance or its representative(s).[75]

3.2.1.2.2.1. The establishment of a contact. Whereas the *establishment of contact* between the sphere of the SC and the BNP was a *coincidence* in the preceding chapter, or took place on the initiative of the BNP, it can also take place *intentionally* in an iNP in which the SC, a RSC or a PNP is the AS. A personal contact needs to be established *before* a

---

[71] "Récits de miracles et récit évangelique. Remarques de grammaires narrative," in *S&B* 10 (1979) [without reference to the author], 27–44, 32.

[72] Ibid., 32.

[73] Ibid., 32–33; cf. also: "De la *motivation* à la *manipulation*, la requête manifeste chez le demandeur une compétence cognitive spécifique" (33).

[74] Ibid., 33.

[75] Ibid., 33.

request can be made. Frequently a *spatial* distance between the BNP and the SC needs to be bridged. The establishment of a spatial contact is often expressed by means of verbs like προσέρχεσθαι or προσφέρειν.[76] The BNP who dwells among the people can be approached directly. In the case of *transcendent* BNPs, the motif of a direct spatial contact is either dropped, or the invokers need to come to a location where the god can be addressed. This is especially clear with regard to the Asclepios-cult at Epidauros: the ἱκέται travel to the *temple* and sleep in the ἄβατον (cf. also Aelian, De nat. animal., 9:33 and 11:32).

3.2.1.2.2.2. Appeals to the vouloir-faire of the BNP. Once contact is established, the activating subject can engage in a performance which aims at involving the BNP in a NP. Various allomotifs can fill this slot:

- various *gestic expressions* of reverence and invocation like πίπτειν ἐπὶ πρόσωπον/πρὸς τοὺς πόδας (Lk 5:12; Mk 5:22/Lk 8:41; Mk 7:25a; Tacitus, Hist. 4:81; cf. 2 Kings 4:27), προσκυνεῖν (Mt 8:2; 15:25), γονυπετεῖν (Mk 1:40a; Mt 17:14),
- the *sleep in the* ἄβατον (Epidauros),
- *explicit expressions of invocation* like δέεσθαι (Lk 5:12; 9:38, 40; Aelian, De nat. animal. 9:33; 11:32, 34), ἱκετεύειν (Josephus, Ant. X 26; Pherecydes, Frg. 114; Epidauros A1 et al.; Oxyrhynchos 11:1381; Aelian, De nat. animal. 9:32; Philostratus, Vita Apol. 3:38), ἐρωτᾶν (Mk 7:26; 8:22; Lk 4:38; 7:3/Joh 4:47), παρακαλεῖν (Mk 1:40a; 5:23/Lk 8:1; Mk 7:2; Mt 8:5/Lk 7:4),
- a *request for mercy* (ἐλεεῖν/ἐλεημοσύνη/רחמים, cf. Mk 10:47–48 parr; Mt 9:27; 15:22; 17:15; Lk 17:13; b.Ber 34b; b.ʿErub 29b; ʿAboda Zara 10b),
- *an outcry for* βοήθεια (Mk 9:22, 24–25; Mt 15:25b),
- התפלל (2 Kings 20:2/Isa 38:2), εὔχεσθαι (Tobit 3:1–6, 10–15),[77] orare (Tacitus, Hist., 4:81/Suetonius, Vesp. 7:2),
- *crying* (2 Kings 20:3b/Isa 38:3b),
- *calculated argumentation aimed at convincing the BNP* (2 Kings 20:3a/Isa 38:3b: Hezekiah reminds Yahweh of his conduct, באמת ובלבב שלם, and his good deeds;[78] Mk 7:28 par, the rhetorically skilled answer of the mother; if Mt 8:7, Ἐγὼ ἐλθὼν θεραπεύσω αὐτόν, is to be understood as a question,[79]

---

[76] Cf. Mk 1:40a/Mt 8:2; Mk 2:3-4 parrs; 5:22/Lk 8:41; Mk 5:27 parrs; 7:25 par; 7:25 par; 7:32; 8:22; 9:17/Mt 17:14, 16; Mt 8:5/Joh 4:47; Mt 12:22/9:32; Philostratus, Vita Apol. III 38; etc.

[77] Here, however, the two SCs do not beg for healing but for their death; for a comparable inconsistence between the lack identified by the SC and the one identified by the BNP, cf. Acts 3:1-11.

[78] The parallel account in Jos., Ant. X 26, presents Hezekiah as rational and unselfish king, who is only concerned with the durability of the Judean kingship.

[79] Cf. U. Luz, *Das Evangelium nach Matthäus (Mt 8-17)*, EKK I/2 (Zürich: Benziger Verlag, 1990), 12, following P. Wendland, *Die urchristlichen Literaturformen*, 275, who refers to Zahn as the first to identify Mt 8:7 as a question.

the centurion's answer might[80] have to be interpreted as a successful attempt to overcome the implied refusal of the BNP Jesus);

– *offering of sacrifices or presents* (Epidaurus A5. 8; Lucian, Philops. 16 and Apollodorus, Bibliotheca II 2, mention a μισθός which has to be paid to the BNP. While in Lucian it is only indicated that the BNP engages in the main performance ἐπὶ μισθῷ μεγάλῳ, the narrative in Apollodoros has the agreement on a contract determining the exact quality of this payment as its pivotal point; cf. Pherecydes, Frg. 114).

Sometimes, in an intermediary step, the SC as activating subject is required to affirm its faith in the numinous ability of the BNP. This *affirmation* or *proof of faith* is the condition of the BNP's agreement to engage in a NP. So in Mt 9:8 where the BNP, Jesus, asks the two blind supplicants: πιστεύετε ὅτι δύναμαι τοῦτο ποιῆσαι; which they affirm; or in Mk 9:23–24 where Jesus informs the invoking father that πάντα δυνατὰ τῷ πιστεύοντι which results in the RSC's affirmation, πιστεύω· βοήθει μου τῇ ἀπιστίᾳ. Another example is Epidauros A3: Asclepios asks the unbelieving supplicant if he is still incredulous of the inscriptions on the tablets (ἔτι ἀπιστησοῖ τοῖς ἐπιγράμμασι τοῖς ἐπὶ τῶμ πινάκων τῶν κατὰ τὸ ἱερόν), which the SC negates.

The activation of a BNP can be complicated by unexpected resistance or circumstances. An obstacle needs to be overcome. In Mk 2:4/Lk 5:19, the carriers of the SC cannot get through to Jesus because of crowds blocking the entrance to the house. Therefore they invent another approach to the BNP, the way through the roof. Mk 7:24–28 describes how a woman, *against* the will of the BNP (οὐδένα ἤθελεν γνῶναι), approaches Jesus and, after his refusal to engage in a performance (ἄφες πρῶτον χορτασθῆναι τὰ τέκνα, οὐ γάρ ἐστιν καλὸν λαβεῖν τὸν ἄρτον τῶν τέκνων καὶ τοῖς κυναρίοις βαλεῖν), is successful in persuading him by means of her rhetorical skills (κύριε, καὶ τὰ κυνάρια ὑποκάτω τῆς τραπέζης ἐσθίουσιν ἀπὸ τῶν ψιχίων τῶν παιδίων).[81] The parallel account in Mt 15:21–28 replaces the first obstacle, namely, that Jesus avoided contact with the people around Tyre and Sidon, by the motif that his disciples wanted to get rid of her since "she keeps shouting after us" (κράζει ὄπισθεν ἡμῶν). This motif is also employed in Mk 10:47–51 parr where an unidentified crowd of people "sternly ordered [the blind Bartimaeus] to be quiet" (ἐπετίμων αὐτῷ ἵνα σιωπήσῃ).[82] All these gospel narratives

---

[80] For an alternative interpretation, cf. Chapter V.

[81] Cf. Mt 8:7–10.

[82] In this case, the people *misinterpret* Bartimaeus' outcry addressing Jesus, Υἱὲ Δαυὶδ Ἰησοῦ, ἐλέησόν με, as a quest for alms. His utterance is ambiguous since ἐλεεῖν (cf. ἐλεημοσύνη in Acts 3:3: the lame beggar ἠρώτα ἐλεημοσύνην λαβεῖν) signifies either the more general "having compassion with" or the more concrete "giving alms." The bystanders assume the latter since it corresponds well to the described situation: ... ὁ υἱὸς Τιμαίου

involving a special effort by the SC or its representatives to activate the BNP call forth a sanction from Jesus: he interprets and praises their endeavor as demonstrations of an extraordinary *faith*, for example,

- when Jesus saw their *faith* ... (ἰδὼν ὁ Ἰησοῦς τὴν πίστιν αὐτῶν; Mk 2:5 parr),
- your *faith* is great! (μεγάλη σου ἡ πίστις; Mt 15:28; cf. Mk 7:29: διὰ τοῦτον τὸν λόγον),
- your *faith* has saved you! (ἡ πίστις σου σέσωκέν σε; Mk 10:52/Lk 18:42).[83]

Another allomotif representing the function of an "obstacle for the activating subject" is the attempt of others to ridicule the faith of the subject. Cf. Epidauros A9: "Some people laugh at the silliness" (ἐγέλων δή τινες ... τὰν εὐηθίαν) of a man missing an eyeball, who resists their temptation and is healed.

While the BNP is usually invoked (appeal to its *vouloir-faire*) to engage in a healing performance, it occasionally seems as if it is forced (*devoir-faire*) to do so. As an example, cf. Apollodoros, Bibliotheca III 3: Minos first *compels* (ἀναγκασθείς) Polyidos to seek his missing son and then again *subjects the will* of the *supposed* BNP to recover the dead son alive (δεῖ καὶ ζῶντα ἀπολαβεῖν αὐτόν). However, it should be noted that Polyidos is, at this stage, not yet bestowed with the numinous knowledge enabling him to engage in the main performance. He is mistaken for a BNP and is, as MNP, the AS of the healing performance.

3.2.1.2.2.3. Preparedness of the invoking subject. Transitive activation of a BNP presupposes a specific competence of the invoking subject. At times, the envisioned NP may include transfer of information about the *method* of healing to the BNP, for example,

- come and lay your hands on her, so that she may be made well, and live (ἵνα ἐλθὼν ἐπιθῇς τὰς χεῖρας (Mt: singular) αὐτῇ ἵνα σωθῇ καὶ ζήσῃ; Mk 5:23),
- they begged him to lay his hands on him (παρακαλοῦσιν αὐτὸν ἵνα ἐπιθῇ αὐτῷ τὴν χεῖρα; Mk 7:32),
- they begged him to touch him (παρακαλοῦσιν αὐτὸν ἵνα αὐτοῦ ἅψηται; Mk 8:22),
- but speak only with a word, and my servant will be healed (ἀλλὰ μόνον εἰπὲ λόγῳ, καὶ ἰαθήσεται ὁ παῖς μου; Mt 8:8/Lk 7:6),

---

Βαρτιμαῖος τυφλὸς προσαίτης ἐκάθητο παρὰ τὴν ὁδόν (10:47). Jesus has to clarify the issue by means of a question: Τί σοι θέλεις ποιήσω; Blind Bartimaeus answers unambiguously, Ραββουνι, ἵνα ἀναβλέψω.

[83] The "obstacle-motif" also appears outside miracle narratives. Cf. Lk 19:3–4, where Zacchaeus wants to see Jesus καὶ οὐκ ἠδύνατο ἀπὸ τοῦ ὄχλου ὅτι τῇ ἡλικίᾳ μικρὸς ἦν καὶ προδραμὼν εἰς τὸ ἔμπροσθεν ἀνέβη ἐπὶ συκομορέαν ἵνα ἴδῃ αὐτόν. Cf. also Mk 14:3–9 par, *The Anointing at Bethany*, where the disciples ἐνεβριμῶντο a woman who anoints Jesus with select ointments.

– and he besought the emperor to deign to moisten his cheeks and eyes with his spittle …, he begged Caesar to step and trample on it (precabaturque principem ut genas et oculorum orbis dignaretur respergere oris excremento … ut pede ac vestigio Caesaris calcaretur orabat; Tacitus, Hist. IV 81; cf. Suetonius, Lives VII 7.[84]

It is interesting to observe that in the three examples from Mark the proposed method is never exactly consistent with Jesus' actually applied method: in Mk 5:41 and 7:33–34, Jesus does not lay on his hands but *touches* the SC in one way or another and undertakes additional preparations, whereas in 8:23–25a, Jesus' *touch* does not *heal*, as had been envisioned and proposed, but has another function, to lead the blind man out of the town (καὶ ἐπιλαβόμενος τῆς χειρὸς τοῦ τυφλοῦ ἐξήνεγκεν αὐτὸν ἔξω τῆς κώμης). In this narrative, Jesus applies the laying-on-of-hands to his *eyes* (ἐπὶ τοὺς ὀφθαλμοὺς αὐτοῦ), after having spat into them. In the gospels, laying-on-of-hands and "touching" are indiscriminately used as expressions of physical contact between a BNP and a SC that effects healing, if this contact is *intentionally* established.

This, sometimes detailed, knowledge of the SC or its representatives poses the question of the *origin* of their preparedness. They might be informed by other humans about the ability of a BNP and how to activate it.[85] Sometimes, however, this bestowal of a SC or its representatives (RSCs) with knowledge already involves the numinous realm: the BNP itself might transfer this knowledge, for example, in a dream[86] or might instruct the SC/RSC in an unspecified manner.[87] Apollodoros, Bibliotheca III 3, presents an interesting case with respect to the preparation of the subject activating the (alledged) BNP:

After the disappearance of his son, who was drowned in a jar of honey, Minos made a great search and consulted diviners as to how he should find him. The Curetes told him that in his herds he had a cow of three different colours, and that the man who could best describe that cow's colour would also restore his son to him alive (τὸν δὲ τὴν ταύτης χρόαν ἄριστα εἰκάσαι δυνηθέντα καὶ ζῶντα τὸν παῖδα ἀποδώσειν). After the diviners were assembled, Polyidos, son of Coeranus, compared the colour of the cow to the fruit of the bramble (which results in his being elected as the one who is supposed to find the missing child and to recover him alive).

---

[84] In Dio's parallel account, Roman History, Epitome of Book LXV 8, Vespasian is depicted as BNP, who is *already* bestowed with a numinous savoir-faire.

[85] 1 Sam 16:15–18; 2 Kings 5:2–4; often ἀκούειν plus genitive: Mk 5:27; 7:25; 10:47 parr; Lk 7:3; Joh 4:47.

[86] Gen 20:3–8; 1QapGen 20:22; Suetonius, Lives 7:2.

[87] Cf. Insc. Creticae I 17:9; Insc. Graecae 14:966: ἐχρημάτισε; Tacitus, Hist. 4:81: monitu Serapidis dei; deo auctore.

This iNP describes a test and a competition. The function of this detailed iNP is to identify an able BNP for the main performance.

Even though the SC/RSC might thus be enabled to *envision* a NP which reverses its predicament, it might still not be able to communicate a NP successfully to a BNP. At this point the PNP (petitioner of numinous power) enters the scene.

3.2.1.2.2.4. The function of the PNP. A PNP appears whenever the invoking subjects SC and RSC are not able to communicate their need directly to the BNP. This applies only where the BNP is *transcendent*. In the material under scrutiny this is a mark of the Jewish-Christian tradition.[88] The PNP has a special, numinous ability which enables it to invoke and thus activate a transcendent BNP who is not directly accessible to the average human being. The competence of the PNP is specific in the sense that it only enables *the PNP* to activate God. The PNP itself is *not* able to perform the miraculous restoration. Furthermore, the PNP itself needs to be activated. Corresponding to the direct activation of the BNP by a SC or its representatives, the invoking subjects focus their activity on the PNP. Thus, the PNP's narrative role is to *mediate* the need of a SC/RSC to a corresponding BNP: SC/RSC → PNP → BNP.

3.2.1.2.2.4.1. The preparedness of the PNP
3.2.1.2.2.4.1.1. Its competence. In the OT, the PNP is chosen by God. The mark of a PNP is its bestowal with the "spirit of Yahweh" (רוח יהוה).[89] This corresponds to Baumgärtel's fundamentally correct assessment: "es gibt keine Vergottung des Menschen in Israel."[90] Standing in the same tradition, the PNPs in Acts, Peter and Paul, are qualified by their bestowal with a certain power (δύναμις) through the πνεῦμα ἅγιον (Acts 1:8; cf. 1:5, 8; 2:1–13; 9:17). This δύναμις, however, does *not* enable them to engage directly in a healing performance. Like the PNPs

---

[88] For rare *pagan* examples, cf. Pherecydes (Frg 114): Melampous effects healing through calming down Hera with implorations and sacrifices (διά τε ἱκεσιῶν καὶ θυσιῶν τὴν ῞Ηραν ἐκμειλιξάμενος). The goddess Hera is the BNP whose healing power restores the daughters of Proitos to health (against H. Maehler, *Die Lieder des Bakchylides. Erster Teil. Die Siegeslieder. II. Kommentar* [Leiden: E.J. Brill, 1982], 202, who maintains that "die Heilung durch Melampous [erfolgt]"); Apuleius, Metamorphoses II 28; Marinos, Vita Proclos 29. The neo-platonic Marinos is of *Samaritan* origin, cf. H. Dörrie, art. "Marinos (Μαρῖνος)," in *Der kleine Pauly* 3 (1979), 1026–1027.

[89] Cf., e.g., Num 11:16–30 (Moses and the seventy elders); 1 Sam 16:13 (David); 2 Kings 2:9, 15 (Elijah, Elisha).

[90] F. Baumgärtel, art. "πνεῦμα, etc. B. Geist im Alten Testament," in *ThWNT* 6 (1956), 363.

of the OT and the rabbinic literature, Peter and Paul have to pray to the BNP or invoke the name of the ascended Jesus as BNP and AS of the healing performance. The author of Acts explicitly states that "God did extraordinary miracles *through* Paul" (δυνάμεις τε οὐ τὰς τυχούσας ὁ θεὸς ἐποίει διὰ τῶν χειρῶν Παύλου; 19:11; cf. 5:12). The following observation by Roloff concerning the role of the PNP Peter and his relation to the BNP is also applicable to Paul:[91] "So zeigt Petrus mit seiner Berufung auf das ὄνομα Jesu (Apg. 3:6) und durch sein Gebet (Apg. 9:40), daß nicht er selbst der Handelnde ist und daß die durch ihn geschehenden Wunder darum als Zeichen und Hinweise auf die Gegenwart des erhöhten Herrn verstanden werden müssen."[92] Roloff correctly compares this mediating function of the apostles as MNPs with the role of the rabbis in Mishna and Talmud.[93] In the miracle material of Acts, the only exception is the already mentioned passage, Acts 14:8–18, where Paul appears to engage in a miraculous performance without divine involvement. Moreover, in 5:15 and 19:12, the shadow of Peter and the clothes of Paul alone effect healing. Acts 5:12 and 19:11 make clear, however, that the author of Acts assumes that God, the BNP, is the AS of these healings and that the apostles are channels of his power (διὰ τῶν χειρῶν of the apostles).

3.2.1.2.2.4.1.2. Its activation. The same allomotifs that occur in the process of the direct activation of a BNP are also employed in the

---

[91] These narratives nevertheless prepared a development which would depict the apostles as self-sufficient BNPs. Cf. the apocryphal Acts of the Apostles from the second century onwards. Acts 14:8–18 is the earliest clear example of this development, where the faith in Jesus' miraculous ability is indeed *replaced* by the faith "an die Kraft des Apostels zum Wunder" (Bultmann, "πιστεύω," 206). Bultmann correctly refers here to Acts 14. Roloff's critique of Bultmann's assessment (cf. above) is valid only insofar as Bultmann does not recognize the *general dependence* of the apostles on the risen Christ. By ignoring the basic function of the apostles as *mediating* men of prayer, Bultmann manipulates the textual evidence for the sake of his preconceived general view of the development of early Christianity: first Jesus and then the apostles were depicted as θεῖοι ἄνδρες. However, it should be noted that Luke, in Acts 5:12–15; 14:8–18; and 19:11–12, *criticizes and corrects* the assessment of these apostles as BNPs in some early Christian communities. Roloff's interest is to demonstrate the *continuity* of the Jesus tradition from the time before to the time after Easter. Consequently, he invalidates traces that indicate an early Christian interpretation of the apostles as all-powerful, cf. Acts 14:8–18. In fact, it seems as if this piece of tradition opposes a view that conceived of Paul as a BNP, giving proof that such an assessment of the apostle indeed existed: καὶ λέγοντες, Ἄνδρες, τί ταῦτα ποιεῖτε; καὶ ἡμεῖς ὁμοιοπαθεῖς ἐσμεν ὑμῖν ἄνθρωποι, εὐαγγελιζόμενοι ὑμᾶς ἀπὸ τούτων τῶν ματαίων ἐπιστρέφειν ἐπὶ θεὸν ζῶντα ὃς ἐποίησεν τὸν οὐρανὸν καὶ τὴν γῆν καὶ τὴν θάλασσαν καὶ πάντα τὰ ἐν αὐτοῖς.

[92] Roloff, *Kerygma*, 191.
[93] Ibid, 200-02.

activation of the PNP. The major difference is that an invoking subject never *prays* to immanent and non-divine PNPs.[94]

A *personal contact* between the SC or its representatives and the PNP is always presupposed or needs to be established.[95] Seldom does the PNP take the initiative to activate itself. This presupposes iNPs which bestow a PNP who is not omniscient with information about a lack or a need. The allomotif *complaint* alone can function as carrier of information about a predicament preparing the PNP to engage in a performance. In the following two examples the complaint is expressed by means of questions:

- What do you have against me, O man of God? Have you come to me to bring my sin to remembrance, and to cause the death of my son? (מה־לי ולך איש האלהיך באת אלי להזכיר את־עוני ולהמית את־בני /Tί ἐμοὶ καὶ σοί, ἄνθρωπε τοῦ θεοῦ; εἰσῆλθες πρός με τοῦ ἀναμνῆσαι τὰς ἀδικίας μου καὶ θανατῶσαι τὸν υἱόν μου; 1/3 Kings 17:18). In this case, the mother of the dead child holds the PNP responsible for her child's death.
- Did I ask my lord for a son? Did I not say, Do not mislead me? (השאלתי בן מאת אדני הלא אמרתי לא תשלה אתי/μὴ ᾐτησάμην υἱὸν παρὰ τοῦ κυρίου μου; οὐκ εἶπα Οὐ πλανήσεις μετ' ἐμοῦ; 2/4 Kings 4:28).

Sometimes, the PNP simply *perceives* a lack, for example, Acts 9:32–33, where Peter on his trip to Lydda found a certain Aeneas who had been bedridden for eight years, for he was paralyzed (εὗρεν δὲ ἐκεῖ ἄνθρωπόν τινα ὀνόματι Αἰνέαν ἐξ ἐτῶν ὀκτὼ κατακείμενον ἐπὶ κραβάττου, ὃς ἦν παραλελυμένος). Another interesting case, which also belongs to narratives involving a reflexive activation of the PNP, is Acts 3:1-6. Peter rejects a NP proposed to him by a lame beggar, namely, to give alms. This rejection is due to Peter's lack of preparedness with respect to the proposed NP, for he is without money. Nevertheless, after having perceived the beggar's lameness, Peter envisions another NP effecting his healing.

Usually, however, the PNP is activated *transitively* by a SC or its representatives who invoke (בעי, δέεσθαι) the PNP.[96] The invoking can be accompanied by presents[97] or by confession of sins.[98]

Sometimes, the activating subject itself is forced and thus prepared (*devoir-faire*) to carry out another NP first as precondition for the ac-

---

[94] The PNPs are usually human beings. An exception is the eleventh ode of victory from Bacchylides where the *goddess* Artemis functions as PNP.

[95] Cf. 1QapGen 20:21; 1 Sam 16:20-22; Num 21:7; 2 Kings 4:45-47a; Acts 3:1-2; 9:33, 38; 16:16-17; 28:7-8; b.Ber 34b, etc.

[96] Num 12:11 [LXX only]; 1QapGen 20:21; Marinos, Vita Procli 29.

[97] Gen 20:14; Bacchylides, Epinicia 11:98-105: Proitos promises sacrifices to the divine Artemis.

[98] Num 12:11; 21:7.

ceptance of the proposed main NP. A *contract* is established, as in Gen 20:14 and 1QapGen 20:27. Here, the return of Sara functions as iNP to activate the PNP for the main NP aimed at the restoration of the king to health. In a fragment from Pherecydes (Frg. 114), Melampous requires a reward (μισθόν) before he engages in any activity to effect healing. He is promised a part of the kingdom and a daughter of the RSC (μέρος τῆς βασιλείας καὶ μίαν τῶν θυγατέρων ἦν ἂν θέληι εἰς γάμον).[99] In Apuleius, Metamorphoses II 28, the RSC has to agree to a "great price" for an Egyptian prophet in order that he might invoke the sun to engage in a healing performance.

As was the case in the direct activation of the BNP by a SC/RSC, the activating subject's proposed NP can be *detailed* and might explicitly describe the *method* of activating the BNP by the PNP. Every example of such a proposal of a method seems to include or indicate *prayer*, although other motifs might be added:

- coming [אתי], praying [צלי], and laying-on-of-hands [-על ידין סמך] (1QapGen 20:21–22; cf. 28a),
- praying to the BNP [Hitpa'el of פלל, εὔχεσθαι] (Num 21:7; cf. Marinos, Vita Procli 29),
- calming down God and praying [חלה, Hitpa'el of פלל, δέεσθαι] (1 Kings 13:6a; LXX omits the reference to prayer),
- asking for mercy [לבקש עליו רחמים] (b.Ber 34b; b.'Erub 29b).

2/4 Kings 5:11 is of special interest in this context. Naaman expects that Elisha

would surely come out, and stand and call on the name of Yahweh his God, and would "wave his hand over the spot [MT]," and cure the leprosy (יצא יצוא ועמד וקרא בשם-יהוה אלהיו והניף ידו אל-המקום /ἐξελεύσεται πρός με καὶ στήσεται καὶ ἐπικαλέσεται ἐν ὀνόματι θεοῦ αὐτοῦ καὶ ἐπιθήσει τὴν χεῖρα αὐτοῦ ἐπὶ τὸν τόπον).

Elisha, however, does not act as PNP, as expected, but bestows Naaman with a numinous *savoir-faire* and thus enables him to be the preparer of his own restoration to health.[100]

---

[99] The parallel account in Apollodoros, Bibliotheca II 2, elaborates this contract-motif. Here, Melampous, now a BNP, asks for the third part of the kingdom, and after the RSC first refuses to pay so high a price but finally has to accept it, the BNP even increases the fee: "Melampous promised to effect a cure whenever his brother Bias should receive just so much land as himself."

[100] Naaman is instructed to go to the river Jordan where he should wash himself seven times (5:10); for a detailed discussion cf. below.

2/4 Kings 5:11 is the only evidence for an action *similar* to the laying-on-of-hands in the context of healing in the Hebrew OT. The Greek tradition interprets this action clearly as *laying-on-of-hands*. It has often been doubted that the Hebrew הניף ידו אל-המקום indicates an action similar to the laying-on-of-hands. While the Hiph'il of נוף = "to swing back and forth" is unusual in the context of healing, its meaning, in connection with יד and מקום,

3.2.1.2.2.4.2. The PNP's activation of the BNP. After having been bestowed with competence and motivation, the PNP is prepared and ready for its specific task, the activation of the transcendent BNP. In the Jewish-Christian tradition, the prophets, apostles, and rabbis do not have to establish a spatial contact with the transcendent BNP[101] but do so right on the spot by means of *raising their voice* in prayer: Num 12:13 (צעק/βοᾶν), 1 Kings 17:20 (קרא/ἀναβοεῖν), cf. 2 Kings 5:11 (קרא/ἐπικα-λεῖσθαι). Occasionally, the PNP prepares the scene by *isolating itself* from other people.[102] The invocations can be accompanied by *gestures of prayer*, cf. Acts 9:40 ("he knelt down" [θεὶς τὰ γόνατα]) and b.Ber 34b ("he put his head between his knees" [הניח ראשו בין ברכיו]). These invocations of the divine BNP usually take on the form of a *prayer* or an *intercession*:

- mild request by means of imperative plus נא/δή (1 Kings 17:21b),
- calming down of God (Pi'el of חלה; 1 Kings 13:6a; Pherecydes, Frg. 114: Melampous calms down Hera by means of invocations and sacrifices and so effects the healing),

---

seems to be unambiguous. The statement that המקום "serait un terme fort obscur pour désigner les plaies de Naaman" and would rather be "une appellation consacrée pour désigner un sanctuaire," [J. Coppens, *L'imposition des mains et rites connexes dans le Nouveau Testament et dans l'Église ancienne. Étude de théologie positive* (Paris: J. Gabalda, 1925), 104–05, who depends here on the fifteenth edition of Gesenius-Buhl's dictionary, cf. art. מקום: "Bisweilen scheint המקום an sich einen Kultusort zu bezeichnen," with references to Gen 28:11–17; 2 Kings 5:11; Ex 29:31; Lev 6:9] is pure speculation and ignores Lev 13:19 which has במקום השחין/ἐν τῷ τόπῳ τοῦ ἕλκους in the context of Lev 13:18–25 dealing with the identification of נגע-צרעת/λέπρα. The LXX as well as the Vulgate ("to touch by hand the locum leprae") can be trusted in their interpretation of 2 Kings 5:11 [Cf. Köhler, Baumgartner, *Lexikon*, 644; A.T. Hanson, art. "Handauflegung I. Altes Testament/Judentum/Neues Testament/Religionsgeschichtlich," in *TRE* 14 (1985), 415–22, 416; H. Ringgren, art. "נוף," in *ThWAT* 5 (1986), 318–22, 319; B.O. Long, *2 Kings*, FOTL 10 (Grand Rapids: William B. Eerdmans, 1991), 71–72; against D. Flusser, "Healing through the Laying-on of Hands in a Dead Sea Scroll," in *IEJ* 7 (1957), 107–8; P. Ackroyd, art. יד, II–V, in *ThWAT* 3 (1982), 425–55; K. Beyer, *Die aramäischen Texte vom Toten Meer samt den Inschriften aus Palästina, dem Testament Levis aus der Kairoer Genisa, der Fastenrolle und den alten talmudischen Zitaten. Aramaistische Einleitung, Text, Übersetzung, Deutung, Grammatik/Wörterbuch, Deutsch-aramäische Wortliste, Register* (Göttingen: Vandenhoeck & Ruprecht, 1984), 176, fn. 1; and C. Vogel, art. "Handauflegung I (liturgisch)," in *RAC* 13 (1986), 482–93, 484, all of whom seem to disregard 2 Kings 5:11 as oldest Jewish evidence for an action similar to the laying-on-of-hands. In any case, *LXX* 4 Kings 5:11 is certainly older than 1QapGen and is also a *Jewish* document]. The relationship between the invocation of God and the laying-on-of-hands as well as their functions will be discussed below (3.3.2).

[101] For a pagan example, cf. Vita Procli 29 by Marinos. Here, the mediating philosopher travels to the *temple* of Asclepios in order to pray there on behalf of a sick girl.

[102] 1 Kings 17:19; 2 Kings 4:33; Acts 9:14.

- various expressions of prayer, like the Hitpaʿel of פלל, בקשׁ, δέεσθαι, προσεύχεσ-θαι, εὔχεσθαι, צלי or בעי (cf. Gen 20:17a; LXX 1 Kings 13:6a; 1QapGen 20:28b; Num 12:13; Jos., Ant. VIII 326; Num 21:7b; Acts 9:40; 28:8; b.Ber 34b; b.ʿAboda Zara 10b; Marinos, Vita Procli 29).

Seldom does the motif "complaint" accompany the invocation. For examples, see 1 Kings 17:20, where the complaint is *not* successful in activating Yahweh, and the parallel in Jos., Ant. VIII 326, where both the complaint and the prayer effect God's decision.[103]

3.2.1.2.2.5. The BNP's sanction of the request: its motivation and decision. After having received information about a predicament, or having been explicitly informed of the proposed NP, the BNP might positively sanction the attempts to activate it. The BNP's *motivation* for its decision to engage in a main performance can be described by means of a variety of allomotifs:

- the BNP might be moved by *compassion* (σπλαγχνίζεται: Mk 1:41a; Mt 20:34; Lk 7:13; κατ-οἰκτείρειν: Jos., Ant. VIII 327; Aelian, De nat. animal. 9:32; ἐλέειν: Homer, Iliad XV 12; Jos., Ant. X 27; cf. Oxyrhychos Papyrus 11:1381),
- its unspecified *will* (Mk 1:41b parr; θέλω),
- out of *rational calculation* (2 Kings 20:4-6: God helps for the sake of himself and his servant David, not because of the prayer and tears of the king; Jos., Ant. VIII 327: besides intervening out of compassion for the mother, God does not want the prophet to appear as one having come to the mother for the purpose of harming her),
- because the BNP witnessed the faith of the supplicant (Mk 2:5 parr; Mt 15:28),
- because of a *contract* (in Epidauros A8, Asclepios agrees to engage in a performance after a boy suffering from a stone promises to give ten dice of *payment* to the good-hearted god: τὸν δὲ θεὸν γελάσαντα φάμεν νιν παυσεῖν).

The acceptance of a supplication can also be expressed by phrases indicating the *granting a prayer* without specification of the reasons:

- Yahweh listens to the voice of Elijah (וישׁמע יהוה בקול אליהו; 1 Kings 17:22a/MT alone),

---

[103] An interesting case is b.Taʿanit 3:8. Choni, the circle-drawer, is approached by people in need of rain in order that he might pray for rain. However, Choni's prayer is not sufficient to prepare God, the BNP, for the performance. After this failed attempt at the activation of God (*vouloir-faire*), Choni draws a circle, enters it, and *swears* that he would not leave the circle until God lets rain fall. Immediately rain falls, but not sufficiently. Only after repeated demands of Choni does the desired amount of rain fall. Choni appears here as *magician* able to subject the will of God (*devoir-faire*). Correspondingly, Schimʿon ben Schatah accuses Choni of sinning. However, since God acts according to Choni's will, he cannot banish him.

– the prayer of the two SCs has been heard before the great glory of Raphael/of God (καὶ εἰσηκούσθη ἡ προσευχὴ ἀμφοτέρων ἐνώπιον τῆς δόξης τοῦ μεγάλου Ραφαηλ [BA]/τῆς δόξης τοῦ θεοῦ [א]; Tobit 3:16).

At times, the BNP's positive santion of the request is expressed in *words of encouragement, promise, and comfort*,[104] indicating the BNP's willingness to engage in a main performance, and its confidence in its own preparedness:

– Yahweh promises Hezekiah that he will heal him (הנני רפא לך/ἰδοῦ ἐγὼ ἰάσομαί σε; 2 Kings 20:5; cf. Jos., Ant. X 27),
– Apollonios comforts the crowd mourning the death of a young woman (ἐγὼ γὰρ ὑμᾶς τῶν ἐπὶ τῇ κόρῃ δακρύων παύσω; Philostratus, Vita Apol. IV 45),
– Asclepios comforts Diana after Hippolytus' violent death (nulla ... causa doloris; Ovid, Fasti VI 746),
– in Mk 5:36/Lk 8:50, Jesus consoles the father of the SC with the words: μὴ φοβοῦ, μόνον πίστευε/πίστευσον καὶ σωθήσεται, reminding the father of the necessary preparedness on his part, faith (cf. also Lk 7:13: Jesus comforts the mother of the dead child: μὴ κλαῖε).

In John 11:1–54, Jesus more than once gives indications of his willingness to engage in a main performance and of his confidence of the successful outcome of such a performance (cf. vv. 4, 11, 23, 40). A common motif expressing encouragement of the SC/RSC is the command θάρσει/θάρρει. Matthew adds it in 9:2 to his Markan *Vorlage* (Mk 2:5) and again in 9:22 to Mk 5:26 where, according to Matthew, the miracle occurs *after* and *through* the words of Jesus. For other examples of this allomotif, cf. Lucian, Philops. 11 and Philostratus, Vita Apol. III 38.[105]

The BNP's sanction of the invoking subject's activity might provoke a negative reaction of disbelief. Jesus negatively sanctions the grief of the mourners since "the child did not die but is sleeping" (τὸ παιδίον οὐκ ἀπέθανεν ἀλλὰ καθεύδει), which causes them to laugh at him (κατεγέλων αὐτοῦ; Mk 5:39 parr). Similarly the mourners of the dead bride misinterpret Apollonios' promise to stay their tears (by raising the bride from her seeming death) as the mere intention to deliver an oration (Philostratus, Vita Apol. IV 45).

---

104   Cf. Theißen, *Wundergeschichten*, 68–69.
105   This encouragment can also be expressed by subjects other than the BNP. In Jos., Ant. VIII 326, the PNP Elijah παρεκελεύετο θαρρεῖν καὶ παραδοῦναι τὸν υἱὸν αὐτῷ· ζῶντα γὰρ αὐτὸν ἀποδώσειν. In Mk 10:49 bystanders encourage blind Bartimaeus: θάρσει, ἔγειρε, φωνεῖ σε.
Apollo's θάρσει νῦν in Homer's Iliad 15:254 does *not*, however, have the function of announcing that the LL is at hand but encourages Hector to engage in the battle. Hector had already been revived by the will of Zeus (242).

Often, however, no explicit reference to the BNP's positive sanction of a request is made. The fact *that* a main performance follows is itself the sole indication that the BNP positively sanctions the attempt at a transitive activation.[106]

3.3. The performance

The *active subject* (AS) refers to the subject whose performance brings about the liquidation of the lack. The AS *can* be identical with the BNP. Often, however, a BNP is not itself the AS but prepares another subject which, after having been bestowed with *vouloir-/devoir-* and/or *pouvoir-/savoir-faire*, is enabled to function as AS for a specific main performance. If the AS is different from the BNP, the following types of subjects are possible: it could be a subject specificially endowed with numinous power for the performance, a mediator of numinous power (MNP), the anti-subject causing the predicament (demons and/or illnesses), the SC, a RSC, or the PNP acting as MNP. Not always, however, are the preparedness and performance of the AS *manifest* in a narrative, even though these phases are always logically presupposed and thus latently present. In those instances where the AS is not explicitly mentioned, as in descriptions of performances by means of passive verbs, it must be inferred from the context.

3.3.1. The BNP as active subject

Since the preparedness of the BNP has already been discussed in the preceding chapter (3.2.1.), it can be presupposed here. After having been activated intransitively by itself or transitively by another subject, the BNP may itself function as AS of the principle performance. In our literature, the following BNPs function as ASs: Yahweh,[107] Moses,[108] Paul,[109] Asclepios,[110] Serapis,[111] Zeus,[112] Hera,[113] the ἰσόθεος son of

---

[106] Cf. "Récits de miracles," 36, with respect to Jesus' miracles: "le miracle est la sanction du croire …" and: "Dans le miracle, Jésus opère à un double niveau: il est sujet opérateur pragmatique dans la transformation des états (par exemple dans la guérison), il est destinateur épistémique quand il sanctionne la performance cognitive (croire) du bénéficiaire."

[107] Gen 20:17; Aristeas the Exegete, Frg. 1; 1 Kings 13:1-10; 4:18-37; rabbinic literature.

[108] Artapanus, Frg. 3:25.

[109] Acts 14:8-18, but only in the miracle itself. Paul rejects the preparedness of a BNP for himself and Barnabas in verse 15.

[110] Epidauros inscriptions; Inscriptiones Creticae I 17:9; Aelian, De nat. animal. 9:33; Oxyrhynchos Papyri 11:1381; Marinos, Vita Procli 29.

[111] Aelian, De nat. anima. 9:32.

[112] Homer, Iliad 15:242.

[113] Bacchylides, Epinicia 11:40-112.

Asclepios Machaon,[114] Melampous,[115] a Babylonian,[116] a Palestinian Syrian,[117] Indians,[118] Jesus (in almost all the restoration miracles in the gospels and Acts with the exception of exorcism, cf. below), and Apollonios of Tyana.[119]

Some motifs concerning the performance are shared by several traditions, while others are particular to a certain tradition. Whenever Yahweh, the exclusive BNP in Jewish literature, functions as AS, the healing performance is never narrated in detail; it is simply indicated *that* Yahweh is the AS of a performance:

- God healed N. N. (ויר פא אלהים את-/καὶ ἰάσατο ὁ θεὸς τόν ...; Gen 20:17),
- God relieved him from his disease (τῆς νόσου αὐτὸν ἀπολῦσαι; Aristeas the Exegete 1:4).

This is also presupposed in miracle stories in rabbinic literature. Here, however, references to God as AS are missing. Usually, rabbis pray (בעא/בקש) for God's mercy for (רהמים על-) some SC.[120] This begging for mercy is followed immediately by a statement of the LL without reference to a performance. It is nevertheless obvious that *Yahweh* is thought of as the AS in these restoration miracles. The reluctance to go into detail with respect to Yahweh's performances is a typical characteristic of Jewish literature. However, also in the pagan milieu of Greco-Roman antiquity the healing performance of a god *can* be depicted in the simplest of terms, indicating the *fact* of divine intervention, cf.

- Zeus revives wounded Hector by an act of his *will* (ἐπεί μιν ἔγειρε Διὸς νόος αἰγιόχοιο; Homer, Iliad 15:242),
- a woman comes as a supplicant to the temple of Asclepius. As soon as she leaves the temple, she is pregnant (Epidauros A1; cf. A2 where Asclepios promises to have a woman give birth to a girl),
- a mute boy can speak all at once after having given sacrifices (A5),
- Asclepios *promises* in a dream to heal a boy (A8),
- a blind man asks Asclepios for help καὶ ὑγιὴς ἐγένετο (A11),
- a dog heals (θεραπευόμενος) a blind boy (A20, cf. B33),
- Asclepios restores a blind man to health (ὑγιῆ κατέστασε; B22),
- the god Serapis simply ἰᾶται a sick man (Aelian, De nat. animal. XI 32).

---

[114] Homer, Iliad 4:192-219.
[115] Apollodoros, Bibliotheca II 2.
[116] Lucian, Philops. 11.
[117] Lucian, Philops. 16.
[118] Philostratus, Vita Apol. 3:39.
[119] Philostratus, Vita Apol. 4:45.
[120] Cf. b.Ber 34b; b.'Erubim 29b; 'Aboda Zara 10b; b.Hagiga 3a.

Similar to rabbinic miracle stories, Marinos (Vita Procli 29) describes how Proclus *prays* to Asclepios for the healing of a girl. During his prayer, the girl experiences a change of her painful condition,

for easily did the savior, inasmuch as he was a god, heal her (ῥεῖα γὰρ ὁ σωτήρ, ὥστε θεός, ἰᾶτο).

Nevertheless, a typical feature of the pagan milieu is its interest in *details* of *how* a BNP brought about the liquidation of a lack. This is especially characteristic of most healing performances by Asclepios attested in the inscriptions of Epidauros. In general, these performances can be characterized as *surgery*. In order to heal *blind* persons, the god cuts eyes open or opens them with his fingers, removes the causes of blindness and even rebuilds eyes by means of special φάρμακα:

- Asclepios cut the diseased eyeball and poured in some drug (ἀνσχίσσαι οὐ τὸν ὄπτιλλον τὸν νοσοῦντα καὶ φάρμακόν τι ἐγχέαι; A4),
- the god prepared some drug, then opening his eyelids, poured it into them (ἑψῆσαί τι φάρμακον, ἔπειτα διαγαγόντα τὰ βλέφαρα ἐγχέαι εἰς αὐτά; A9),
- the god opened his eyes with his fingers (τοῖς δακτύλοις διάγειν τὰ ὄμματα; A18),
- a man who carries a spearhead in his eyes dreams that Asclepios pulled out the missile and then fitted into his eyelids again the so-called "pupils" (ἐξελκύσαντα τὸ βέλος, εἰς τὰ βλέφαρα τὰς καλουμένας κόρας πάλιν ἐναρμόξαι; B32).

The surgical manipulations of Asclepios are even more apparent when it comes to inner sicknesses. In these cases, Asclepios cuts open patients, removes the cause (e. g., leeches [A13; B23; 25], water [B21], a tumor [B27]), and is also able to close the opened body after surgery, usually by means of stitches (A13; B23; 25; 27).[121] In the case of arrowheads that are stuck deeply in the body of a patient, Asclepios is able to remove them without killing the SC (A12; B30; 31).[122] Incorporated in a dog or snake, Asclepios heals sores and wounds by licking the ill spot with his tongue (A17; B26). The god heals a man with paralyzed fingers (τοὺς τᾶς χηρὸς δακτύλους ἀκρατεῖς ἔχων πλὰν ἑνός) by jumping onto his sick hand (τὸν θεὸν ἐφαλέσθαι ἐπὶ τὰν χῆρα καὶ ἐκτεῖναί οὐ τοὺς δακτύλους; A3). As is obvious for this example, Asclepios at Epidauros does *not*

---

[121] Cf. also Insc. Creticae I 17:9: Asclepios ἔταμε the patient while he was sleeping. As an example of the whole process, cf. B27: a man who has a tumor in his stomach dreams that after he is bound Asclepios ἀνσχίσσαντα τὰγ κοιλίαν, ἐκταμεῖν τὸ ἕλκος καὶ συρράψαι πάλιν, καὶ λυθῆμεν ἐκ τῶν δεσμῶν.

[122] Concerning an assessment of these surgical performances attributed to Asclepios, cf. the apt comment of Herzog, *Wunderheilungen*, 76, "Die Phantasie der Außenseiter ist also hier wie beim Flugproblem der zünftigen Wissenschaft vorausgeeilt."

heal by means of mere *touch*, be it with his feet or his hand.[123] This holds true also for B31: a woman comes to the temple because of her need of offspring. She dreams that a beautiful young man uncovers her (παῖς τις ὡραῖος ἀγκαλύψαι) and that the god touches her with the "hand" (τὸν θεὸν εὐψεσθαί οὐ τᾶι [χη]ρί). To interpret this performance as "die für Asklepios typische Auflegung der milden Hand"[124] is an assessment nurtured by depictions of Asclepios of later times.[125] In the context of the inscriptions from Epidauros,[126] however, it is more realistic to interpret χῆρ as a symbol for the phallus.[127] Thus, in B31, 39, and 42 the god Asclepios himself begets the requested child.[128]

The motifs of surgery as means of an AS's performance seem to be limited to, and are thus characteristic of, the Asclepios cult from the fifth to the third century B.C.E. One example resembling the performances of Asclepios can be found in Homer's Iliad 4:192-219, where the *son of Asclepios* Machaon removes a poisoned arrow from wounded Menelaos, sucks out the blood, and spreads onto the wound soothing medicine (ἤπια φάρμακα) which Cheiron had given to his father a long time earlier. However, this performance also is part of the Asclepios tradition and proves that, from earliest times,[129] surgery and the use of φάρμακα were attributed to Asclepios. While surgery became the primary means of healing at Epidauros, the use of φάρμακα and the prescriptions of cures[130] replaced surgery from the second century B.C.E. onwards. Oxyrhynchos papyrus 1381 witnesses the use of medicine in the second century C.E. for the Asclepios tradition: Imouthes-Asclepios cured a sick mother with simple remedies (ἀπήλλαξεν βοηθήμασιν; col. IV).

However, during the first two centuries C.E., BNPs were not limited to the use of medicine for their miraculous healing performances. The

---

[123] Cf. Herzog, *Wunderheilungen*, 99.

[124] Ibid., 74.

[125] Cf. among the evidence from the second century C.E. the Apellas-inscription, ἥψατο δέ μου καὶ τῆς δεξιᾶς χιρὸς καὶ τοῦ μαστοῦ. For the time before the turn of eras, however, the assessment of Blinkenberg, quoted in Weinreich, *Heilungswunder*, 30, fn. 2, seems adequate, "Am Ende geht die Heilkraft der göttlichen Hand wohl einfach darauf zurück, daß die älteste Heilkunde besonders χειρουργία war. Es ist die Hand des Arztes, die in den gewöhnlichen Fällen die Hilfe bringt, in den außergewöhnlichen also die Hand des Gottes."

[126] Cf. especially the B39 and 42: a snake has sexual intercourse (συγγενέσθαι) with a woman asking for offspring.

[127] Cf. Weinreich, *Heilungswunder*, 19-21 for similar examples. He, however, does not count B31 among these examples, cf. 28.

[128] Cf. the "miraculous pregnancies" in the OT (Gen 17:16-19; 18:1-15; 1 Sam 1:1-28; 2 Kings 4:8-17) where the pregnancies are always decreed and thus depend on the *will* of the BNP alone.

[129] By the latest the eightth century C.E.

[130] Cf. below.

seer (μάντις) Melampous first chases the mad women in a bevy with shouts (μετ' ἀλαλαγμοῦ) and a sort of frenzied dance (τινος ἐνθέου χορείας) before he heals and purifies them (Apollodoros, Bibliotheca II 2). Lucian describes the performance of a Babylonian (Philops. 11) who removes the anti-subject causing the predicament of a SC by *drawing it out* of the body. The Babylonian ἀνέστησε τὸν Μίδαν ἐπῳδῇ τινι ἐξελάσας τὸν ἰὸν out of the body and attaches a piece of gravestone from a virgin's grave on the SC's toe. In this case, it is the BNP's *knowledge* of certain oral formulas (ἐπῳδή) which effects the healing.

Another means of miraculous healing in the pagan Greco-Roman world is attested in writings from around 200 C. E. Dio Cassius describes how the BNP Vespasian[131] heals a lame hand by means of *trampling on it* and blind eyes by means of spittle (τοῦ μὲν τὴν χεῖρα πατήσας τοῦ δὲ τοῖν ὀφθαλμοῖν προσπτύσας, ὑγιεῖς ἀπέφηνε; Roman Hist. 65:8). In Philostratus (Vita Apol. III 39), Indian wise men treat a man with a dislocated hip by *touching* it with their hands (αἱ χεῖρες αὐτῷ καταψῶσαι τὸν γλουτόν). In IV 45, Apollonios raises a dead girl by means of *touching* her and adding a secret spell (προσαψάμενος αὐτῆς καί τι ἀφανῶς ἐπειπῶν). In all these cases, a touch or other *physical contact* is an essential part of the miraculous healings by non-transcendent BNPs. The physical contact provides for the transfer of numinous power from the BNP to the SC. Apollonios adds to the physical contact secret oral formulas (ἀφανῶς ἐπειπῶν). For another pagan example of touching and speaking as means of healing, cf. the widespread mythological legend about Hippolytus' resuscitation from around the turn of the eras: Asclepios touched the youth's breast thrice and thrice he spoke healing words (pectora ter tetigit, ter verba salubria dixit; Ovid, Fasti VI 753). From the context it is suggested that the BNP touches the SC with herbs (gramina, herbae).

Compared with the material listed above, the restoration miracles of the *BNP Jesus as AS* are characterized by distinct features. According to the overwhelming majority of the gospel miracle narratives, Jesus heals by means of *physical contact* and/or simply *decrees* healing by means of his *powerful word*. The healing performance is sometimes preceded by the *separation* of Jesus and the SC from the crowd. This motif is found in Mk 5:40/Mt 13:25 and Mk 8:23 (cf. 7:33 in the context of an apparent exorcism). For the motif "physical contact" it is presupposed that the contact is *intentionally* established between the BNP and the SC.[132] In Mk 8:22–25, e. g., Jesus is asked to touch (ἵνα ... ἅψηται) the

---

[131]   In Tacitus' and Suetonius' accounts of the same event, Vespasian is *not* depicted as BNP.

[132]   Cf. also the discussion of Mk 5:25–34 below.

blind man (v. 22). Jesus' first action is to separate himself and the SC from the town (ἐπιλαβόμενος τῆς χειρὸς τοῦ τυφλοῦ ἐξήνεγκεν αὐτὸν ἔξω τῆς κώμης; v. 23). The motif "taking the SC by the hand"[133] clearly does not have the function of healing him. Even though it is presupposed in this case that Jesus *touches* the SC with his hand in this act, the man is not healed. The SC is healed only when Jesus *intentionally* touches ("lays his hand on") him. This pericope also makes clear that ἐπιτίθεναι τὰς χεῖρας does not imply a laying-on-of-hands on the *head* of the SC.[134] While the location of the laying-on-of-hands is not mentioned in verse 23, it is made explicit in verse 25:

> once again he laid his hands on his *eyes* (εἶτα πάλιν ἐπέθηκεν τὰς χεῖρας ἐπὶ τοὺς ὀφθαλμοὺς αὐτοῦ).[135]

Furthermore, "touching" and "laying-on-of-hands" are *indiscriminately* used as indications of the establishment of physical contact between the BNP and the SC. Everything depends on the *intentionality* of the physical contact, be it on the part of the BNP or the SC.[136] Thus, a proposed ἅπτεσθαι in Mk 8:22 corresponds to the actual laying-on-of-hands in verses 23 and 25. In Mk 7:32, however, where Jesus is also asked ἵνα ἐπιθῇ αὐτῷ (the deaf man with speaking problems) τὴν χεῖρα, contrary to the coordination between expectation and actual performance in 8:22, 23 and 25, he does not "lay his hand" on the man. Rather, he engages in various actions which include physical contact (v. 33: ἔβαλεν τοὺς δακτύλους αὐτοῦ εἰς τὰ ὦτα αὐτοῦ καὶ πτύσας ἥψατο τῆς γλώσσης αὐτοῦ). A similar case is Mk 5:21–24, 35–43. Jairos asks Jesus ἵνα ἐλθὼν ἐπιθῇς τὰς χεῖρας αὐτῇ (v. 23). Jesus, however, after taking the hand of the child (κρατήσας τῆς χειρὸς τοῦ παιδίου) raises her with a command (v. 41). These examples also make obvious that the ancient writers saw no difference between the laying-on of *one* or *both* hands.[137] Finally, it should be clear that "physical contact," especially in the form of laying-on-of-hands, is not limited to physical healings, but could also be used

---

[133] It should be noted that in miracle stories, this single motif can appear as filler of three distinct motifemes: to prepare the base-performance, to transfer numinous power, and to demonstrate the successful outcome of the performance (cf. Acts 3:7; 9:41).

[134] Against P. Trummer, *Die blutende Frau. Wunderheilungen im Neuen Testament* (Freiburg: Herder, 1991), 82.

[135] For additional evidence, cf. LXX 4 Kings 5:11: ἐπιθήσει τὴν χεῖρα αὐτοῦ ἐπὶ τὸν τόπον.

[136] Cf. F. Preisigke, "Die Gotteskraft der frühchristlichen Zeit," in *Der Wunderbegriff im Neuen Testament* (Darmstadt: Wissenschaftliche Buchgesellschaft, 1980), 210–47, esp. 213.

[137] Cf. the *Jewish* evidence of laying-on-of-hands in antiquity: 2 (LXX: 4) Kings 5:11 has the singular ידו/τὴν χεῖρα αὐτοῦ while ידי in 1QapGen 20:22,29 can either be the singular or dual plus suffix of the first person singular, cf. K. Beyer, *Texte*, 593.

in *exorcisms* (cf. 1QapGen 20:22, 29; Lk 13:10–17; and maybe Mk 1:31).[138]

The performances of a healing effected by physical contact by Jesus as AS are expressed with the following phrases:

ἐκτείνας τὴν χεῖρα ἥψατο αὐτοῦ (Mt 8:3; cf. the parallels), κρατήσας τῆς χειρὸς τοῦ παιδίου (Mk 5:41/Mt 13:25; cf. Lk 8:54 and Mk 9:27), ἐπιθεὶς τὰς χεῖρας αὐτῷ/ἐπὶ τοὺς ὀφθαλμοὺς αὐτοῦ (Mk 8:23,25), ἥψατο τῶν ὀμμάτων/ὀφθαλμῶν αὐτῶν (Mt 20:34; 9:29), ἥψατο τῆς σοροῦ (Lk 7:14),[139] ἐπιλαβόμενος (Lk 14:4).

Jesus can heal by mere physical contact (Mt 13:25; Mk 9:27; Mt 20:43; Lk 14:4; 22:51). Frequently, however, the establishment of physical contact is accompanied by a word, *commanding or decreeing healing*.[140] But Jesus is also able to heal by *merely* commanding or decreeing. In fact, this kind of performance is prevalent among the restoration miracles attributed to him.[141] This ability of Jesus is emphasized in the only extended healing narrative from the Q-tradition:[142] the centurion is convinced that Jesus can heal by only saying a word (μόνον εἰπὲ λόγῳ; Mt 8:8; Lk 7:7), which indeed happens (cf. Joh 4:50).

Among the healing words of Jesus, one can distinguish three types based on their different functions. First, Jesus *effects* the liquidation of the lack by means of a command. In Mt 8:3,[143] after having touched

---

[138]   For a discussion of the function of this motif in exorcism-stories, cf. below.

[139]   Wiefel, *Evangelium*, 146, seems to suggest that this touch of Jesus caused the carriers of the bier to stand still. G. Petzke, *Das Sondergut des Evangeliums nach Lukas*. Zürcher Werkkommentare zur Bibel (Zürich: Theologischer Verlag, 1990), 91, is undecided about the function of this action of Jesus. However, this action does clearly not have the function of stopping the carriers of the coffin from moving. There is no evidence that would suggest that ἅπτεσθαι a coffin *could* have this function. The usual function of ἅπτεσθαι in restoration stories strongly suggests that Jesus touches the coffin in order to transfer his power *through* the coffin to the dead boy. Cf. also the very similar story in Philostatus, Vita Apol. IV 45, which supports this interpretation: Apollonios *commands* the carriers to stop before he, προσαψάμενος αὐτῆς (referring to the dead girl) καί τι ἀφανῶς ἐπειπών, wakes up the girl. Likewise does Asclepios, appearing in the shape of a young man to a woman being carried back home on a stretcher after she had failed to activate the healing god at Epidauros, *order* the carriers of the woman to set down on the ground the stretcher before he engages in a healing-performance: ἐκελήσατο θέμεν τὰν κλίναν, ἐφ' ἇς τὰν Σωστράταν ἔφερον (Epidauros B25). According to Lk 7:14, Jesus' restoration performance *consists* in his touching the bier. The following command, however, is *not* a "healing-word." Its function is rather to prepare the SC for the demonstration of the LL, cf. below concerning the classification of the words of Jesus.

[140]   Such is the case in Mt 8:3; Mk 5:40–41; Mt 9:29; Lk 7:14; 13:12–13.

[141]   Cf. Mk 2:10–11; Mt 15:28; Mk 10:52/Lk 18:14; Mk 3:5 parr; Mt 8:8. 32/Lk 7:7/Joh 4:10; Mt 15:28; Joh 5:8; 11:33.

[142]   The other healing-story in Q is Mt 9:32–33/Lk 11:14. Here, however, the healing of a mute man possessed by a demon is simply stated, but not narrated in detail.

[143]   The parallel accounts in Mk 1:40–45 and Lk 5:12–16 do not have Jesus as AS of the performance but the λέπρα; cf. below.

the leper with his hand, Jesus expresses his *will* (*vouloir-faire*) to engage
in the proposed performance and commands, καθαρίσθητι, "you be healed!" A statement of the success of the performance follows: "and
immediatly his leprosy was purified" (καὶ εὐθέως ἐκαθαρίσθη αὐτοῦ ἡ
λέπρα).[144] Matthew employs a specific formula for this type of performance: Jesus decrees healing by means of an imperative in the third person
singular, γενηθήτω, addressed either to the SC or the RSC. This decree-
formula always relates to the πίστις of the supplicant, cf.

- Jesus tells the centurion, ὕπαγε, ὡς ἐπίστευσας γενηθήτω σοι (Mt 8:13),
- Jesus, after having touched the eyes of two blind men, answers them: κατὰ
  τὴν πίστιν ὑμῶν γενηθήτω ὑμῖν (Mt 9:29),
- Jesus answers the Syro-Phoenician woman: μεγάλη σου ἡ πίστις· γενηθήτω σοι
  ὡς θέλεις (Mt 15:28).

In each case the decree is followed by a motif indicating the liquidation
of the lack. Thus, according to Matthew, Jesus heals by means of his
powerful, commanding word. Only such oral expressions can correctly
be termed "healing-words."

Secondly, the word of Jesus in the context of the liquidation of a lack
prepares the SC to *demonstrate* the successful outcome of a manifest or
latent performance. Mk 3:1-6 parr can serve well as an example for this
type. It seems to be presupposed *that* Jesus is the AS of the healing
performance for the man with a withered hand, but *how* and *when* he
did it is not made explicit. Jesus' command, ἔκτεινον τὴν χεῖρα, *prepares*
the SC to demonstrate the success of a hidden and silent performance
but is not a healing-word.[145]

---

[144] In contrast with his Markan *Vorlage*, Matthew identifies the SC as the λέπρα.
According to his formulation, the *leprosy* is cleansed, not the *man* (cf. Mk 1:42, where
the leprosy first *leaves* the man before *he* is healed, cf. Lk 5:13). Cf. H.J. Held, who
notices "die merkwürdige Aussage, daß der Aussatz rein wurde" (203), but does not interpret it. "Matthäus als Interpret der Wundergeschichten," in G. Bornkamm, G. Barth,
H.J. Held (eds.), *Überlieferung und Auslegung im Matthäusevangelium* (Neukirchen: Neukirchener Verlag, 1960), 155-287. Against W. Bauer, K. Aland, *Wörterbuch*, who translate
Mt 8:3b: "sein Aussatz verschwand" (786).

[145] Against R. Pesch, *Das Markusevangelium. I. Teil. Einleitung und Kommentar zu Kap.
1, 1-8, 26*, HThKNT 2 (Freiburg: Herder, 1976), who states, "Die Heilung vollzieht Jesus
durch ein Heilwort, das zugleich Demonstrationsbefehl ist ...; die Kopplung von Heilwort
und Demonstrationsbefehl ist bei Lahmenheilungen topisch (vgl. zu 2, 11)" (194).
The identification of the described state of facts is important for the recognition of the
point of the story. Jesus is observed εἰ τοῖς σάββασιν θεραπεύσει αὐτόν, ἵνα κατηγορήσωσιν
αὐτοῦ (v. 2). Besides the theological question whether one is allowed to heal on the Sabbath
at all (cf. Lk 13:10-17; 14:1-6), this pericope presents the decision of the Pharisees and
Herodians to kill Jesus (v. 6) as absurd, since Jesus did not explicitly and openly engage
in a performance of healing. Thus, Jesus' behavior is well thought out and basically not
incriminating, and puts all blame for his persecution and death on his enemies. For a

The man can stretch out his hand only *after* being healed.[146] Thus, ἀπεκατεστάθη states the successful outcome of a performance and not its execution. Therefore, it is not to be translated, "it was being restored," but, "it was restored."[147] Other examples of commands of Jesus preparing the SC to demonstrate the successful outcome of a latent performance are the following:

- I say to you, stand up, take your mat and go to your home! (σοὶ λέγω, ἔγειρε ἆρον τὸν κράβαττόν σου καὶ ὕπαγε εἰς τὸν οἶκόν σου; Mk 2:11 parr),[148]
- Little girl, get up! (Ταλιθα κουμ/τὸ κοράσιον, σοὶ λέγω, ἔγειρε; Mk 5:41: here Jesus heals by means of a physical contact),
- Go! Your faith has saved you! (ὕπαγε· ἡ πίστις σου σέσωκέν σε; Mk 10:42),
- Young man, I say to you, rise! (νεανίσκε, σοὶ λέγω, ἐγέρθητι; Lk 7:14: Jesus heals by means of a physical contact),
- Stand up, take your mat and walk! (ἔγειρε ἆρον τὸν κράβαττόν σου καὶ περιπάτει; Joh 5:8: the performance of an AS is not made explicit),
- Lazarus, come out! (Λάζαρε, δεῦρο ἔξω; Joh 11:43: the performance of an AS is not made explicit).

In all of these cases the subjection of the will of the SC leads to a performance by the SC corresponding exactly to the command. These performances demonstrate the outcome of a (latent) main performance.

Thirdly, a command by Jesus in the context of a healing miracle story

---

similar presentation of Jesus' behavior, cf. Mk 12:13-17 parr, "The Question concerning Tribute to Caesar" (this is the only other evidence, besides 3:6, for an alliance of Pharisees and Herodians against Jesus).

[146] For similar cases, cf. Herzog, *Wunderheilungen*, 99, who quotes Hippocrates, Epid. V 23 (V 222 L.): "N.N. ἐπάγη [cf. ξηραίνειν!] τὰ σκέλεα καὶ χεῖρας ..., καὶ οὐκ ἠδύνατο οὖτε ἐκτείνειν οὖτε ξυγκάμπτειν ...," or 1 Kings 13:4: the king's *arm* (יד; cf. Ackroyd, art. "יד," 4-7; also χεῖρ which the LXX employs, can mean "arm") ἐξηράνθη. Since the arm was stretched out when it suddenly withered, he is unable to ἐπιστρέψαι αὐτὴν πρὸς ἑαυτόν. Here we have, compared with Mk 3:5, the inverse case: the king is unable to draw his יד/χεῖρ to his body, while the SC in Mk 3:1-6 is unable to stretch out his χεῖρ. However, both circumstances are due to ξηραίνειν. Concerning both movements, cf. again the text from Hippocrates (ἐκτείνειν, ξυγκάμπτειν) as well as Epidauros A3: a man with δακτύλους ἀκρατεῖς dreams that, after Asclepios jumped onto his hand and thus stretched out his fingers, he himself seems συγκάμψας τὰν χῆρα καθ' ἕνα ἐκτείνειν τῶν δακτύλων.

[147] In German, "sie war wiederhergestellt" and not "sie wurde wiederhergestellt."

[148] In Mk 2:1-12, the main performance of Jesus seems to be manifest in verse 5: activated by the πίστις of the SC and its representatives, Jesus says to the paralyzed man: τέκνον, ἀφίενταί σου αἱ ἁμαρτίαι. The passive makes it ambiguous here, if Jesus is really the AS of the act of forgiving sins, or if he simply recognizes that *God* has forgiven the sins. Verse 10, however, explicitly states that the son of man has the ἐξουσία to forgive sins on earth. In any case, the base-performance is implied in v. 5. The SC could walk off already at this point. However, his departure is delayed since it is supposed to demonstrate not only the successful base-performance but also the validity of Jesus' statement concerning the authority of the son of man. Therefore, Jesus introduces his command with the words ἵνα δὲ εἰδῆτε.

can have the function of orally *sanctioning* a performance. The sanction indicates the *miraculous knowledge* of Jesus who knows what happens in distant locations, for example,

- Because of this word, the demon has left your daughter! (διὰ τοῦτον τὸν λόγον ὕπαγε, ἐξελήλυθεν ἐκ τῆς θυγατρός σου τὸ δαιμόνιον; Mk 7:29),
- Go, your son lives! (Πορεύου· ὁ υἱός σου ζῇ; Joh 4:50).

Lk 13:12–13 is a special case since Jesus announces the LL, ἀπολέλυσαι τῆς ἀσθενείας σου (v. 12b) *before* he heals the woman with a spirit of infirmity by means of laying-on-his-hands, καὶ ἐπέθεκεν αὐτῇ τὰς χεῖρας (v. 13a). The context indicates that an action of Jesus drove out a demon (cf. 13:16).

Each of these three types of healing words represents a distinct function: healing words as a means of performing the miracle (only in Matthew), preparation of the demonstration of the LL, and orally sanctioning the successful outcome of a performance.

There are three pericopes that go more into detail about the healing activity of Jesus: Mk 7:31–37;[149] 8:22–26; and Joh 9:1–7. All of these narratives mention the use of spittle, which was considered a remedy for physical ailments in the ancient world.[150] In Mk 8:22–26, Jesus, after having spat into the eyes of the blind SC, has to repeat the laying-on-of-hands ἐπὶ τοὺς ὀφθαλμοὺς αὐτοῦ in order to effect the LL. Both, the use of spittle and the step by step success of Jesus' performance, present Jesus as not an *authorative* BNP, who is able in every case to heal effectively by his will or command alone. He also, even if only sometimes, employs touching as means of transferring healing power. It is probably for that reason that this passage, as well as Mk 7:31–37, was dropped by Matthew and Luke. The detailed accounts in Mk 7:31–37 and 8:22–26, which borrow from folk-material and certain magical practices may have stood in too great a tension with powerful statements, such as, Mt 8:8/Lk 7:7 (ἀλλὰ [μόνον] εἰπὲ λόγῳ, καὶ ἰαθήσεται ὁ παῖς μου; cf. Mt 8:16), Mt 9:32–33; 12:22–23/Lk 11:14 and Mt 12:28/Lk 11:20 (Jesus ἐκβάλλει τὰ δαιμόνια ἐν πνεύματι/δακτύλῳ θεοῦ). Matthew and Luke could not reconcile these Markan accounts with the Q material.

3.3.2. Prophets and apostles as PNPs and MNPs channeling divine power

The OT prophets and the apostles in Acts usually function as PNPs who activate a transcendent BNP. These subjects assume at times an addi-

---

[149] This text will be dealt with in the next section concerning demons as ASs since Jesus does not seem to function as active subject here but as BNP who prepares (devoir-faire) an AS (a demon).

[150] For references, cf. Pesch, *Markusevangelium*, 392–94.

tional function as mediators of numinous power (MNP) who *channel* the healing power of a transcendent BNP to a SC.

In the OT Yahweh usually acts without mediators for the transfer of the divine healing power. God decides, after having been invoked by a PNP, and then immediately *decrees* healing. This is also the usual procedure in the rabbinic miracle traditions: the rabbi invokes God for healing and God heals without mediators.

There are, however, two narratives in the OT which reflect an *understanding* of miraculous healing in which prophets function as MNPs. This is expressed in the virtual miracle which had been expected by Naaman in 2 [LXX:4] Kings 5:11. Naaman *expected* that Elisha might get into direct contact with him (ἐξελεύσεται πρός με καὶ στήσεται),[151] invoke the name of his god (ἐπικαλέσεται ἐν ὀνόματι θεοῦ αὐτοῦ),[152] and lay his hand on the sick spot (ἐπιθήσει τὴν χεῖρα αὐτοῦ ἐπὶ τὸν τόπον) in order to heal the leprosy. Elisha's first function in the proposed program is to activate the BNP, Yahweh, by means of an invocation, and then to mediate the healing power of Yahweh to the SC by means of direct physical contact.[153]

2 Kings 4:31–35, Gehazi's attempt to resuscitate the child by laying the stick of Elisha onto his face, reflects a similar understanding. The reason for his failure is that *Yahweh* was not involved.[154] This is suggested by the following, successful attempt of Elisha, who, as PNP, first of all *prays* to Yahweh (ויתפלל אל יהוה/καὶ προσηύξατο πρὸς κύριον) before he engages in a performance guaranteeing physical contact between him and the dead child (this performance has to be repeated once according

---

[151] The Hebrew text expresses the same action as the LXX. For the sake of the terminology, however, I quote from the Greek tradition.

[152] The Hebrew has וקרא בשם־יהוה אלהיו = "that he invokes Yahweh, his god" or "that he invokes his god by means of the name Yahweh." ἐν renders ב and is, in this context, unusual in Greek, but not for the LXX. Cf. Rom 10:14, where ἐπικαλεῖσθαι is followed by the preposition εἰς plus relative pronoun. εἰς or ἐν introduce the direct object here.

[153] Cf. P. Ackroyd, "יד," 447: "In einigen Beispielen kann die göttliche Macht durch Menschenhand weitergegeben werden, wobei die Macht von Gott durch einen Vermittler an den Empfänger gelangt ..."

[154] Cf. 1 Kings 17:20–22 where one can distinguish a failed and a successful performance. Verses 20–21aα describe first how Elijah accuses Yahweh for being responsible for the death of the child and secondly how he himself tries to resuscitate the child by stretching out on it three times (LXX has ἐνεφύσησεν ... τρίς). This three-fold attempt suggests that the performance of Elijah did not effect the intended result. Therefore, after recognizing that he is not able to succeed without the help of Yahweh, he implores God (LXX: ἐπεκαλέσατο τὸν κύριον) to have the נפש/πνεῦμα of the child return to him (v. 21). Yahweh is persuaded and the soul of the child returns. In this narrative two things are stressed: first, Elijah cannot act as BNP, since he is and remains a PNP; and secondly, only Yahweh is BNP and is *not* dependent in the healing performance on the PNP Elijah functioning as channel.

to the MT; the seven times according to the LXX are due to the omission of עלָ]יו ויזורר). The physical contact makes possible the transfer of divine power, mediated by the prophet to the child, and effects its re-suscitation. Yahweh is the AS of the performance.[155]

In these two stories we encounter an extraordinary subject with the two functions *invoking of a transcendent BNP* and *mediating the divine power*. An example from Qumran is the recasting of Gen 20:1–18 in 1QapGen 20:21–29. In the OT story Abraham prays to God who mysteriously and transcendently heals Abimelech without physical contact. In the Qumran version, Abram *prays* for the healing of the king (וצלית עלוהי על רפאוהי) and then *lays his hands on his head* (וסמכת ידי על ראישה)· *God* is the BNP in 1QapGen 20:28–29 with Abram functioning as *mediator* of the divine power. The result of the transfer of divine power by means of laying-on-of-hands is that "the plague was removed (אתפלי, Itpaʿal of פלא) from him and the evil spirit was driven out of him (אתגערת, Itpaʿel of גער = "to drive out a demon [with screaming]")[156] and he was restored (ואתוקם)." The passive verbs indicate that Yahweh is thought to be the AS of the main performance.[157]

---

[155] Cf. J. Behm, *Die Handauflegung im Urchristentum. Nach Verwendung, Herkunft und Bedeutung in religionsgeschichtlichem Zusammenhang untersucht* (Darmstadt: Wissenschaft-liche Buchgesellschaft, 1968 [orig. 1911]), whose analysis of 1 Kings 17 and 2 Kings 4 leads to the following conclusion: "… so soll durch diese körperlichen Aktionen der Pro-pheten die neue Lebenskraft auf die Toten übertragen werden. In beiden Fällen ist aber letztlich *Jahve der Vollbringer der Wundertat* …" (106; italics are mine). With respect to the performance of Elisha in 2 Kings 4 and parallels, cf. Weinreich, "Wundertypus" who declares, "daß ein Heiltumträger … die gesamte okkulte Kraft ausnützt, die aus seinem in den anderen Leib überfließen und ihm [dem anderen Leib; W.K.] neue Kraft geben soll, sei es, daß er [der Heiltumträger; W.K.] selbst Träger einer Eigenkraft ist oder als Vermittler einer allgemeineren, ihm von Gott verliehenen Kraft gilt, die durch ihn wirkt" (246). Blackburn, *Theios Anēr and the Markan Miracle traditions. A critique of the Theios Anēr Concept as an Interpretative Background of the Miracle Traditions Used in Mark*. WUNT 2/40 (Tübingen: J.C.B. Mohr [Paul Siebeck], 1991), 115, in his discussion of 2 Kings 4:29–34, disregards the fact that Elisha first *prays* to Yahweh. He fails to recognize that the prophet's repeated laying down on the SC has the function of *channeling* the divine power. Thus Elisha (in 2 Kings 4), and likewise Elijah (cf. the preceding fn.), on the one hand, and Jesus, on the other hand, do not represent the same "miracle-working" type. Blackburn's treatment of 1QapGen 20 in this context is misleading.

[156] Cf. Beyer, *Texte*, 545.

[157] Blackburn, *Theios Anēr*, refers to this passage as the "most striking example" for the fact that the rebuking of a demon (גער) with a spokesperson of God as subject of his activity can already be found in Palestinian sources. Consequently, "if Jesus' rebuking activity represents assimilation to Yahweh" [it is Blackburn's intention to invalidate the usage of a Hellenistic Theios Anēr concept for the interpretation of Jesus' depiction in the Gospels], this had to be assumed also for Abram in the Genesis Apocryphon (134). Black-burn, however, disregards the motif of Abram's *prayer* (to God!). This motif indicates that Abram does not have the exorcizing power at his own disposal. Jesus, on the other hand, *never* invokes God or another BNP for the healing of a SC. He is clearly the *subject* of

Prayer as the means of invoking God occurs twice in Acts with regard to the miracle working activity of the apostles Peter and Paul (Acts 9:40 and 28:8). A comparison of the parallel[158] resuscitation miracles in Mk 5:40–42 and Acts 9:40–41 demonstrates the decisive difference between the function of Jesus as BNP and/or AS of a miracle performance and the apostle as PNP. In both narratives the main actor isolates himself and the SC from others (ἐκβαλὼν πάντας) before engaging in a miraculous performance. But while Jesus holds the hand of the child (κρατήσας τῆς χειρὸς τοῦ παιδίου), Peter kneels down and prays (θεὶς τὰ γόνατα προσηύξατο). Then both command the SC to rise (ταλιθα κουμ/Ταβιθα ἀνάστηθι[159]). This command is followed by demonstrations of the success of the miracle performance:

- and immediately the girl got up and began to walk around (καὶ εὐθὺς ἀνέστη τὸ κοράσιον καὶ περιεπάτει; Mk 5:42),
- then she opened her eyes, and after seeing Peter, she sat up (ἡ δὲ ἤνοιξεν τοὺς ὀφθαλμοὺς αὐτῆς, καὶ ἰδοῦσα τὸν Πέτρον ἀνεκάθισεν; Acts 9:40).

Only *then* does Peter *touch* the woman, but here the touch has a function different than in the case of Jesus in Mk 5:41! By means of giving her a hand, Peter *helps her up*: δοὺς δὲ αὐτῇ χεῖρα ἀνέστησεν αὐτήν.[160] Peter does not effect the resuscitation by means of touching. He does so by *praying*. His prayer implies that he invokes a transcendent BNP, the resurrected Christ, to engage in the performance. His command, Ταβιθα ἀνάστηθι, has the function of *channeling* the divine power to the SC. He does not touch the woman as part of the performance and has to *turn towards* her before giving the command: καὶ ἐπιστρέψας πρὸς τὸ σῶμα εἶπεν ... The addition ἐν τῷ ὀνόματι τοῦ κυρίου ἡμῶν Ἰησοῦ Χριστοῦ in some traditions (it sy[h] Cyp Spec) after the command emphasizes that Jesus Christ as BNP is thought to be the AS of this performance, and not Peter. Peter is a MNP.

---

the rebuking activity (cf. Mk 1:25; 9:25). Thus, Gnilka's assessment is correct: "Jesus tritt an die Stelle Jahwes" (*Markus*, vol. I, 81). Abram in the Genesis Apocryphon, however, does not replace Yahweh. He depends on God whom he is able to activate by means of prayer. *This* is Abram's extraordinary ability.

[158] The identical structure, the same allomotifs (cf. the motif ἐκβάλειν πάντας) and especially the Aramaic name Ταβιθα (טביתא), whose consonants closely resemble the Aramaic טליתא in Mk 5:41, suggest the possibility of a common origin of both stories. Cf. also the tendency of copyists in later centuries to replace טליתא in Mk 5:41 with טביתא from Acts 9:40 (D W a r¹).

[159] Even though Mk 5:41 translates the Aramaic command קום (cf. Beyer, *Die aramäischen Texte*, 123) with ἔγειρε, ἀνάστηθι would have been the alternative possibility (both verbs are frequently used in the LXX to render forms of קום).

[160] The NRSV (Graded Press, 1990) correctly translates, "He gave her his hand and helped her up."

In all restoration miracle stories in Acts, Christ is referred to as the miracle working BNP, and the apostles are always depicted as the mediators of this BNP, the channel of his power.[161] In Acts 3:6-7, Peter commands the lame man "in the name of Jesus Christ of Nazareth" (ἐν τῷ ὀνόματι Ἰησοῦ Χριστοῦ τοῦ Ναζωραίου) to rise and walk. Peter's action which follows, taking him by the right hand, is probably not to be understood as a means of transferring power, but *helping* the man to his feet (καὶ πιάσας αὐτὸν τῆς δεξιᾶς χειρὸς ἤγειρεν αὐτόν). Therefore, he *holds* him by the *right* hand. Neither πιέζειν nor δεξιὰ χεῖρ as point of contact *ever* appear elsewhere in miracle narratives in the NT. In addition, if ἔγειρε καὶ is, in fact, original,[162] a physical contact with the function of transfering power would be superflous, for this command implies that the lame person had already been enabled to do so. In contrast, Jesus, in his miracles, touches the SC *before* he gives a command (Mk 1:41; 5:41; 7:33-34; Lk 7:14; Mt 9:29). Everything suggests that verse 7a has the same function as 9:41: Peter assists the SC to get up.[163] Prayer and the appeal to the name of Jesus demonstrate that the apostles in Acts do not function as BNPs but as PNPs *and* MNPs channeling the BNP's power. The apostles do not effect miracles through their own power, "sondern das ὄνομα Jesu war das *handelnde Subjekt.*"[164] So, also Acts 9:17, where Ananias, after having been instructed by the resurrected κύριος to do so, goes to Paul and, laying the hands on him (ἐπιθεὶς ἐπ᾽ αὐτὸν τὰς χεῖρας), declares that he is sent by Jesus so that he might see again and be filled with the Holy Spirit (ὅπως ἀναβλέψῃς καὶ πλησθῇς πνεύματος ἁγίου).

In 9:34, Peter, before giving the command to the paralyzed man to get up (ἀνάστηθι καὶ στρῶσον σεαυτῷ), explicitly points out to the SC that *Jesus* is the one who healed him (ἰᾶταί σε Ἰησοῦς Χριστός)! When Paul exorcizes a spirit of divination (πνεῦμα πύθωνα) from a maiden (16:16-18) he turns towards the spirit (ἐπιστρέψας τῷ πνεύματι; cf. 9:40), and then commands it ἐν ὀνόματι Ἰησοῦ Χριστοῦ to leave her.[165] Here,

---

[161] The only exception is 14:8-18, where Paul, without referring to another BNP, commands the lame man μεγάλῃ φωνῇ to get up on his feet. Consequently, Paul and Barnabas are thought to be incorporations of the gods Zeus and Hermes and treated as such. Many manuscripts, under the influence of 3:6, add to the command, σοι λέγω ἐν τῷ ὀνόματι τοῦ κυρίου Ἰησοῦ Χριστοῦ, in order to make Paul's action conform with the "proper" role of an apostle.

[162] This is suggested in Nestle-Aland, [26]1979.

[163] Roloff, *Kerygma*, 191, misinterprets Acts 3:7 as "auslösende Handlung" and ascribes to it the same function 9:40 (the prayer of Peter) has in its context. This does neither make sense to Roloff who, a little helpless, points to the "typische(n) Topik der Wundergeschichten" as an explanation.

[164] Ibid., 197; italics are mine.

[165] The continuation, καὶ ἐξῆλθεν αὐτῇ τῇ ὥρᾳ, indicates that the πνεῦμα is here the AS

Paul, calling upon the "name of Jesus Christ," functions as a means of invoking the BNP Jesus. It is presupposed that the BNP, thus activated, coerces the anti-subject to become the AS of the main performance and to leave the maiden. In Acts 28:8, Peter effects healing[166] by praying and the laying-on-of-hands (προσευξάμενος ἐπιθεὶς τὰς χεῖρας αὐτῷ). In all these cases, it is evident that the resurrected Christ functions as BNP when not also as AS (cf. the exception in the exorcism 16:18). This is obvious wherever *prayer* is employed. The appeal to the "name of Jesus Christ" has the same function.

Heitmüller's declaration, "das Aussprechen des Namens, schliesslich der Name selbst, war das Mittel"[167] of the miraculous performances, reflects an incorrect assessment of the evidence. The understanding of Acts is that the "name of Jesus" could *not* be used as a magical means as argued.[168] This is the point in Acts 19:13–20. Some Jews tried to exorcize evil spirits (τὰ πνεύματα τὰ πονηρά) by means of using τὸ ὄνομα τοῦ κυρίου ᾿Ιησοῦ. Among them were seven sons of a certain high priest Sceva. However, one evil spirit refuses to recognize the authority of the self-proclaimed exorcists (ὑμεῖς δὲ τίνες ἐστέ;) and, instead of leaving the possessed man, the spirit attacks and forces the Jews to flee from that house (ἐκφυγεῖν ἐκ τοῦ οἴκου ἐκείνου; v. 16).[169] The implication is that the "name of Jesus" *cannot* be used as *magical means*.[170] With "magic" I refer to a *technique* which can be used by anyone who knows it. This

---

while the BNP Jesus forces the AS into the performance. Paul functions here as channel of Jesus' power.

[166] Acts has ἰάσατο αὐτὸν with Peter as subject. However, it is understood that Paul is *not* the BNP nor the AS of the performance but simply the channel of divine power.

[167] W. Heitmüller, *"Im Namen Jesu." Eine sprach- und religionsgeschichtliche Untersuchung zum Neuen Testament, speziell zur altchristlichen Taufe.* (Göttingen: Vandenhoeck & Ruprecht, 1903), 56.

[168] Against idem, 60: "Damit sind sie (die Wörter ἐν τῷ ὄνομα) zur [Zauber-?] Formel geworden."

[169] Cf., for this motif, 1QapGen 20:20–21. The Egyptian phycisians, magicians, and wise men fail to free the king from his demonic possession with the result that "the spirit afflicted all of them and they fled" (רוחא כתש לכולהון וערקו). This similarity has also been observed by Blackburn, *Theios Anēr* 208, fn. 134.

[170] Heitmüller's exegesis of Acts 19:13 comes to an opposite conclusion, because he does not take into account the immediate context of this passage. However, the Jewish exorcists are *not* successful in their usage of the "name of Jesus Christ!" Heitmüller's comparison of the Jewish and Christian exorcists according to Acts 19 overlooks the fact that some Jews *tried* (ἐπεχείρησαν) to do what the apostles did. While the apostles were successful (cf. 19:11–12), these Jews were not! Cf. S.R. Garrett, "Magic and Miracle in Luke-Acts" (Ph.D. diss., Yale University, 1988), 221: "... what really matters is whether the demons 'know' that a wonderworker has the divinely bestowed authority needed to invoke that sacred name;" and H. Bietenhard, art. "ὄνομα etc.," *ThWNT* 5 (1954), 242–283, 277: "Die Heilung wird nicht durch eine ausgesprochene Formel vollzogen, sondern durch den Herrn auf das Gebet hin, das ihn gläubig anruft."

technique enables the magician to *impose* his or her will on nature, on human beings, or gods.[171] If the technique is not meticulously followed, magical formulas not only do not work in the intended way but may have a dangerous effect on the magician.[172]

Usage of the "name of Jesus" implies that Jesus himself as BNP is the AS who heals.[173] Only those who have a special ability can successfully involve Jesus in a performance.[174] However, it should be noted that there are traces in the synoptics which indicate a magical use of the "name of Jesus" in miracle healings. Mk 9:38-40 par refers to an exorcist casting out demons "in the name of Jesus" (εἴδομέν τινα ἐν τῷ ὀνόματί σου ἐκβάλλοντα δαιμόνια). This exorcist is the AS of the exorcizing performance. When the disciples object to this exorcist's activity, Jesus replies, "Do not forbid him; for no one who does a mighty work in my name will be able to speak evil against me" (ὃς ποιήσει δύναμιν ἐπὶ τῷ ὀνόματί μου ...).

What has been demonstrated for the "name of Jesus" corresponds to the gesture of "laying-on-of-hands." Acts 8:14-24 can serve as a key text for understanding this gesture: people in Samaria had only been baptized "in the name of Jesus" (εἰς τὸ ὄνομα τοῦ κυρίου Ἰησοῦ). The πνεῦμα ἅγιον, however, had not yet fallen onto them (οὐδέπω γὰρ ἦν ἐπ᾽ οὐδενὶ αὐτῶν ἐπιπεπτωκός). Therefore, Peter and John, coming from

---

[171] Cf. G. Luck, *Arcana Mundi. Magic and the Occult in the Greek and Roman Worlds* (Baltimore: The John Hopkins University Press, 1985), 3-4, and H.C. Kee, *Medicine*, 3-4, 123-24.

[172] Cf. Apuleius, *Metamorphoses*, III 23-25.

[173] Incantations in the *name of God* were known in Qumran as a means to expell demons, cf. 11QPsApᵃ according to the reconstruction of E. Puech, "11QPsApᵃ: Un rituel d'éxorcismes. Essai de reaconstruction," in *RevQ* 55 (1990), 377-403. The second and third psalm both of which are ascribed to David (לדויד), are of special interest here, since both are introduced by the formula על דברי לחׁשׁ בשׁם יהוה] = "concerning words of invocation in the name of Yahweh." The third psalm, col. IV:4-V:3, continues, "invoke at all times the God of heaven when Belial comes to you and say to him ..." (על וא]מרתה אליו] קרא בכו]ל עת אל אל השמ]ים אשר] יבוא אליך בלי; the incantation addressing the demon follows). With regard to the function of Yahweh as BNP and the function of the one invoking his name, cf. the concluding remarks of Puech: "l'invocation du nom divin YHWH occupe la place centrale afin que le Dieu unique agisse contre les esprits malfaisants et hostiles et guérisse celui pour lequel l'invocation a été faite. *Il s'agit moins d'avoir pouvoir sur Dieu que de se confier en Lui*" (403; italics are mine).

[174] Cf. D. Georgi, *The Opponents of Paul in Second Corinthians* (Philadelphia: Fortress Press, 1986 [tr. from the revised German edition of 1964]), who correctly suggests "that the name and with it also the Kerygma may not be separated from the person of the miracle-working missionary. Non-'Christians' may not use this decisive tool ... The missionary has become a *medium of the power of Jesus (Acts 19:13, 15)*. The concept of Jesus-faith proclaimed here would apparently be abandoned if the union between name and proclaimer were denied. An obvious powerful reality stands behind the proclaimer, but only behind him" (169-70; italics are mine).

Jerusalem, first "prayed for them that they might receive the Holy Spirit" (προσηύξαντο περὶ αὐτῶν ὅπως λάβωσιν πνεῦμα ἅγιον; v. 15), and only "then did they lay their hands on them" (τότε ἐπετίθεσαν τὰς χεῖρας ἐπ᾽ αὐτούς) before the baptized people received the Holy Spirit (v. 17). The apostles *transfer* the spirit, which they themselves had received in Acts 2:1–13,[175] *by means of laying-on-of-hands*. However, this gesture alone would not be sufficient to have the effect, even for those who are already bestowed with the spirit. For, first of all, Christ needs to be invoked since he is the BNP. The apostles can only function as *mediators* of the transfer of τὸ πνεῦμα.

This interpretation is sustained by the fact that Simon Magus, who had become a believer and was also baptized (v. 13) and thus among those who received the Holy Spirit through the mediation of Peter and John (v. 17), is still not able to channel the Holy Spirit. His request for power which might enable him to transfer the Holy Spirit by the lay-ing-on-of-hands (δότε κἀμοὶ τὴν ἐξουσίαν ταύτην ἵνα ᾧ ἐὰν ἐπιθῶ τὰς χεῖρας λαμβάνῃ πνεῦμα ἅγιον; v. 19) reveals that the "laying-on-of-hands" for the transfer of the spirit depends on an authority other than the spirit itself. The prayer suggests that this authority lies in God or Christ. The human being can only invoke God or Christ, but it is God or Christ who decides, and who ultimately acts. This is also true for the installment of the seven διάκονοι in Acts 6:6: "and after having prayed they laid their hands on them" (καὶ προσευξάμενοι ἐπέθηκαν αὐτοῖς τὰς χεῖρας). The power of God is transmitted through the hands of the apostles to the receiving subjects. In Acts 19:11, Luke explicitly states that *God* performed miracles *through* Paul (ὁ θεὸς ἐποίει διὰ τῶν χειρῶν Παύλου).[176]

The following sequence may serve to summarize the functions of the "name of Jesus" and the "laying-on-of-hands" in Acts: the apostle as PNP prays to Christ, the BNP (and AS) → Christ transfers the healing power to the PNP → the PNP as MNP establishes a physical contact to or verbally addresses the SC, channeling the power to the receiver. Whenever the formula ἐν τῷ ὀνόματι τοῦ Ἰησοῦ is used, the first two steps are presupposed. For that reason, prayer and the onoma-formula never occur *together* in a single miracle story.[177]

---

[175] Cf. the prophecies in Acts 1:5, 8, 16.

[176] Cf. 5:12: Διὰ δὲ τῶν χειρῶν τῶν ἀποστόλων ἐγίνετο σημεῖα καὶ τέρατα πολλὰ ἐν τῷ λαῷ. Only in this context can the apparent characteristics of a θεῖος ἀνὴρ in Acts with regard to Peter (5:15: the shadow of Peter) and Paul (19:12: the clothes of Paul heal) be correctly assessed: Luke presents these apostles not as θεῖοι ἄνδρες but as *channels* of divine power.

[177] These observations might also illuminate the understanding of Mk 9:38–39/Lk 9:49–50, the pericope about "The Strange Exorcist," who drives out demons in the name

A similar understanding of the process of Christian miraculous healing lies behind James 5:14–15: if someone is sick, the elders of the church are supposed to

pray for him and anoint him with oil in the name of the Lord. The prayer of faith will save the sick one, and the Lord will raise him up (προσευξάσθωσαν ἐπ᾽ αὐτὸν ἀλείψαντες [αὐτὸν] ἐλαίῳ ἐν τῷ ὀνόματι τοῦ κυρίου· καὶ ἡ εὐχὴ τῆς πίστεως σώσει τὸν κάμνοντα, καὶ ἐγερεῖ αὐτὸν ὁ κύριος).

Here, again, the κύριος is the BNP, as well as the AS of the healing performance, while the prayers serve to invoke him to intervene. The anointing with oil has the same function as the laying-on-of-hands: it mediates divine power.[178]

Rabbinic literature resumes the OT conception of a PNP who only invokes God, stressing the total independence of God who decrees health without a mediator. For the pagan miracle tradition, only Insc. Graecae XIV 966a from the second century C.E. seems to indicate the involvement of an invoking subject as MNP: Asclepios reveals to a blind SC to go to the base of the Asclepios-statue in order προσκυνῆσαι after which he is supposed to

go from the right to the left and place his five fingers on the base of the altar and raise his hand and lay it on his own eyes (εἶτα ἀπὸ τοῦ δεξιοῦ ἐλθεῖν ἐπὶ τὸ ἀριστερὸν καὶ θεῖναι τοὺς πέντε δακτύλους ἐπάνω τοῦ βήματος καὶ ἆραι τὴν χεῖρα καὶ ἐπιθεῖναι ἐπὶ τοὺς ἰδίους ὀφθαλμούς).

The SC is bestowed with a numinous *savoir-faire*. He knows now what to do: first he has to invoke the god, and thus function as PNP, while afterwards he touches the statue of the god with his fingers in order to receive divine δύναμις. This transfer of divine power depends on the will of the god who is activated by the prayer in order that he might send out his power. Now, with this numinous power in his hand, the SC is supposed to "lay his hands on his own eyes" (τὴν χεῖρα ... ἐπιθεῖναι ἐπὶ

---

of Jesus even though he does not follow him. His *success* may demonstrate that he must be bestowed with divine authority to do so. This might explain Jesus' confidence expressed in his command not to hinder him, "for no one who does a deed of power in my name will be able soon afterward to speak evil of me" (οὐδεὶς γάρ ἐστιν ὃς ποιήσει δύναμιν ἐπὶ τῷ ὀνόματί μου καὶ δυνήσεται ταχὺ κακολογῆσαί με; Mk 9:39). However, the interpretation of this passage remains elusive. While it could be presupposed that the apostles first invoke the risen Christ when effecting healing "in the name of Jesus," it must be considered here that the "strange exorcist" does *not follow* Jesus and the disciples. This may indicate a *magical use* of the name of Jesus in this case.

[178] Cf. H.D. Betz, *Lukian von Samosata und das Neue Testament. Religionsgeschichtliche und paränetische Parallelen. Ein Beitrag zum Corpus Hellenisticum Novi Testamentum* (Berlin: Akademie-Verlag, 1961), 151, who quotes Dibelius, *Jakobusbrief*, 233: "Die Substanzen dienen 'als Vermittler einer durch den göttlichen Namen beschworenen göttlichen Kraft.'"

τοὺς ἰδίους ὀφθαλμούς).[179] By means of this action, the SC *channels* the divine power to the sick spot and thus effects healing. The difference compared with the stories about Elijah, Elisha, Abraham, Peter, and Paul, is that here the channeling subject is the SC himself, not a PNP. Thus, it can be concluded that the concept of an PNP who has the additional function of a MNP channeling divine healing power is a feature prevalent in *Jewish* traditions around the beginning of the turn of ages and in Acts. This concept, however, is already attested in the OT[180] and might have its origin in Mesopotamia:

> Im Zweistromland betet ein Beschwörungspriester um die Hilfe Marduks für die erfolgreiche Berührung des Kranken: "Laß mich gesegnet sein, wohin immer ich gehe. *Gib deinen Segen dem Mann, den ich jetzt berühre.*"[181]

The function of the MNPs dicussed in this chapter is to channel divine healing power to the SC, predominantly through physical contact. These PNPs who also function as MNPs are not bestowed with numinous competence which would enable them to function as ASs in a healing performance. A transcendent BNP is the AS in these cases.

3.3.3. The anti-subject as AS

The anti-subject causing the original need[182] can also function as AS of the performance which reverses the initial circumstance marked by the absence of health or life. This is often, and especially, but not exclusively, the case in exorcism stories. The BNP is, in this case, different from the AS. Its function in these NPs is to *subject the will (devoir-faire) of the anti-subject* to force it to engage as AS in the main performance. Sometimes, however, the BNP is not directly involved in the preparation

---

[179] For this motif in narratives about the healing of the blind, cf. Mk 8:25: εἶτα πάλιν ἐπέθηκεν τὰς χεῖρας ἐπὶ τοὺς ὀφθαλμοὺς αὐτοῦ.

[180] The differentiation between these two functions of PNPs, mediating the request for the LL to a transcendent BNP and mediating the divine power to the SC, is also important with regard to the question of a divine-man Christology in the Gospels. Blackburn, *Theios Anēr*, does not distinguish these two mediating functions and takes prayers of a PNP and commands of a BNP as expressions of the one motifeme: "the Jewish and apostolic miracle stories apparently do not understand prayer miracles to be of a completely different order than miracles performed by decree or command of the miracle worker" (131; cf. 144). This misinterpretation leads him to the false conclusion "that the tradents of the Markan miracle stories would not necessarily have interpreted Jesus' miracle-working as an *absolutely* autonomous activity, i.e., as the activity of a 'second god'" (132). As has been shown above, Jesus *never* prays before engaging in a miracle performance. He *incorporates* miraculous power (contra Blackburn, ibid., 127–28) and is always the BNP.

[181] K. Groß, *Menschenhand und Gotteshand in Antike und Christentum*. Ed. by W. Speyer (Stuttgart: Anton Hiersemann Verlag, 1985), 279, who quotes here H. E. Sigerist, *Anfänge der Medizin* (Zürich 1963); italics are mine.

[182] Cf. above, 3.1.2.

of the AS, but instructs a PNP or RSC (transfer of *savoir-faire*) how to force the AS out of the SC.

In antiquity, various ways and means were considered as effective for exorcisms. In the Egyptian legend of the possessed princess, preserved in the Bentresh-Stele, it is the mere *presence* of the god Khonsu-the-Carrier-out-of-Plans, which motivates the demon causing the sickness of Bintresh to consider leaving the woman. There is only one exorcism story in the Hebrew OT, 1 Sam 16:14–23. The lyre-playing of David makes the evil spirit temporarily leave Saul (ἀφίστατο ἀπ' αὐτοῦ; v. 23).[183] The LXX has an additional exorcism in Tobit: the angel Raphael, sent by God (3:16–17), bestows Tobias with information on how to drive out a demon (6:8).[184] Tobias then applies this knowledge and forces the demon to leave his bride: after Tobias burnt the liver and heart of the fish

the demon smelled the odour and fled to Egypt, where the angel bound him (ὠσφράνθη τὸ δαιμόνιον τῆς ὀσμῆς, ἔφυγεν εἰς τὰ ἀνώτατα Αἰγύπτου, καὶ ἔδησεν αὐτὸ ὁ ἄγγελος; 8:3 BA).

The Talmud also knows of some rabbis who had the power to prepare demons for a main performance. In b.Meila 17 a-b, rabbi Simeon ben Yohai commands a demon to leave the daughter of the Roman emperor (בן תמליון צא בן תמליון צא), which the demon does.[185]

For the pagan Greco-Roman environment, the earliest written evidence of an exorcism *narrative* goes back to the second century C.E. It is found in Lucian, Philops. 16. A well known Syrian from Palestine, after questioning the demon "from where he came into the body," drives out the demon (ἐξελαύνει τὸν δαίμονα) while adjuring (ὅρκους ἐπάγων) and threatening him (ἀπειλῶν) if he does not obey. This activity of the BNP forces the demon to leave the body. Again, it is a performance of the demon as AS which brings about the liquidation of the lack.

Philostratus, who wrote some fifty years after Lucian, incorporated a number of exorcism stories in his Vita Apollonii. Only those that concern a restoration to health are to be considered here. In 3:38 an Indian sage prepares a life-threatening demon to let go of a young boy by means of

---

[183] Cf. Pseudo-Philo LX, which focuses on the activity of David driving out the demon. Here the psalm, causing the demon to leave Saul, is given in detail. Concerning the use of psalms in exorcisms of a Jewish milieu at the turn of eras, cf. 11QPsAp[a] and Josephus, Ant. VIII 45–47 (ἐπῳδαί).

[184] Ἡ καρδία καὶ τὸ ἧπαρ [τοῦ ἰχθύος, W. K.], ἐάν τινι ὀχλῇ δαιμόνιον ἢ πνεῦμα πονηρόν, ταῦτα δεῖ καπνίσαι ἐνώπιον ἀνθρώπου ἢ γυναικός, καὶ οὐκέτι οὐ μὴ ὀχληθῇ [BA]/... καὶ φεύξεται ἀπ' αὐτοῦ πᾶν ἀπάντημα καὶ οὐ μὴ μείνωσιν μετ' αὐτοῦ εἰς τὸν αἰῶνα [א].

[185] Cf. b. Pesahim 112b, where Hanina ben Dosa commands the demon Agrath not to wander around in populated places anymore.

a *letter* which he sends with the SC's mother: the letter is addressed to the demon "with a threat and a terrifying matter" (ξὺν ἀπειλῇ καὶ ἐκπλήξει). Apollonios, of course, is also capable of driving out demons. In 4:20 he gazes at the demon possessing a young man (ὁρῶντος τε ἐς αὐτὸ τοῦ ᾿Απολλωνίου) with the effect that the demon utters cries of fear and rage swearing that he "would leave the young man (ἀφέξεσθαί τε τοῦ μειρακίου ὤμνυ) and never take possession of any person again (καὶ μηδενὶ ἀνθρώπων ἐμπεσεῖσθαι)."[186] But Apollonios addresses him with anger (ξὺν ὀργῇ), "as a master might a shifty, rascally, and shameless slave" and so on, and he orders him (καὶ κελεύοντος αὐτῷ) to leave with a visible sign (ξὺν τεκμηρίῳ ἀπαλλάττεσθαι). The demon agrees and leaves the boy.

An example for an anti-subject functioning as AS of the main performance outside the realm of exorcisms is 6:43: Apollonios *orders* (ἐκέλευσε) the dog which caused the wound and madness of a boy "to lick the wound all around (περιλιχμήσασθαι τὸ δῆγμα) so that the agent of the wound might in turn be its physician (ὡς ἰατρὸς αὐτῷ πάλιν ὁ τρώσας γένοιτο)."

Generally, Jesus expels demons and illnesses by means of touch and/or command. The prevalent means, however, is the *command*. In Mk 1:25–26/Lk 4:35, Jesus rebukes (ἐπετίμησεν) the unclean spirit: Shut up and leave him! (φιμώθητι καὶ ἔξελθε ἐξ αὐτοῦ). The demon obeys imediately.[187]

At times, however, even though a δαίμων, δαιμόνιον, πνεῦμα ἀκάθαρτον or πονηρὸν might not be explicitly mentioned in a pericope, the actions of the BNP involved and the AS might still indicate an exorcism. This is obvious for Lk 13:10–17, "The Healing of the Woman with a Spirit of Infirmity." Jesus' performance (a word sanctioning the performance: ἀπολέλυσαι τῆς ἀσθενείας σου, followed by the laying-on-of-hands) does not necessarily indicate an exorcism. The immediately following *passive* description of the main performance or its outcome, ἀνωρθώθη, gives a hint that Jesus is not thought of as AS but rather as a preparing BNP. Indeed, verse 11 ascribes the woman's condition to her conjunction with a πνεῦμα ... ἀσθενείας, and verse 16 explicitly states that ὁ σατανᾶς bound (ἔδησεν) the woman for the eighteen years of her illness. The

---

186   For this motif in exorcism-stories, cf. Mt 12:43–45/Lk 11:24–26 and Jos. Ant. 8:47.

187   καὶ σπαράξαν αὐτὸν τὸ πνεῦμα τὸ ἀκάθαρτον καὶ φωνῆσαν φωνῇ μεγάλῃ ἐξῆλθεν ἐξ αὐτοῦ; Luke adds: μηδὲν βλάψαν αὐτόν. For other examples of exorcisms by means of a command, cf. Mk 5:8/Lk 8:29 and Mk 9:25–26/Mt 17:18/Lk 9:42. Jesus' preparing action is described as ἐκβάλλειν δαιμόνια (Lk 11:14/Mt 9:33; Mk 1:34,39; 3:22–23; 6:13; 7:26; 9:28; etc.) while the demon's performance is always described as ἐξέρχεσθαι (cf. Acts 16:18 where *Jesus* is the BNP and Paul the channel of his power which forces the demon out: καὶ ἐξῆλθεν [τὸ πνεῦμα πύθωνα] αὐτῇ τῇ ὥρᾳ; and also Mk 7:29: ἐξελήλυθεν ... τὸ δαιμόνιον; cf. Lk 11:14).

woman, however, had been in need of being freed from this bond (λυ-θῆναι ἀπὸ τοῦ δεσμοῦ τούτου). Thus, the sanction of Jesus, "You are set free from your ailment" (ἀπολέλυσαι τῆς ἀσθενείας σου), implies the woman's being freed from her illness-*demon*. Even though the AS of the performance is not explicitly mentioned, it is probable that the demon, as is common in exorcisms, is the AS of the healing performance, prepared by Jesus (*devoir-faire*) to engage in the restoration performance.

Against this background it can be assumed that also Mk 7:31-37, "The Healing of the Deaf Mute," does not depict Jesus as AS of a healing performance, but rather as BNP who *prepares* an unmentioned but implied *demon* to leave the SC. This is suggested by five observations: 1. the performance in verse 35 is described by means of passive verbs (καὶ [εὐθέως] ἠνοίγησαν αὐτοῦ αἱ ἀκοαί, καὶ ἐλύθη ὁ δεσμὸς τῆς γλώσσης αὐτοῦ), and the AS is not made explicit; 2. as has been indicated above (Lk 13:16), demons are expected to bind their victims and thus need to be loosened[188] (the expression καὶ ἐλύθη ὁ δεσμὸς τῆς γλώσσης αὐτοῦ [Lk 13:16: λυθῆναι ἀπὸ τοῦ δεσμοῦ τούτου] may presuppose that a demon caused this sickness);[189] 3. also the command of Jesus, εφφαθα, which is translated διηνοίχθησαν, points in this direction, since these passive verbs eliminate the possibility that the SC might be regarded as AS;[190] 4. the detailed description of the performance of Jesus, which involves thrusting his fingers into the ears of the man, touching the man's tongue with his saliva, looking up into heaven before sighing (ἐστέναξεν), and finally, giving the command,[191] presents him as an exorcist who, by

---

[188] Cf. also Tobit 3:17 [ℵ]: λῦσαι Ασμοδαιον τὸ δαιμόνιον τὸ πονηρὸν ἀπ' αὐτῆς, and already Homer, Odyssey 5:397-398: στυγερὸς δέ οἱ ἔχραε δαίμων, ἀσπάσιον δ' ἄρα τόν γε θεοὶ κακότητος ἔλυσαν.

[189] Cf. T.A. Burkill, "The Notion of Miracle with Special Reference to St. Mark's Gospel," in *ZNW* 50 (1951), 33-48, 44.

[190] εφφαθα is imperative singular masculine Itpa'el of the Aramaic פתח. Thus, it has either a reflexive or passive meaning. Both Beyer, *Texte*, 673 and H.P. Krüger, art. "Aramäisch II. Im Neuen Testament," in *TRE* 3 (1978), 602-609, 606, propose here the reflexive meaning. However, the Greek translation διανοίχθητι, as well as the following ἠνοίγησαν/διηνοίχθησαν (v. 35; both ἠνοίγησαν [text Nestle/Aland] and διηνοίχθησαν, are well attested; Greeven's ἠνοίχθησαν seems to be a mistake [but cf. codex L]) suggest the passive meaning which also occurs in Babylonic-talmudic Aramaic (cf. Beyer, ibid.; Krüger, ibid.).

[191] Mark kept this command in the original Aramaic because it would leave a mysterious impression on his readers. It was expected in the 1st century C.E. that exorcists make use of secret and mysterious formulas (cf. Lucian, Philops. 9; Jos., Ant. 8:46-48; and also Philostratus, Vita Apol. IV 45). This piece of tradition might well stem originally from the area which is mentioned in this context: the Dekapolis. It can be expected that Greek was the predominant language in these Hellenistic cities. Jesus' mother-language, however, was Aramaic which is reflected in this passage.

means of these manipulations, prepares a demon to depart;[192] and 5. finally, a variant reading demonstrates that in fact people of late antiquity saw an exorcism here: the manuscripts W L N Δ al[193] read μογγιλάλον instead of μογιλάλον, and so shift the meaning from "talking with difficulty" or "being unable to speak" to "speaking hoarsely," like one possessed by a demon.[194] All the evidence suggests that Mk 7:31–37 describes an exorcism.

Two other miracle stories present Jesus as BNP who prepares an anti-subject as AS for a main performance. Both stories have affinities to explicit exorcism narratives: Mk 1:29–31, "The Healing of Peter's Mother in Law," has the *fever* engage in the main performance: "and the fever left her" (καὶ ἀφῆκεν αὐτὴν ὁ πυρετός). It is this performance which brings about the LL; the fever was forced to move away from the SC due to Jesus' touch (ἤγειρεν αὐτὴν κρατήσας τῆς χειρός). Even though the preparing activity of Jesus does not seem to have been intentionally aimed at the subjection of the will of the anti-subject-for he grasps her hand in order to raise her or to wake her up-it has this effect. Matthew's parallel account in 8:14–15 omits the confusing detail about the ἐγείρειν and clearly has Jesus ἥψατο her hand in order for the fever to leave her. Luke, on the other hand, has Jesus prepare the AS as he would activate a demon: "he rebuked the fever and it left her" (ἐπετίμησεν τῷ πυρετῷ, καὶ ἀφῆκεν αὐτήν; 4:39). Luke personifies the fever in his recasting of the story in two ways (v. 38: the mother-in-law ἦν συνεχομένη πυρετῷ μεγάλῳ; v. 39: the fever is *addressed* by Jesus). He clearly interpreted Mk 1:29–31 in the form of an exorcism and rewrote the pericope accordingly.

The other miracle story presenting the sickness as AS is Mk 1:40–45/Lk 5:12–16:[195] "immediately the leprosy left him" (εὐθὺς ἀπῆλθεν ἀπ' αὐτοῦ ἡ λέπρα).[196] This performance makes leprosy the AS of the NP. Jesus functions again as a preparing BNP who subjects the will of the AS by means of his touch (v. 41: ἐκτείνας τὴν χεῖρα αὐτοῦ ἥψατο) and

---

[192]   Cf. J. M. Hull, *Hellenistic Magic and the Synoptic Tradition* (Naperville, IL: Alec R. Allenson Inc., 1974), 78–85, especially his remark: "in short there is nothing in the description of this man which would lead the ancient reader to suppose that the man was not possessed by a demon ... Jesus was therefore thought of as exorcizing a demon and using this particular technique in order to do so (81)."

[193]   Cf. F. Blass, A. Debrunner, F. Rehkopf, *Grammatik des neutestamentlichen Griechisch* (Göttingen: Vandenhoeck & Ruprecht, [16]1984), 28. This variant reading is mentioned in neither Nestle/Aland nor in Huck/Greeven.

[194]   Cf. Philostratus, Vita Apol. III 38: the possessed boy οὐδὲ τὴν φωνὴν ... τὴν ἑαυτοῦ ἔχει, ἀλλὰ βαρὺ φθέγγεται καὶ κοῖλον, ὥσπερ οἱ ἄνδρες; cf. also Hull, *Magic*, 80–81.

[195]   For Mt 8:1–4, cf. above since in Matthew the leprosy does not function as AS.

[196]   Luke simply rearranges the sequence of the words for stylistic reasons.

the command καθαρίσθητι. As in Mk 7:34, the passive voice is chosen. It refers neither to Jesus nor to the SC as possible ASs, but presupposes another, the anti-subject λέπρα, as AS.

The anti-subject functioning as AS is, however, not always a sickness-causing demon. In 1/3 Kings 17:17–24, Elijah's request to Yahweh (v. 21b) already introduces the AS:

Let the child's life come into him again (תשב נא נפש-הילד הזה על-קרבו/ἐπιστραφ-ήτω δὴ ἡ ψυχὴ τοῦ παιδαρίου τούτου εἰς αὐτόν).

The נפש-הילד/ψυχὴ τοῦ παιδαρίου which left the child, causing its death,[197] is the AS of the main performance: "and the child's life returned into him and he revived" (ותשב נפש-הילד על-קרבו ויחי). It is, however, understood that Yahweh, after having been prepared by Elijah, in turn prepares the AS to engage in this performance: "and Yahweh listened to the voice of Elijah" (וישמע יהוה בקול אליהו), even though this preparation is not made explicit.[198] For a similar NT example, cf. Luke's version of Mk 5:41–42 in 8:54–55: Jesus commands the girl to get up after having grasped her hand. But while in Mark the girl immediately gets up and in so doing demonstrates the success of the performance, Luke introduces an AS different from Jesus as the BNP: "and her *soul* returned" (καὶ ἐπέστρεψεν τὸ πνεῦμα αὐτῆς; v. 55a).

Three other motifs should be mentioned here since they are sometimes employed with regard to the preparation of the anti-subject as AS. First, the demon is ordered *not to return* once it is driven out (Mk 9:25; Jos., Ant. 8:46–47; Philostratus, Vita Apol. 4:20; cf. also the Q tradition Mt 12:43–45/Lk 11:24–26, where the phenomenon of a returning demon is discussed).[199] Secondly, the demon, once it has accepted that it *has to* leave a human body, might beg for a *concession* which is then regularly granted by the exorcist. In Mk 5:12–13 parr the demons beg (παρεκά-λεσαν) Jesus to be sent into a herd of pigs, which Jesus permits (καὶ ἐπέτρεψεν αὐτοῖς). One encounters this motif already in the Bentresch-Stele where the sickness demon asks the exorcist-god for a common festival before leaving the girl. The exorcist-god grants this request.[200]

---

[197] Cf. verse 17: the child's sickness is so severe that finally לא-נותרה-בו נשמה/οὐχ ὑπε-λείφθη ἐν αὐτῷ πνεῦμα. נשמה/πνεῦμα and נפש/ψυχὴ are here identical terms.

[198] The LXX is reluctant in determining the AS and simply states, καὶ ἐγένετο οὕτως, καὶ ἀνεβόησεν τὸ παιδάριον. Josephus (Ant. VIII 325–7) presents God as BNP and the ψυχὴν as AS: Elijah prays to God that τὴν ψυχὴν εἰσπέμψαι πάλιν τῷ παιδὶ καὶ παρασχεῖν αὐτῷ τὸν βίον. Accordingly, God παρὰ πᾶσαν προσδοκίαν ἀνεβίωσεν.

[199] Cf. in this context also Tobit 8:3 [BA]. The angel *binds* the demon. This implies that it cannot return to the woman.

[200] This motif also occurs in rabbinic literature, but not in the context of healing miracles. Granting her plea for a concession, Hanina ben Dosa allows the demon Agrath to spend appointed periods of times in populated areas (b.Pes 112b).

Thirdly, the exorcist might *prepare himself* (in our literature always males) with knowledge about the condition of the SC or the nature of the possession, asking representatives of the SC or the demon itself for background information. In Mk 5:9 Jesus asks the demon for its name (τί ὄνομά σοι;), and in Mk 9:21 Jesus asks the father of the possessed child about the history of his illness, "How long has this been happening to him" (πόσος χρόνος ἐστὶν ὡς τοῦτο γέγονεν αὐτῷ)? Lucian, Philops. 16, mentions a Syrian exorcist from Palestine who asks the demon from where it entered the body (ὅθεν εἰσεληλύθασιν εἰς τὸ σῶμα;).

3.3.4. The MNP or SC as AS or as preparer of an AS

In those cases where the BNP is neither involved in the main performance directly as AS (cf. 3.2.2.1) nor as preparer of an anti-subject as AS (*devoir-faire*), its function might be to bestow a distinct subject, a MNP, or even the SC itself with knowledge (*savoir-faire*) and/or sometimes with the necessity (*devoir-faire*) either to engage in a main NP or to prepare another AS for the healing performance. These subjects are never *permanently* bestowed with numinous power; they can use it only for a specific purpose.

If the BNP is a transcendent god, it might get into contact with the SC or a subject chosen to function as MNP through a *dream* (ὄναρ) or *vision* (ὄψις). This motif is common in a Greco-Roman environment, cf. especially the inscriptions from Epidauros where the supplicants slept in the incubation-room (ἄβατον) where they would see a dream appearance (ὄψιν εἶδε . . . ἐδόκει ...).[201] But it is not necessarily explicit *how* the contact was established. The point is *that* a god instructed a SC or related subjects. This activity of a transcendent BNP can be expressed by verbs such as,

- אמר/λέγειν introducing a command (in the OT, God can communicate immediately with his prophets, cf. Num 21:8; LXX 4 Kings 20:7; cf. Insc. Graecae IV² 1:126),
- κέλεσθαι/κελεύειν (Metagyrtes; Epidauros A6; Insc. Graecae IV² 1:126),
- πείθειν (Insc. Graecae IV² 1:125),
- χρηματίζειν (Insc. Graecae XIV 966 a.b.c.d),
- προσ/συντάσσειν (Aelian, De nat. animal. 9:34; Plutarch, Pericles 8; Galen, Sub. Emp. X), or
- δεικνύναι (Diodorus of Sicily, Bibliotheca XVII 103:7).

---

[201] Pausanias, Description of Greece 38:13; Livius, Ab urbe II 36:2; Diodorus of Sicily, Bibliotheca XVII 103:7; Plutarch, Pericles 8; Galen, Sub. Emp. X; Suetonius, Lives of Ceasars VIII 7:2. Only Suetonius has the motif in this story. The parallel account in Tacitus, Histories IV 81, only knows that the two men were somehow instructed by Serapis (deo auctore).

Non-transcendent BNPs may communicate *savoir-faire* in the form of a command, for example, "Go, wash in the pool of Silo'am!" (Joh 9:7)[202]

3.3.4.1. The MNP as AS or as preparer of an AS

This section presents subjects other than the SC who are bestowed with numinous competence by a transcendent BNP for a specific healing performance.

Philo, Mos. I 79–80, presents a clear example of this iNP. In an interpretation of Ex 4:1–9, Philo compares God, the BNP, with a *teacher* who bestows Moses with numinous knowledge (ταῦτα μὲν οὖν ὑπὸ μόνος ἐπαιδεύετο, ὡς παρὰ διδασκάλῳ γνώριμος), as well as with the *instruments of the miracles* (τὰ τῶν τεράτων ὄργανα; *pouvoir-faire*). In this passage Philo stresses the dependence of Moses on a transcendent BNP. God's iNP conjoins the MNP Moses with numinous competence (ἔχων παρ' ἑαυτῷ ...).[203]

In the case of MNPs, the BNP may make the MNP familiar with *natural* remedies which possess a magical power.

In 2 Kings 20:7a, Isaiah prepares ASs for the healing of Hezekiah by subjecting their wills and bestowing them with numinous *savoir-faire*: "Bring a lump of figs!" (קחו דבלת תאנים). The undetermined ASs are obedient: "and they brought it and applied it to the boil." This is the main performance whose success is stated in verse 7bβ: וַיֶּחִי. The LXX, however, has the whole of verse 7 as preparation of the ASs. Furthermore, it does not indicate whether Yahweh or Isaiah is the preparing subject. The context, however, seems to suggest that *Yahweh* is the subject of εἶπεν·

and he said, "They shall take a lump of figs and lay it on the boil, and he will become healthy!" (καὶ εἶπεν Λαβέτωσαν παλάθην σύκων καὶ ἐπιθέτωσαν ἐπὶ τὸ ἕλκος, καὶ ὑγιάσει).

Here, neither the main performance nor its outcome is explicitly narrated.[204]

The application of a secret medicine or herbs is especially prevalent in the pagan Greco-Roman material. In Antiphanes, Metagyrtes frg. 154,

---

[202] Cf. 2 Kings 20:7; Lk 17:14; Pausanias, Desc. Graecae X 38:13.

[203] For a detailed discussion of Philo's understanding of divine-human relationships, cf. C. R. Holladay, *Theios Aner in Hellenistic-Judaism: A Critique of the Use of This Category in New Testament Christology* (Atlanta: Scholars Press, 1977), 103–98, esp. 155–63.

[204] In Jos. Ant. X 25, the motif of the lump of figs is completely missing. From Josephus' perspective and image of God, it is sufficient to note that God granted the request of Hezekiah, and thus simply decreed healing. Thus the LXX and Josephus sensed a tension in the Masoretic text between God's decision to add years to Hezekiah's life and the necessity of a healing practice as proposed by Isaiah. Josephus' account, beyond the adjustments in the LXX, stresses the total almightiness of God.

a girl receives a certain ointment (ἀλείμματα) from a goddess and is instructed by the goddess to anoint, first the feet and then the knees, of a SC who is unable to walk. As soon as the girl touches his feet and rubs them, the man gets on his feet (ὡς θᾶττον ἡ παῖς δ᾽ ἥψατ᾽ αὐτοῦ τῶν ποδῶν ἔτριψέ τ᾽, ἀνεπήδησεν). The girl's performance brings about the LL. Similarly, Alexander, according to Diodoros of Sicily (Biblio- theca, Hist. XVII 103:4–8) is numinously bestowed with knowledge about the location of a secret plant with healing power (δύναμις). After having found and grounded the plant (iNP), Alexander applies it to the body of wounded Ptolemy, gives him to drink from it, and so restores him to health.[205] Alexander, as MNP, is the AS of the healing perform- ance.

An interesting case concerning the bestowal of a subject with numinous *savoir-faire* is preserved in Apollodoros, Biblotheca III 3. The diviner and *supposed* BNP Polyidos finds himself in an apparently desperate situation. He is locked in a room with a dead body whom he is expected to revive.

And while he was in great perplexity, he saw a serpent going towards the corpse. He threw a stone and killed it, fearing to be killed if any harm befell the body. But another serpent came, and, seeing the former one dead, departed, and then returned, bringing a herb (πόαν), and placed it on the whole body of the other; and no sooner was the herb so placed upon it than the dead serpent came to life. Surprised at this sight (θεασάμενος δὲ Πολύιδος καὶ θαυμάσας), Polyidos applied the same herb to the body of Glaucus ...

This iNP, representing a miraculous restoration to life, bestows the AS with the necessary knowledge for the main performance.[206] In this way, Polyidos becomes the MNP who is now endowed with numinous *savoir-faire* concerning the application of an herb with healing power. The MNP engages successfully in the performance restoring the SC to life.

In Plutarch, Pericles 8, the goddess Athena bestows a RSC with the knowledge about a cure which makes it the MNP and enables it to heal the SC quickly and easily (θεραπείαν, ἧ χρώμενος ὁ Περικλῆς ταχὺ καὶ ῥᾳδίως ἰάσατο τὸν ἄνθρωπον).

Both Tacitus, Hist. IV 81, and Suetonius, Lives VII 2–3, describe how the AS Vespasian is prepared by the two SCs who approach him with a proposal (*savoir-faire*) for a NP based on a dream, and secondly by

---

[205] ἐγερθεὶς οὖν ὁ ᾿Αλέξανδρος καὶ τὴν βοτάνην ἀναζητήσας καὶ τρίψας τό τε σῶμα τοῦ Πτολεμαίου κατέπλασε καὶ πιεῖν δοὺς ὑγιῆ κατέστησεν.

[206] This motif is found in numerous folk-tales from around the world, cf. J.G. Frazer, "Appendix VII. – The Resurrection of Glaucus," in idem, ed. and translator, *Apollodorus. The Library*. II, LCL (London: William Heinemann, 1921), 363–70.

the persuasion (*vouloir-faire*) of his friends and physicians to engage in a performance. Vespasian is *not* the BNP and in fact strongly *doubts* that he will be able to carry out the proposed performance successfully. This corresponds to the fact that he is not bestowed *permanently* with the ability to heal as proposed by means of "spitting into the eyes" and "jumping onto the hand"[207]/"touching the leg with his heel." He does neither have the *savoir-faire* nor the *pouvoir-faire* for this perform-ance.[208] Only after having been bestowed by the BNP Serapis, through the SCs' mediation, with the required competence for this performance, thus becoming a MNP, is Vespasian able to engage as AS successfully in the main performance.

There is one example of a detailed *exorcism* narrative in which the demon is not the AS of the main performance: Josephus (Ant. 8:45–49) mentions one Eleazar who had been bestowed with secret knowledge concerning "the art used against demons" (τὴν κατὰ τῶν δαιμόνων τέχνην) by Solomon, who himself received his knowledge from God. In this case God is the ultimate BNP. Solomon had been bestowed with numinous *savoir-faire* from God, thus becoming a MNP. Against this background it is understood also that Eliazar is a MNP. Eleazar would "put to the nose of the possessed man a ring which had under its seal one of the roots prescribed by Solomon, and then, as he smelled it (ὀσφρομένῳ, cf. Tobit 8:3 BA: ὠσφράνθη with the demon as subject), *drew out* (ἐξεῖλκεν) the demon through the nostrils, and when the man at once fell down,[209] adjured the demon never to come back into him,[210] remembering the conjuration of Solomon and reciting the incantations (τὰς ἐπῳδάς)[211] which he had composed." In this case the will of the demon is not subjected to become the AS of the main performance; it is *drawn out* by the MNP as AS.

3.3.4.2. The SC as AS or as preparer of an AS

At times the BNP gets in contact (directly or mediated) with a SC and, instead of healing it immediately and actively in a main performance, prepares it for its own healing performance. In this way, the SC itself

---

[207] Cf. for this motif, Epidauros A3.

[208] This has correctly been observed by A. Henrichs, "Vespasian's Visit to Alexandria," in *ZPE* 3 (1968), 51–80: "The true wonderworker, however, acts on an inner impulse, because he is sure of his power ..." Henrichs suggests that not Vespasian but *Serapis* is here the AS: "It was in fact, the foot of Serapis which healed the crippled hand" (71). If this is correct, one should notice the closeness of this healing-story to those narrated about the apostles in Acts.

[209] Cf. for this motif in the context of an exorcism, Mk 9:26.

[210] Cf. for this motif in the context of exorcisms, the Q tradition Mt 12:43–45/Lk 11:24–26 and Philostratus, Vita Apol. 4:20.

[211] Cf. Lucian, Philops. 11 in the context of driving out poison.

either becomes the AS or is enabled to prepare a different subject (for example, a demon) as AS for a main performance by subjecting its will (*devoir-faire*).

Prescriptions of remedies are not given for the Asclepios cult at Epidauros. As has been pointed out above, the god himself is usually the AS. Only in later centuries is the image of Asclepios changed from a superhuman surgeon to a superhuman pharmacist. This development reached its climax in the second century C.E., but was prepared for already in the centuries before the turn of eras. This is the case in Insc. Creticae I 17:18, where the SC, a man with pain in his right shoulder, is instructed to

apply a plaster of barley-meal mixed with old wine and of a pine cone ground down with olive oil, and at the same time a fig and goat's fat, then milk with pepper, wax-pitch and olive oil boiled together ...

In 17:19 a SC is given the following detailed prescription:

she was healed by the God who ordered her to apply the shell of an oyster, burnt and ground down by her with rose-ointment, and to anoint with mallow, mixed with olive oil.

These two examples,[212] dating from the second to the first centuries B.C.E., indicate that Asceplios was increasingly perceived more as a superhuman pharmacist than as a surgeon.

For corresponding examples in the second century C.E., cf. Insc. Graecae IV² 1:125 b.c.d., where Asceplios appears as a revealer of prescriptions. For example, in 125 d, the SC, a blind soldier, is instructed to

take the blood of a white cock along with honey and compound an eye ointment and for three days apply it to his eyes (ἐπιχρεῖσαι ἐπὶ τοὺς ὀφθαλμούς).

Galen, in Sub. Emp. X, describes how a SC was instructed by the god

that he should drink every day of the drug produced from the vipers (τοῦ διὰ τῶν ἐχνιδῶν φαρμάκου) and should anoint the body from the outside (χρίειν ἔξωθεν τὸ σῶμα).

In all these examples, the SC carries out these instructions, functioning as the AS whom Asclepios bestowed with numinous *savoir-faire*. It seems as if the perception of Asclepios as surgeon determined his cult in the beginning of his rise as a healing god, especially in Epidauros. However, this was a temporary phase and his image changed in later centuries.

In addition to the prescription of ointments, the god was believed to prescribe certain other *cures* in the second century C.E. The SC is or-

---

[212] Cf. Insc. Creticea I 17:17.

dered to engage in activities like bathing in cold water or running bare-foot while being put on a strict diet. The god retreats more and more into transcendence and the miraculous factor is limited to the bestowal of knowledge with the focus on the detailed main performance by the SC.[213] This development may already be foreshadowed in an epigram on a heavy stone found at Epidauros dating from the end of the third century B.C.E. (Insc. Graecae IV² 1:125).[214] It is a recasting of Epidauros A15: the paralyzed Hermodicos of Lampsacos was healed by Asclepios. The epigram is written in the first person singular as expression of the SC's thankfulness. The stone in which the epigram is inscribed is supposed to be the stone the SC carried. Concerning the *function* of the motif "carrying of the stone," a remarkable difference between Epidauros A15 and this epigram can be observed. While in A15 the stone is carried by the SC as a *demonstration* of the success of the performance executed by Asclepios (τοῦτον ἐγκαθεύδοντα ἰάσατο), the epigram indicates that the healing was accomplished *by means* of the stone-carrying which was *ordered* by Asclepios.[215] According to this epigram, Asclepios subjected the will of the SC to carry out the main performance (πεῖσάς με ἄρασθαι τόνδε [πέτρον, W.K.]). The SC who carried out this *task* is the AS of the main performance. This is also indicated at the end of the epigram stating the success. The god's function is described as ἄνοσον διάγειν. Asclepios effected the healing as the AS in an iNP preparing the AS for the main performance. He himself is not the AS of the main performance.[216]

This motif, *healing through the accomplishment of a task*, is also found in other traditions. Livius, De urbe II 36, describes how a certain plebeian, due to his repeated failure to obey a divine order to mediate a message to the city consuls, became very sick. However, immediately after he does communicate the message, he becomes healthy.

In Pausanias, Desc. Graecae X 38:13, Asclepios orders the poetess Anyte (*devoir-faire*) to bring a sealed tablet to blind Phalysios and com-

---

[213] Cf. the Apellas stele from about 160 C.E., Insc. Graecae IV² 1:126, and especially the orations of Aelius Aristides.

[214] For the dating, cf. Herzog, *Wunderheilungen*, 100-1.

[215] Herzog, ibid., 101, observes this difference but does not seem to notice that it was this very act of carrying which *brought about* the healing: "Das Epigramm erweckt auch den Eindruck, als ob die Kraftleistung die Vorbedingung der Heilung sei. Der Wunderbericht dagegen sagt mit voller Deutlichkeit, daß der Gott zunächt den Kranken heilte (ohne nähere Angabe ...) und ihm dann einen Befehl für später, d.h. nach der Heilung, erteilte." Cf., however, already A16: a boy steals the stick of a lame man who ἀστὰς ἐδίωκε καὶ ἐκ τούτου ὑγιὴς ἐγένετο. The man is here not ascribed a task. The ἐκ τούτου, however, makes clear that it was this performance of the SC which brought about LL.

[216] Cf. A15, where Asclepios is the subject of the unspecified ἰάσατο.

mand him to read it after having taken away the seal. She prepares the SC accordingly. In spite of his doubts (τῷ δὲ ἄλλως μὲν οὐ δυνατὰ ἐφαίνετο ἰδεῖν τὰ γράμματα …), he has some hope in Asclepios' ability (ἐλπίζων δέ τι ἐκ τοῦ Ἀσκληπιοῦ χρηστόν), opens the seal, and becomes healthy (καὶ ἰδὼν ἐς τὸν κηρὸν ὑγιής τε ἦν). These two acts of the SC, opening of the seal and watching the tablet, constitute the main performance which has the SC as its AS. Cf. in this context Lk 17:14, where Jesus instructs the ten lepers to show themselves to the priests: καὶ ἐγένετο ἐν τῷ ὑπάγειν αὐτοὺς ἐκαθαρίσθησαν. All these examples portray the SC as AS, instructed by the BNP or a MNP to fulfill a certain task: the performances exemplify the SC's obedience which immediately effects the healing. If the instructions are followed, a successful outcome of the performance is guaranteed. If not, the lack will not be liquidated (cf. Livy, Ab urbe II 26).

The book of Tobit describes a sequence of preparations with respect to the healing of Tobit's blindness: Raphael being sent by God (3:16–17) bestows Tobias with knowledge concerning the use of the fish's bile:

- Anoint a man who has white spots in his eyes with the bile, and he will become healthy (ἡ δὲ χολή, ἐγχρῖσαι ἄνθρωπον, ὃς ἔχει λευκώματα ἐν τοῖς ὀφθαλμοῖς, καὶ ἰαθήσεται; 6:9 BA)[217]
- Now, anoint his eyes with the bile! And being stung [by it], he will rub his eyes and thus remove the white spots, and he will see you (σὺ οὖν ἔγχρισον τὴν χολὴν εἰς τοὺς ὀφθαλμοὺς αὐτοῦ, καὶ δηχθεὶς διατρίψει καὶ ἀποβαλεῖ τὰ λευκώματα καὶ ὄψεταί σε; 11:8 BA).[218]

Tobias, thus bestowed with savoir-faire, acts accordingly and applies the bile (11:11).[219] However, this is not the main performance. The procedure of applying medication *prepares* the father for the main performance. The bile has a burning effect on Tobit's eyes as Raphael had predicted (11:8). This forces him (*devoir-faire*) to rub his eyes with his hands, an action which takes away the λευκώματα from his eyes.[220] The SC Tobit is the AS prepared by a MNP, the RSC Tobias, who himself was prepared by a BNP, Raphael, who is endowed with numinous *savoir-faire*, who was in turn activated by another BNP, God (*devoir-faire*).

Cf. in this context Joh 9:6–7: Jesus *prepares* the healing of the blind man, first, by applying dirt mixed with his saliva to the eyes of the SC (καὶ ἐπέχρισεν αὐτοῦ τὸν πηλὸν ἐπὶ τοὺς ὀφθαλμούς), and secondly, by

---

[217] ℵ adds: ἐμφυσῆσαι ἐπ' αὐτοὺς ἐπὶ τῶν λευκωμάτων.

[218] ℵ has: … καὶ ἀποστρύψει τὸ φάρμακον καὶ ἀπολεπίσει τὰ λευκώματα ἀπὸ τῶν ὀφθαλμῶν αὐτοῦ …

[219] ℵ has φάρμακον and adds that first Tobias ἐνεφύσησεν εἰς τοὺς ὀφθαλμοὺς αὐτοῦ.

[220] ὡς δὲ συνεδήχθησαν, διέτριψε τοὺς ὀφθαλμοὺς αὐτοῦ, καὶ ἐλεπίσθη ἀπὸ τῶν κανθῶν τῶν ὀφθαλμῶν αὐτοῦ τὰ λευκώματα (11:12 BA, similar ℵ).

instructing the SC to wash himself in a certain pool. The SC, thus prepared and bestowed with competence (*savoir-faire*) becomes the AS of the main performance: "then he went and washed and came back able to see" (ἀπῆλθεν οὖν καὶ ἐνίψατο, καὶ ἦλθεν βλέπων; v. 7; cf. v. 11). For an OT example, see Num 21:1–9. Upon the instructions of Yahweh, Moses makes a serpent of bronze and puts it on a pole. The people who were bitten by snakes would *look at the serpent* and live.

The numinous competence (*savoir-faire*) with which a SC is bestowed does not necessarily enable it to carry out the main performance itself. However, it might be bestowed with the ability to subject the will (*devoir-faire*) of another AS. This is the case in 2/4 Kings 5:10–13: Elisha instructs leprous Naaman to wash himself seven times in the river Jordan. After having been persuaded by his friends to do so, he goes to the Jordan and washes himself seven times according to the instructions by the prophet (וירד בירדן שבע פעמים כדבר איש האלהים/καὶ ἐβαπτίσατο ἐν τῷ Ἰορδάνῃ ἑπτάκι κατὰ τὸ ῥῆμα Ελισαιε; v. 14a). This action *effects* the main performance, bringing about the liquidation of the lack. The SC is here not the AS but prepares a different subject as AS: "and his flesh *turned* like the flesh of a small child" (וישב בשרו כבשר נער קטן /καὶ ἐπέστρεψεν ἡ σὰρξ αὐτοῦ ὡς σὰρξ παιδαρίου μικροῦ; 14b). The בשר/σάρξ of Naaman functions as AS of the main performance.[221]

Aelian, De nat. animal. 11:34, knows of an example where a poisoned SC is instructed by the god Serapis to "buy a live moray and thrust his hand into the creature's tank." After having been bestowed with this numinous *savoir-faire* the SC acts accordingly. Thrusting his hands into the moray's tank and the pulling off of the moray *prepares* the animal's main performance: "And the moray fastened on and clung to him but when it was pulled off *it pulled away* the sickness from the young man at the same time" (ἀποσπωμένη δὲ καὶ τὴν νόσον τὴν ἐν τῷ νεανίᾳ συναπέσπασεν).

There is only one example in the gospels where a SC prepares an AS other than Jesus for a main performance: in Mk 5:25–34/Lk 8:43–48[222]

---

[221] For a similar case where the subject of שוב/ἐπιστρέφειν is the AS of a main performance, cf. 2/4 Kings 20:11b. After Isaiah has implored God that the shadow might retreat ten intervals, *God* did retreat the shadow: וישב את־הצל. The LXX, however, has the *shadow* as AS of this performance and God as implied preparer of the AS (devoir-faire): καὶ ἐπέστρεψεν ἡ σκιὰ ἐν τοῖς ἀναβαθμοῖς εἰς τὰ ὀπίσω δέκα βαθμούς. The success of the main performance is stated by the following ויטהר/καὶ ἐκαθαρίσθη.

[222] Mt 9:20–22 is different from the parallels in Mark and Luke. The woman is not healed by touching the fringe of Jesus' cloak. By means of her touch, she rather draws Jesus' attention to her: ὁ δὲ Ἰησοῦς στραφεὶς καὶ ἰδὼν αὐτήν ... (v. 22). The δύναμις is here replaced by the woman's πίστις. The focus is on σωθῆναι/σώζειν, which appears three times in these few verses. Matthew recasts this pericope from the perspective of eschatological

the woman, by means of her ἅπτεσθαι, *forces* the δύναμις which dwells in Jesus to engage in a performance bringing about the liquidation of her lack. This story is distinct insofar as the woman had *not been instructed* by divine advice to do so. She *has* the will and knowledge needed for the direct preparation of the healing δύναμις. The extraordinary nature of this miracle story is due to the fact that she does not invoke Jesus but, in his place, immediately subjects the will of his δύναμις. Concerning the preparedness of the the "fluidum" δύναμις as AS in Mk 5:25–34, see the apt discussion of F. Preisigke, who observes, "daß die am Mantel haftende Kraft mit *Bewußtsein* ausgestattet ist: sie kann unterscheiden, ob eine Berührung mit oder ohne Absicht geschieht, und je nach Lage des Falles trifft sie (ganz ohne Mitwirkung Christi) ihre *Entscheidung*, überzuströmen oder nicht; nur wenn jene *Absicht* vorliegt, *muß* sie überströmen."[223]

3.4. The sanction of the main performance and of the preparedness of a BNP or MNP

The successful main performance leading to the LL may be followed by the *recognition* of the outcome of this *performance* and/or the *preparedness* of the subject(s) bringing about the LL.

Occasionally, a single action of the SC may have the double function of demonstrating the success of a main performance and sanctioning the preparedness of the BNP. This is the case in Lk 1:64, where Zechariah, after his tongue was loosened, begins to praise God (καὶ ἐλάλει εὐλογῶν τὸν θεόν). The same is true for Tobit 12:1–14:1, where Tobias' and Tobit's μισθός to Raphael is replaced by their praise of God. The *written* prayer of formerly blind Tobit (ἔγραψεν προσευχὴν εἰς ἀγαλλίασιν) demonstrates the success of the main performance and, at the same time, sanctions God's preparedness.

As a pagan example for this phenomenon of a double-function of one action, cf. Apollodoros, Bibliotheca II 2:

---

salvation. Therefore, the concrete situation of physical sickness is neglected, even though its description heavily pervades the accounts of Mark and Luke (cf. Mk 5:26: the failure of the physicians; v. 29: the source of blood dries up; ἴαται v. 34: to be ὑγιής; Lk 8:43: θεραπεύειν; v. 44: the flow of the blood stands still; v. 47: ὡς ἰάθη παραχρῆμα). H.J. Held, "Interpret," assesses the interpretation in Matthew correctly with the following statement: "Das Wort vom rettenden Glauben ... (Mt 9:22) enthält gleichsam das Thema der matthäischen Neuerzählung" (169). Cf. also U. Luz, *Matthäusevangelium*, 53: "Die Rettung ist aber mehr als die Heilung: Das drückt Matthäus aus, indem er zuerst erzählt, daß Jesus der Frau aufgrund ihres Glaubens die Rettung zuspricht und erst hinterher von der Heilung berichtet."
[223] "Gotteskraft," 213.

Proitos [the father of mad women] gave them [his daughters after Melampous had healed them] in marriage to Melampous [the BNP and AS] and Bias [Melampous' brother] ...

This action demonstrates the recovery of the SCs and is, at the same time, part of the reward of the BNP and AS, Melampous.[224]

Usually, however, the sanction of the main performance and of the preparedness of the BNP or MNP are clearly distinguishable.

3.4.1. The sanction of the main performance

A successful main performance effects the liquidation of the initial lack. The demonstration of the LL sanctions the outcome of a main performance. Sometimes the verb describing the performance of an AS already indicates its positive outcome, for example, an AS *heals* a SC. In this case the LL does not necessarily have to be stated or demonstrated. Usually, however, the LL is explicitly stated and/or demonstrated. The demonstration of the LL is a performance carried out by the SC and/or the anti-subject[225] which caused the lack and functioned as AS of the main performance. The subject demonstrating the LL can be prepared by the BNP to do so. In those instances, the BNP subjects the will (*devoir-faire*) of the SC or anti-subject.

A common motif in connection with the LL is the *suddenness* of the restoration[226] indicated by adverbs like εὐθέως, ταχέως, παραχρῆμα et al.[227] Matthew typically employs the following formula:

ἰάθη/ἐσώθη/ἐθεραπεύθη a subject of circumstance ἀπὸ τῆς ὥρας ἐκείνης/ἐν τῇ ὥρα ἐκείνῃ.[228]

The LL is stated by means of passive constructions or by descriptions of the SC's new condition. The LL can be stated in more general terms

---

[224] For additional examples, cf. Mk 5:18–20 par and Philostratus, Vita Apol. IV 20 as well as Mk 10:52 par: formerly blind Bartimaeus is now able to follow Jesus on his way (demonstrating the LL; this action also sanctions Jesus' preparedness).

[225] In the case of some exorcism narratives, cf. Mk 5:13–15; Philostratus, Vita Apol. 4:20.

[226] Cf. Weinreich, *Heilungswunder*, 197–98.

[227] Cf., e.g., Mk 5:29, 42; 10:25b; Lk 1:64; 4:39; 5:25; 8:44, 47; 13:13; 18:43; Acts 3:7; Tobit 8:3 [ℵ]; Jos., Ant. VIII 47; X 25–29; Epidauros A1; Marinos, Vita Procli 29; Tacitus, Hist. IV 81; Plutarch, Pericles 13:8. This motif, indicating the immediate change of the initial condition, has the function of emphasizing the BNP's competence. It corresponds to another motif with the same function which ocasionally occurs in healing miracle stories: an indication of the *effortlessness* of the BNP's performance. Asclepios restores a woman ἀμάχῳ τινί (Aelianos, De nat. animal. IX 33) and restores a sick girl to health over a distance ῥεῖα (Marinos, Vita Procli 29). Cf. Delling, "Wunder-Allegorie," 77, fn. 20, who shows that Philo employs this motif with respect to the divine δύναμις which πάντα δρᾶν εὐμαραές (Mos. I 94).

[228] Mt 8:13; 9:22; 15:28; 17:18; cf. Joh 4:53; b.Ber 34b; Acts 16:18.

like ἰάθη (Mt 8:13b; cf. Lk 7:10; Joh 4:53) or וְאִתְקִם (1QapGen 20:29b) = ἀπεκατέστη (Mk 8:25). The inscriptions from Epidauros use a more formulized language: ὑγιὴς ἐξέρχεσθαι by daylight/ὑγιὴς γίνεσθαι.[229] In other narratives, the statement of LL is more explicit and concrete:

- the withered hand ἀπεκατεστάθη (Mk 3:5b; cf. Tacitus, Hist. IV 81),
- a leper טָהֵר/ἐκαθαρίσθη (Mk 1:42b; Lk 17:14; Num 12:16 LXX; 2 Kings 5:14b),
- the source of blood ἐξηράνθη (Mk 5:29; cf. Lk 8:44),
- τὸ δαιμόνιον ἐξεληλυθός (Mk 7:30),
- the bent woman immediately ἀνωρθώθη (Lk 13:13),
- ἐστερεώθησαν οἱ βάσεις of a lame man (Acts 3:7),
- a forehead is now free of στίγματα (Epidauros A6),
- a blind man leaves the incubation room being able to see (A9; cf. Joh 9:7; Tacitus, Hist. IV, 81; ac caeco reluxit dies),
- the man with fever is now τοῦ πυρέτου ἀπηλλαγμένον (Oxyrh. 1381).

In all these examples, the initial circumstance appears to be reversed as the result of a successful main performance.

The motifemic slot of the sanction at times involves iNPs as in Tobit 8:10–14 where a maid is sent (devoir-faire) to determine whether Tobias is still alive or whether the demon of his bride has killed him overnight. The maid investigates (καὶ εἰσῆλθεν ἡ παιδίσκη ἀνοίξασα τὴν θύραν), finds out that Tobias is alive (καὶ εὗρεν τοὺς δύο καθεύδοντας), and informs the father of the bride (καὶ ἐξελθοῦσα ἀπήγγειλεν αὐτοῖς ὅτι ζῇ).

3.4.1.1. The SC as subject demonstrating the LL

If the SC functions as the subject which demonstrates the successful outcome of the main performance, its action indicates that what was previously impossible for it due to its handicap is now possible. The description of its performance demonstrating the LL is the direct antithesis to the description of the inabilities of the SC at the beginning of a narrative.

Sometimes, the SC is prepared by the BNP to engage in a demonstration-performance. In those cases the BNP subjects the will of the SC by means of a command (devoir-faire). This is a common feature in narratives depicting Jesus' miraculous performances. Cf. Mk 2:10–11 parr, in which Jesus says to the paralyzed man:

I tell you, get up, take up your stretcher and go to your house (σοὶ λέγω, ἔγειρε ἆρον τὸν κράβαττόν σου καὶ ὕπαγε εἰς τὸν οἶκόν σου).

---

[229] A3,4,5,8,11,16,17,18,20,B21,23,26,27,29,32; but cf. also the Apellas-stele; Insc. Creticae I 17:9; Pausanias, Desc. Graecae X 38:13.

The SC obeys and acts accordingly. This action demonstrates the success of Jesus' silent performance and in addition proves that "the Son of Man" indeed "has the power to forgive sins on earth" (ἐξουσίαν ἔχει ... ἀφιέναι ἁμαρτίας ἐπὶ τῆς γῆς; v. 10).[230]

In Epidauros A15, Asclepios, after healing a paralyzed man orders him that he should, after leaving, bring to the temple as large a stone as he is capable of carrying (ἐκελήσατο ἐξελθόντα λίθον ἐνεγκεῖν εἰς τὸ ἱαρὸν ὁπόσσον δύναιτο μέγιστον). The man's performance corresponds to the order: he carries the rock which is now located before the incubation room (ὁ δὲ τὸμ πρὸ τοῦ ἀβάτου κείμενον ἤνικε). In other traditions, the demonstrating actions of formerly *paralyzed or lame* SCs are often similar to those at Epidauros.

- the paralyzed man gets up, carries his stretcher and walks away (Mk 2:12a; cf. Joh 5:9; Lucian, Philops. 11, both of whom have the detail with the stretcher; cf. Acts 9:34b),
- the χωλός, after being healed by Jesus through Peter, ἐξαλλόμενος ἔστη καὶ περιεπάτει ... (Acts 3:8, cf. Acts 14:10),
- the SC who was carried on a litter to the consuls (ad consules lectica defertur), after accomplishing the task demanded and thus being restored to health, goes home on his own feet (pedibus suis domum redisse; Livius, Ab urbe II 36).

These SCs demonstrate that they can use their limbs which were formerly useless.

Various performances of formerly dead SCs indicate their successful *resuscitation*.

- the child ἀνεβόησεν (MT: ויחי; 3. Kings [LXX] 17:22; cf. 2 Kings 4:35 where the child sneezes seven times according to the MT),
- a man, after returning to life (ויחי/καὶ ἔζησε), gets to his feet (ויקם על־רגליו/καὶ . ἀνέστη ἐπὶ τοὺς πόδας αὐτοῦ; 2 Kings 13:21),
- a little girl ἀνέστη ... καὶ περιπάτει (Mk 5:42; cf. Lk 8:55), while a young man ἀνεκάθισεν καὶ ἤρξατο λαλεῖν (Lk 7:15; cf. Philostratus, Vita Apol. 4:45: φωνήν τε ἡ παῖς ἀφῆκεν and returns to her father's house),
- Tabitha ἤνοιξεν τοὺς ὀφθαλμοὺς αὐτῆς, καὶ ἰδοῦσα τὸν Πέτρον ἀνεκάθισεν (Acts 9:40), and
- Lazarus leaves his grave (ἐξῆλθεν; Joh 11:44).

In order to demonstrate the LL, formerly dead SCs give signs of life like getting up from a stretcher, walking around, talking, and opening their eyes. Cf. the detailed account in Apuleius, Metamorphoses II 29:

---

[230] For other NT examples, cf. Mk 3:5-6 parr; Lk 7:14; Mk 5:41; Joh 5:8; 11:14; Acts 3:6; 9:34, 40; 14:10.

Now his chest rose with a swell; now his health-giving artery pulsated; now his body was filled with breath; and the corpse rose and the young man spoke (Et assurgit cadaver, et profatur adulescens).

Ovid indicates similarly the successful resuscitation of Hippolytus who lifts his head from the ground (Fasti VI 754).

Blind SCs are enabled to *see* again:

- the SC [a: ὀϱθὸν] ἀνέβλεψεν (Insc. Graecae 14:966 a and d),[231]
- Tobit ἰδὼν τὸν υἱὸν αὐτοῦ ἐπέπεσεν ἐπὶ τὸν τϱάχηλον αὐτοῦ (Tobit 11:13),
- a blind man first saw the people like trees, but finally ἐνέβλεπεν τηλαυγῶς ἅπαντα (Mk 8:24–25 describes here a gradual restoration) [232]

Formerly *mute or deaf* SCs can now *speak*:

- καὶ ἐλάλει ὀϱθῶς (Mk 7:35),
- καὶ ἐλάλει εὐλογῶν τὸν θεόν (Lk 1:64),[233]
- ἐλάλησεν ὁ κωφός (Lk 11:14; cf. Mt 9:33/12:22).

SCs suffering from *fever*, lying on their beds and unable to do anything, now ask for water or food (b.Ber 34b: שׁאל לנו לשחות; cf. y.Ber 9d) or engage in daily activities: καὶ διηκόνει αὐτοῖς (Mk 1:31 parr).

Those who could not give birth before, do so now (cf. Gen 20:17–18). In Epidauros A1, the SC, after a five-year pregnancy, gives birth to a son who acts like a five year old: "she bore a son who, immediately after birth, washed himself at the fountain and walked about with his mother" (cf. A2; B31).

A man with a *headache*, after being healed, is instructed by Asclepios in fist-fighting. After leaving the incubation room, the man wins a fist-fight (Epidauros B29).

At Epidauros, an especially explicit demonstration is described in A12: after extracting the spearhead from the SC's jaw, Asclepios gives it into his hands. The SC departs with the spearhead in his hands (ἁμέϱας δὲ γενομένας ὑγιὴς ἐξῆϱπε τὰν λόγχαν ἐν ταῖς χεϱσὶν ἔχων; cf. A13: leeches; A14: stone; B30: arrowhead).

---

[231] Cf. Mk 10:52b; Mt 12:22; Acts 9:18; Epidauros A9.

[232] Epidauros B18 (the blind SC "saw a dream. It seemed to him that the god came up to him and with his fingers opened his eyes and that he first saw the trees of the sanctuary. At daybreak he walked out sound") does *not* mention a stepwise restoration (with Gnilka, *Markus*, 314, against Pesch, *Markusevangelium*, 419). The final sentence indicates the *real* LL, while the observation of the trees is part of a dream-vision. The final statement can thus not be regarded as the perfection of a former inferior state.

[233] This action of the SC has an additional function besides demonstrating the success of the main performance: the sanction of the BNP God who brought about healing.

In the case of *demonic possessions* various performances of the SC can indicate its recovery. After the demon has left, the SC is likely to fall down or lie down:

- πεσόντος εὐθὺς τἀνθρώπου (Jos., Ant. VIII 47),
- καὶ ἐγένετο ὡσεὶ νεκρός (Mk 9:26),
- τὸ παιδίον βεβλημένον ἐπὶ τὴν κλίνην (Mk 7:30).

The *conduct* of a SC freed from a demon is contrary to its behaviour while being possessed. This is decribed in detail by Philostratus, Vita Apol. IV 20:

But the young man rubbed his eyes as if he had just woke up, and he looked towards the rays of the sun, and won the consideration of all who now had turned their attention to him; for he no longer showed himself licentious (ἀσελγές τε οὐκέτι ἐφαίνετο), nor did he stare madly about (οὐδὲ ἄτακτον βλέπον), but he had returned to his own self (ἀλλ᾽ ἐπανῆλθεν ἐς τὴν ἑαυτοῦ φύσιν) ...; and he gave up his dainty dress and summery garments and the rest of his sybarite way of life, and he fell in love with the austerity of philosophers, and donned their cloak, and stripping off his old self modelled his life in future upon that of Apollonios (καὶ ἐς τὰ τοῦ Ἀπολλωνίου ἤθη ἀπεδύσατο).

A close parallel is Mk 5:15, 18, 20, καὶ θεωροῦσιν τὸν δαιμονιζόμενον καθήμενον ἱματισμένον καὶ σωφρονοῦντα ... παρεκάλει αὐτὸν ὁ δαιμονισθεὶς ἵνα μετ᾽ αὐτοῦ ᾖ ... καὶ ἀπῆλθεν καὶ ἤρξατο κηρύσσειν ... In both narratives, the SC is depicted as quiet and reasonable, contrary to its prior wild behaviour (cf. Philostratus, Vita Apol. VI 43), choosing as its new role model the BNP. Cf. Apollodoros, Bibliotheca II 2: after the mad women have been purified and *recovered their wits* (σωφρονῆσαι), they are given in marriage.

3.4.1.2. The anti-subject demonstrating the LL

In the case of exorcisms, a performance of the departing demon can be the only or an additional demonstration of the successful outcome of the main performance. The Bentresh-stele simply notes that the sickness-demon went to its location (cf. Tobit 8:3: the demon goes away to Egypt). Sometimes, the demon is *forced* by the BNP to demonstrate its departure. Cf. Josephus, Ant. VIII 48–49: in order that he ἐπιγνῶναι τοῖς ὁρῶσιν that the demon has left, Eleazar commands the demon to overturn a cup or footbasin full of water, which then also happens. An *additional* function of this demonstrating performance is to convince the bystanders that Eleazar has this ability, βουλόμενος δὲ πεῖσαι καὶ παραστῆσαι τοῖς παρατυγχάνουσιν ὁ Ἐλεάζαρος ὅτι ταύτην ἔχει τὴν ἰσχύν.[234]

---

[234] Cf. C. Bonner, "The Technique of Exorcism," in *HTR* 36 (1943), 39–49, 47.

Ultimately, however, the performance of the demon reveals the σύνεσις καὶ σοφία of Solomon who had received knowledge in the art of exorcism from God. This knowledge was then handed down to Eleazar.

Philostratus, Vita Apol. IV 20, describes how Apollonios orders the demon to depart with a sign (ξὺν τεκμηρίῳ). The demon decides to throw down a statue which first moves and then falls down. In Mk 5:13, the demons, after being allowed by Jesus to do so, enter a herd of pigs and drown in a lake.[235] In both the Philostratus and the Markan account, which share the common feature of a following demonstration of the LL by the SC, the anti-subject's demonstrating-performance presents an *act of destruction*.[236]

3.4.1.3. *The BNP or PNP demonstrating the LL*

At times, a performance of the BNP or PNP demonstrates the successful outcome of the main performance. As examples, cf. the following: the BNP or PNP *returns* the SC to the people to whom it belongs, cf. 1 Kings 17:23a:

Elijah took the child, brought him down from the upper chamber into the house and gave him to his mother (ויקח אליה את־הילד וירדהו מן־העליה הביתה ויתנהו לאמו/καὶ κατήγαγεν αὐτὸν ἀπὸ τοῦ ὑπερῴου εἰς τὸν οἶκον καὶ ἔδωκεν αὐτὸν τῇ μητρὶ αὐτοῦ).

This "return-motif" occurs often in resuscitation narratives, cf. 2 Kings 4:36; Lk 7:15; Acts 9:40–41; 'Aboda Zara 10b (ושדריה).[237] Jesus *sends away* the healed SCs: ἰάσατο αὐτὸν καὶ ἀπέλυσεν (Lk 14:4; cf. Mk 5:19, 34; 8:26). Jesus' command to provide the resuscitated girl with food (Mk 5:43: καὶ εἶπεν δοθῆναι αὐτῇ φαγεῖν) indicates once more the successful outcome of the main performance (correspondingly, Luke, in 8:55, has this command between the demonstrating performance of the SC and the sanction of her parents). After Lazarus left his grave, Jesus gives the order to unbind him and to let him go: λύσατε αὐτὸν καὶ ἄφετε αὐτὸν ὑπάγειν (Joh 11:44). The command of Jesus affirms the LL which had already been demonstrated by Lazarus' leaving the grave.

3.4.1.4. *Witnesses sanctioning the main performance*

The usual reaction of witnesses to a successful main performance effecting healing is marked by *joy* (χαρὰ and χαίρειν). In the literature under

---

[235] εἰσῆλθον εἰς τοὺς χοίρους, καὶ ὥρμησεν ἡ ἀγέλη κατὰ τοῦ κρημνοῦ εἰς τὴν θάλασσαν, ὡς δισχίλιοι, καὶ ἐπνίγοντο ἐν τῇ θαλάσσῃ.

[236] Cf. Bonner, "Technique," 47–49.

[237] In Philostratus, Vita Apol. IV 45, this motif also appears. Here, however, it is the SC who ἐπανῆλθέ τε ἐς τὴν οἰκίαν τοῦ πατρός.

scrutiny here, χαρά is commonly employed to describe the emotional involvement of bystanders witnessing a restoration, cf.

- the blind SC "could see clearly while the people stood by (τοῦ δήμου παρεστῶτος) and *rejoiced* (συνχαιρομένου) that glorious deeds lived (ὅτι ζῶσαι ἀρεταὶ ἐγένοντο) under our emperor Antonius" (Insc. Graecae XIV 966a; cf. 966b: καὶ ὁ δῆμος συνεχάρη αὐτῷ),
- and there was *joy* among all his brothers in Ninevi (καὶ ἐγένετο χαρὰ πᾶσι τοῖς ἐν Νινευη ἀδελφοῖς αὐτοῦ; Tobit 11:18 [BA]; א has: πᾶσιν τοῖς Ἰουδαίοις τοῖς οὖσιν ἐν Νινευη),
- and the entire crowd was *rejoicing* at all the wonderful things that he was doing (καὶ πᾶς ὁ ὄχλος ἔχαιρεν ἐπὶ πᾶσιν τοῖς ἐνδόξοις τοῖς γινομένοις ὑπ' αὐτοῦ; Lk 13:17).

However, χαίρειν can also occur with respect to the emotions of the SC after its healing (Tobit 11:16 with respect to Tobit; in 11:15, Tobias in his function as RSC is the subject of χαίρων). While χαρά generally denotes a certain inner disposition of a person and sanctions the main performance, χάρις is a concretion of this disposition and ultimately aims at the retribution of the subject which caused the χαρά, implying a sanction of that subject's preparedness. Χάρις presupposes χαρά. Χάρις and other expressions of the sanction of the BNP's or MNP's preparedness are to be discussed in the following subsection.

3.4.2. The sanction of the preparedness of the BNP or MNP

While the *demonstration* of the LL points back to the *performance*, sanctioning its outcome, the *sanctions* to be discussed now concern the *preparedness* of the BNP and MNP. Distinct types of allomotifs can fill this motifemic slot.

3.4.2.1. Spreading of information

In cases where the main performance happened in secret, for example, in a hidden place, information regarding the performance of a subject with miraculous healing abilities is often mediated to the outside world. The transfer of information can be prepared explicitly and might involve distinct iNPs.

The BNP itself can *command* the spreading of the information about a LL. This is documented twice for the Asclepios cult. The Apellas-stele, Insc. Graecae IV² 1:126, ends with the order of Asclepios to record what happened (ἐκέλευσεν δὲ καὶ ἀναγράψαι ταῦτα). In Oxyrh. 1381 (col. IX 191–198), the same god rejects the sacrifices and votive offerings of the SC and requires the completion of the composition of a divine book in Greek. The SC agrees and admits that a written record is much more worthy as an expression of gratitude than sacrifices:

for every gift of a votive offering or sacrifice lasts only for the immediate moment, and presently perishes, while a written record is an undying meed of gratitude, from time to time renewing its youth in the memory (πᾶσα γὰρ ἀνα-θήματος ἢ θυσίας δωρεὰ τὸν παραυτίκα μόνον ἀκμάζει καιρόν, ἔφθαρται δὲ τὸν μέλλοντα, γραφὴ δὲ ἀθάνατος χάρις κατὰ καιρὸν ἀνηβάσκουσα τὴν μνήμην).

In both the stele and the papyrus describing the deeds of Asclepios, affirming the BNP's *preparedness* (*pouvoir-faire*), the sanction is *manifest*. A *written and public* sanction seems to be a feature of the Asclepios cult. The Apellas-stele and the Oxyrh. papyrus 1381 date from the second century C. E.; an inscription on a stone dating from the end of the third century B. C. E. (Insc. Graecae IV² 1:125) attests the same. Here, the SC inscribed, upon an order from the god, his praise of Asclepios on the stone he carried during the main performance:[238]

as an example *of your power*, Asclepios, I have put up this rock which I had lifted up, manifest for all to see, *an evidence for your art* (σῆς ἀρετῆς [παράδειγμ]', Ἀσκληπιέ, τόνδε ἀνέθηκα πέτρον ἀειράμενος, πᾶσι[ν ὁρᾶν] φανερόν, ὄψιν σῆς τέχνης ...).

In this case, clear reference to the competence of Asclepios is made: σῆς ἀρετῆς and ὄψιν σῆς τέχνης. The oldest evidence for written and public sanctions, however, are the inscriptions from Epidauros. A1 in-cludes the quotation of a verse a healed SC inscribed on her offering praising Asclepios:

admirable is not the greatness of the tablet, but *the divinity* . .., and he made her sound (οὐ μέγεθος πίνακος θαυμαστέον, ἀλλὰ τὸ θεῖον [the description of the initial lack and the preparation of the god follows], καί μιν ἔθηκε ὑγιῆ).[239]

The purpose of these inscriptions is to make known the power of Asclepios so that everyone might praise the god (cf. Oxyrh. 1381, col. IX 197–202).

The motif of a *written* documentation of Yahweh's miraculous acti-vities and those of his messengers is manifest with regard to healings in Jewish literature in the *Book of Tobit*, which is a written account of miracle healings with the intention of glorifying God, thus sanctioning his preparedness. In 12:20, just before ascending to God, the angel Raphael instructs Tobit and Tobias to write everything that happened in a book (γράψατε πάντα τὰ συντελεσθέντα εἰς βιβλίον).

Jesus, on the other hand, tries to *prevent* the SCs from spreading the news about their healing and restoration in an attempt to keep his iden-

---

[238] Cf. above.

[239] For a discussion of this verse and its relation to the story presented in A1, cf. Dibelius, *Formgeschichte*, 166, and Herzog, *Wunderheilungen*, 71–72.

tity secret. In Mk 1:43-44 he emphatically warns the healed leper not to tell anybody anything, but to go and present himself, in accordance with the purity laws,[240] to the priest and sacrifice:

after sternly warning him he sent him away at once, saying to him, "See that you say nothing to anyone .. ." (καὶ ἐμβριμησάμενος αὐτῷ εὐθὺς ἐξέβαλεν αὐτόν, καὶ λέγει αὐτῷ, "Ορα μηδενὶ μηδὲν εἴπῃς ...).[241]

The same is intended when Jesus sends the healed SC home.

- And he sent him to his house, saying, "Do not go into the village." (καὶ ἀπέστειλεν αὐτὸν εἰς οἶκον αὐτοῦ λέγων, Μηδὲ εἰς τὴν κώμην εἰσέλθῃς; Mk 8:26),
- Go to your house to your family, and tell them how much the Lord has done for you, and what mercy he has done for you ("Υπαγε εἰς τὸν οἶκόν σου πρὸς τοὺς σούς, καὶ ἀπάγγειλον αὐτοῖς ὅσα ὁ κύριός σοι πεποίηκεν καὶ ἠλέησέν σε; Mk 5:19/Lk 8:39).

This limits the spreading of information to the family of the SC. However, Jesus' attempts fail. The more he commands SCs not to let anyone know what happened, the more do they proclaim what Jesus had done to them.[242] The healing performances point back to the pre-paredness of Jesus, indicating his extraordinary healing abilities. Jesus is unable to keep the news about his preparedness from spreading:

At once *his fame* began to spread throughout the surrounding region of Galilee (καὶ ἐξῆλθεν ἡ ἀκοὴ αὐτοῦ εὐθὺς πανταχοῦ εἰς ὅλην τὴν περίχωρον τῆς Γαλιλαίας; Mk 1:28).[243]

3.4.2.2. Assessment of the subject effecting the healing

The miraculous event usually raises the question of the *identity* of the subject which effected, in one way or another, the healing. This applies especially in the case of miracles attributed to Jesus. The instant reaction of bystanders indicates that they are usually aware of a numinous realm present in the BNP, PNP or MNP. This is brought to expression by means of actions implying

- θαυμάζειν (Tobit 11:16; cf. Philostratus, Vita Apol. 4:20: the people clapped their hands ὑπὸ θαύματος; Mk 5:20; Mt 9:33/Lk 11:14),
- θαμβεῖσθαι (Mk 1:27; Lk 4:36; Acts 3:10),

---

[240] Cf. Lev 13-14.
[241] Cf. Lk 5:14/Mt 8:4; Mk 5:43/Lk 8:56: καὶ διεστείλατο αὐτοῖς πολλὰ ἵνα μηδεὶς γνοῖ τοῦτο; Mk 7:36: καὶ διεστείλατο αὐτοῖς ἵνα μηδενὶ λέγωσιν.
[242] ὅσον δὲ αὐτοῖς διεστέλλετο, αὐτοὶ μᾶλλον περισσότερον ἐκήρυσσον; Mk 7:36; cf. Mk 5:20/Lk 8:39; Mk 1:45/Lk 5:15.
[243] Cf. Lk 4:14, 37; 7:17; Mt 4:24; Mk 5:14 parr; Mt 13:26.

– ἐξιστάναι (Mk 2:12/Lk 5:26; Mk 5:42b/Lk 8:56; Mt 12:23; Acts 3:10),
– φοβεῖσθαι (Mt 9:8; Mk 5:16/Lk 8:35; Lk 7:16), or
– ἐκπλήσσεσθαι (Mk 7:37; Lk 9:43).

These emotional reactions are neutral in the sense that they alone do not indicate a positive or negative assessment of the BNP or the PNP and their performances. Φοβεῖσθαι, e. g., can effect a positive (Lk 7:16: ἔλαβεν δὲ φόβος πάντας, καὶ ἐδόξαζον τὸν θεὸν λέγοντες …) as well as a negative (Mk 5:15-17: after witnessing the LL, the people ἐφοβήθησαν … καὶ ἤρξαντο παρακαλεῖν αὐτὸν ἀπελθεῖν ἀπὸ τῶν ὁρίων αὐτῶν) reaction towards the BNP.

Miracles in the Jewish tradition usually provoke and settle the question of the competence and identity of a BNP or PNP. In 1/3 Kings 17:24, the mother of the resuscitated child recognizes that Elijah is a "man of God" (איש אלהים/ἄνθρωπος τοῦ θεοῦ) who truly speaks the word of Yahweh (ודבר־יהוה בפיך אמת/καὶ ῥῆμα κυρίου ἐν στόματί σου ἀληθινόν; cf. Jos., Ant. VIII 327: the woman clearly realized ὅτι τὸ θεῖον αὐτῷ διαλέγεται). Whereas in 1/3 Kings 17:24 the competence of the PNP is sanctioned, 2/4 Kings 5:15a states that the Syrian Naaman acknowledges Israel's monotheism: ידעתי כי אין אלהים בכל־הארץ כי אם־בישראל/ἰδοὺ δὴ ἔγνωκα ὅτι οὐκ ἔστιν θεὸς ἐν πάσῃ τῇ γῇ ὅτι ἀλλ' ἢ ἐν τῷ Ισραηλ. In 'Aboda Zara 10b, the king realizes that even the most inferior among the rabbis is able to raise the dead.

The pagan people of Lystra (Acts 14:11-18) take it for granted that Barnabas and Paul are incorporations of Zeus and Hermes. Compared with these examples, it is peculiar that Jesus' identity remains *controversial* in spite of his miraculous healings, or more accurately, that the miraculous performances of Jesus *provoke* a controversy concerning his identity among those present, which of course does not apply from the point of view of the gospels themselves. After the first miracle of Jesus narrated in Mark and Luke, *The Healing of a Man with an Unclean Spirit* (Mk 1:23-27/Lk 4:33-35), the people wonder, Τί ἐστιν τοῦτο; (Luke has: Τίς ὁ λόγος οὗτος, ὅτι ἐν ἐξουσίᾳ καὶ δυνάμει ἐπιτάσσει τοῖς ἀκαθάρτοις πνεύμασιν, καὶ ἐξέρχονται;). In contrast, the *demon* who provoked the exorcism by revealing the identity of Jesus, *knows* who Jesus is: οἶδά σε τίς εἶ, ὁ ἅγιος τοῦ θεοῦ (Mk 1:24; cf. 5:7 parr). The demon sanctions Jesus' preparedness. Jesus contributes to the confusion of the people when he *shuts up* the demon (Mk 1:25: φιμώθητι …).[244] The

---

[244] This attempt of Jesus to hide his identity corresponds with his commands at the healed SCs *not* to talk about the performance of Jesus. In this context, it seems clear that the silencing-command corresponds well to Mark's Messianic secret theory (cf. 1:34; 3:12), cf. B. Kollmann, "Jesu Schweigegebote an die Dämonen," in *ZNW* 82 (1991), 267-73. It is difficult to decide if the command "to shut up" addressing a demon is generally a

people are not sure about what is happening. This is new for them: οὕτως οὐδέποτε εἴδομεν (Mk 2:12/Lk 5:26).

For a lengthy discussion of the identity of Jesus which is provoked by a miracle healing, cf. Joh 9:8–34. Jesus is branded a "sinner" (ἁμαρτωλός; v. 24), one who is not "from God" (παρὰ θεοῦ; v. 16). In Q (Lk 11:14–23/Mt 12:22–37; cf. Mt 9:32–34 and Mk 3:22–30) an exorcism leads to the assessment that Jesus exorcizes ἐν Βεελ Ζεβουλ. These charges against him (ungodly sinner, agent of the leader of demons) are contradicted by those who, under the influence of his miraculous ability, revere him as a prophet (Joh 9:17; cf. Lk 7:16: προφήτης μέγας ἠγέρθη ἐν ἡμῖν). This contrary assessment of Jesus as either an agent of God (from the perspective of the Gospel of John a correct and positive sanction) or the anti-God (from the persective of the Gospel of John a mistaken and negative sanction) entails and determines the quality of additional actions sanctioning Jesus.

3.4.2.3. Rewarding the subject effecting the healing

Distinct types of allomotifs describe the rewarding of a BNP or MNP for its restoration performance. These sanctions imply a recognition of the BNP's or MNP's extraordinary preparedness.

3.4.2.3.1. Presents, offerings, and sacrifices.

In the pagan environment, presents, offerings, or sacrifices are a common means to express one's satisfaction with the outcome of a performance effecting healing. In fact, these signs of gratitude are often *expected* and failure to offer them to a god might result in punishment. Cf. Epidauros B22: a man healed from blindness did not bring the required thank-offerings with the result that the god made him blind again (μετὰ δὲ τοῦτο τὰ ἴατρα οὐκ ἀπάγοντα ὁ θεός νιν ἐπόησε τυφλὸς αὖθις; cf. A7). Refusal to express one's gratitude for healing is, however, the exception.

At Epidauros, thank-offerings do not have to be of great value. A man dedicates to the temple the band with the sign which had formerly been on his forehead (A6), while a little boy promises to give "ten dice" if he gets cured (A10). A woman gives an offering with an inscription praising Asclepios (A1). In Insc. Graecae XIV 966b.c.d., the offer is not specified: δημοσίᾳ ηὐχαρίστησεν τῷ θεῷ. In later times, the expected sign

---

traditional motif of exorcism stories (Bultmann, *Geschichte*, 239) or not (Kollmann, ibid.). Bultmann, among others, refers, for the assessment of the silencing-command as a traditional motif, to magical papyri of the third century C.E. Kollmann, on the other hand, concludes that the silencing-command is not a traditional exorcism motif in exorcism stories, drawing on material from the second and third centuries C.E. which do not mention any such command (Lucian, Philops 16; Philostratus, Vita Apol. IV 20, et al.). The difficulty in deciding whether the silencing-command is a traditional topos in ancient exorcism stories or not is due to the obscure πεφίμωσο in Mk 4:39.

of gratitude can be of much higher value. Pausanias, Desc. Graecae X 38:13, mentions that a man had to give 2000 staters of gold. Around the same time, Oxyrh. 1381 describes that the god Asclepios received χάριτας in form of θυσίων (cf. Acts 14:13: the priest of Zeus is about to sacrifice [θύειν] to the apparent gods Paul and Barnabas). Apollonios, after effecting the resuscitation of the bride, is to receive 150,000 sesterces (Philostratus, Vita Apol. IV 45), but he refuses to take the money for himself and decides to give it to the revived bride.

This motif of a refusal of presents also occurs in the Jewish tradition: a man of God refuses to accept the present offered to him by the healed king, due to orders from Yahweh (1 Kings 13:7-9). Similarly Elisha does not accept the ברכה/εὐλογίαν from Naaman (2/4 Kings 5:15-16). The same reaction can be observed with respect to Raphael in Tobit 12:1-15: Tobias offers Raphael half of all his possessions as an expression of his gratitude for Raphael's help, but Raphael who has not yet revealed himself as angel instructs Tobit and Tobias to present their εὐλογία to God. This passage makes clear that angels as well as prophets are only *means* of God's work (cf. Tobit 12:20 where Raphael proclaims: ἀναβαίνω πρὸς τὸν ἀποστείλαντά με). Therefore, all reverence has to be shown to *God*.

Apollonios, a self-sufficient BNP, is motivated in his rejection of the offer (Philostratus, Vita Apol. IV 45) by a different reason: as a Neopythagorian he is not supposed to own any material goods.

With regard to the Jewish tradition, however, it is not *necessary* that presents always be rejected by the PNP. 1QapGen 20:29-32 narrates that the Egyptian king, after being healed, showers Abram and his family with various kinds of gifts. Another example is b.Me'il 17b which describes an exorcism that is calculated to ensure the offer of presents by the Roman emperor after his daughter is freed from the demon. As expected, the emperor offers to fulfill their every wish. This promise binds him to destroy the Roman decrees against Jewish religious practices.

It should be noted in this context that Jesus never receives presents as expressions of gratitude for his healing performances, nor does he require material goods (as Asclepios does; cf. Lucian, Philops. 16, describing how the exorcist has to be payed for his performance with μισθῷ μεγάλῳ). Jesus does not even ask the healed SCs to offer sacrifices or thank-offerings to God (as Raphael in Tobit does), but in one case he has the SC go to the temple to show himself to the priest and to give sacrifices εἰς μαρτύριον αὐτοῖς.[245]

---

[245] The function of these sacrifices is not to thank God but seems to be a concession to the Jewish tradition (Lev 13-14) in order not to arouse suspicion.

3.4.2.3.2. Gestures and oral and written expressions. The χαρὰ of the SC often takes on concrete forms of χάρις expressed orally and/or gesturally. A typical gesture expressing gratitude in antiquity is the proskynesis (προσκύνησις).

- after her child is resuscitated, the mother falls at the feet of Elisha and bows to the ground (ἡ γυνὴ ἔπεσεν ἐπὶ τοὺς πόδας αὐτοῦ· καὶ προσεκύνησεν ἐπὶ τὴν γῆν; 4 Kings [LXX] 4:37; the MT has ותשתחו ארצה ותפל על־רגליו),[246]
- Hezekiah is restored from his sickness and goes up to the temple and, worshipping God, gives offerings of thanks (ἄνεισιν εἰς τὸ ἱερὸν καὶ τῷ θεῷ προσκυνήσας εὐχὰς ἐποιήσατο; Jos., Ant. X 29 in his recast of 2 Kings 20:1–11),
- the healed SC prostates himself at Jesus' feet and thanks him (ἔπεσεν ἐπὶ πρόσωπον παρὰ τοὺς πόδας αὐτοῦ εὐχαριστῶν αὐτῷ; Lk 17:16),
- the blind SC, after being healed and after being revealed the identity of Jesus as the "Son of Man," expresses his faith in him καὶ προσεκύνησεν αὐτῷ (Joh 9:38),
- the mother of a SC does reverence to the manifestation of the god (τὴν μὲν τοῦ θεοῦ προσεκύνησεν ἐπιφάνειαν; Oxyrh. 1381:113–114).

These examples indicate that προσκύνησις as an expression of gratitude was widespread throughout the ancient Mediterranean world and was, in the context of miracle stories, shown to the BNP itself, and only occasionally to a PNP (2 Kings 4:37).[247]

The προσκύνησις can be accompanied by oral expressions of gratitude (cf. Jos. Ant. X 29: εὐχὰς ποιεῖν; Lk 17:16: εὐχαριστεῖν). Often, expressions of thanksgiving are oral: the mother of the resuscitated child εὐχαρίστει Elijah (Jos. Ant. VIII 327); in the Book of Tobit, the grateful subjects express their thanks by praise (εὐλογεῖν; 8:4–8: Tobit and his bride towards God; 8:15–17: Ragouel towards God; 11:14,16: Tobit towards God; 11:15 [א]: Tobias towards God).

With respect to the NT it is striking that the motif of *joyful thanksgiving* is a prevalent feature of Luke's miracle stories, while it is almost non-existent in Mark and Matthew, where it is replaced by the motifs of "fear" and "confusion."[248] The only exception is Mk 2:12 parr where

---

[246] Cf. v. 27, where the similar motif ותחזק ברגליו/καὶ ἐπελάβετο τῶν ποδῶν αὐτοῦ has another function, namely, to *activate* the PNP.

[247] It should be noted that προσκύνησις can have additional functions in miracle stories. Always, however, it indicates submissiveness. In Mk 5:6, προσκύνησις in connection with the demon's plea that Jesus might not torment it, has the function to resist the threatening expulsion of the demon. In Mk 5:33, the woman, after having directly and successfully activated the AS δύναμις which dwells in Jesus, being motivated by fear and trembling (φοβηθεῖσα καὶ τρέμουσα) προσέπεσεν αὐτῷ. The function of this action is probably to request forgiveness (against Trummer, *Die blutende Frau*, 98–99).

[248] For Mark, this could be due to his Messianic secret theory, cf. Theißen, *Wundergeschichten*, 172.

it is mentioned that, besides being amazed or filled with fear, everybody praised God for the unexpected deed (πάντας καὶ δοξάζειν τὸν θεὸν λέγοντας ὅτι Οὕτως οὐδέποτε εἴδομεν; cf. Mt 15:31). The tendency of Luke to emphasize the praise of *God* at the end of a miracle story can be observed here. While in the parallel accounts only the people praise God, Luke adds that also the SC was δοξάζων τὸν θεὸν on his way home (5:25). Similarly, in 18:43, Luke adds to his *Vorlage*, which only mentions that the healed SC became a follower of Jesus, that he was δοξάζων τὸν θεὸν while πᾶς ὁ λαὸς ἰδὼν ἔδωκεν αἶνον τῷ θεῷ. This tendency of Luke is especially manifest in the miracle stories in his Sondergut.

- the people, even though they are full of fear, glorified God saying, "A great prophet has risen among us" and "God has looked favorable on his people" (ἐδόξαζον τὸν θεὸν λέγοντες ὅτι Προφήτης μέγας ἠγέρθη ἐν ἡμῖν, καὶ ὅτι Ἐπεσκέψατο ὁ θεὸς τὸν λαὸν αὐτοῦ; 7:16),
- the healed woman immediately glorified God (ἐδόξαζεν τὸν θεόν; in 13:13), while the whole crowd rejoiced at all the wonderful things that he was doing (πᾶς ὁ ὄχλος ἔχαιρεν ἐπὶ πᾶσιν τοῖς ἐνδόξοις τοῖς γινομένοις ὑπ' αὐτοῦ; v. 17).

The thanksgiving to God after a miraculous healing is even the *theme* of the miracle story in 17:14-24, "The Healing of the Ten Lepers:"

only a Samaritan returns, glorifying God with a great voice (μετὰ φωνῆς μεγάλης δοξάζων τὸν θεόν; v. 15) so that Jesus wonders if this foreigner is the only one to praise God (οὐχ εὑρέθησαν ὑποστρέψαντες δοῦναι δόξαν τῷ θεῷ εἰ μὴ ὁ ἀλλογενὴς οὗτος; v. 18).

For further evidence, cf. Acts 3:8, where again both the SC *and* the bystanders praise God (αἰνεῖν τὸν θεόν), and the two eulogies in Lk 1:46-55 and 68-79, the latter of which functions at the same time as demonstration of the successful outcome of a hidden main performance which is attributed to God: καὶ ἐλάλει (Zachariah) εὐλογῶν τὸν θεόν (v. 64).[249] The motif of joyful thanksgiving never occurs in John in the context of restoration miracle narratives. For John, the miracles of Jesus pose the question of a *decision of faith* or rejection of Jesus as sanction of his preparedness.

The eulogies can be more detailed and might turn into whole psalms praising the power and help of the transcendent BNP. While Josephus in Ant. X, 29 only mentions that Hezekiah εὐχὰς ἐποίησε, Isa 38:9-20, in an addition to the story, presents a prayer of thanksgiving to the king (מכתב is translated in the LXX with προσευχή): οὐ παύσομαι εὐλογῶν σε

---

[249] Theißen, ibid., 167, aptly calls these expressions of thanksgiving to God "kultischen Dank."

μετὰ ψαλτηρίου (v. 20). A similar psalm of praise to God, in the context of a miracle story, is Tobit 13:2–18. This eulogy is said to have been a *written* composition: καὶ Τωβιτ ἔγραψεν προσευχὴν εἰς ἀγαλλίασιν (v. 1). Besides praising God, Tobit urges the Jews to turn to God. For additional material from the pagan world concerning written expressions of thanksgiving, especially stelai, cf. the Epidauros inscriptions, Insc. Graecae IV² 1:125 (the stone of Hermodicus), 126 (the Apellas inscription), as well as Oxyrhynchos papyrus 1381. These written expressions of thanksgiving have more than just the function to give thanks: they *witness* the greatness and power of the BNP and have, at the same time, a missionary intention, cf. Oxyrh. 1381:

And I hope to extend by my proclamation the fame of thy inventiveness … Every Greek tongue will tell thy story, and every Greek man will worship the son of Ptah, Imouthes.

For a Christian equivalent, cf. the SCs' oral proclamation (κηρύσσειν) of the healing performances and the preparedness of Jesus, a feature that almost exclusively occurs in Mark (Mk 1:45; 5:20/Lk 8:39; Mk 7:36) where this action always happens *against* the will of Jesus.

3.4.2.3.3. The establishment of a permanent contact with the BNP. The deepest expression of gratitude towards a BNP is a commitment of the SC or RSC which seeks a permanent contact with the BNP and might include an identification with the value-system it represents.[250] In the pagan Greco-Roman world, this commitment is often expressed by the SC's decision to build a temple or a statue for the respective god. This decision, however, can be prepared by the BNP itself or another numinous instance: in Epidauros B33, the people of Halieis wonder what to do with a sacred snake that traveled from Epidauros to their city in order to heal a citizen there. An oracle at Delphi decides that "they should leave the serpent there and put up a sanctuary of Asclepios, make an image of him, and set it up in the temple." Pausanias (Desc. Graecae X 38:13) describes how a restored SC, formerly blind, gave 2000 staters of gold (στατῆρας δισχιλίους χρυσοῦ) to the mediator sent by Asclepios, corresponding to what was written on the table he read. Pausanias seems to indicate that this money was used to build the sanctuary of Asclepios at Naupactus where the SC lived. While these two examples attribute the buildings of sanctuaries for Asclepios to the subjection of the will of the SCs (*devoir-faire*) who then agree to the proposal, there is evi-

---

[250] Cf. Groupe d' Entrevernes, *Signs and Parables. Semiotics and Gospel Texts.* (Pittsburgh, PA: Pickwick, 1978 [French orig.: 1972]), who describe the "entering into *active obedience*" as ratification and acceptance of Jesus' value-system.

dence also from a pagan environment that assumes the *will* of the SC (*vouloir-faire*) to commit itself to the BNP: in Plutarch, Pericles 8, Pericles sets up a "bronze statue of Athena Hygieia on the Acropolis near the altar of that goddess." The Bentresh-stele describes this desire to be close to the BNP in a different way: after having brought the statue of "Khonsu-the-Carrier-out-of-plans" from Egypt to Bekhten, and after the BNP expelled a demon, the prince of Bekhten refuses to return the statue: "Then he schemed with his heart, saying: 'I will cause this god to stay *here* in Bekhten. I will not let him go (back) to Egypt.'" After a period of almost four years, a dream-appearance subjects the will of the prince of Bekhten, and the statue is sent back. In this context cf. Jos., Ant. VI 169: Saul, after experiencing the healing power of David's songs, asks his father to leave David with him, "since both the sight of the boy and his presence gave him pleasure (ἥδεσθαι γὰρ αὐτῷ βλεπομένῳ καὶ παρόντι)."

If the BNP is a non-transcendent figure, the erection of sanctuaries and statues is replaced by other expressions the identification of the healed SC with the value-system of its healer. This is the case in Philostratus, Vita Apol. IV 20: the young man, after being freed from a demon, changes his lifestyle totally,

he fell in love with the austerity of philosophers, and donned their cloak, and stripping off his old self modelled his life in future upon that of "Apollonios" (ἐς ἔρωτα ἦλθεν αὐχμοῦ καὶ τρίβωνος καὶ ἐς τὰ τοῦ Ἀπολλωνίου ἤθη ἀπεδύσατο).

This motif, the identification with the value-system of the healing-effecting BNP,[251] is a common feature in John's healing stories. Here, the restoration miracle *effects faith* in the BNP, cf.

– and he himself *believed*, along with his whole household (καὶ ἐπίστευσεν αὐτὸς καὶ ἡ οἰκία αὐτοῦ ὅλη; 4:53b; cf. the parallel-accounts in Mt 8 and Lk 7, where this motif is missing, since the πίστις of the centurion is the motivation of Jesus to engage in a hidden main performance),
– the formerly blind man confesses: "I believe, Lord" (πιστεύω, κύριε; 9:38)
– many of the Jews, therefore, who had come with Mary and had seen what Jesus did, *believed* in him (πολλοὶ οὖν ἐκ τῶν Ἰουδαίων οἱ ἐλθόντες πρὸς τὴν Μαριὰμ καὶ θεασάμενοι ἃ ἐποίησεν, ἐπίστευσαν εἰς αὐτόν; 11:45)

The πίστις-motif also occurs in Acts stressing the *success* of the apostles' activities,[252] cf. 9:35 and 42:

---

[251] Cf. already Wendland, *Literaturformen*, 304–5, fn. 4: "Eine Konsequenz davon, daß nicht vor dem Wunder schon der Glaube geweckt wird, ist, daß das ... im Epilog nachgeholt wird."

. [252] Cf. ibid., 330. Wendland concludes: "Die Wunderauffassung steht etwa auf der Stufe des Joh."

- and all the residents of Lydda and Sharon saw him and turned to the Lord (καὶ εἶδαν αὐτὸν πάντες οἱ κατοικοῦντες Λύδδα καὶ τὸν Σαρῶνα, οἵτινες ἐπέστρεψαν ἐπὶ τὸν κύριον),
- this became known throughout Joppa, and many believed in the Lord (γνωστὸν δὲ ἐγένετο καθ' ὅλης τῆς Ἰόππης, καὶ ἐπίστευσαν πολλοὶ ἐπὶ τὸν κύριον).

In the Synoptics where the faith of the SC or its representatives is usually the motivation for Jesus' activation, the restoration to health can *effect* the identification of the SC with the value-system of Jesus; in Mk 5:18/Lk 8:38 the man from whom the demon went out asks Jesus "to be with him" (ἵνα μετ' αὐτοῦ /εἶναι σὺν αὐτῷ). Jesus rejects this request. In Mk 10:42 parr, blind Bartimaeus, who vividly expressed his faith in Jesus in the beginning of the miracle story, after being healed, *followed* Jesus on his way (ἠκολούθει αὐτῷ [τῷ Ἰησοῦ] ἐν τῇ ὁδῷ).

3.4.2.3.4. The rejection of the BNP. While in all other traditions under scrutiny the BNP is *positively* received and rewarded by the witnesses of a miraculous restoration, its rejection is a feature exclusive to the gospels.[253] Jesus is a *controversial* BNP. His rejection, negatively corresponding to *positive* sanctions like believing, following, or praising, can be expressed by different motifs:

- the Pharisees and Herodians decide to liquidate Jesus (Mk 3:6/Mt 12:14; cf. Joh 11:46–53),
- people flee away from Jesus and beg him to leave their area (Mk 5:14,17),
- he is accused of being an agent of Beelzebul (Mt 12:24/9:34/Mk 3:22/Lk 11:15),
- a leader of a synagogue accuses Jesus to have disregarded the Sabbath (Lk 13:14).

The controversy about Jesus is a characteristic feature especially of *John's* miracle narratives. Some Jews persecute Jesus because he healed on a Sabbath (5:16) and because he identifies himself as "Son of God" (5:18). They depict Jesus as sinner and not as a "Man of God" (9:16) and remain unbelievers (9:18–34). Finally, they decide to kill Jesus (11:46–53).[254] In Acts 16:16–24, Paul and Silas are thrown into prison

---

[253] The motif of the rejection of a BNP in spite of its clear signs has a parallel in the OT description of the ten plagues in Egypt. The attitude of the Egyptians is especially emphasized in Philo's account of the event, Mos. I 95: "But though they were compelled by the clear evidence of the facts (ὑπὸ τῆς τῶν γινομένων ἐμφανοῦς ἐναργείας) to admit the truth, they did not abate their audacity, but clung to their old inhumanity and impiety (ἀπανθρωπίας καὶ ἀσεβείας) as though it were the surest of blessings ... God had shown His will by the proofs of signs and wonders which are clearer than oracles (ἅτε δὴ τοῦ θεοῦ τρανοτέραις χρησμῶν ἀποδείξεσι ταῖς διὰ σημείων καὶ τεράτων τὸ βούλημα δεδηλωκότος).

[254] The widespread negative assessments of Jesus' competence and performances seem to reflect the controversy with which Jesus was perceived before *and* after his death.

after Paul expelled a spirit of divination from a maiden who brought her owners "a great deal of money by fortune-telling." Her owners are enraged about the expected loss of income and punish the two.

3.4.2.3.5. The effect of the sanction. The sanction of Jesus' preparedness can provoke different reactions and further NPs of Jesus. Since many people got to know about him against his will, Jesus, who had the intention to remain unknown (at least according to Mark), retreats to deserted places.[255] The people, however, follow him with their sick. In Joh 11:54, the decision to kill Jesus has the effect that he

no longer walked openly among the Jews (οὐκέτι παρρησίᾳ περιεπάτει ἐν τοῖς Ἰουδαίοις), but went from there to a town called Ephraim in the region near the desert (ἀπῆλθεν ἐκεῖθεν εἰς τὴν χώραν ἐγγὺς τῆς ἐρήμου, εἰς Ἐφραὶμ λεγομένην πόλιν) and he remained there with the disciples.

Here, it can be observed that Mk 1:45b and Joh 11:54 use the same motifs, "inability to remain secret" and "retreat to deserted places" to describe the situation of Jesus. This situation, however, is caused by different factors: in Mk 1:45 the people value Jesus positively, while in Joh 11:54 the reverse is the case. According to Mk 5:18 parr Jesus departs by ship. There are other examples where Jesus confronts his enemies and *defends* himself against their accusations. This is the case in the speeches of Jesus in Mk 3:23–30/Mt 12:25–37/Lk 11:16–23; Lk 13:15–16; Joh 5:17,19–47 and 9:39–41.

---

[255] μηκέτι αὐτὸν δύνασθαι φανερῶς εἰς πόλιν εἰσελθεῖν, ἀλλ' ἔξω ἐπ' ἐρήμοις τόποις ἦν (Mk 1:45/Lk 5:16).

V. Evaluation of the Morphological Analysis: Structure, Types, and Function of Miracle Stories; the Question of Acculturation

1. The structure of miracle narratives

A miracle healing story can be described in the following way: the circumstance of a subject marked by conjunction with sickness or – which amounts to the same – disjunction from health is reversed through a performance by an active subject who is prepared for the performance by numinous power. The phrase "numinous power" denotes an ability to heal *beyond* normal human competence. In ancient miracle stories, "numinous power" always indicates and presupposes involvement of the divine.

Investigation of structure in literature has shown that every narrative development describes at least one move from Lack (L) to Lack Liquidated (LL). The investigation of *miracle healing* stories focuses on narratives which share a common theme with respect to the initial lack (absence of *health*) as well as to the preparedness of an AS (who is prepared through *numinous power*). All narratives which do not involve these two features have not been considered here.[1]

The previous chapter has shown that one can distinguish a certain number of motifemes as structural components of miracle stories. The syntagmatic sequence of these motifemic slots transcends cultural borders because it depends on a universal *logic of narrativity* which is transcultural diachronically and synchronically.[2] What follows is a description of the structural components of healing miracle narratives.

---

[1] For this reason the account of how Asclepiades, the famous physician from the first century B.C.E., raised a man considered dead is excluded, cf. Pliny, Nat. Hist. 7:37; 26:8; Celsus, On Medicine 2:6; Apuleius, Florida 19. All three sources presuppose that the man being carried at the funeral procession was only *thought* to be dead, but was in reality still alive. Cf., e.g., Apuleius, Florida 19: et invenit in illo vitam latentam. confestim exclamavit vivere hominem. This "raising of an apparently dead man" is not ascribed to miracle powers but to Asclepiades' "remarkable powers of observation."

[2] Cf. H. Jason, "Genre in Folk Literature: Reflections on Some Questions and Problems," in Fabula 27 (1986), 167–94, who discusses the "level of universals" with respect to genres in folk literature: "The biological qualities and among them the nervous system

1.1. The initial lack (L)

The main NP of a healing miracle story requires and presupposes as obligatory element an *initial lack* (L) of health. This initial lack of the subject of circumstance (SC), the initial motifeme of the the main NP of a healing miracle story, can be stated, described, or otherwise established in various ways, that is, in the form of a wide range of allomotifs as discussed in IV. 3.1.1. and 3.1.2., above.

1.2. Preparedness of the AS

The next necessary motifeme concerns the preparedness of an active subject (AS) for the healing performance. Distinctive of miracle stories compared with other narratives is that this phase includes as part of the preparedness of the AS access to a numinous power, by a bearer of numinous power (BNP) on its own initiative, or invoked by the SC, its representative(s) RSC, or a subject specifically endowed with the preparedness to petition the BNP, a petitioner of numinous power (PNP). The BNP may not engage immediatly in a miracle NP, but do so through a mediator endowed with numinous power, a mediator of numinous power (MNP).

1.2.1. Activation of the BNP

The BNP is either itself the AS or the preparer of an AS different from itself. Since the BNP's *competence* is always assumed, only the question of its *activation* is at stake (ActBNP). Distinct types of iNPs can function as allomotifs filling this slot (IV. 3.2.1.2.), for example, if the BNP itself does not engage in an act of self-activation (IV. 3.2.1.2.1.), it needs to be transitively activated by other subjects (IV. 3.2.1.2.2.). The transitive activation of the BNP presupposes a certain preparedness on the part of the invoking subjects. The invoking subjects (either the SC, an RSC, or a PNP) need to be bestowed with motivation (*vouloir-* or *devoir-faire*) and the capability (*savoir-* and *pouvoir-faire*) to make appeals to the *vouloir-faire* of a BNP. This phase, the preparation of the BNP, can involve a *sequence of preparations* by these other mediating subjects. For example, in b.Ber 34b the SC (the sick child) does not have the preparation to invoke the BNP (God), and neither are its representatives, the

---

of humans being identical everywhere, some elements of culture created by humans may be similar in all human cultures, however diverse these cultures are and however different their way through history has been" (172).

This observation also accounts for Bultmann's reference to RGL material from all over the world up to the twentieth century in his collection of parallels to NT miracle stories, cf. *Geschichte*, 236–53.

father (rabbi Gamaliel)[3] and the two disciples sent out in order to appeal to the *vouloir-faire* of the PNP, Hanina ben Dosa. Only Hanina is bestowed with the specific ability to invoke God successfully by means of appeals to God's *vouloir-faire*.[4] It should be noted that the figure of a PNP is *often* employed in Jewish miracle narratives and also appears occasionally in pagan sources (cf., for example, Pherecydes, Frg. 3; Marinos, Vita Procli 29).

Another common way to realize the transitive activation of a BNP is by *repeated* actions of one and the same subject to invoke the BNP. This allomotif is employed in Apollodoros, Bibliotheca II 2. The RSC, Proitos, refuses to agree to the contract proposed by the BNP, Melampous. Thus, his appeal to the *vouloir-faire* of the BNP fails. Only after the lack becomes more severe is Proitos prepared (motivated) to pay the required price. For a NT example, see Mk 9:22b-24, in which the BNP, Jesus, sanctions the invocation of the RSC, the father, as an insufficient attempt to activate him: *"But* (δέ) Jesus said to him, 'If you are able! – all things are possible for the one who believes'"* (τὸ εἰ δύνῃ – πάντα δυνατὰ τῷ πιστεύοντι; v. 23). At the same time, the BNP, Jesus, encourages the imploring RSC to avail itself of the required competence (*savoir-faire*) for the activating process. *Faith* is what is required. Accordingly, the RSC repeats his attempt to invoke Jesus with a manifestation of his faith: "I believe. Help my unbelief!" (πιστεύω· βοήθει μου τῇ ἀπιστίᾳ; v. 24). As a consequence Jesus engages in the expected performance and exorcizes the demon.[5]

1.2.2. Preparing an AS other than the BNP

In cases where the BNP is *not* identical with the AS, additional motifs account for the *preparedness of the AS*. In such cases, the AS is ultimately prepared by the BNP. The allomotifs which fill this aspect of the preparedness are of distinguishable types.

The BNP might *directly* bestow the AS with preparedness necessary for the main performance. For example, in exorcism stories (IV. 3.3.3.),

---

[3] Cf. also b.Ber34 for the parallel account where the healing of the son of rabbi Yohanan ben Zakkai by Hanina ben Dosa is described. Here, Yohanan ben Zakkai, comparing himself with Hanina ben Dosa, sanctions his own incompetence with respect to the activation of God: "If ben Zakkai had squeezed his head between his knees all day, no notice would have been taken of him."

[4] For other examples, cf. Lk 7:1–10; Acts 9:36–43; Gen 20:1–17; 1QapGen 20:21–22; Num 12:1–16; 21:4–9; 2 Kings 4:18–37; y.Ber 9d; Marinos, Vita Procli 29; Bacchylides, Epinicia 11:95–109; Pherecydes, Frg. 3.

[5] For more examples of this type of realizing the phase preparedness of the BNP, cf. Mk 7:24–30 par; Mk 10:46–52 parr; Mt 8:5–13; Joh 4:46–53; 1QapGen 20:21a–28a; Epidauros A2.

the BNP *forces* the AS (the demon) to leave its dwelling place (devoir-faire). The exorcist (e.g., the BNP) has to use force to prepare the demon for its performance, because the equilibrium produced by the demon (LL in the NAP) directly corresponds to the disequilibrium of the SC (L in the miracle NP). It is the demon's intention to *maintain* its own state of equilibrium. The narrative trajectory of the exorcist is thus contrary to the narrative trajectory of the demon. In exorcism stories the polemical structure of narratives is *manifest*. A *confrontation* between the BNP and the demon as AS is predetermined. This conflict of interest is usually dissolved by the BNP's subjection of the AS's will (*devoir-faire*). The BNP's ability to subject the will of the AS is always stronger than the demon's ability to maintain its position. A specific feature of exorcism stories is thus the *domination* of the demon, which "caractérise la position du sujet d'un énoncé de faire lorsqu'il exerce son pouvoir-faire rendant ainsi impossible toute action contraire de l'anti-sujet."[6]

In miracle stories, the preparedness of an AS different from the BNP always requires a (mediated) involvement of a superhuman numinous power. It was shown that in cases where the equilibrium of an anti-subject directly causes the disequilibrium of a SC, as in the case of demonic possession, the BNP needs to subject the will of the anti-subject. This allomotif is regularly employed in exorcism stories. This feature can be expressed in numerous ways, for example, by means of commanding, rebuking, swearing, touching, staring, by the mere presence of a BNP, etc. (IV. 3.3.3.). However, *subjecting the will of the AS* is not limited to stories describing the expulsion of demons or other anti-subjects like sicknesses (Mk 1:29–31). The BNP can also *force* other subjects, such as the SC, RSC, or the PNP into a main performance (cf. IV. 3.3.4.). For example, in Plutarch, Life of Pericles 13:7–8, the goddess appears to a RSC and *commands* a cure (συνέταξε θεραπείαν) for the SC. In cases where the SC, RSC, or PNP function as ASs, the BNP usually bestows them with a numinous *savoir-faire* necessary for a successful main performance. An example is Diodoros of Sicily, Bibl. Hist. XVII 103:4–8, where Alexander (RSC) receives numinous knowledge about a healing plant which enables him to become the AS of the main performance bringing about health for Ptolemy.

Whereas the BNP in such cases *directly* prepares the AS by an appeal to its *devoir-faire* and/or by its bestowal with competence (*savoir-* and *pouvoir-faire*), there are other cases in which the BNP is only *indirectly* involved in the preparation of the AS. In such cases, the BNP activates *mediators* whose function it then becomes to prepare an AS. The exorcism

---

[6] Greimas, Courtés, *Sémiotique* 110; ET: 95.

and subsequent healing in Tobit can serve as an example. Raphael is sent by God with the mission to heal Tobias and Sarah (*devoir-faire*; 3:16–17). He bestows Tobias with a numinous *savoir-faire* concerning the means and method of the exorcism and the healing (6:8–9; 11:8). Tobias, bestowed with this magical knowledge, is able to subject the will of the demon (*devoir-faire*) and forces it to become the AS of the main performance: it leaves Sarah (8:2–3). This knowledge also enables him to prepare the healing of his father, who *has to* to rub his eyes (*devoir-faire*) with the result that the white spots on them disappear (11:12). The father thus becomes the AS of his own healing. This passage also demonstrates that the mediating process can be complex, involving a number of mediators.

A comparison of the motifs expressing *preparedness of the BNP* and those that express *preparedness of the AS* reveals a distinct difference between the two. The preparation of the BNP is limited to its motivation, since its competence is always presupposed. Its activation, if it does not activate itself, is usually further limited to appeals to its will (*vouloir-faire*). In all traditions under scrutiny, all that human beings in need can do is to invoke a BNP for help. The exception in Mk 5:25–34 proves the rule. Here, the SC (the bleeding woman) *is* already bestowed with a numinous *savoir-faire* enabling it to subject the will (*devoir-faire*) of a miracle-effecting power. The SC's competence is ascribed to its faith (5:34 parr). The extraordinary nature of this story is due to the implication that the woman, the social outcast,[7] is able to do what is normally reserved for Jesus, activation of his miracle power by subjecting that power to effect the healing (*devoir-faire*).

The preparation of an AS different from the BNP *never* involves the AS's volition. Rather, the AS has to be prepared with miraculous power. The BNP, directly or indirectly, bestows the AS with a numinous competence (*savoir-faire*) and/or subjects its will (*devoir-faire*).

1.3. The main performance (P)

Once the AS is sufficiently prepared, it engages in a *main performance* (P) bringing about the transition from L to LL. It was shown that the main performance is not reserved for the BNP, but that the SC, the RSC, the PNP, the anti-subject, or other subjects can function as AS as well (cf. IV. 3.3.2. to 3.3.4.). Numerous allomotifs are employed to describe this motifeme in healing miracle stories: touching, surgery, oral

---

[7] Cf. Trummer, *Die blutende Frau*, 95.

formulas, departure of a demon, application of ointments and herbs, etc. It should be noted that most of these motifs also occur as allomotifs of other motifemes, for example, the preparedness of the AS (cf. above). Thus it is important to identify carefully the functions of these actions from case to case, and not to presuppose that, for example, "taking somebody by the hand," would always indicate the healing performance of an AS. This motif, like others, can have *multiple* functions in the context of healing narratives. It can be utilized in the phase *preparedness of the AS*, "and taking the blind man by the hand, Jesus led him out of the town" (Mk 8:23); in the phase *main performance*, "and taking the child by the hand, Jesus said, Talitha koum" (Mk 5:41); or in the phase *sanction*, after the dead woman had already been resuscitated and opened her eyes, Peter, "giving her a hand, helped her up," and thus prepared for the sanction of others (Acts 9:41).

As in the case of other motifemes, also the main performance can be realized in various ways. The condition of the SC might require a *repetition* of the performance by the AS, as in the following examples.

- Elisha got up on the bed and lay upon the child, putting his mouth upon his mouth, his eyes upon his eyes, and his hands upon his hands; and while he lay bent over him, the flesh of the child became warm. He got down, walked once to and fro in the room, then got up *again* and lay bent over him ... (2 Kings 4:34-35a; cf. LXX which reads that Elisha lay down on the child *seven times*: καὶ συνέκαμψεν ἐπὶ τὸ παιδάριον ἕως ἑπτάκις),
- and when Jesus had put saliva on his eyes and laid his hands on him, he asked him, "Can you see anything?" And the man looked up and said, "I can see people, but they look like trees, walking." Then Jesus laid his hands on his eyes *again* ... (Mk 8:23-25).

Both examples have in common that the first performance is not a total failure, but only partly successful. The full success is gradually accomplished.

1.4. The sanction (S)

In the case of the sanction, it is possible to distinguish allomotifs which sanction the main performance from those which focus on the preparedness of the subjects representing the powers which brought about the liquidation of the initial lack.

1.4.1. Sanctioning the performance

The main performance can be sanctioned by *oral statements* of its outcome by either a narrative figure (cf., "See, your son is alive;" 1 Kings 17:23) or the narrator (cf., "his hand was restored," Mk 3:5). Often, however, is the main performance sanctioned by iNPs explicitly *demon-*

strating the LL. The bestowal with *competence* of the SC, necessary to demonstrate LL, is provided for by the main performance. The demonstration of the LL may be preceded by an iNP concerned with the *activation* of the sanctioning (demonstrating) subject, be it the SC, the anti-subject, the BNP, or any other subject. While often intransitive activation is only presupposed (cf., "and she began to serve them;" Mk 1:29) and thus not *manifest* in a narrative, transitive activation, usually in the form of commands (*devoir-faire*),[8] is a common feature of miracle healing stories, especially with respect to the SC or the anti-subject as demonstrating subjects, as the following examples show.

- I tell you, get up, take up your stretcher and go to your house (Mk 2:11),
- Eleazar placed a cup or footbasin full of water a little way off and commanded (προσέταττεν) the demon, as it went out of the man, to overturn it and to make known to the spectators that he had left the man (καὶ παρασχεῖν ἐπιγνῶναι τοῖς ὁρῶσιν ὅτι καταλέλοιπε τὸν ἄνθρωπον; Jos., Ant. VIII 48).

After being thus prepared (*pouvoir-* and *devoir-faire*), the demonstrating subject engages in an action which *proves* the success of the main performance. The *demonstration of the LL* is the direct antithesis to the initial demonstration of L and marks the establishment of an equilibrium for the SC. The ways of realizing this motifeme are unlimited (for examples, cf. IV. 3.4.1.) and, to a certain degree, but not absolutely, predetermined by the nature of the initial lack. A SC, for example, whose demonstrating performance consists in *seeing* would have had an initial conjunction with blindness. Not always, however, is it possible to conclude from the nature of the demonstrating performance of a SC the specifics of the initial lack:

- Peter's mother-in-law *serves* Jesus and his first disciples after being healed from *fever* (Mk 1:31),
- a man *wins a fist-fight* after being healed from a *headache* (Epidauros B21).

In the case of demonic possessions, it should be noted that the success of an exorcism could be demonstrated by performances of the anti-subject as well as the SC, as in the following:

and the *unclean spirits* came out and entered the swine; and the herd, numbering about two thousand, rushed down the steep bank into the sea, and were drowned in the sea ... ; they saw the *demoniac* sitting there, clothed and in his right mind ... (Mk 5:13,15; cf. Philostratus, Vita Apol. IV 20).

---

[8] In Mk 5:13, the BNP, Jesus, after having subjected the will of the demon(s) (v. 8) for the main performance, *allows* the anti-subject(s) functioning as AS(s) and as demonstrating subject(s) to enter the pigs. Cf. Philostratus, Vita Apol. IV 20, where the demon *chooses* the demonstrating sign of its expulsion.

Even though the healing miracle narrative reaches its equilibrium, with regard to the health of a SC as the result of the successful performance of the AS, an additional type of allomotif may be identified as filler of the motifeme sanction.

1.4.2. Sanctioning the preparedness

The subjects sanctioning the competence of subjects representing numinous abilities (the BNP, PNP, and MNP) need to be prepared to do so. The preparation of sanctioning subjects is only seldom manifest in miracle healing stories but nevertheless presupposed. This preparedness is realized by allomotifs reflecting a transfer of information about the successful performance and the forces behind it (cf. IV. 3.4.2.1.). The sanctioning subjects need to be *informed* about the LL, either through witnessing the main performance, or indirectly. At times, the sanctioning subjects SC and/or its representative(s) are prescribed a certain form of sanction (*devoir-faire*), as in the following:

- Rafael *orders* the SC (Tobit) and the RSC (Tobias) to praise God, which includes an ethical dimension (ἀγαθὸν ποιήσατε καὶ κακὸν οὐχ εὑρήσει ὑμᾶς; Tobit 12:6–7),
- Asclepios *orders* Apellas to inscribe what has happened to him (ἐκέλευσεν δὲ καὶ ἀναγράψαι ταῦτα; Insc. Graecae IV² 1:126).

In other instances the sanction of the preparedness of the BNP, MNP, and/or PNP can be expressed according to a contract agreed upon as part of the *preparedness of the BNP*. As has been shown above (IV. 3.4.3.2.), the *sanction of the preparedness* can be realized by various allomotifs, ranging from oral expressions of joy or fear to the offer of gifts, to admiration, following, or persecution. At times, the sanction of the preparedness, as the sanction of the performance, involves numerous and complex iNPs.

1.5. Conclusion

It is thus possible to distinguish four main *motifemes* (L, Prep, P, and S) as structural components of miracle stories. These motifemes correspond to the four phases of the Narrative Schema and are shared by narratives of various themes. *Restoration miracle* stories are distinct with respect to the features on the level of *motifs*: first, the initial lack is marked by the absence of health or life, and second, a BNP is involved in the narrative development at the phase of the preparedness and/or performance. Not all four motifemic slots need to be filled, that is, realized in a miracle story. So, for example, the motifeme concerned with the preparedness of the active subject is often presupposed, especially in the case of intransitive activation. In Lk 22:49–51 the creation of the initial lack in a NAP comprises verses 49–59a, whereas only the performance of the miracle NP is depicted in half a verse. By means of touching the ear, Jesus healed the servant of the high priest (καὶ ἀψάμενος τοῦ ὠτίου ἰάσατο αὐτόν; v. 51b). An extreme case is Mk 6:5a, a rudimentary miracle story consisting of a negative sanction of the preparedness of the BNP for the performance of miracles.

With respect to the *choice of motifemes* that are activated, the narrator is restricted to the structurally fixed sequence of these components. The narrator's freedom is limited to the choice of the motifemes to be actualized. With respect to the *choice of allomotifs* realizing the motifemic slots, the narrator's freedom is almost unlimited, restrained only by *cultural* factors. Even within those restraints the narrator still has a great freedom of expression, as the following analysis will show.

2. Examples of structural analysis

Before presenting two analyses, one pagan and one Jewish-Christian, the problem of *how to identify* narratives from different sources as versions of one and the same story needs to be addressed briefly. The synoptic gospels can help to answer this question. Even though Matthew and Luke at times alter their Markan *Vorlage* considerably by means of omissions, additions, replacement of motifs, and refinements of style, it is generally easy to identify parallel stories. This is made possible by, on the one hand, an identical or at least almost identical employment of motifemes, accounting for the same *structure*, and, on the other, to a certain number of identical or similar characters and types of allomotifs used as realizations of the underlying motifemes. The more features conform, the easier it is to identify parallel stories.

2.1. The healing of Proitos' daughters from madness

The tale about the healing of the mad daughters of Proitos was widespread in antiquity.[9] For our purpose it is sufficient to select three versions preserved in *Bacchylides*, Epinicia 11:40–112 [first half of fifth century B.C.E.],[10] *Pherecydes*, frg. 114 [first half of fifth century B.C.E.],[11] and *Apollodoros*, Bibliotheca II 2 [around the turn of eras].[12]

---

[9] Cf. the references in J.G. Frazer, *Apollodorus*, I 146, fn. 2.

[10] For a critical text-edition, German translation and explanation, cf. the recent work of H. Maehler, *Die Lieder des Bakchylides. Erster Teil. Die Siegeslieder; I. Edition des Textes mit Einleitung und Übersetzung; II. Kommentar* (Leiden: E.J. Brill, 1982).

[11] The Greek text is easily accessable in idem, *II. Kommentar*, 196–97.

[12] Text, translation and annotations in Frazer, *Apollodorus*.

All three versions agree on the nature of the initial lack, a kind of madness (μανία) which befalls the daughters of Proitos (Pherecydes determines the number of mad daughters to be two and knows their names: Lysippe and Iphianasse). The creation of the lack had been provoked by the daughters' religious shortcomings. They went into the temple of Hera and maintained that their father's riches exceeded by far those of Hera (Bacchylides 11:47–52), which Pherecydes interprets as sinning (ἁμαρτουσῶν εἰς "Ηραν). Apollodoros, however, is not sure, due to different sources, Hesiod and Acusilaus, if they did not accept the rite of Dionysos or if they disparaged the wooden image of Hera. Only Bacchylides mentions the actual performance which created the lack: Hera grew angry at them (preparedness of AS: χολωσαμένα; 53), caused their minds to be distracted (παλίντροπον ἔμβαλεν νόημα; 54)[13] and drove them away from their father's house (43–45). Hera is here the AS of the NAP bringing about the lack. In Pherecydes and Apollodoros the actual performance is not manifest. Only its result is described (Pherecydes: διὰ τοῦτο μανεισῶν; Apollodoros: γενόμεναι δὲ ἐμμανεῖς). In all three versions, however, a motifeme sequence interdiction-violation-consequence/creation of lack[14] seems to be presupposed. The resulting punishment sanctions the success of the NAP performance which is at the same time the lack for the new program presented in the following ways:

- The girls flee (φεῦγον; Bacchylides: 55,84,94) into wooded mountainous regions (55; cf. 93) and utter terrible cries (σμερδαλέαν φωνὰν ἱεῖσαι; 56). This condition lasts for exactly one year (τριακαιδέκα μὲν τελέους μῆνας; 92–93). Their father's hopelessness for a change of his daughters' condition is expressed by his failed attempt to commit suicide (85–95),
- The daughters' madness (μανεισῶν) lasts for ten years (δεκαετής) and causes pain to them and others [Pherecydes],
- The daughters roam over the whole Argive land (ἐπλανῶντο ἀνὰ τὴν Ἀργείαν ἅπασαν) and afterwards, passing through Arcadia and the Peleponesos, they run through the desert in the most indecently fashion (μετ' ἀκοσμίας ἁπάσης διὰ τῆς ἐρημίας ἐτρόχαζον). With time their condition worsens, they affect other women who abandon their homes and kill their own children and also flock into the desert [Apollodoros].

All three versions describe the resulting lack, but each in a distinct way. The differences in shaping and embellishing (*Ausgestaltung*) are even more obvious with regard to the *preparedness of the BNP* (PrepBNP). While Bacchylides and Pherecydes introduce a PNP (Artemis and Melampous, respectively) for the preparation of the BNP (appeals to the *vouloir-faire* of Hera), Apollodoros has the RSC Proitos

---

[13] For the interpretation and translation of verse 54, cf. Maehler, *II. Kommentar*, 224–26.
[14] Cf. Dundes, *Morphology*, 64–72.

directly prepare the BNP Melampous. All three accounts agree that the BNP is *identical* with the AS of the main performance, but not as the same character in the story.

- According to Bacchylides 11:95–109, the RSC Proitos prepares himself by washing in the river Lusos for the preparation of the PNP Artemis whom Proitos, by lifting his hands towards the sun, implores to save his daughters from their madness. He promises to sacrifice twenty selected oxen for her (*vouloir-faire*). The goddess yields to his prayer (εὐχομένου; acceptance of the request) and is thus activated for her preparation of the BNP and AS Hera. By persuading Hera, Artemis brings about the end of the daughters' condition (πιθοῦσα δ' "Ηραν παῦσεν καλυκοστεφάνους κούρας μανιᾶν ἀθεῶν). The main performance itself is not depicted, but it is implied that Hera, and not Artemis, functions as AS.
- In Phercydes' account, the divine PNP Artemis is replaced by the diviner and seer (μάντις) Melampous. He is activated to engage in the preparation of the AS by the RSC Proitos. Proitos, in this version, does not activate the PNP by invocation and promises of sacrifices, as in Bacchylides, but by agreeing to a contract proposed by the PNP: Melampous promises help only for a worthy reward (εἰ λάβοι κατάξιον τῆς θεραπείας τὸν μισθόν) and prepares the RSC for a corresponding action (bestowal of *savoir-faire*). Motivated by the seriousness and endurance of his daughters' condition, Proitos offers part of his kingdom to Melampous. In addition, the PNP is allowed to choose one of his daughters for marriage. Melampous, sufficiently prepared by this promise, effects the healing by calming down Hera with invocations and sacrifices (ἰάσατο τὴν νόσον ὁ Μελάμπους διά τε ἱκεσιῶν καὶ θυσιῶν τὴν "Ηραν ἐκμειλιξάμενος). It is implied that *Hera* is the AS of the main performance since Melampous' function is limited to preparing her for the performance (appeals to her *vouloir-faire*). It should be noted that the motifs "invocations" and "sacrifices" are here employed to describe the preparation of the BNP by the PNP, while in Bacchylides they function to activate the PNP Artemis by the RSC. Again, the main performance is not made explicit.
- Apollodoros' story conforms with Pherecydes in that a *contract* is made between Proitos and Melampous. However, this motif is now embellished. It is not the RSC Proitos who makes the offer to give part of his kingdom, but Melampous *requires* it. He offers his service on the condition that he might get the third part of the kingdom (εἰ λάβοι τὸ τρίτον μέρος τῆς δυναστείας). An additional motif, delaying the engagement of Melampous, is the RSC's refusal to accept this contract. Only after the condition of his daughters worsens, is the RSC prepared to agree to the terms brought forth by Melampous. However, Melampous, knowing that Proitos has no other choice, raises the price and adds to the contract that his brother Bias should get the same portion of land as he does.[15] The RSC has to accept these terms. A major

---

[15] Cf. Herodotos, *The Histories*, 9:34, who mentions this episode as an example for a situation where implorers in need of help are totally vulnerable to those who bring relief and have to accept any demands made by the helpers.

difference compared with the two older accounts is that in Appolodoros' narrative *Melampous* functions as BNP and AS of the main performance. The involvement of divine beings is excluded. Only here is the main performance described in detail: Melampous gathers some strong young men and, with their help, chases the women in a bevy from the mountains to Sicyon with shouts and a sort of frenzied dance (μετ' ἀλαλαγμοῦ καί τινος ἐνθέου χορείας). One woman dies in this process, but the others are purified and so recover their wits (ταῖς δὲ λοιπαῖς τυχούσαις καθαρμῶν σωφρονῆσαι συνέβη).

While Pherecydes' account breaks off with the depiction of how Melampous prepares Hera resulting in the SCs' healing, Bacchylides and Apollodoros explicitly mention a sanction following the main performance:

- Bacchylides 11:110–112 narrates how the healed SCs immediately erect a temple and an altar for the divine PNP *Artemis*, sacrifice there and institute choirs of women.[16]
- In Apollodoros the RSC Proitos gives his daughters in marriage to Melampous and his brother, which implies the demonstration that they are restored to health and, at the same time, sanctions Melampous' preparedness as successful AS.

The juxtaposition of these three narratives reveals how differently a single miracle story can be realized. Even where subjects are realized by identical characters, they are embellished in various ways that can, at times, vary greatly. Two additional conclusions can be drawn.

The narrator has the freedom to insert narrative material, like background information, at any point of the narrative. For example, Bacchylides inserts background information concerning the struggle between the twin brothers Proitos and Acrisios in the phase describing the lack of the SCs (between 51 and 81). While this information is lacking in Pherecydes' account, in Apollodoros it immediately *precedes* the miracle story. The other conclusion is that the same story can function differently in different contexts. In Bacchylides, the miracle story (11:40–112) moves from mentioning the altar of Artemis to an account of *why* this altar was erected. The miracle narrative functions here as an *etiological* story. Pherecydes narrates the story as an example of why a *most glorious reward* was given to Melampous. This intention is made explicitly by the introductory line:

Melampous, the son of Amythaonos, did many different miracles through divination; this was the most glorious reward given to him ... (οὐχ ἥκιστα δὲ αὐτῶι καὶ οὗτος ὁ ἐνδοξότατος ἆθλος ἐγένετο).

---

[16] This motif demonstrates, at the same time, the success of the main performance. The women are not mad anymore. After having experienced the help of the goddess, they worship her. Cf., as a motif with an identical function, Mk 5:18–20 par and Philostratus, Vita Apol. IV 20: a formerly possessed man becomes a follower of a BNP.

Apollodoros has his story as part of the *family history* of Inachos. In all three cases, the cultural background and the intentions of the narrators distinctly shape their accounts of the same basic story. They are free to *refocus* the narrative so that it fits a new context as well as the authors' intention.

An impressive example for narrative freedom is Apuleius' *Golden Ass*, two thirds of which consists of tales incorporated in the development of a main NP describing the restoration of Lucius from an ass to a human being. This is a miraculous restoration narrative which, in the widest sense, can be interpreted as a *healing* miracle story: like sick and dead people, Lucius is restored to *full human life*. Some of the tales are inserted in the NAP resulting in the creation of the initial lack, Lucius becoming an ass (I-III 24). The bulk of tales is inserted in III 25-X 35 and, in the widest sense, serves to *demonstrate* the predicament of Lucius. H. van Thiel[17] correctly states: "Ihre Zahl [of the tales] ließe sich beliebig verändern ... Formal lassen sich also die Abenteuer des Esels als *Erweiterung und Retardierung der Haupthandlung* ansehen."[18] The entire narrative exhibits a structure identical with the one identified in other, shorter miracle healing stories: XI 1 describes Lucius' preparedness to engage in a performance to activate the BNP. He feels hopeful that the goddess might help him and, before praying, purifies himself through a bath in the sea (cf. Bacchylides 11:96-97). In XI 2, he prays for help (appeal to *vouloir-faire*). The goddess Isis appears in a dream and agrees to a counter-action. She bestows the SC with knowledge how to find roses serving as his remedy (XI 3-6). Lucius is thus prepared with the necessary *savoir-faire* to become the AS of the main performance which takes place in XI 7-13 (chapter 13 describes the LL). The crowd witnessing the metamorphosis and, being amazed, immediately "pays homage to this clear manifestation of the power of the mighty deity ..." In so doing, Isis' preparedness is sanctioned (XI 13). The rest of the book (XI 14-30) describes further sanctions of Isis by the SC: Lucius becomes a follower of the Isis cult and is initiated into various other cults.

The next example demonstrating the narrators' freedom of choice with regard to the individual embellishments of a given story, this time from a Jewish-Christian milieu.

---

[17] *Der Eselsroman. I. Untersuchungen* (München: C. H. Beck'sche Verlagsbuchhandlung, 1971).

[18] 204; italics are mine.

2.2. A SC is healed at a distance

I propose taking the narratives in Mt 8:5-13; Lk 7:1-10; Joh 4:46-53; and b.Ber 34b (the healing of the son of rabbi Gamaliel)[19] as variations of one and the same story. Again, the purpose of the juxtaposition of these narratives is not to establish their *traditionsgeschichtliche* evolution. It is difficult, if not impossible, to find sound criteria for the illumination of such a *Traditionsgeschichte*. The synchronic approach, however, makes it evident *that* there are dependencies among these narratives, but it also shows that each version exhibits distinct features corresponding to its narrative and cultural contexts.

In comparing these narratives, one should keep in mind that all versions not only locate the event in Galilee but also ascribe it to "men of deeds" who lived before 70 C.E.[20] Furthermore, it should be noted that *Cana*, where Joh 4:46 locates the episode, lies in the neighborhood of *Arab* where Hanina ben Dosa is reported to have lived. In addition, Hanina's hometown is situated approximately only ten miles north of Jesus' hometown Nazareth. This local and the temporal closeness of the Christian and Jewish versions suggests a *common* origin. The same remarkable incident was attached to different local heroes, three Christian sources (Matthew, Luke, and John) attributed it to Jesus and two Jewish writings (the Babylonian and Palestinian Talmuds) to Hanina. Fiebig's judgment

> daß solche Erzählungen *völlig unabhängig voneinander* sind und nur deswegen einander so sehr ähneln, weil sie *derselben Zeit, demselben Ort und Milieu entstammen*,[21]

is unjustified: if similar narratives originate at the same time, location, and milieu, it would be inconceivable that they were "totally independent" from each other.[22]

---

[19] Cf. y.Ber. 9d which contains a shortened version of the one extant in b.Ber. 34b. This version is not further analyzed here.

[20] G. Vermes, *Jesus*, 72-73, and "Hanina ben Dosa," in idem, *Post-Biblical Jewish Studies* (Leiden: E.J. Brill, 1975), 178-14, especially 208-210, following a proposal by J. Neusner, assumes that this is rabbi Gamaliel *I* and makes a strong case in dating Hanina in the middle of the first century C.E.

[21] "Wunder," 170 (italics are mine).

[22] In *Jüdische Wundergeschichten* from 1911, Fiebig is more to the point when suggesting that Joh 4:46-53 and the Hanina story "nur insofern zusammenhängen, als sie demselben Milieu entstammen" (22). Cf. U. Wegner, *Der Hauptmann von Kafarnaum (Mt 7, 28a; 8, 5-10, 13 par Lk 7, 1-10). Ein Beitrag zur Q-Forschung*. WUNT 2. Reihe 14 (Tübingen: J.C.B. Mohr [Paul Siebeck], 1985), who admits, after having devaluated the parallels between the Q version and b.Ber. 34b, that "gewisse formale Gemeinsamkeiten ... höchstens darauf hindeuten (könnten), daß beide Geschichten möglicherweise aus einem ähnlichen Milieu entstanden sind" (356).

The SC is in each case *dependent* on an *authority* figure as RSC. Matthew and Luke have παῖς/δοῦλος of a centurion while John and b.Ber 34b clearly determine the SC as *son* (υἱός/בן) of, respectively, a βασιλικὸς and the famous rabbi Gamaliel (I or II). The initial condition of the SC is described in Matthew as a paralyzed man (παραλυτικός) in a bad condition, while Luke mentions that the SC was about to die. John and b.Ber 34b agree in stating that the son was sick (ἠσθένει/חלה).

With regard to the motifeme *preparedness of the BNP* each version exhibits different features. In Mt 8:5–12, the RSC gets in touch with Jesus, and invoking his help (παρακαλῶν αὐτόν) bestows Jesus with information about the lack. In so doing, the RSC establishes the lack. However, its παρακαλεῖν is unspecific. The RSC does not propose a NP to Jesus, as is the case of the other versions. It is unclear if Jesus is invoked as BNP or possibly as PNP (as in b.Ber 34b). Thus, Jesus' question (ἐγὼ ἐλθὼν θεραπεύσω αὐτόν) does not necessarily need to be interpreted as indignant refusal,[23] but might simply be a request for *clarification*: "[Do you want that] I, after *coming* [with you], *heal* him?"[24] Now the RSC specifies the request and explicitly proposes a NP to Jesus. The centurion does not want Jesus to *come* to his house, since he does not feel worthy of it. He rather expects Jesus to effect the healing "with a word" (μόνον εἰπὲ λόγῳ; unusual instrumental dative). The comparison which follows in verse 9 implies that Jesus also has ἐξουσία, but on another level than the military commander. This comparison is intended to *illustrate* the *power of the word* of someone with ἐξουσία. In the military realm this commanding word subjects the will of subordinates and forces them into a performance: "I say to this one, 'go!,' and he goes."

Whose will does Jesus subject? The will of a sickness-demon (cf. Lk 4:36 par), the will of God (like Honi the Circle-drawer in m.Taan 3:8), or is Jesus expected to command the SC to be healed? Neither the meaning of verse 8b nor the relation between verses 8b and 9 is clear. Thus the expected *function* of Jesus also remains *uncertain*. However, in verses 10–12 Jesus positively sanctions the preparedness of the RSC when he praises its faith and juxtaposes it with the faith in Israel, sanctioned negatively (cf. the included words of an eschatological judgment in vv. 11–12). Verse 13 demonstrates what verses 10–12 strongly suggest:

---

[23] This would be the other alternative, cf. Luz, *Matthäus*, I/2, 12, fn.1, who argues here from the perspective of Mt 15:21–28, where Jesus rejects the imploration of a *pagan* woman. In this case, the RSC's answer in vv. 8–9 would function like Mt 15:27 par: as a rhetorically skilled persuasion of the BNP in a performance.

[24] For a similar case, cf. Mt 20:32: τί θέλετε ποιήσω ὑμῖν;

the explication of the RSC's faith in verse 8-9 was sufficient to activate Jesus (appeal to his *vouloir-faire*).

Lk 7:2-9 utilizes different motifs with respect to the preparation of Jesus. The RSC's own preparedness is alluded to: the centurion "had heard the things concerning Jesus" (cf. Mk 7:25). Motivated by the distress of a servant to whom he felt especially close (ὅς ἦν αὐτῷ ἔντιμος) the Roman heathen sends Jewish elders as *mediators* to Jesus, hoping that they might be able to appeal to Jesus' *vouloir-faire* in order that he might engage in a NP effecting the healing of the SC. Their mission is to propose the NP to Jesus. The elders are supposed to ask Jesus to come and heal the servant (ἐρωτῶν αὐτὸν ὅπως ἐλθὼν διασώσῃ τὸν δοῦλον αὐτοῦ). Jesus is expected to function as BNP and AS of the main performance of healing. The corresponding iNP of the mediators consists of their contacting Jesus and imploring him for help (v. 4).

A distinct feature of Luke's version is that Jewish mediators try to activate the BNP by pointing out the preparedness of the RSC who is depicted as extraordinarily friendly towards Judaism. It might be implied that the RSC sends *Jewish elders* precisely for the purpose that they might testify to his worthiness. Jesus accompanies them to his house and thus demonstrates that he accepted the proposed NP (v. 6). However, even though the AS is sufficiently prepared to engage in the required main performance and is about to do so, the RSC changes its mind with respect to the proposed *method* of this performance. The readers are not told why. Parallel to verse 3, the RSC sends *mediators* (this time φίλους; v. 6) through whom a new appeal to the *vouloir-faire* of the BNP is made. The first delegation transferred information about the lack, invoked Jesus to engage in a main performance, proposed that he might do so *where the SC is located* (ὅπως ἐλθὼν διασώσῃ τὸν δοῦλον αὐτοῦ), and pointed out the preparedness of the RSC (who ἄξιός ἐστιν of Jesus' engagement) as a means of activating Jesus: the second delegation proposes a change of the healing-method (*savoir-faire*) due to the RSC's *humbleness* which is also given as the reason for the RSC's decision not to get directly in contact with Jesus:

> Lord, do not trouble yourself, for I am not worthy (ἱκανός) to have you come under my roof; therefore, I did not presume (οὐδὲ ἐμαυτὸν ἠξίωσα; literally: "I did not find myself worthy") to come to you. But effect the healing of my servant with a word (ἀλλὰ εἰπὲ λόγῳ, καὶ ἰαθήτω ὁ παῖς μου; literally: "Speak with a word; and my child be healed!").

The function of verses 6b-8 is not, as in Matthew, to engage Jesus in the healing performance since this has already been accomplished in verses 3-6a. For the sake of his humbleness, the RSC appeals to the *vouloir-faire* of the BNP to agree to a *method of healing* (*savoir-faire*) which avoids direct personal contact: the healing at a distance through a word. In verse 9, Jesus positively sanctions the preparedness of the RSC by pointing out the centurion's faith in contrasting it with the faith in Israel. It is implied that Jesus agrees to the RSC's proposal.

A comparison of the versions in Matthew and Luke shows that Mt 8:5–12 (the entire miracle narrative, except for the concluding v. 13!) focuses on only one motifeme, the transitive activation of Jesus which is effected by the preparedness of the invoking RSC, its *faith*. All the allomotifs serve the one purpose to activate Jesus. In Lk 7:3–9, the transitive activation of Jesus as BNP is accomplished by the first delegation (vv. 3–6a). The RSC's *faith* does not play a role in this first attempt but does so in the *second* iNP of the phase preparedness of the BNP which aims at the BNP's acceptance of a different method of healing.

In Joh 4:47–49, the RSC (τις βασιλικός) intentionally encounters Jesus and implores him to descend (from Cana to Capernaum) and heal his *son* who is about to die (ἵνα καταβῇ καὶ ἰάσηται αὐτοῦ τὸν υἱόν, ἤμελλεν γὰρ ἀποθνῄσκειν; v. 47). Through this request the lack is established and an appeal made to Jesus' *vouloir-faire* to act as the AS of the main performance. Jesus' answer in verse 48 is a general sanction of the people's preparedness with regard to faith:

Unless you see signs and wonders you will not believe (ἐὰν μὴ σημεῖα καὶ τέρατα ἴδητε, οὐ μὴ πιστεύσητε; v. 48, cf. Mk 9:19 parr).

This general sanction includes the RSC's preparedness. Different from the parallels in Matthew and Luke, the *faith* of the RSC in John plays no role in the preparation of the BNP. Jesus' answer in verse 48 seems to criticize the *method* implied in the proposed NP, namely, that Jesus has to *come* (καταβῇ) in order to heal.[25] As has been suggested above, this also seems to be the critical point in Mt 8:7, whereas it is missing from Luke's account in which Jesus willingly travels to the house of the SC in order to perform the healing. However, the invoking RSC does not get the message across, as indicated in its repeated attempt to activate Jesus to *come*, this time stressing the seriousness of the SC's condition (Κύριε, κατάβηθι πρὶν ἀποθανεῖν τὸ παιδίον μου; v. 49).

In the rabbinic text b.Ber 34b, the RSC rabbi Gamaliel sends two messengers (from Jerusalem) to rabbi Hanina ben Dosa's house (in Arab in Galilee) so that they might ask him to pray for mercy for the sick son (לבקש עליו רחמים). While this motif of a delegation proposing a NP is also found in Luke's version (7:3–6), the function of this motif in

---

[25] Cf. Mt 8:8–10 and Lk 7:7–9 where the proposed healing *at a distance* by means of a word is taken as an indicator for the RSC's *faith*.

b.Ber 34b is distinct: different from Luke, the reason for a *mediated* activation is not the humbleness of the RSC but is due to the *distance* between Jerusalem and Arab. Furthermore, its function is not to activate a BNP as AS but a *PNP* who is able to prepare the BNP *God* to bring about the healing. However, due to Hanina's numinous foreknowledge, the messengers do not need to express their request orally. As soon as he *sees* them (שׁראה אותם), Hanina is prepared to activate God. For this purpose, he mounts to an upper room and does what is expected of him: he asks (God) for mercy for the sick child.

The detailed analysis and comparison of the phase of the BNP's preparedness clearly shows the distinct embellishments of this motifeme. The freedom and creativity of the four redactors can be studied further with respect to the choice of motifemes following the preparedness of the BNP and their realization.

Only in *Matthew* is the motifeme *main performance* realized by Jesus as the AS. He decrees the healing by means of a word, corresponding to the proposed method in verse 8:

Go; let it be done for you according to your faith! (Ὕπαγε, ὡς ἐπίστευσας γενηθήτω σοι; v. 13).

The successful outcome of this performance, LL, is stated by means of a phrase commonly used in Matthew in similar contexts (cf. 9:22; 15:28; 17:18):

And the child was healed in that hour (καὶ ἰάθη ὁ παῖς [αὐτοῦ] ἐν τῇ ὥρᾳ ἐκείνῃ; v. 13).

Luke, without mentioning the main performance, only attests the LL when he describes how the previously ill slave was found in a healthy condition by the returning messangers (7:10).

In *John*, the attestation and sanction of the LL play a major role in the narrative, already indicated by the fact that these two moves occupy the second half of it. First, Jesus *sanctions* the outcome of a healing performance, which is subsequently made explicit in the text. Thus Jesus exhibits a *numinous knowledge* which transcends local distances. The RSC *trusts* and thus sanctions this *word* of Jesus (ἐπίστευσεν ὁ ἄνθρωπος τῷ λόγῳ ὃν εἶπεν αὐτῷ ὁ Ἰησοῦς καὶ ἐπορεύετο; v. 50) and returns home. The following verses 21–22 serve to demonstrate that the healing occurred exactly at the time that the conversation between Jesus and the RSC took place. In a statement sanctioning the healing performance, the fever is depicted as AS: "Yesterday at the seventh hour *the fever* (ὁ πυρετός) *left* him (ἀφῆκεν αὐτόν). The RSC, after recognizing the connection between Jesus' word and the healing, sanctions the preparedness of Jesus by *becoming a believer*, together with his entire household:

The father realized that this was the hour when Jesus said to him, "Your son lives." So he himself believed, along with his whole household (ἔγνω οὖν ὁ πατὴρ ὅτι [ἐν] ἐκείνῃ τῇ ὥρᾳ ἐν ᾗ εἶπεν αὐτῷ ὁ Ἰησοῦς, Ὁ υἱός σου ζῇ, καὶ ἐπίστευσεν αὐτὸς καὶ ἡ οἰκία αὐτοῦ ὅλη; v. 53).

The continuation of b.Ber 34b is close to the one in John. Again, however, it should be kept in mind that Hanina functions as a PNP, not a BNP. After invoking the BNP (God), Hanina, displaying a numinous knowledge, sanctions a main performance which took place at a distant location: "Go, for the fever has left him" (לכו שחלצתו חמה). This sanction closely resembles Joh 4:50, Jesus' mysterious sanction of the main performance. Again, the anti-subject *fever* is the AS of this performance. But different from the account in John, the addressees of the sanction doubt the word uttered by Hanina. Instead of leaving for Jerusalem they engage Hanina in a discussion about his preparedness with respect to his claim that the healing performance has taken place: "Are you a prophet?" (אמרו לו וכי נביא אתה). Hanina explains to them his extraordinary ability to make such a prediction with certainty:

I am not a prophet nor a son of a prophet; but I have learnt this, if my prayer (תפלתי) is fluent (שגורה) in my mouth I know that he (שהוא) is accepted (מקובל); if not, I know that he (שהוא) is rejected (מטורף).[26]

As a means of verifying his prediction the two delegates note the exact hour and return. Rabbi Gamaliel attests that the healing performance took place at exactly that time. It was then that the SC requested to drink (שאל לנו לשתות). This request *demonstrates* the LL. For the motif "comparison of time" as a means of attesting the preparedness of a

---

[26] A problem of translation is posed by the fact that it seems unclear to what שהוא refers. Fiebig ("Wunder Jesu," 169; *Jüdische Wundergeschichten*, 20) suggests that it refers back to Hanina. However, this would be unusual. In addition, the masculine participles מקובל and מטורף cannot refer to the acceptance and rejection of a *prayer*. The problem is that תפלה is feminine! Due to the *parallelism* of the two sentences introduced by שהוא which function as apodoces of the conditional clause, it is, also, not sound to take the first personal pronoun as reference to the *sick person* because the corresponding verb indicating acceptance fits his condition while the second personal pronoun is taken as substitute for his *disease* since this would fit better the corresponding verb מטורף indicating destruction or rejection (cf. the translation offered by Vermes, *Jesus*, 75). The context as well as grammatical considerations make it clear that שהוא refers to the male SC. With regard to the "fluency" of the prayer in the mouth of Hanina, cf. the suggestion of Vermes, "Hanina ben Dosa," 179: "since in similar literary units the verb *hishgir* means 'to improvise', [reference to y.Ber 9c] the fluent (*shegurah*) supplication in question must refer to a free composition. Expressed differently, Hanina humbly asserts that if the words of his prayer are not his own, but are placed in his mouth by God, they are efficacious. If, on the other hand, inspiration is lacking and no healing words emerge, there is no cure for none is intended by heaven."

person predicting an event in a distant location, cf. especially Joh 4:52–53 and Mt 8:13.

The comparison and structural analysis of these four variants suggests that they are versions of one and the same story. It has become clear that Matthew and Luke represent variations of the Q-tradition, whereas John and the Babylonian Talmud have many features in common. The source Q, consisting basically of Palestinian material, locates the episode in Capernaum of Galilee at the northern end of the lake Genezareth. The tradition represented by John and the Babylonian Talmud suggest that the area of Cana and Arab might have been the location where this story originally circulated. In any case, this narrative is clearly of *Palestinian* origin.

Each version represents a distinct variation of a common theme. A SC dependent on an authority figure functioning as RSC is healed at a distance. The fact that certain data and allomotifs vary from author to author, especially between the Christian and the Jewish tradition, is for the most part self-explanatory: the hero of the Christian versions is Jesus while rabbi Hanina ben Dosa is the main actor in the rabbinic source.[27] The authority functioning as RSC in Q is a pagan centurion (probably due to the beginning of Christian missionary activity among pagans), while in the Jewish tradition it is a rabbi, Gamaliel. The localization in the Q tradition is Capernaum. Much of Jesus' activity is localized there. The rabbinic tradition presupposes Arab as localization since Hanina ben Dosa settled here. Jesus is taken as BNP while Hanina is the PNP whose function it is to implore God, the BNP.[28] This difference is determined by the two religions under consideration, Christianity and Judaism. A comparison of Christian and Jewish miracle stories clearly demonstrates that in Judaism throughout its history the concept of God

---

[27] It is interesting that this rabbi from Galilee, Hanina ben Dosa, who lived around 50 C.E. in a place about ten miles north of Nazareth, is also well-known for his emphasis on good deeds in connection with a "positive embrace of poverty inspired by absolute reliance on God" (Vermes, *Jesus*, 77); cf. Vermes, "Hanina ben Dosa," 195–98, and H. Kremers, "Die Ethik der galiläischen Chassidim und die Ethik Jesu," in K. Ebert (ed.), *Alltagswelt und Ethik* (Wuppertal: Peter Hammer Verlag, 1988), 143–56.

[28] Against Fiebig, "Die Wunder Jesu," who, in a comparison of these four narratives, concludes: "Jesu Wunder sind genauso 'Gebetserhörungen' wie die Wunder der Rabbinen" (174). Even though Jesus is not depicted as AS in the accounts of Luke and John, according to Matthew he decrees healing by means of his word without any reference to another BNP. The phase of preparedness of Jesus clearly points into the same direction: the people *expect* Jesus to *heal* the SC, be it at a distance by means of his word (Mt 8:8; Lk 7:7) or by some physical contact (Lk 7:3; Joh 4:47, 49). Hanina ben Dosa, however, is expected to act as PNP: rabbi Gamaliel "sent out two disciples to rabbi Hanina ben Dosa that he may ask for mercy for him."

(almost) totally excludes *human* BNPs: *God* is the one and only BNP.[29] Notwithstanding this difference, further attention to these few verses of a distant healing story will reveal a certain closeness of the Johannine and rabbinic versions compared with the Q versions.

3. The question of classification and function of restoration miracle stories

3.1. The problematic

It will be shown in this section that the function of a miracle story can usually be identified by noting on which motifeme a story is *focused*. The story about the healing of a SC dependent on an authority figure as RSC analyzed above in its various versions (2.2.) is often classified as "a healing at a distance."[30] However, from a broad RGL perspective, this classification has no relation to the *functional* significance of the different versions of the story. Pesch and Kratz[31] claim that the theme and structure of NT miracle stories describing a healing at a distance allows for the establishment of a distinct *genre* (*Gattung*) which has its "Sitz im Leben" in the missionary activity of the early Christian church among pagans. Even from a NT perspective, this delimitation is problematic. How far away from the SC does a BNP have to be in order for the condition of a "healing at a distance" to be fulfilled? Cf. Lk 7:6 where Jesus is οὐ μαϰράν away from the house while in Joh 4:46–53 the SC is located in Capernaum and the sanction of Jesus with regard to the SC's recovery is given in Cana. One would also have to ask why Lk 17:11–19 (the SCs stand πόρρωθεν with respect to Jesus) is not counted as a "*Fernheilungswunder.*" Futhermore, what is the difference when, for example, in Mk 5:1–20 (and most other exorcism stories) Jesus commands the anti-subject to depart, without any physical contact? Finally, are healings directly effected by a transcendent god also to be considered as "miracles at a distance?" This makes it clear that classification based on the *method of the main performance* or the *method of the BNP/AS* are not helpful means.

A recent example of a problematic classification of miracle stories is

---

[29] Dibelius, *Formgeschichte*, 146, is basically correct when he states: "Diese Wunderrabbinen sind nicht große Könner, sondern große Beter." However, it should be emphasized that the extraordinary pouvoir-faire of these rabbis consists of their ability to activate God. In *this sense*, they are "große Könner," too.

[30] Cf. Pesch, Kratz, *So liest man synoptisch*, III/II, 70–83.

[31] Ibid., 70–83.

J. L. Bailey and L. D. Vander Broek, *Literary Forms in the New Testament. A Handbook* (1992).[32] The authors, who reflect especially Bultmann's, Theißen's, and Wire's research concerning the matter, distinguish between *exorcism, controversy story containing a miracle, story of healing as a response, provision story, rescue story,* and *epiphany.* A closer look at the definitions of these six "subforms" of miracle stories reveals that this classification is useless. This is due to the fact that not every story is classified according to the same criterion. For example, the subtypes "exorcism," "provision," and "rescue story" are differentiated according to *theme,* established by the *nature of the need.* The category "A Controversy Story Containing a Miracle," however, is delineated by purely *structural or formal* observations, while "A Story of Healing as Response to a Petitioner" seems to involve a judgment on the *focus* of the story.

In addition, non-NT material is not considered at all. In exorcism stories, according to this classification, for example, the "struggle is central."[33] This, however, can neither be verified for Lk 13:10–17 or Mt 12:22–37 par nor for 1QapGen 20–29 or Tobit 8:1–3. Also the assertion that Mk 9:14–29 *"focus(es)* on this overthrow of demonic power,"[34] needs to be questioned. The focus seems to be rather on the preparedness of the subject activating the BNP, namely its *faith* (cf. vv. 18–19, 22–24, 28–29). Mk 9:14–29, however, would also fit the category *story of healing as a response to a petitioner,* where "a sick person or an intermediary approaches Jesus, directly or indirectly entreating him for help,"[35] since the RSC, the father, clearly requests help of Jesus (vv. 22, 24; cf. v. 17). Also Mk 2:1–12 would have to be listed here (cf. vv. 3–4), and it is, at the same time, a *controversy story containing a miracle.* Furthermore, the *rescue story* Mk 4:35–41 contains an exorcism (cf. v. 39). The *epiphany* Mk 6:45–52 is also a *rescue story,* while Mk 1:23–28, here listed as an *exorcism,* seems to focus on the "divine manifestation of Jesus" and also evokes strong reactions "in those who witnessed it," cf. verses 27–28.[36] The *provision story,* finally, is described as a "type of story [which] depicts Jesus' response to a situation of need."[37] This is certainly true also for the healing miracle stories. The provision of *food* is a variation on the level of motif. With respect to the observation that this type is characterized by an *intransitive* activation of Jesus, one at least has to take miracle stories with other themes, where this is also

---

[32] (Louisville, Kentucky: Westminster/John Knox Press).
[33] Ibid., 137.
[34] Ibid., 137 (italics are mine).
[35] Ibid., 138.
[36] Cf. ibid., 138.
[37] Ibid., 138.

the case, into consideration.[38] If, for example, the OT provision story in Ex 17:1-7, which presents a case of *transitive* activation (v. 2), is taken into account, it must be concluded that the NT "provision story" of a miraculous feeding in its various versions *accidentally* realizes the motifeme *preparation of the BNP* with the allomotif "intransitive activation."[39]

What has been explicated with respect to this classification is also applicable to Theißen's distinction of six *themes*. The critique of Kl. Berger is to the point:

> Die Einteilung der Wundergeschichten in Exorzismen, Therapien, Epiphanien, Rettugswunder, Geschenkwunder und Normwunder, wie sie etwa G. THEISSEN vornimmt, ist, speziell was die drei letztgenannten Kategorien betrifft, *modern und rein inhaltlich* gedacht.[40]

Also Bultmann's differentiation of miracle stories in "Heilungswunder" und "Naturwunder"[41] is artificial and reflects a modern rather than an ancient concept of "nature."[42] The allotment of the material among the two genres "Erzählungsstoff" and "Apophthegmata"[43] is *fundamentally* correct, even though some stories need to be regrouped (cf. below). Bultmann's as well as Dibelius' ("Paradigmen," "Novellen") classifications often distort the material (cf. the literary- and tradition-critical decisions) due to their preconceived opinions concerning the *development* of early Christianity.[44] However, these two eminent scholars introduced a classification which basically *transcends* themes and pays attention to the *form* and *function* of miracle stories. Their analyses of the *form* of miracle stories are often arbitrary and led by intuition, since a clear structural criterion of classification was not at their disposal.[45] Bultmann's

---

[38] Cf. Mk 1:23-24; 3:1; 5:1-7 parr; Lk 7:11-12; 13:10-11; 14:1-2; 22:5; etc.

[39] Theißen also states: "Die Spontanität des wunderbaren Handelns zeigt sich darin, daß die Geschenkwunder *nie* durch Bitten provoziert werden, sondern durch einen Akt des Wundertäters. Formgeschichtlich gesprochen: Das Motiv 'Initiative des Wundertäters' hat in besonders ausgezeichneter Weise seinen Haftpunkt in Geschenkwundern" (*Wundererzählungen*, 111-12; italics are mine). Theißen refers to 1 Kings 17 and 2 Kings 4 since these texts sustain his argument. Ex 17:1-7 is, however, not taken into consideration.

[40] "Hellenistische Gattungen," 1214 (italics are mine).

[41] *Geschichte*, 223-33.

[42] For a critique of this position, cf. C. F. D. Moule, "Excursus 2. The Classification of Miracle Stories," in idem (ed.), *Miracles. Cambridge Studies in their Philosophy and History* (London: A. R. Mowbray & Co. LTD, 1965), 239-43, esp. 239-40.

[43] Cf. Theißen: *Normwunder*

[44] Cf. the history of research, above.

[45] This is true not only for scholars of the early FGS but applies to folklore studies in the first half of the twentieth century in general. Cf. the remarks by B. N. Colby ("On the Scientific Study of Folktales," in Fabula 30 [1989], 230-233): "In the century ahead folklorists are likely to look back upon the 20 th Century as a time of transition in which

and Dibelius' approaches were nurtured basically by a *sociological* interest, namely, to determine the "Sitz im Leben" of a certain form of tradition. Thus they focused on the *eternal functions* of traditions, that is, their functions in and for a Christian community as, for example, sermons, legendary material, etc.[46]

For the question of classification and function of healing miracle narratives I abandon the static *formal* and *external* functional approach and replace it with a *structural* and *inner-narrative* functional investigation. With the term "inner-narrative function" I refer to the narrative function a miracle story *bears in itself.* It is assumed that this inner-narrative function of a story is reflected by the choice of motifemes realized and the allomotifs and types of allomotifs chosen as fillers of the chosen motifemic slots. Since all miracle stories are based on one and the same *sequence* of motifemic slots and since distinct *morphic* subtypes could not be established, I will undertake a classification which takes the inner-narrative function of a story into account. The task will be to identify those motifemes on which miracle narratives *focus.* This identification of the *dramatic stress*[47] will help to determine the specific function of a given narrative.[48]

----

analyses of folk phenomena evolved from intuitive ideas to more empirically based findings with stricter standards of rhetoric and defensibility. The work of Vladimir J. Propp is a landmark in this direction, ..." (230). Cf. Perels' attempt at an analysis and description of the *structure* of synoptic miracle stories in *Wunderüberlieferungen.* His observations point into the right direction. However, also Perels' investigation falls short of useful conclusions. His approach is too formal and does not take the *function* of actions into account.

[46] G. Schille, *Die urchristliche Wundertradition. Ein Beitrag zur Frage nach dem irdischen Jesus.* Arbeiten zur Theologie I, 29 (Stuttgart: Calwer Verlag, 1967), identifies etiology and mission as the two main motivations for the origination and spreading of early Christian miracle traditions. Cf. also the assessment of this contribution in Theißen, *Wundergeschichten,* 90.

[47] For this term, cf. Bailey, Vander Broek, *Literary Form,* 139.

[48] A classification according to inner-narrative functions appears to be presupposed by Delling, "Zur Beurteilung des Wunders durch die Antike," in *Studien,* 53–71; cf. 55–56, where he points to the "Gruppe der Wunder ..., die in der Hauptsache ihren Sinn darin haben, die Macht und das außergewöhnliche Wesen des Täters zu erweisen" (55). He calls these miracle stories "Erweiswunder." It seems that Delling's category "Erweiswunder" (miracle to prove something) needs to be further differentiated with respect to the reference of the proof: the intention to prove the preparedness of the BNP, the PNP, the SC/RSC, etc. Cf. also Berger, "Gattungen," 1215–18, who proposes a classification of miracle stories *as* "Ätiologie," "Erscheinungsberichte," "Verherrlichung eines Ortes," "Prodigien," and "Anekdoten mit chrienhafter Struktur." Theißen, *Wundergeschichten,* 90–94, does not consider the possibility of a classification according to the inner-narrative function of miracle stories.

3.2. An example of a classification according to inner-narrative function

The story represented by the four versions in Mt 8:5-13; Lk 7:1-10; Joh 4:46-53; and b.Ber 34b analyzed above can serve as an example of how one story can have different inner-narrative functions in different versions due to a refocalizing process.

The version presented by Matthew clearly emphasizes the *preparedness of the RSC* in the phase of the preparation of the BNP. Almost the entire narrative (vv. 5-13a) concentrates on this aspect of the story. In verses 5-9 the attempt by the RSC to prepare the BNP is depicted, and in verses 10-13a the RSC's preparedness is positively sanctioned by the BNP. On the level of motifs, the *faith* of the invoking centurion is pointed out. More can be said with respect to the choice of allomotifs. The RSC needs to *repeat* its attempt to motivate the BNP (vv. 7-9). In addition, the RSC employs a *comparison* (v. 9) for its persuasion of Jesus, *paralleling* the RSC's authority with respect to the military and Jesus' authority with respect to healing. This comparison, drawing on the RSC's authority as centurion in the realm of military structure, also serves to highlight the *humble* attitude of this person towards *Jesus* (v. 8: οὐκ εἰμὶ ἱκανός). For the positive sanction of the RSC's preparedness, pointing out its faith, Jesus juxtaposes this faith with the lack of faith in Israel and thus utilizes an *antithetic* comparison (vv. 10-12). Also Jesus' promise of healing includes a reference to the centurion's preparedness: "Go; let it be done for you according to *how you believed*" (ὡς ἐπίστευσας; v. 13). Whereas the RSC's preparedness is the main focus of this version, the depiction of which occupies almost the entire narrative, only a short reference to the main performance is given in the concluding verse 13b. The function of the narrative in Matthew is to emphasize that *faith* is the proper *preparedness of a subject invoking Jesus.* It will be shown below that this emphasis corresponds to Matthew's reshaping of other miracle stories as well.

Luke's version, an edition of the narrative he, like Matthew, found in Q, also concentrates on the *preparedness of the RSC* in the phase of the preparation of the BNP. The performance is not manifest in the story. An indication of its successful outcome is pushed to the periphery (v. 10). As has been shown above, however, Luke chooses different allomotifs compared with Matthew. While Matthew points out the *faith* of the imploring subject as its outstanding quality, Luke's version is concerned with the *worthiness* of the RSC. In the two different moves aiming at the activation of the BNP (vv. 2-6a, 6b-9), replacing the repetition of the RSC's request after an apparent refusal by the BNP in

Matthew, the *worthiness* of the centurion plays a crucial role. Luke embellishes this motif which was already present in Q (v. 6: οὐκ ἱκανὸς εἰμὶ ἵνα ὑπὸ τὴν στέγην μου εἰσέλθῃς = Mt 8:8). In verse 4, the Jewish elders assure Jesus that the centurion "is worthy" (ἄγξιός ἐστιν) of his engagement in a healing performance. This worthiness is substantiated by a reference to the centurion's love of the Jewish people which found its concretion in his building the synagogue in Capernaum. In verse 7, the centurion, explaining why he himself did not come to Jesus points out his unworthiness and demonstrates a *humbleness* exceeding its depiction in the Matthean parallel: "I did not find myself *worthy* to come to you" (οὐδὲ ἐμαυτὸν ἠξίωσα πρὸς σὲ ἐλθεῖν).

While both Matthew's and Luke's versions focus on the *preparedness of the subject imploring the BNP*, each of them emphasizes a different quality as crucial: Matthew is interested in the RSC's *faith*, while Luke is concerned with a *worthiness* which finds expression in *humbleness* and *deeds of love* (cf. v. 5: "For he loves our people and the synagogue *he* has built for us").[49]

Different from these two synoptic versions based on Q, the accounts in Joh 4:46–53 and b.Ber 34b have in common a shift away from the question of the preparedness of the invoking subject to a focus on the *numinous ability*, respectively, of the BNP and PNP. In Joh 4:46–49, describing the repeated attempt of the RSC to activate Jesus, the *faith* of the RSC plays a role only insofar as it is lacking, made clear in Jesus' general negative sanction of a faith called forth by a miracle (v. 48). The detailed account on how the RSC comes to realize that the promise of Jesus in fact meets the reality of his child's restoration to health (vv. 51–53) suggests that the *ability (pouvoir-faire) of Jesus* is the center of interest in John's version. This assessment is supported by the conclusion of the story in which the RSC and its whole household become believers after recognizing that Jesus effected the cure. In this context, the motif of faith has the function of *sanctioning Jesus' preparedness*.

A comparison of Matthew's, Luke's, and John's versions also demonstrates that the one motif *faith* can serve as a filler of *different* motifemes in miracle stories. While Matthew in particular, in this and other miracle stories, utilizes this motif in the phase of the preparation of the BNP, John always places it at the phase of the sanction of the BNP. While

---

[49] This difference between Matthew's and Luke's accounts has also been observed by Achtemeier: "Lucan Perspective," 549: "The major point has thus become that the centurion was worthy to receive the requested miracle (v. 4), a point confirmed by his own humility (v. 7; both points are absent in Matthew). Thus, while Matthew's point concerns the power of faith in healing, Luke emphasizes the worthiness of a non-Jew to receive the benefits of Jesus' power."

faith in Matthew and Luke is the *presupposition* of the main performance, it becomes its *consequence* in John. The function of John's version is to emphasize the *preparedness of the BNP*, whereas in Matthew and Luke the focus is on the *invocation of the BNP* (InvBNP). This aspect, Jesus' ability (*pouvoir-faire*), is enhanced by the motif of the great *distance* between Cana and Capernaum. In the synoptic versions both the location of the SC and the RSC's activation of the BNP are placed in Capernaum. In Lk 7:6, Jesus even comes in close range of the location of the SC: ἤδη δὲ αὐτοῦ οὐ μακρὰν ἀπέχοντος ἀπὸ τῆς οἰκίας.

The version in b.Ber 34 focuses on the *preparedness of the PNP*, the parallel figure to John's BNP. A great distance between the location of the PNP, Arab in Galilee, and the SC, Jerusalem, is presupposed (cf. Joh 4:46). The emphasis is reaffirmed by the *sanction* of the PNP's ability. Activated by the question, "Are you a prophet?," which is provoked by Hanina's declaration that the SC is restored to health, he sanctions his own ability by explaining how he can tell if his prayer is successful or not. The motif of the comparison of the time of the promise and the time of the SC's restoration to health, which occurs in John, is also found here. The concurrence of these two events confirms the significance of Hanina's involvement as PNP in the healing of the SC. His extraordinary ability, not as BNP, but as PNP, is also stressed by the additional motif describing how he engages in the performance of invoking the BNP, God, after *seeing* the RSCs come to him. He is bestowed with a mysterious ability of knowing.

The immediately following narrative in b.Ber 34b describes a similar incident, but without the motif of a healing at a distance. This incident of a healing through the mediation of Hanina ben Dosa causes a discussion on his preparedness. Rabbi Yohanan ben Zakhai positively sanctions the special ability of Hanina ben Dosa as PNP, by comparing Hanina's preparedness with his own incompetence: "If ben Zakhai had squeezed his head between his knees all day, no notice would have been taken of him ...; he [Hanina] is like a servant before the king, and I am like a nobleman before the king." Both rabbinic stories have the function of *pointing out the PNP's preparedness*. Rabbi Hanina ben Dosa is not honored by faith in him, as in Joh 4:53, with respect to the BNP Jesus, but by the *recognition* that he is able to bring a prayer successfully before God, that is, in his activity as a PNP.

The analysis of these narratives from the perspective of their respective foci has led to the identification of two distinct narrative functions with emphasis on

- either the preparedness of the subject invoking the BNP
- or the preparedness of the BNP.

It is interesting to observe that Joh 4:46–53 and b.Ber 34b employ a story with similar motifs to focus on different kinds of preparedness, in terms of the Jewish tradition the preparedness of a PNP (Hanina ben Dosa), and in terms of the Christian tradition, the prepardness of a BNP (Jesus). This phenomenon will be discussed further below with regard to the process of acculturation.

3.3. The inner-narrative functions of restoration miracle narratives

In "The Principles of Classifying Folklore Genres" from 1964,[50] Propp determines three features as guidelines for the classification of folklore genres. His proposal is worth being considered here: 1) "The selected feature must reflect *relevant* aspects of the phenomenon."[51] It has been suggested above that categories like "healing miracles" vs. "nature miracles" are irrelevant for the classification of miracle stories insofar as they impose a modern world view on the ancient material. Like other thematic classifications, these categories remain on the level of motifs and are artificial and ambiguous. A classification which tries to categorize from the perspective of the social function of miracle traditions ("Sitz im Leben") is also arbitrary and unreliable. By contrast, a classification that makes use of the criterion "inner-narrative function" (cf. V. 2.2.) takes into account structural features of the stories. By determining the focal point(s) of a narrative, it tries to illumine the reason for the existence of a given miracle story: *why* did a narrator choose to tell or write a story in a particular way? It will be shown below that the number of inner-narrative functions of miracle stories can be limited to a few distinct types.

2) "The selected feature must remain *the same* throughout the classification; it cannot vary."[52] This principle is often disregarded, as was shown in my critique of Bailey's and Vander Broek's approach.

3) "The basic feature must be formulated *clearly*, so as to preclude the possibility of different interpretations."[53]

The analysis of the structure of healing miracle stories reveals that there exists only one fundamental structure. Therefore, consideration of motifemic sequences *alone* is not sufficient for a categorization of the material. The classification which follows is based on the criterion of

---

[50] Translated in V. Propp, *Theory and History of Folklore*, ed. by A. Liberman (Minneapolis, MN: The University of Minnesota Press, 1984), 39–47.

[51] Ibid., 43 (italics are mine).

[52] Ibid., 44 (italics are mine).

[53] Ibid., 44 (italics are mine).

"inner-narrative function." The question for the following investigation will be: what happens with respect to the inner-narrative function of a miracle story when the focus is on this or that motifeme? The focal point of a narrative can often be determined by identifying the motifeme which is clearly embellished with allomotifs over and against the absence, or only scanty realization, of other motifemes (cf. the examples in 3.2.). The means by which the correctness of a classification can be controlled are occasional remarks by a narrator explicitly pointing to the significance of a miracle story.

3.3.1. Stories with the focus on the initial lack

Miracle healing stories with the focus on the initial lack are the exception. The only example in the NT is Lk 22:49–51:

When those who were around him saw what was coming, they asked, "Lord, should we strike with a stroke?" And one of them struck the slave of the high priest and cut off his right ear.

But Jesus answered and said, "No more of this!" And he touched his ear and healed him (καὶ ἁψάμενος τοῦ ὠτίου ἰάσατο αὐτόν).

The question of the followers of Jesus concerning the use of force (v. 49) refers to the creation of a lack of health or life with respect to aggressors in order to prevent another, impending, lack, namely, the capture of Jesus. This *consideration of a possibility* to repulse the aggression of the armed servants of the high priest is transformed into a reality before Jesus has a chance to answer (v. 50): one of his followers cuts off the ear of one of the servants. In this way a lack is created, and a formerly hypothetical situation is realized (at least partly). Jesus' reaction consists of a verbal sanction (Εᾶτε ἕως τούτου) and a non-verbal performance. Jesus' sanction rejects the option of creating a lack through military resistance. His healing performance in a NP opposed to the disciples' NAP, which resulted in the L, restores the opponent to health, LL. From the point of view of the miracle story the focus is on the creation of a lack of health in a specific situation. Jesus sanctions the proposed program negatively and reinforces the negative sanction of the lack creating NAP with a performance in an opposed NP, the miracle healing. It should be noted that this miracle story is distinct from most other miraculous healing narratives in the NT insofar as the NAP leading to the L is *manifest* in the narrative and that in the main NP *only* the motifeme P is realized. The performance of the main NP is directly juxtaposed with the performance of the preceding NAP and reverses its outcome. The imbalance in the narrative moves of the two programs can be diagrammed as follows:

NAP = PrepAS:P:(neg.) Sanction of PrepAS / NP = P.

It is clear that the negative sanction concentrates on the preparedness to create the lack and not on the restoration to health. This becomes obvious when the episode is schematized according to the Narrative Schema. The initial lack of the NAP is formulated as a sanction of the feared circumstance that is expected to occur. The lack for the NP was created by the performance of the NAP.

	Lack	Preparedness	*Performance*	*Sanction*
NAP	(49a) When those who were around him saw what was coming,	(49b) they asked, "Lord, should we strike with a stroke?"	(50) And one of them struck the slave of the High Priest and cut off his right ear.	(51a) But Jesus answered and said, "No more of this!"
NP	[(50) And one of them struck the slave of the High Priest and cut off his right ear.]		(51b) And he touched his ear and healed him	

The healing performance is a supplement in the narrative as a whole. It reinforces the negative sanction of the disciples' *preparedness* to create the lack which is liquidates. A synoptic comparison confirms this analysis. Mk 14:47 reports only the performance which creates the lack; Mt 26:51–54 also consists of only the performance (v. 51) followed by an extended speech in which Jesus, as in Luke, negatively sanctions the preparedness of the AS (vv. 52–54). In neither case is the performance in Matthew and Mark related to a miracle story. Only The significance of Jesus' healing performance in Luke is clearly supplementary to the non-miracle story NP, reinforcing Jesus' decision and negative sanction in that program. By adding the healing performance, Luke transforms the NP describing the creation of the lack into a NAP creating the lack liquidated in the performance of the miracle story NP. The focus of the episode as a whole clearly remains on this NAP, concerned with the issue of armed resistance in a specific situation. It should be noted that the NP describing the restoration to health consists only of the assumed L and the P, whereas the "NAP" actualizes the motifemes Prep, P, and S. The story is at the fringes of the morphology of a healing miracle narrative. It can more correctly be classified as a *dispute* (on violence), which concludes with a miraculous healing performance reinforcing the sanction in the main narrative (anti-)program.

Another example of a healing miracle story which focuses on the motifeme L is Aelian, De nat. animal. XI 32. Roughly four-fifth of this narrative is a description of the creation of the initial lack and its severity:

A husbandman was digging a trench in a vineyard in order to plant some fine, choice cutting, when he brought down his mattock upon a sacred snake (ἀσπίδα ἱεράν) that had its lair below the soil and was far from hostile to man, and without knowing it cut the snake in half ... After seeing this, he was horror-struck, went out of his mind, and passed into a state of real madness of the most acute description (ἐκπλήττεται, καὶ ἔκφρων γενόμενος ἐς τὸ ὀρθὴν μανίαν καὶ ὡς τὰ μάλιστα ἰσχυρὰν ἐκφοιτᾷ). By day he lost control of himself and of his reason (ἑαυτοῦ τε καὶ τοῦ λογισμοῦ ἦν ἀκράτωρ) ...

So when his affliction had lasted for some time, his relations took him as a suppliant (ἄγουσιν ἱκέτην) to the temple of Serapis and implored the god (ἐδέοντο) to remove and abolish the phantom of the aforesaid snake. Well, the god took pity on the man and cured him (οἰκτείρει μὲν οὖν τὸν ἄνδρα ὁ θεὸς καὶ ἰᾶται).

The story describes (εἴρηται) how the snake had not to wait long for its revenge, and a very sufficient revenge.

The NP which describes the creation of the lack is detailed and given at length. A husbandman unwittingly severely injures a sacred snake. It is understood that an aggression against a sacred snake inevitably brings about punishment of the aggressor. The husbandman is immediately inflicted with madness. After the severity of his condition has been described, the RSCs implore a BNP, Serapis, for help (InvBNP). The BNP, identical with the AS, is persuaded by this invocation and heals the SC. The creation of the lack is reversed and the SC restored to health. The concluding interpretation of the narrator, stressing that the immediate consequence of an aggression against a sacred snake will be the punishment of the aggressor, reinforces the initial lack as the focus of the story. The main NP, therefore, is not concerned with a restoration to health but the demonstration of the effectiveness of the revenge of a sacred asp. Only in connection with the following NP that describes the restoration to health does this main NP become an NAP, providing the lack for the miracle NP which follows. In this example the healing miracle NP is a mere interlude in the main non-miracle NP. It actualizes the motifeme PrepAS = BNP and P, depicted by [ὁ θεὸς] ἰᾶται. A sanction of the healing performance or the preparation of the BNP is missing. The motif "pity" (οἰκτείρει) with respect the motivation of the BNP = AS, Serapis, is apparently related to the *accidental* nature of the aggression against the snake by the SC.[54]

---

[54] As is often the case with Jesus' motivation to engage in a healing performance in the synoptic miracle stories, also this *pagan* BNP is moved by pity. The motif *pity of the BNP* with a SC is thus not limited to the Christian tradition.

In both stories the miracle NP is subordinate to a non-miracle NP, which creates the lack for the miracle NP. The example from Luke is a NP (a dispute) concerning violence which ends with a healing performance, and the Aelian narrative is a *punishment story* with an intervening restoration to health. The function of the latter story is to demonstrate the instant revenge of an endangered sacred asp, while the former exemplifies Jesus' rejection of the creation of lack by military force.

3.3.2. Stories with the focus on a subject invoking a BNP (InvBNP)

The inner-narrative function of the miracle stories to be discussed under this category is to highlight the activity of the subject invoking a BNP to activate the BNP for a healing performance.[55] This focus can occur at the phase of preparedness or the sanction.

In 3.2. we have seen that in Mt 8:5–13 and Lk 7:1–10, the story of the centurion of Capernaum, the focus is on the invocation of the BNP. In both versions the *activity* of the *invoking subject*, the centurion as RSC, is emphasized, in contrast with John 4:46–53 and b.Ber 34b, which have their focus on the preparedness of the BNP and PNP (PrepBNP and PrepPNP) respectively. It was shown that Matthew and Luke each chose a distinct allomotif, faith and humbleness, as a filler of this motifemic slot. In focusing on the activity of an invoking subject, other narrative moves recede into the background of the narrative development. In Mt 8:5–13 and Lk 7:1–10 the focus on the InvBNP is at the *phase of preparedness*. The faith or humbleness of the invoking subject, the father, is exemplified by his actions aimed at activating the BNP.

Other examples which belong to this category include the following:

In Mk 7:24–30, verses 25–29 describe how a pagan woman, whose daughter is possessed by a demon, is able to *persuade* Jesus to engage in a healing performance by means of her rhetorical skills. She has to overcome two obstacles in order to accomplish the task of activating Jesus. First, she approaches Jesus against his intention to remain hidden. Secondly, she overcomes the negative sanction of Jesus with regard to her request (v. 27). Jesus' final positive sanction attributes his motivation to the woman's response, her λόγος (v. 29). The main performance is not manifest but sanctioned by Jesus (ἐξελήλυθεν ἐκ τῆς θυγατρός σου τὸ δαιμόνιον; v. 29b). Again, as in Mt 8:5–13/Lk 7:1–10, the *motif* "healing at a distance" is employed to highlight the preparedness of an invoking subject during the invocation of the BNP. This episode concludes with

---

[55] Since InvBNP is an iNP in a miracle story which aims at the *preparation* (motivation) of a BNP, thus involving PrepBNP, I prefer to speak here of a focus on the "activity" of the invoking subject, and not of its "preparedness." It should be clear, however, that this "activity" usually assumes the *preparedness* of the invoking subject as the AS in the iNP.

a DLL. The mother returns home to find her daughter freed of the demon and resting on her bed. This narrative has its focus on InvBNP at the phase of *preparedness*, reinforced by the positive *sanction* of the activity of the invoking subject.

The parallel account in Mt 15:21–28 has an identical structure. The same motifemes are realized. With regard to the choice of allomotifs, however, Matthew differs from Mark. Instead of being refused help *once* (Mark), the woman's supplications are rejected *twice* in Matthew (vv. 23–24, 26). In addition, the woman is not only confronted by a BNP unwilling to help her, but also by Jesus' disciples, who encourage him to disregard her request (v. 26). By means of these motifs the obstacles to the invoking RSC are described as much more difficult to overcome than in Mark. In order to have the woman accomplish her task, Matthew typically employs allomotifs which indicate her *faith* in Jesus:

– Have *mercy* on me, *Lord, Son of David* ... (Ἐλέησόν με, κύριε, υἱὸς Δαυίδ; v. 22),
– But she came and *knelt before him*, saying, "*Lord, help me*" (ἡ δὲ ἐλθοῦσα προσεκύνει αὐτῷ λέγουσα, Κύριε, βοήθει μοι; v. 25).

The woman addresses Jesus three times with κύριε, which is used only once in the Markan story. Furthermore, κύριος in Matthew is clearly qualified *theologically* (cf. Lord, Son of David). She does not simply fall to Jesus' feet, as in Mark (ἐλθοῦσα προσέπεσεν πρὸς τοὺς πόδας αὐτοῦ), but engages in proskynesis (προσεκύνει αὐτῷ). Finally Jesus sanctions her invocations as expressions of *faith* (πίστις), whereas the Markan Jesus acknowledges the woman's convincing answer (λόγος) without referring to her faith. For the conclusion of the story, Matthew utilizes a stereotypical formula to state the LL:

and her daughter was healed from that hour (καὶ ἰάθη ἡ θυγάτηρ αὐτῆς ἀπὸ τῆς ὥρας ἐκείνης; cf. 8:13; 9:22; 17:18).

Notwithstanding the different expressions (allomotifs), λόγος and πίστις, the *preparedness of the invoking subject* is highlighted in both cases. The invoking actions are depicted at length and in detail. The positive sanction of the activity of the invoking subject by the BNP, Jesus, corresponds to this focus.

The narrative in Mk 10:46–52 parr also focuses on the invocation of the BNP at the phase of preparedness. Blind Bartimaeus has to repeat his attempt to activate Jesus after being hindered by the crowd in his first attempt. His repeated outcry, "Jesus, Son of David, have pity on me" (vv. 47–48), expressing his confidence in the extraordinary power of the BNP, is sanctioned by Jesus as proof of his *faith*. Jesus is motivated by the SC's πίστις to effect the healing. Again, the main performance is not manifest in this narrative, only its sanction by the BNP:

Go! Your faith has saved you ("Υπαγε, ἡ πίστις σου σέσωκέν σε; v. 52).

This positive sanction of the invoking subject's activity is at the same time a sanction of the LL which is demonstrated in verse 52b. The SC immediately regains his sight. He sanctions Jesus as the BNP of the non-manifest main performance by becoming a follower of Jesus. As in the previous examples, the activity of the invoking subject is emphasized by the motif "overcoming of an obstacle." Again, a positive sanction of the activity of the invoking subject, here the SC, confirms this inner-narrative function.

Matthew's and Luke's parallel accounts exhibit the same structure with special attention given to the invoking subject. However, some motifemic slots are realized differently. Mt 20:29-34 adds the typical κύριε three times to his Markan *Vorlage*. Instead of one, Matthew mentions two SCs. Instead of having Jesus explicitly sanction the SC's preparedness, Matthew employs the motif of the BNP's *pity* and describes briefly Jesus' main performance:

Moved with compassion, Jesus touched their eyes (σπλαγχνισθεὶς δὲ ὁ ᾽Ιησοῦς ἥψατο τῶν ὀμμάτων αὐτῶν; v. 34).

Luke embellishes the motif sanction according to his predilection for stressing the glorifying of *God* for a miracle:

Immediately he regained his sight and followed him, *glorifying God*; and all the people, when they saw it, *praised God* (18:43).

The focus of Matthew's version remains the same as Mark, namely on the InvBNP at the phase of preparedness emphasizing the extraordinary faith of the invoking subject. All additional realized motifemes play subordinate narrative roles.

In the case of Luke (18:35-43), however, a new group of allomotifs is emphasized. By adding a twofold sanction of the preparedness of God (Lk 18:43), Luke, in a way typical of his gospel, refocalizes the story from the InvBNP to the PrepBNP at the phase of the sanction. The competence of *God*, of whom Jesus here becomes a representative, a MNP, is emphasized by the sanctions of the SC and the bystanding people. In the story itself, however, as in Mark and Matthew, the focus is on InvBNP, with Jesus evidently as the BNP.

A similar shift of focus also occurs in the parallel story in Mt 9:27-31. Here the phase of preparedness (InvBNP) has been abreviated. However, the motif of the invoking subject's faith, a typically Matthean feature, is still manifest in the story. The obstacle-motif is replaced by a question of Jesus,

> Do you *believe* (πιστεύετε) that I am *able* (δύναμαι) to do this?

This question is an allomotif for the obstacle-motif in Mk 10:48; Mt 20:31; and Lk 18:39. Jesus' question, pointing to his healing *ability* (δύναμαι) and the sanction of his competence (acclamation), reveals a new focus on the PrepBNP. Lk 18:35–43 and Mt 9:27–31, thus, do not belong to the category discussed at this point. These two stories have different inner-narrative functions, namely a focus on PrepBNP at the phase of preparedness (Mt) and of the sanction (both). They were discussed here to show again the shift of focus from the InvBNP to PrepBNP in a single miracle story tradition. In Luke God is reinterpreted as the BNP, whereas in Matthew Jesus remains the BNP.

An OT example for miracle stories which focus on the InvBNP with the invoking subject, in this case a PNP, is 1 Kings 17:17–24. After the initial lack has been established (vv. 17–18), Elijah, the PNP, engages in actions invoking God, the BNP, to effect the restoration of the SC to life (vv. 19–21). The BNP's positive sanction of the request and the main performance are described briefly in verse 22. The narrative concludes with a sanction of the performance (v. 23) and a sanction of Elijah's extraordinary preparedness as PNP. The mother of the SC recognizes that Elijah is a "man of God" in whose mouth the word of Yahweh is truth (עתה זה ידעתי כי איש אלהים אתה ודבר יהוה בפיך אמת; v. 24). This story, like the other narratives in this category, has the inner-narrative function of focusing on the activity of a subject invoking a BNP, thus pointing out the PNP's ability to activate God.[56] The focus is on Elijah's activation of God, the BNP. Elijah's various actions are depicted in detail (vv. 19–21). The concluding sanction of the SC's mother corresponds to this emphasis, even if it is the prophet's preparedness as PNP which she sanctions positively.

Another OT example may be found in Num 21:4–9.

> From Mount Hor they set out by the way to the Red Sea, to go around the land of Edom; but the people became impatient (ותקצר נפש־העם/ὠλιγοψύχησεν ὁ

---

[56] Cf. R. Kilian, "Die Totenauferweckungen Elias und Elisas – eine Motivwanderung?," in *BZ* 10 (1966), 44–56: "Gattungsmäßig ist diese poetische Erzählung als *prophetische Erweislegende* zu bestimmen, die in ihrem Schlußsatz ihr Ziel findet … Der Sinn dieser Legende ist also nicht das Wunder als solches, gleich gar nicht wird das Wunder nur um des Wundersamen willen erzählt, einzig der Erweis des Elia als Gottesmann, der in Wahrheit das Wort Jahwes verkündet, ist die angezielte Aussage (46; italics are mine)." Cf. K. Schubert, "Wunderberichte und ihr Kerygma in der rabbinischen Tradition," in *Kairos* 24 (1982), 31–37, esp. 32. For other narratives with the same function, cf., for example, Num 12:1–16; 2 Kings 20:1–11; Josephus, Ant. X 25–29; Marinos, Vita Procli 29.

λαός) on the way. The people spoke against God and against Moses (וידבר העם באלהים ובמשה/καὶ κατελάλει ὁ λαὸς πρὸς τὸν θεὸν καὶ κατὰ Μωυσῆ), "Why have you brought us up out of Egypt to die in the wilderness? For there is no food and no water, and we detest this miserable food."

Then Yahweh sent poisonous serpents among the people, and they bit the people, so that many Israelites died.

They came to Moses and said, "We have sinned (חטאנו/ἡμάρτομεν) by speaking against Yahweh and against you; pray to Yahweh to take away the serpents from us."

So Moses prayed for the people.

And Yahweh said to Moses, "Make a poisonous serpent, and set it on a pole; and everyone who is bitten shall look at it and live."

So Moses made a serpent of bronze, and put it upon a pole; and whenever a serpent bit someone, that person would look at the serpent of bronze and live.

The story consists of two basic narrative moves. Verses 4–6 describe a punishment, a NAP which creates the lack for the miracle story NP: the peoples' criticism of Yahweh and his mediator, Moses, prepares Yahweh to engage in a performance which creates a lack of the security of life. He sends serpents among the people. These serpents function as the ASs in this NAP. Verses 7–9, in a second narrative move, describe the restoration to health, the miracle story NP: after having been thus punished, the SCs acknowlege their negative contribution to Yahweh's preparedness in the NAP, a disbelief in him and Moses' leadership, as the cause of the lack. The SCs now reverse this contribution to Yahweh's preparedness. The reversal is manifest in their characterization of their former attitude as *sinning* against Yahweh and Moses. This earlier negative activity is replaced by repentence and faith in Moses and Yahweh. The people request that Moses, the PNP, invoke Yahweh, the BNP, in order that Yahweh might engage in a performance that would result in a LL. In so doing, the people express their recognition of Moses' ability to function as PNP and Yahweh as BNP. This new activity is sufficient to activate Yahweh via Moses. The BNP bestows Moses, who now also functions as MNP, with a numinous *savoir-faire* for the healing performance. Moses acts according to the divine instructions and makes a serpent of bronze, which he sets on a pole. In so doing, Moses prepares for the healing performance. The people's active involvement in the healing performance, their having to look at the serpent of bronze in order to be healed, points back to their activity in the preparedness of Yahweh. The focus of this narrative in both its moves is on the *activity of the invoking subject*, the Israelites. The purpose of stories such as this is not primarily to emphasize the power of the BNP, but to focus on the *activity of the invoking subject*. The main performance is often simply alluded to, if it is manifest at all. It can be observed that the activity of the invoking subject is often also *explicitly* sanctioned, whereas sanctions of the main performance or the BNP's preparedness are absent or play a minor role.

The *quality* of the activity of the invoking subject differs from tradition to tradition. Various motifs can serve as allomotifs for this feature of a story. So, in addition to the examples given above, note the following narratives from Epidauros:

- A mute boy: He came as a suppliant to the temple for his voice. When he had performed the preliminary sacrifices and fulfilled the usual rites, the temple servant who brings in the fire for the god, looking at the boy's father, demanded that he should promise to bring within a year the *thankoffering* for the cure if he obtained that for which he had come. But the boy suddenly said, "I promise." His father was startled at this and asked him to repeat it. The boy repeated the word and since then was well (καὶ ἐκ τούτου ὑγιὴς ἐγένετο; A5),
- Euphanes, a boy of Epidauros: Suffering from a stone, he slept in the temple. It seemed to him that the god stood by him and asked: "What will you give me if I cure you?" "*Ten dice*," he answered. The god laughed and said to him that he would cure him. When day came he walked out sound (A8).

In both cases a *contract* is established between the SC and the BNP. The spontaneous expression of the *willingness* of the SCs to *retribute* the BNP for a successful performance motivates the BNP to engage in a healing performance. The main performance is not manifest in the narrative; only its successful outcome; the focus rests solely on the InvBNP.

While the above-mentioned narratives point out the *proper* activity of invoking subjects as positive examples, there are miracle stories which do the same by means of *negative* activity, as in Epidauros A4:

Ambrosia of Athens, blind in one eye: She came as a suppliant to the god. As she walked about in the temple, she *laughed at some of the cures* as incredible and impossible, that the lame and the blind should be healed by merely seeing a dream. In her sleep she had a vision. It seemed to her that the god stood by her and said that he would cure her, but that in payment he would ask her to dedicate to the temple *a silver pig as a memorial of her ignorance* (ὑπόμναμα τᾶς ἀμαθίας). After saying this, he cut the diseased eyeball and poured in some drug. When day came she walked out sound.

The ἀμαθία of the SC is illustrated by her laughing at the cures. This ignorance is sanctioned by the BNP's demand to dedicate a specific item as a memorial of her lacking preparedness, functioning as a rebuke of her ignorance. The focus is nevertheless on the deficient activity of the invoking subject, that is on the InvBNP.[57]

---

[57] For a similar example, cf. A3.

The discussion above has shown that stories that have their focus on the activity of the invoking subject at the phase of preparedness, have, in some cases, a coordinating sanction of that focus. The following story focuses on the InvBNP at the phase of preparedness as well as the sanction. It is from a pagan milieu, Epidauros A2. The sanction phase is in italics.

A three-years' pregnancy: Ithmonice of Pellene came to the temple for off-spring (ὑπὲϱ γενεᾶς). After she had fallen asleep she saw a vision. It seemed to her that she asked the god that she might get pregnant with a daughter (κυῆσαι κόϱαν), that Asclepios said that she would be pregnant (ἔγκυον ἐσσεῖσθαί νιν), and that if she asked for something else he would grant it to her too, but that she answered that she did not need anything else. When she became pregnant she carried in her womb for three years (ἔγκυος δὲ γενομένα ἐγ γαστϱὶ ἐφόϱει τϱία ἔτη), until she approached the god as a suppliant concerning the birth (ἱκέτις ὑπὲϱ τοῦ τόκου). When she had fallen asleep she saw a vision; *it seemed to her that the god asked her if she had not obtained all she had asked for and was pregnant (ἔγκυος εἴη); about the birth (ὑπὲϱ δὲ τόκου) she had added nothing, and that, although he had asked if she needed anything else, she should say so and he would grant her this too. But since now she had come for this as a suppliant to him, he said he would accord even it to her.* After this, she hastened to leave the Abaton, and when she was outside the sacred precincts she gave birth to a girl (ἔτεκε κόϱαν).

The focus of this narrative is on the inadequate activity of the invoking SC at the phase of preparedness as well as the sanction. The first (failed) NP is due to the invoking subject's inability to formulate her need properly. She only asks the god to become pregnant but not to give birth. The god's sanction addresses this incorrectness of the SC's invocation. The liquidation of the lack is mentioned only briefly in the conclusion of this narrative.

We have a single example of this type in the synoptics, Mt 13:53–58. That the focus in this case comes only at the phase of the sanction may be due to the fact that the "miracle story" is very brief, no more than a fragment. It is interesting to compare Mt 13:53–58 with Mk 6:1–6a, from which it is drawn. Mk 6:5 states that "Jesus was *unable* to do any powerful deeds in Nazareth (οὐκ ἐδύνατο ἐκεῖ ποιῆσαι οὐδεμίαν δύναμιν), except that he laid his hands on a few sick people and cured them." In verse 6 Jesus sanctions the people's unbelief: "and he was amazed at their unbelief" (καὶ ἐθαύμαζεν διὰ τὴν ἀπιστίαν αὐτῶν). Thus we have two sanctions: first the narrator sanctions negatively the PrepBNP, Jesus' inability to perform miracles, and then Jesus sanctions negatively the Nazarenes' faith. However, Jesus' sanction is not explicitly related to his inability to do powerful deeds. There is no explicit reason given for Jesus' failure in Mark.

In Matthew's version the tension between "no powerful deed at all" and "but a few sick people he cured" is resolved, "and Jesus did not do many powerful deeds there *because of their unbelief*" (καὶ οὐκ ἐποίησεν ἐκεῖ δυνάμεις πολλὰς διὰ τὴν ἀπιστίαν αὐτῶν; Mt 13:58). Furthermore, while Jesus, according to Mark, was *not able* to perform miracles (PrepBNP), Matthew's recasting of the incident indicates that Jesus *refused* to perform many miracles because the people in Nazareth lacked faith. Mark and Matthew here present a miracle story in a *fragmentary* form. While Mark indicates a *lack of competence* (*pouvoir-faire*) on the part of the BNP (PrepBNP), Matthew's account sanctions a deficiency in the activity of the invoking subjects (lack of faith), the cause of Jesus' unwillingness (*vouloir-faire*) to engage in a healing performance. According to Matthew, Jesus only engages in healing performances if the invoking subjects have faith in him. Matthew's refocusing is intended to avoid the notion of Jesus' inability as BNP. A typical Matthean allomotif is employed to reshape the story: the focus is shifted from the preparedness of the BNP to the lack of *faith* of the invoking subjects.[58]

Acts 9:10–19a also has a focus on the quality of the invoking subject at the phase of the sanction. After Saul was inflicted with a lack of health (blindness; 9:1–9) and prayed to Jesus for help as can be inferred from verses 11–12 (ἰδοὺ γὰρ προσεύχεται ...), Jesus appears to Ananias in a vision (ἐν ὁράματι; v. 10) and commands him to lay his hands on Saul so that he might be restored to health (vv. 11–12). Ananias who is supposed to function as MNP channeling the divine healing power, first objects (vv. 13–14) but finally follows the order. It is explained to him that the SC is to be restored for the sake of divine plans with Saul:

Go, for *he is a chosen instrument for me* (σκεῦος ἐκλογῆς ἐστίν μοι οὗτος) to bring my name before Gentiles and kings and before the people of Israel. I myself will show him how much he must suffer for the sake of my name (vv. 15–16).

This story focuses on the sanction of the invoking SC, Saul. Ananias sanctions the SC's activities negatively. The BNP Jesus invokes the *devoir-faire* of the MNP Ananias, and bestows him with the necessary *savoir-faire* for the healing performance in which Ananias is supposed to channel the divine healing power through the laying-on-of-hands on

---

[58] Cf. here Mk 8:11–12 par and Mt 12:38–42 par, "The Pharisees Seek a Sign." Jesus refuses to give a "sign from heaven." He refers to the negative preparedness of the invoking subjects who want to test him (πειράζοντες αὐτόν): "No sign will be given to it (the evil generation) except the sign of Jonah." Due to the lack of preparedness of the invoking subjects, Jesus does not engage in the required performance (vouloir-faire).

the SC. Saul's preparedness as invoking SC is qualified by his being "a chosen instrument" of the transcendent Jesus for the purpose of universal missionary work.

3.3.3. Stories with the focus on the preparedness of the BNP or MNP

The analysis which follows concerns stories with a focus on the preparedness of either the BNP (most stories discussed here focus on this subject) or the MNP. In this case the focus can be established at the phase of the preparedness and/or at the phase of the sanction, as well as at the phase of the performance.

3.3.3.1. The preparedness of the BNP

Philostratus, Vita Apol. III 38, presents a healing miracle story which, at first glance, seems to have its focus on the initial lack which is described at length and in detail. A woman comes as a supplicant (ἱκετεῦον) to Indian sages on behalf of her son who is possessed by a demon. Her invocation of the BNP includes a detailed description of the condition of the SC, which suggests a very severe and life threatening case of demonic possession. The description also includes a failed NP: the mother herself was not able to cure her son.

A closer analysis reveals that the information given about the difficulties faced by the invoking subject, the mother, has the function of pointing out the *preparedness of the BNP*, the Indian sage. The focus on the BNP is already established at the beginning of the story by its setting in the gathering of the sages. The RSC's invocation consists of references to the length (two years) and the condition of the SC (δαιμονᾶν). When the mother describes the anti-subject as a "mocker and liar" (εἴρωνα εἶναι καὶ ψεύστην), one of the sages asks for the reasons for this characterization. The major part of the narrative is devoted to the mother's explanation. The focus of this part, taken by itself, is indeed on the description of the severity of the L, but the inner-narrative function relocates the focus of the story on the PrepBNP. In terms of the inner-narrative function, the phrase "mocker and liar" primarily depicts the anti-subject's *resistance* to face the BNP:

> but he promised, if I would only not denounce him to yourselves (ὑπισχνεῖτο δέ, εἰ μὴ διαβάλλομαι αὐτὸν πρὸς ὑμᾶς), to endow the child with many noble and good things. As for myself, I was influenced by these promises; he has put me off and off for such a long time now, that he has gained sole control of my household, yet has no honest or true intentions (οὐδὲν μέτριον οὐδὲ ἀληθὲς φρονῶν).
> Here the sage asked afresh, if the boy was at hand; and she said not, for, although she had done all she could to get him to come with her, the demon had threatened her with steep places and precipices and declared that he would kill her son, "in case," she added, "I haled him hither for trial."

The consistent refusal of the anti-subject to encounter the Indian sages indicates its acknowledgement of their competence (preparedness).[59] The description of the lack embellishes the PrepAS with special attention to the anti-subject's refusal to allow preparation for the main performance. Its function in the story as a whole, however, is to emphasize the BNP's preparedness.

The narrative concludes with the bestowal of the RSC with numinous power in the form of a magical helper, a letter addressed to the demon. The letter contains threats against the anti-subject that are supposed to keep the demon from killing her son. The narrative ends with this prep-aration of the RSC. The actual subjection of the will of the anti-subject and its performance are not manifest in the narrative. It is simply pre-supposed *that* the promise of the sage will certainly turn out:

Take courage ..., for he will not slay him when he has read this (θάρσει ..., οὐ γὰρ ἀποκτενεῖ αὐτὸν ἀναγνοὺς ταῦτα).

This sanction of the success of the activation of the AS and its main performance points in the same direction as the broad description of the anti-subject's resistance, the emphasis on the PrepBNP at the phase of preparedness.

In the Asclepios traditions of the second century C. E., the healing god immediately bestows a SC with a numinous *savoir-faire*, usually without being invoked to do so. The bestowal with numinous *savoir-faire* in these cases consists of the communication of prescriptions or instruc-tions for specific cures, as in the following examples:[60]

- In those days he [Asclepios] revealed to Gaius, a blind man that he should go to the holy base [of the statue] and there prostate himself (προσκυνῆσαι); then go from the right to the left and place his five fingers on the base and lay it on his own eyes (καὶ θεῖναι τοὺς πέντε δακτύλους ἐπάνω τοῦ βήματος καὶ ἆραι τὴν χεῖρα καὶ ἐπιθεῖναι ἐπὶ τοὺς ἰδίους ὀφθαλμούς). And he could see again clearly while the people stood by and rejoiced that glorious deeds (ἀρεταί) lived again under our emperor Antonius (Insc. Graecae 14:966a),
- To Valerios Aper, a blind soldier, the god [Asclepios] revealed that he should go and take the blood of a white cock along with honey and compound an eye salve and for three days should apply it to his eyes. And he could see again and went and publicly offered thanks to the god (Insc. Graecae 14:966d).

In these cases the ASs, identical with the SCs, are not the point of interest. What is at stake is their preparation by the BNP. Thus, the

---

[59] Cf. Mk 1:23–24; 5:6–7; 9:20; Acts 16:17 and 19:15. In all these cases the anti-sub-ject's reaction towards the BNP has the function of pointing out Jesus' competence. Bult-mann, *Geschichte*, correctly identifies the function of this reaction of the anti-subject: "er [the demon] kennt die Macht des Beschwörers" (239).

[60] Cf. also the Apellas Stela with its detailed descriptions of cures.

bestowal of the SC with numinous *savoir-faire* is described in detail. Insc. Graecae 14:966a is especially interesting. The BNP Asclepios himself instructs the SC what has to be done in order to activate the god (προσκυνῆσαι) before the transfer of miracle power can take place.[61] In both examples the main performance is not manifest. The emphasis lies entirely on Asclepios' bestowal of the SC with numinous *savoir-faire*. The god's extraordinary healing power is highlighted. Correspondingly, the concluding sanction in 14:966d[62] expresses thanks to the healing god. In 966a the ἀρεταὶ of Asclepios are sanctioned as an extraordinary qualification of the emperor Antonius. Both stories focus on *PrepBNP* at the phase of preparedness, which is exemplified by the detailed description of its bestowal of the AS with numinous *savoir-faire*, indicating the BNP's competence. This focus is enhanced by the concluding sanction of the BNP's preparedness.

Some miracle narratives in this category describe the healing performance in detail as a means of focusing on the miraculous power of a BNP as AS. These stories are prevalent among the Epidauros inscriptions, but also in the Jesus tradition. Note the following two examples,

- Aristagora of Trozen: She had a tapeworm in her belly, and she slept in the temple of Asclepios at Trozen and saw a dream. It seemed to her that the sons of the god, while he was not present but away in Epidauros, cut off her head, but, being unable to put it back again, they sent a messenger to Asclepios asking him to come. Meanwhile day breaks and the priest clearly sees her head cut off from her body. When night approached, Aristagora saw a vision. *It seemed to her the god had come from Epidauros and fastened her head on to her neck. Then he cut open her belly, took the tapeworm out, and stitched her up again. And after that she became well* (Epidauros B23).
- They came to Bethsaida. Some people brought a blind man to him and begged him to touch him. *He took the blind man by the hand and led him out of the village; and when he had put saliva on his eyes and laid his hands on him, he asked him, "Can you see anything?" And the man looked up and said, "I can see people, but they look like trees, walking."* Then Jesus laid his hands on his eyes again; and he looked intently and his sight was restored, and he saw everything clearly. Then he sent him away to his home, saying, "Do not even go into the village" (Mk 8:22–26).

Epidauros B23 not only gives a detailed account of the main performance in order to *demonstrate Asclepios' competence*; it also *juxtaposes the main performance with a failed NP* of the servants of Asclepios who lack the ability to heal the SC. Through their attempt at a healing they worsen

---

[61] Cf. Gen 20:1–18 where Yahweh informs the SC Abimelech that Abraham will be able to function as PNP if Abimelech fullfills certain preconditions.

[62] Cf. 966b and c.

the condition of the SC. The initial lack is aggravated. Against this background, the *competence of the BNP* is, in addition to the impression left by its successful performance, highlighted.[63] After stating the LL, the narrative breaks off. The focus lies *between* the InvBNP and the LL, namely on the *main performance as demonstration of PrepBNP.*

Mk 8:22–26 also describes Jesus' healing performance in great detail. First, he separates himself with the SC from the crowds, and then he applies saliva to the blind man's eyes and lays on his hands. The condition of the SC is so severe that the procedure has to be repeated in order to accomplish full success.[64] As in the example from Epidauros, the InvBNP recedes into the background of the narrative. A concluding sanction is also missing. Thus, the attention of the reader is focused on the main performance, described in detail and at length, as demonstration of the PrepBNP.

Miracle stories at Epidauros occasionally concentrate on the sanction of the performance by demonstrating the LL, as in the following two examples:

- Hermodicos of Lampsacos paralyzed in body: While sleeping in the temple, the god healed *and ordered him that, after leaving, he should bring the largest possible stone to the temple. It is what lies to this day in front of the temple* (A15),
- Hagestratos with headaches: He suffered from insomnia on account of headaches. When he came to the Abaton he fell asleep and saw a dream. It seemed to him that the god cured him of his headaches *and, making him stand up naked, taught him the lunge used in the pancratium. When day came he departed well, and not long afterwards he won in the pancratium in the Nemean games* (B29).

In these two examples L, InvBNP, and P are mentioned only in passing. The stories focus on the healing god preparing the restored SCs for a demonstration of the LL. This focus has the purpose of pointing out the extraordinary power of the BNP who was able to prepare the SCs sufficiantly for their DLL.

Miracle healing narratives with a clear focus on the motifeme sanction are found primarily in Christian traditions. In these examples the preparedness of the BNP, Jesus, his extraordinary competence, is usually at stake. In order to determine the purpose of a miracle story belonging to this category, it is important to identify the *reference-point* of a sanction.

---

[63] This motif is even more emphasized in Aelian's parallel account in De nat. animal. IX 33, where he points out that the god heals the SC "with a certain effortless divine power," a task that was "beyond the wisdom" of his servants.

[64] Cf. Mk 7:31–37 as another NT example of this type.

The analysis in 3.2. revealed Joh 4:46–53 as an example of a miracle story which focuses on the sanction of the BNP's preparedness at the phase of the sanction. A royal official whose son was about to die from illness in Capernaum meets Jesus in Cana and invokes him to engage in a healing performance. Jesus, after generally sanctioning a faith that is based on signs and wonders negatively, sanctions the healing performance over a great distance and sends the RSC home. The RSC trusts this sanction of Jesus. On his way he meets some of his slaves who attest that his son began to recover at exactly the time when Jesus sanctioned the healing performance. After recognizing Jesus' preparedness to foresee a healing performance that took place in a distant location, the RSC together with his whole household become believers in Jesus, in this way focusing on his extraordinary competence.[65]

Mk 1:21–28 consists of two NPs. NP I (vv. 21–22, 27a) describes Jesus' teaching in the synagogue and the people's sanctioning of his preparedness. Jesus teaches *with authority*. NP II is an exorcism (vv. 23–26; 27b). These NPs present two extraordinary abilities of Jesus: his teaching and his exorcizing power. Jesus' fame (ἡ ἀκοὴ αὐτοῦ), which is spreading throughout Galilee (v. 28), is a result of both his teaching and his exorcisms. The restoration miracle story in NP II describes the BNP's subjection of the anti-subject, the demon. The anti-subject attempts to repulse the threatening exorcizing performance of Jesus (v. 24). At the same time, this verse indicates the BNP's competence which is recognized by the demon. Jesus the BNP is, however, able to subject the will of the anti-subject by commanding it to leave the possessed person (v. 25). This exorcizing activity is successful, as demonstrated by the following main performance. The anti-subject, forced by the BNP to function as AS of the main performance, leaves the SC (v. 26). The witnesses of this exorcism react with amazement (καὶ ἐθαμβήθησαν ἅπαντες; v. 27aα). They *sanction Jesus' action* of subjecting the anti-subject as AS:

He commands even the unclean spirits, and they obey him (καὶ τοῖς πνεύμασι τοῖς ἀκαθάρτοις ἐπιτάσσει, καὶ ὑπακούουσιν αὐτῷ; v. 27b).

In this miracle story an invocation of Jesus is missing. The focus of the story is on Jesus' *extraordinary ability*, his preparedness. This focus is accomplished, first, by the description of how Jesus subjects the will of the anti-subject to become the AS. The preparedness of the AS (the anti-subject) is clearly not the purpose of this story. The performance of the AS points back to the authority of the BNP which is able to activate it. The focus on PrepBNP becomes especially obvious in the

---

[65] Lk 18:35–43 and Mt 9:27–31 also belong in this category.

following sanction (vv. 27-28). This sanction, referring to both Jesus' teaching and exorcizing power, is the aim of the entire narrative (vv. 21-28) and results in the spreading of Jesus' *fame* all over Galilee.

Mk 9:14-29; Mt 17:14-20 and Lk 9:37-43a present the story of "The Healing of an Epileptic Child." Each version has the focus on PrepBNP. However, as will be shown in detail, each gospel refers to a *different* BNP.

Mk 9:14-29 is a miracle story describing an exorcism (vv. 14-27) followed by a supplement (vv. 28-29). Several motifs in the miracle story establish its focus on PrepBNP = Jesus. His preparedness is enhanced by the disciples' failed NP sanctioned by the RSC, the father of the possessed boy (καὶ οὐκ ἴσχυσαν; v. 18) as well as by the description of the severity of the SC's condition (vv. 17b-18, 20-22a). While the disciples were not able to accomplish the requested exorcism, the demon, upon seeing Jesus (ἰδὼν αὐτόν; v. 20), reacts by producing convulsions in the SC. This reaction manifests the anti-subjects' knowledge of the power of Jesus, pointing out Jesus' preparedness.[66] Furthermore, the people, immediately on seeing Jesus, are *overcome with awe* (ἐξεθαμβήθησαν), run towards him, and greet him (v. 15). This reaction of the people indicates their being familiar with his extraordinary competence. Jesus is able to subject the will of such a violent and resistant anti-subject (vv. 18 and 20-22; cf. v. 29: τοῦτο τὸ γένος). The request of the RSC, the father, also refers to Jesus' *ability* (εἴ τι δύνῃ).

The miracle story itself (vv. 14-27) is followed by a sanction of the disciples' inability to subject the will of the anti-subject (vv. 28-29) as a supplement. This supplement is only loosely connected with the miracle story itself, where the disciples' unpreparedness was only casually referred to, and is not the focus of the story. Their unpreparedness becomes the issue in this supplement, looking back at their failed NP. The unpreparedness of the disciples is due to their lacking knowledge of the proper *means* (prayer [and fasting]) required for the successful expulsion of this kind of a demon (τοῦτο τὸ γένος).

It is interesting to note that Jesus' answer in verse 29 refers to the disciples' preparedness, not as BNPs, but as PNPs. While Jesus, the BNP, was able to subject the will of the demon (*vouloir-faire*), the disciples are instructed to *pray*, thus invoking a BNP (God). "Fasting" (καὶ νηστείᾳ), regardless of its textcritical value, points in the same direction. In Jewish and Christian literature from around the turn of the

---

[66] For this motif, describing the demon's attempt to escape the immanent expulsion (disequilibrium from the perspective of the anti-subject) out of fear for the exorcist's power, cf. Mk 1:24; 5:7 and Philostratus, Vita Apol. III 38.

eras, *fasting* can accompany, often in an enforcing sense, prayer.[67] In this case the disciples assume the same role as the apostles in Acts; they depend on a BNP in their healing activities.[68]

It should also be noted that the focus in the miracle story itself is *not* on the disciples' incompetence due to *their* lack of faith. This is also shown by Jesus' sanction in verse 19 which is of a *general* nature. The father's attitude (v. 22b) seems to reflect the condition of the γενεὰ ἄπιστος, negatively sanctioned in verse 19. It seems to be implied that this lack of faith was responsible for the disciples' failure. According to Mk 9:22b-24, Jesus rejects the RSC's request since it addresses Jesus' competence only in hypothetical form (εἴ τι δύνῃ) without implying the RSC's faith. Jesus instructs the RSC that everything is possible to the one who *believes*. Now the father expresses his faith in a dialectic statement (v. 24). Only after having established the RSC's faith does Jesus engage in the miracle performance. The focus of Mark's version is, however, clearly on *PrepBNP = Jesus.*[69]

Matthew's version has a different focus:

When they came to the crowd, a man came to him, knelt before him, and said, "Lord, have mercy on my son (Κύριε, ἐλέησόν μου τὸν υἱόν), for he is an epileptic and he suffers terribly; he often falls into the fire and often into the water.

And I brought him to your disciples, but they could not cure him" (καὶ οὐκ ἠδυνήθησαν αὐτὸν θεραπεῦσαι). Jesus answered, "You faithless (ἄπιστος) and perverse generation, how much longer must I be with you?

Bring him here to me." And Jesus rebuked the demon, and it came out of him, and the boy was cured in this hour.

Then the disciples came to Jesus privately and said, "Why could we not cast it out" (διὰ τί ἡμεῖς οὐκ ἠδυνήθημεν ἐκβαλεῖν αὐτό;)? He said to them, "Because of *your* little faith (διὰ τὴν ὀλιγοπιστίαν ὑμῶν). For truly I tell you, if *you* have faith (ἐὰν ἔχητε πίστιν) the size of a mustard seed, you will say to this mountain, 'move from here to there,' and it will move; and nothing will be impossible for you" (καὶ οὐδὲν ἀδυνατήσει ὑμῖν)!

This pericope, a typically Matthean recasting of a Markan story, shifts the focus from the preparedness of Jesus as BNP to the (un-)preparedness of the disciples on whom the criticism of a lack of faith now comes

---

[67] Cf. Dan 9:3; 2 Makk 13:11-12; Tobit 18:8; Jos., Ant. XX 89; Contra Apionem I 308; Lk 2:37; Acts 13:3; 14:23; et al.

[68] This piece of tradition is opposed by Mk 6:6b-13 parr, describing how Jesus bestows his disciples with ἐξουσίαν τῶν πνευμάτων τῶν ἀκαθάρτων.

[69] It should be noted that, from the *perspective of the focus on PrepBNP = Jesus*, there are, against the common *literarkritische* opinion, no literary tensions to be discovered in the miracle story in Mk 9:14-27.

to rest. The *inability* of the disciples as BNPs to heal the possessed boy (cf. the repeated sanctions of the failed NP by the father in v. 16 and the disciples themselves in v. 19) is due to the disciples' *lack of faith*. In stating this causal relationship, Matthew differs from his Markan *Vorlage*, which seems to draw a connection between the lack of faith of "this generation," in general, and of the RSC, the *father* (cf. Mk 9:22b-24), in particular, and the failed NP of the disciples. As a result of the refocalizing process, Matthew depicts the invoking father from the beginning as a RSC who *believes* in Jesus. This is expressed by his *kneeling* before the BNP and addressing him with "*Lord*, have mercy on my son" (v. 15), a formula typical for Matthew's depiction of faithful invoking subjects.[70] In his refocalizing of the narrative, Matthew omits Mark's second establishment of the lack (Mk 9:20-22a). The seeming failure of Jesus' performance in Mk 9:26-27 is also omitted. In Matthew, the preparation of the anti-subject and its performance are mentioned only in passing (Mt 17:18), in part due to his refocusing on the disciples' lack of preparedness as BNPs. The LL is stated with a formula typical for Matthew: "and from that hour onwards the child was healed."

Most of these changes are motivated by the intention to focus the narrative on the disciples' lack of preparedness throughout the story.[71] The preparedness of the invoking subject, the RSC, marked by the *presence* of faith (vv. 14-15), enhances the unpreparedness of the supposed BNPs, the disciples, who lack faith. While Jesus sanctions the father's preparedness positively with the exorcism (v. 18), he sanctions the disciples' preparedness as BNPs negatively (v. 17). Different from Mark, Matthew integrates the discussion on the (lack of) preparedness of the disciples as BNPs (vv. 19-20) into the miracle story. This theme is then highlighted in verses 19-20. Throughout this version, the disciples' inability is directly related to their lack of faith as the focus of the story. In order to express the connection between a lack of faith on the part of the disciples and their failed NP Matthew makes use of a chiastic figure. This chiasm is marked by a reverse parallelism which is, in addition, enhanced by an *anti-thetical* relation between the first and second phrase:

A. Then the disciples came to Jesus privately and said, "Why *could we not* (ἡμεῖς οὐκ ἠδυνήθημεν) cast it out?

B. He said to them, "Because of your *little faith*" (ὀλιγοπιστίαν).

---

[70] Cf. 9:27; 20:30.

[71] Cf. Luz, *Matthäus*, 523: "Ihr Ziel erreicht die Erzählung erst mit V 19f. Hier steht das Unvermögen der Jünger, den Dämonen auszutreiben, zur Debatte." However, the inability of the disciples is already the focus of verses 14-18.

B'. For truly I tell you, if you *have faith* (ἐὰν ἔχετε πίστιν) the size of a mustard
seed,
A'. you will say to this mountain, 'move from here to there,' and it will move; and *nothing will be impossible* for you (οὐδὲν ἀδυνατήσει ὑμῖν)!

A and B sanction the disciples' unpreparedness and give the reason for their failed attempt at the exorcism whereas A' and B' give a positive example of a preparedness marked by the presence of faith. The double negation, οὐδὲν ἀδυνατήσει ὑμῖν, expresses the same as the positive phrase in Mk 9:23, πάντα δυνατὰ τῷ πιστεύοντι. It should be noted that Mk 9:14–29 at no point refers to the *faith* of the disciples. This is a feature introduced into the story by Matthew, whose intention it is to have the story focus on the (lack of) *PrepBNP = disciples* at the phase of the sanction.

Luke's version of the story in 9:37–43a has the same focus as Matthew but a different reference point. While Matthew introduced the topic of the disciples' *unpreparedness* as BNPs due to a *lack of faith*, Luke refocuses with a different intention. The most obvious change to his Markan *Vorlage* is the omission of the negative sanction of the disciples' preparedness in Mk 9:28–29. The motif of the enhancement of Jesus' preparedness as BNP by contrasting it with the disciples' lack of preparedness, as was the case in Mark, is not utilized in Luke. Compared with Mark, also the effect of Jesus on the demon recedes into the background of the narrative. The anti-subject's reactions which serve in Mark to highlight Jesus' competence is missing in Luke's account: in Mk 9:20 the demon engages in convulsions as soon as it notices Jesus (ἰδὼν αὐτόν), thus attesting Jesus' power. The parallel verse in Luke 9:42 lacks this motif. Here the demon, *while getting close* (ἔτι δὲ προσερχομένου αὐτοῦ), is still involved in convulsions. These convulsions are not related to the demon's noticing Jesus. In addition, Luke drops the performance of the anti-subject, its leaving the body. While Luke omits *these* features from his *Vorlage*, indicating that he is not interested in the depiction of the preparedness of Jesus as BNP, his *additions* make clear where he sets the focus. He concludes the story with a positive sanction of *God*, a typical feature in miracle narratives of this gospel:

and all were astounded at the greatness of *God* (ἐξεπλήσσοντο δὲ πάντες ἐπὶ τῇ μεγαλειότητι τοῦ θεοῦ; v. 43a).

By means of the conclusion, Luke shifts from Jesus as BNP to him as MNP, as the representative of God to whom all praise is directed.

Luke adds other motifs absent in the Markan and Matthean versions. The possessed child is the *only* son of a father (μονογενής). Luke has a predilection for the circumstance expressed by this term in the context of miracle stories (cf. 7:12; 8:42). This motif is probably derived from 1 Kings 17:17–24 and 2 Kings 4:18–37. That Luke's reshaping is indeed informed by these OT texts, narrating the involvement of *prophets* in miraculous restorations, is suggested by another motif which Luke has in common with the two narratives from 1 and 2 Kings: after the child is healed, Jesus returns him to the parent. Compare the following Greek phrases,

– καὶ ἀπέδωκεν αὐτὸν τῷ πατρὶ αὐτοῦ (Lk 9:42),
– καὶ ἔδωκεν αὐτὸν τῇ μητρὶ αὐτοῦ (Lk 7:15 = 1 Kings 17:23),
– λαβὲ τὸν υἱόν σου (2 Kings 4:36).

Luke's depiction of Jesus is informed by the OT accounts describing miracles connected with Elijah and Elisha. While Jesus is more powerful than these PNPs and MNPs, Luke seldom misses the opportunity to have *God* sanctioned for a miracle Jesus did or effected. In Luke's miracle stories in general, and in 9:37–43a in particular, the BNP, God, is positively sanctioned. Jesus is reinterpreted as a MNP who is, nevertheless, *permanently* bestowed with numinous *pouvoir-faire*. Luke's version with its focus on Jesus' preparedness as MNP is a manifestation of his Christology presenting Jesus, while walking on earth, as subordinate to God.

Some restoration miracle stories in the NT which *concentrate* on the motifeme *sanction* provoke not only a positive-but sometimes also a negative-reaction towards the BNP. The BNP Jesus is negatively sanctioned by his opponents. This usually leads to a dispute between the BNP and his enemies. In these cases the miracle itself can have a merely *introductory* function for the following dispute on the preparedness of the BNP, as in the case of Mt 9:32–34; 12:22–37 par; Mk 3:22–30.

Mk 3:22–30 begins with a negative sanction of Jesus' preparedness by scribes from Jerusalem. This provokes Jesus' reaction; he rejects the accusation that he might be in alliance with the leader of the demons. Jesus' defense of his preparedness (vv. 23–27) is combined with his sanctioning negatively the preparedness of his opponents as characterized by blasphemy against the "Holy Spirit" (vv. 28–29). The concluding verse 30 (ὅτι ἔλεγον· πνεῦμα ἀκάθαρτον ἔχει) reminds the readers that the question of Jesus' preparedness is at issue here. This pericope focuses on the PrepBNP at the phase of the sanction without any other parts of the miracle story.

Mt 12:22–37 and Lk 11:14–30 combine a short miracle story, which has a parallel in Mt 9:32–34, and the discussion on Jesus' sanction in Mk 3:22–30, adding a few verses of Q material. In this way their versions become fuller miracle stories, and the sanction of Mk 3:22–30 becomes more specific. Through this combination, the focus is now much stronger on Jesus' sanction than in Mt 9:32–34.

Luke omits the reference to the blasphemy against the "Holy Spirit" and replaces it with a general statement of Jesus sanctioning that there are those who are on his side and those who oppose him (v. 23).

Matthew, in contrast, elaborates on the general issue of eschatological judgment (cf. 12:31–36). While Mark identifies blasphemy against the "Holy Spirit" with the accusations against Jesus (ὅτι ἔλεγον· πνεῦμα ἀκάταρτον ἔχει; v. 30) insofar as Jesus *represents* the "Holy Spirit," and thus focuses his version on the PrepBNP at the phase of the sanction, Matthew leaves the boundaries of the miracle story and instrumentalizes it as an *introductory* story to the following words of general judgment. This becomes evident in his separation of words against the "Son of Man" and words against the "Holy Spirit" (v.32). Only the latter lead to eternal condemnation. In so doing, the focus is no longer on the preparedness of Jesus at the phase of sanction, but on the preparedness of his opponents.[72] While this theme is present, but not dominant, in the accounts in Mark and Luke, Matthew makes it the focus of his story.

Mt 9:32–34 presents a short narrative, a parallel to the miracle story in Mt 12:22–37 par, with the focus on the PrepBNP = Jesus at the phase of the sanction. Jesus heals a mute man by expelling the demon causing his condition. The SC demonstrates, and thus sanctions, the success of the miracle performance (DLL). The sanction following the miracle performance and the DLL is twofold: the people are amazed (ἐθαύμασαν) and sanction the extraordinary nature of the performance:

Never has anything like this been seen in Israel (οὐδέ ποτε ἐφάνη οὕτος ἐν τῷ Ἰσραηλ; v. 33b)

The Pharisees add to this a negative sanction of Jesus' *preparedness*:

By the ruler of the demons he casts out the demons (ἐν τῷ ἄρχοντι τῶν δαιμονίων ἐκβάλλει τὰ δαιμόνια; v. 34).

While the performance is sanctioned by the DLL and the peoples' amazement, the Pharisees introduce the issue of Jesus' alliance with the demons and thus move away from his accomplishment to his preparedness. The sanction of Jesus' opponents does not question *that* Jesus has extraordinary ability. The *origin and nature* of his competence are at stake in this sanction. All of this reinforces the focus on PrepBNP.

---

[72] For another example of the *tendency* of Matthew to shift from the issue of the preparedness of Jesus to the (lack of) preparedness on the part of his opponents, cf. his reshaping of Mk 6:5–6 in 13:58.

3.3.3.2. *The preparedness of the MNP*

Whenever the preparation of a MNP who functions as AS is the focus of a miracle story, the extraordinary competence of the MNP, selected by a god as its representative is highlighted, and not the power of a transcendent BNP itself. This is obvious for the narrative describing how Vespasian was bestowed with *savoir-faire* by the BNP Sarapis, mediated by the SCs, and how he became, unexpectedly, able to heal the SCs. Vespasian functions here as MNP in the role of the AS of the main performance:[73]

> Vespasian as yet lacked prestige and a certain divinity, so to speak, since he was an unexpected and still new-made emperor; but these were also given to him.
> A man of the people who was blind, and another who was lame, came to him together as he sat on the tribunal, begging for the help of their disorders which Sarapis had promised in a dream; *for the god declared that Vespasian would restore the eyes, if he would spit upon them, and give strength to the leg, if he would deign to touch it with his heel. Though [Vespasian] had hardly any faith that this could possibly succeed, and therefore shrank even from making the attempt, he was at last prevailed upon by his friends* and tried both things in public before a large crowd; and with success (Suetonius, Vesp. 7:2–3; cf. Tacitus, Hist. 4:81; Dio, Roman Hist. 65:8).

The *preparation* of the MNP Vespasian as AS is clearly the focus of this narrative. He is not only bestowed with numinous *savoir-faire* but also needs to be especially *motivated* for the main performance. The successful main performance itself is only alluded to. The introduction to the episode agrees with the emphasis of the narrative on Vespasian as MNP. By focusing on the *PrepMNP* at the phase of preparedness, it demonstrates that the new-made emperor was favored by the gods.

In pagan miracle stories, especially in those with a MNP as AS, the InvBNP is rarely realized. Instead, these stories usually begin with allomotifs filling the motifeme *preparation of the MNP as AS* after the initial lack has been established. So in the following example from Dio-

---

[73] Cf. Henrichs, "Vespasian's Visit," who correctly observes that Vespasian is not permanently bestowed with healing power like a BNP. He functions as MNP: "It was, in fact, the foot of Sarapis which healed the crippled hand. In rationalistic terminology we could probably say that Vespasian acted as a *representative* of the god" (71; italics are mine). Henrich's observation has consequences for the comparison of this, and other, pagan miracle healing stories with those of the Jesus tradition. Jesus is usually depicted as BNP who acts independently while Vespasian functions as MNP. Only in Luke is Jesus to be considered a MNP rather than a BNP (cf., however, Acts 2:22). This is not explicit within the miracle stories as he incorporated them into his gospel, but in the following sanctions in which God is sanctioned as BNP.

doros of Sicily, Bibl. Hist. 103:7–8 (for the establishment of the initial lack, see below).

The king saw a vision in his sleep. It seemed to him that a snake appeared carrying a plant in its mouth, and showed him its nature and efficacy and the place where it grew. When Alexander awoke, he sought out the plant, and grinding it up plastered it on Ptolemy's body. He also prepared an infusion of the plant and gave Ptolemy a drink of it. This restored him to health.

The focus is on the preparation of Alexander (PrepMNP), his bestowal with an extraordinary *savoir-faire* enabling him for his healing performance. A comparison of the preceding two examples shows that different allomotifs are utilized as fillers of identical motifemic slots. Alexander is instructed by a snake appearing in a dream whereas Vespasian is bestowed with numinous *savoir-faire* by Serapis who uses the SCs as invoking subjects. Alexander makes use of a certain powerful plant whereas Vespasian heals by means of touching and spittle.

As in the story about Vespasian, the introduction of the miracle story about Alexander focuses on the MNP:

So the wounded were dying in this fashion, and for the rest *Alexander was not so much concerned, but he was deeply distressed about Ptolemy*, the future king who was much beloved by him. *An interesting and quite extraordinary event* (παράδοξον) occurred in the case of Ptolemy, which some attributed to divine Providence (εἰς θεῶν πρόνοιαν). For he was loved by all because of his character and his kindness to all, and he obtained a succor appropriate to his good deeds (οἰκείας τῆς φιλανθρώπου βοηθείας ἔτυχεν).

Alexander's distress indicates both his wish that the condition of the SC were reversed (*vouloir-faire*) and his inability to transform Ptolemy's condition from L to the LL (lack of *pouvoir-* and *savoir-faire*). This introduction to the story is concerned with the demonstration of the specific preparedness of the MNP Alexander, marked by the tension between his will and his inability to carry out his will. The detailed description of the SC's qualities enhances the motif of the distress and the need for miraculous help.

The conclusion of the story reinforces the focus on the MNP Alexander:

Now that the value of the remedy had been demonstrated, all the other wounded received the same therapy and became well. Then Alexander prepared to attack and capture the city of Hamatelia, which was large and strongly fortified, but (δέ) the inhabitants came to him with suppliant branches and handed themselves over. He spared them any punishment.

Even though Alexander is not so much concerned for the wounded soldiers (ἐπὶ μὲν τοῖς ἄλλοις οὐχ οὕτως ὁ βασιλεὺς ἐλυπήθη), they too profit from the remedy which proved to be successful in the case of Ptolemy. The immediately following preparation for the fight demonstrates the LL. The enemies of the strongly fortified city recognize the strength of Alexander and his army and, through their coming to him as supplicants and handing themselves over to him, positively sanction Alexander's preparedness. Thus healing miracle stories with the focus on the preparation of a MNP as AS have the purpose of demonstrating the divine selection of a MNP.

Acts 14:8–18 is a story in which the preparedness of the MNP is mistaken for that of a BNP. The miracle itself is briefly narrated in verses 8–10. The condition of the SC is described in detail. It is stressed that the SC was lame from birth and has, therefore, *never* (οὐδέποτε) before walked (v. 8). The description of the severity of the SC's condition has the function of enhancing the demonstration of the ability of what appears as BNP. Paul is motivated by the *faith* he notices in the SC to engage in a healing performance (v. 9). Without invoking Jesus or God, Paul *directly* commands and thus prepares the SC, in a loud voice, to stand upright on his feet (v. 10a). The man does accordingly. His walking demonstrates and sanctions the success of the performance (v. 10b). The pagan witnesses of this incident, in Lystra in Minor Asia, immediatly sanction the preparedness of Paul and his travel companion Barnabas as divine BNPs:

The gods have come down to us in the likeness of men (οἱ θεοὶ ὁμοιωθέντες ἀνθρώποις κατέβησαν πρὸς ἡμᾶς; v. 11b).

Paul is sanctioned as the incorporation of the god Hermas and Barnabas is taken as Zeus (v. 12). The priest of Zeus, together with the people of Lystra, is about to prepare sacrifices for the apparent gods (v. 13). The story is focused on the PrepMNP at the phase of the sanction. Paul, who always functions as a PNP and/or MNP in Acts, is here taken for a BNP. However, it should be noted that the healing performance in verse 10 indeed presents Paul as a divine healing authority. This is the only instance in Acts where an apostle does not heal with a reference to the risen Christ as the BNP and AS of the healing performance. Paul himself *appears* here as an independent BNP who commands the healing with authority (εἶπεν μεγάλῃ φωνῇ). Thus the pagan inhabitants of Lystra have good reason to believe that Paul (and also Barnabas) is the incorporation of a god, a BNP. The rest of the narrative (vv. 14–18) depicts Paul's endeavors to convince the people of Lystra of his human nature. After being elevated to the dignity of a god and BNP by the people of Lystra, Paul publicly sanctions his and Barnabas' preparedness as humans, that is, as MNPs.

Men, why are you doing this? We are also human beings of like nature with you... (ἄνδρες, τί ταῦτα ποιεῖτε; καὶ ἡμεῖς ὁμοιοπαθεῖς ἐσμεν ὑμῖν ἄνθρωποι ...; v. 15a).

The focus of this narrative is clearly on the PrepMNP with a unique twist insofar as the MNP not only *appears* and is *conceived* of as a BNP, but also sanctions his own preparedness as a non-BNP.

3.3.4. Conclusions

The preceding investigation was an attempt to classify miracle stories by means of the criterion of inner-narrative function. In the examples analyzed it became obvious that the focus on one motifeme usually entails the recession of others. Often the motifeme emphasized is embellished while other motifemes are actualized only in passing, if they are manifest at all. It thus becomes evident that while a specific motifemic slot *favors* a certain inner-narrative function, *definite clarity* about the purpose of a story can only be reached after the relationship to other motifemes has been identified. However, it also became clear that healing miracle narratives favor purposes that are concerned with the *demonstration of the preparedness* of a certain subject. This subject is most likely a BNP. In such a case the competence (*pouvoir-faire*) of a BNP is usually highlighted. However, the focus of miracle stories do not necessarily have to refer to *this* subject. Frequently the demonstration of the preparedness of another subject, a SC or MNP, is the purpose of a miracle story. If this is the case, the competence of the invoking subjects necessary for the *activation* of a BNP (iNP) is the focus of the story.[74]

Miracle stories with no apparent emphasis on one specific motifeme can nevertheless be categorized according to the identified inner-narrative functions. If, for example, no motifeme is especially embellished, the purpose of such a story will most likely be to point out the power of the subject effecting the transformation from one state to another, as in the following two examples,

- Lyson of Hermione, a blind boy: While wide-awake he had his eyes cured (θεραπευόμενος) by one of the dogs in the temple and went away (Epidauros A20),
- When Jesus entered Peter's house, he saw his mother-in-law lying in her bed with fever; he touched her hand, and the fever left her, and she got up and began to serve them (Mt 8:14–15).

---

[74] Bultmann, *Geschichte*, 234–35, downplays the importance of this inner-narrative function. According to him, also the InvBNP points *primarily* to the competence of the BNP: "Da die πίστις die Anerkennung Jesu bedeutet, so fällt auf Jesus, dem sie gilt, nicht auf den Kranken, *alles Licht*" (235; italics are mine).

The example from Epidauros has the motifemic sequence L → P → DLL. The purpose of this story is to indicate the power of Asclepios who is represented here by a sacred dog. In Mt 8:14–15 the motifemic sequence can be rendered L → PrepAS → P → DLL. Jesus is able to effect the restoration in his function as BNP subjecting the will of an anti-subject. The PrepBNP = Jesus at the phase of the performance is the focus of this narrative.

3.4. The miracle story as an iNP

While in the preceding categories the liquidation of a lack related to health was the concern of a main NP incorporating iNPs, a miraculous healing is sometimes utilized as an *iNP* and thus becomes subordinate to a main NP describing the liquidation of a lack unrelated to the issue of health. In the narratives belonging to this category, the liquidation of the lack related to health has an *additional* function, namely to liquidate, at the same time, another lack. Thus, the main performance of these narratives has a *double function*. Regarding the utilization of *healing* miracle stories as iNPs, numerous examples can be found in Jewish and Christian traditions. It is possible to distinguish distinct ways of relating the miracle iNP to the superior NP.

3.4.1. The iNP follows a legal statement

Even though it has often been maintained that in rabbinic literature miracles are not used as an argument in a legal dispute,[75] there are instances where this is the case. In 'Erubin 29a-b a healing miracle story narrates how Hanina ben Dosa once ate half an onion whereupon he fell seriously sick because of poison contained in the onion. Only after other rabbis implored God to have mercy with him does he recover. This miracle healing story is narrated as support for a legal decision stated immediately before the narrative:

the rabbis taught: one is not allowed to eat onions because of the poison contained in them (תנו רבון לא יאכל אדם בצל מפני נחש שבו).

See also in this context Pesahim 112b-113a which contains a miracle story describing how Hanina ben Dosa restricted the demon Agrath's activity to Wednesday and Sabbath nights. This story is used as an argument for the legal statement prohibiting someone from walking alone on Wednesday and Sabbath nights.

---

[75] For references, cf. A. I. Baumgarten, "Miracles and Halakah in Rabbinic Judaism," *JQR* 73 (1983), 238–53, esp. 238–42.

Do not go out alone at night; for it is taught: One must not go out alone at night, neither on the night of the fourth day, nor on the night of the Sabbath (אל תצא יחיד בלילה דתניא לא יצא יחיד בלילה לא בלילי רביעיות ולא בלילי שבתות) ...

The prohibition introduces the miracle story of how Hanina ben Dosa restricted the demon's actions.

Hagiga 3a has the miraculous healing story of how two mute men were healed through the mediation of Rabbi. The story is set in the context of a discussion of the question whether *mute* persons are able to learn Mosaic and oral law when it is read and/or discussed in gatherings of the Jewish community. This legal discussion is concerned in particular with the exegesis of Dtn 31:11–12 prescribing that the Mosaic law be read every seventh year "before all Israel in their hearing (באזניהם) ... so that they may hear and learn" (למען ישמעו ולמען ילמדו). The miracle story is employed at this point to refute the interpretation (ותניא) that "one who can hear but not speak" is excluded from the Mosaic prescription. Two mute persons used to attend Rabbi's teaching sessions and would nod their heads and move their lips. After Rabbi prayed as PNP for the SCs (InvBNP), they were cured: "and it was found that they were versed in Halakah, Sifre, Sifra, and the whole Talmud!"

The miracle story functions as a means to decide a legal debate. As iNP it is subordinate to the goal of demonstrating that mute persons can indeed *learn* the Mosaic, as well as, oral law. By means of this example, a legal decision is sustained.

In these examples the miracle story is only loosely connected with a preceding legal statement. The miracle stories of this category are simply adduced to legal statements in order to sustain them.

3.4.2. The iNP is embedded or interlocked in a main NP

In serveral narratives of Jewish origin a healing miracle story as iNP is embedded in the broader framework of a main NP concerned with the liquidation of a lack unrelated to health. The relation between the iNP and the main NP can be depicted schematically in the following way:

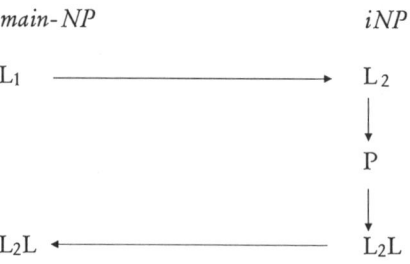

In this case, one performance liquidates two lacks simultaneously. An example from the OT is Ex 4:1–9. Moses anticipates that the Israelites would reject his claim to the leadership inaugurated by Yahweh. As a *means* of convincing his people that he is indeed the divinely appointed leader, Yahweh bestows Moses with numinous *savoir-faire* enabling him to perform certain extraordinary miraculous deeds. Among them is a miracle which allows Moses to change his healthy hand instantly to a leprous hand and back to health.

In Me'ila 17a-b, the demon Ben-Tamaljon makes himself available to a delegation of rabbis sent to the Roman emperor with the mission of effecting the annulment of decrees against Jews. The demon is sent into the daughter of the emperor by the rabbis, and rabbi Simeon ben Yohai is able to free the girl of her demonic possession. Now the emperor is indebted to the Jewish delegation and offers to fulfill any request they have. In this way, the rabbis effect the annulment of the decrees against Jewish religious practices. The miracle story functions clearly as an iNP. It is the *means* for the liquidation of a superior lack in a distinct main NP.

The same can be observed in the following example. 'Aboda Zara 10b describes how the Roman emperor Antonius secretly visits Rabbi in his house on a regular basis. He demands that no human being (גבר) other than Rabbi be present when he comes for a visit. The visits are so secret that Antonius would kill one of his accompanying two servants at the entrance of the tunnel leading from his house to Rabbi's house and the other at the end of the tunnel. Once, however, rabbi Hanina ben Hama happens to be present when Antonius arrives. In order to convince the enraged emperor that he did not disregard the agreement that no other human being be present, Rabbi points out that rabbi Hanina ben Hama is not a "son of men" (בר איניש). In order to demonstrate his extraordinary nature, Hanina ben Hama is sent to revive one of the dead servants of the emperor. This task is accomplished through an invocation of God. Hanina ben Hama functions as PNP. This iNP of a miraculous resuscitation leads to the emperor's general recognition of rabbinic qualities which he sanctions in the following way: "I am well aware that the least one among you can bring the dead to life ..."

In the narratives belonging to this category, an initial lack of a main NP, unrelated to the issue of health, is established. In order to overcome this lack a distinct NP, concerned with the liquidation of a lack of health, is introduced into the story. The miracle story functions as iNP in a dominant main NP. The liquidation of the lack of health directly effects the liquidation of the lack in the main NP.

An OT example is 2 Kings 5:1–19, in which Elisha agrees to engage in a healing performance in order that he [the SC] may learn that there is a prophet in Israel (וידע כי יש נביא בישראל/γνώτω ὅτι ἔστιν προφήτης ἐν Ισραηλ; v. 8b).

Here, the fundamental purpose of the miraculous healing of the Syrian commander Naaman by Elisha (apparently the BNP, but it can be pre-supposed that he is rather functioning as a MNP depending on God) is to liquidate a lack with respect to the SC's *ignorance* of the Jewish religion, and only secondarily to heal a sick SC, the same Naaman. Thus the miraculous healing becomes an iNP for a superior NP, the bestowal of the SC with faith in Yahweh. The iNP as well as the main NP are successful. The SC is restored to health and sanctions the preparedness of Yahweh positively, while other gods are negatively sanctioned:

Now I know that there is no God in all the earth except in Israel (הנה-נא ידעתי כי אין אלהים בכול-הארץ כי אם-בישראל/ἰδοὺ δὴ ἔγνωκα ὅτι οὐκ ἔστιν θεὸς ἐν πάσῃ τῇ γῇ ὅτι ἀλλ' ἢ ἐν τῷ Ισραηλ; v. 15a).

What has been observed with regard to the Jewish material applies to the Synoptics as well. In Mk 3:1-6 and Lk 14:1-6, probably presenting two versions of the same story as suggested by the identical structure and agreement in a number of allomotifs,[76] Jesus chooses to heal a SC *in order to* demonstrate his opinion in a legal debate, namely the question if it is lawful to engage in life-supporting activities on the Sabbath. The SCs are accidentally present. Their healing functions within the frame-work of a legal argument concerning the general question of the kind of work permitted on the Sabbath which, in turn, has an effect on the treatment of sick people. In both versions, the principal lack, convincing adversaries, is liquidated only insofar as no counter argument is brought forth. On the level of argumentation, Jesus is the winner:

and they could not reply to this (καὶ οὐκ ἴσχυσαν ἀνταποκριθῆναι πρὸς ταῦτα; Lk 14:6).

However, this does not necessarily mean that the adversaries come to agree with Jesus' argument. In Mk 3:6 the enemies' inability to counter Jesus on an argumentative level motivates them to plan his death.

Mk 2:1-12 parr presents a case in which the miracle healing narrative is interlocked with another NP rather than embedded in it.[77] While a huge crowd is gathered at the house where Jesus is staying in Capernaum, some people try to carry a paralyzed man to him. Due to the crowds, they have no direct access to Jesus. However, they are determined and able to accomplish their mission by letting the paralytic man down to

---

[76] Cf. Bultmann, *Geschichte*, 10: "Eine Variante der vorigen Geschichte [with respect to the relation between Lk 14:1-6 and Mk 3:1-6]."

[77] Scholtissek, *Vollmacht*, correctly speaks of a "Schachtelkomposition" (148).

Jesus from the roof of the house through a hole which they dug for this purpose. Jesus sees their faith and attests to the paralytic that his sins are forgiven. Some scribes who are present at the scene interpret this attestation as blasphemy, since only God could forgive sins. In order to demonstrate that he, the "Son of Man," has the power to forgive sins on earth, Jesus commands the paralytic to stand up, take his mat, and walk. The man acts accordingly which amazes the people and leads them to glorify God.

The miracle story begins with allomotifs expressing the InvBNP in verses 1–4. Prepared by the *faith* of the SC and the RSC (v. 5a), Jesus does not immediately perform the expected miracle but sanctions a performance (not explicit in the narrative) in which the SC's sins were forgiven (v. 5b). Jesus' sanction does not necessarily make him the active subject of the performance which he sanctions, but that is the way his opponents understand it, and in verse 10 he claims authority (*pouvoir-faire*) to do so. There is an implication in the story that the SC's condition of a lack of health is the result of a preceding narrative program (NP 1) in which the SC lost its health as punishment for its sins.[78] Implicitly, the liquidation of the SC's lack of health required that its sins be forgiven before its health could be restored. The SC's sins created the need of punishment, the performance through which it was punished with a lack of health (NP 1). In the NAP Jesus sanctions a performance (not made explicit in the narrative) in which the SC's conjunction with sins is transformed into a disjunction from sin. The controversy which arises from this sanction now draws the PrepAS in the NAP into the focus of the narrative. The demonstration of the SC's restoration to health in verse 12 functions to confirm the success of the performance in the miracle story as well as the PrepAS in the NAP.

---

[78] This relationship between sin, divine punishment, lack of health, forgiveness of sins, and restoration to health is, with respect to the Synoptics, presupposed only in this miracle story, Mk 2:1-12 parr.

Lack of health as the consequence of divine punishment for sins is twice alluded to in John in the context of miracle healing stories. In Joh 5:14, Jesus warns the restored SC not to sin anymore: Ἴδε ὑγιὴς γέγονας· μηκέτι ἁμάρτανε, ἵνα μὴ χεῖρόν σοί τι γένηται. While Jesus clearly seems to embrace the ancient Jewish concept of divine punishment for sins in this context, he denies it in 9:3. Asked by his disciples who is responsible for a blind man's condition, Jesus answers: Οὔτε οὗτος ἥμαρτεν οὔτε οἱ γονεῖς αὐτοῦ, ἀλλ' ἵνα φανερωθῇ τὰ ἔργα τοῦ θεοῦ ἐν αὐτῷ. Güttgemann's *general* statement concerning the structure of miracle stories, derived from an analysis of Mk 2:1-12, needs to be limited to *this story*: "In *a* MIRACLE STORY the protagonist liquidates a lack ... which a recipient experiences. The lack presupposes the violation ... of an interdiction ..." ("Fundaments of a Grammar of Oral Literature," 77–97, 87; italics are mine). "Divine punishment for sins" is an *allomotif* for an anti-NP creating the lack of a main NP.

The focus in the miracle story is on the InvBNP at the phase of preparedness. The invoking subjects' overcoming an obstacle is described at length (vv. 2–4). Their *faith* prepares Jesus for his performance (v. 5a). However, he does not perform the miracle, but draws into the miracle story an opposed narrative program (NAP) standing in opposition to a previous program (NP 1) which created in the SC a lack of health. This NP/NAP shifts the focus of the narrative from the InvBNP (invocation by the SC and RSC) to PrepAS, Jesus' preparedness *(pouvoir-faire)* to be the active subject in a program, in which he transforms the SC's conjunction with sins into a disjunction from sins. The SC's conjunction with sins created the need of punishment in NP, which at the same time created the lack of health in the miracle story. Even though this preceding NP functions to create the lack of health for the miracle story, it is not integral to it but is an independent narrative program correlated with the NAP in which Jesus forgives the SC's sins. These opposed programs (NP 1/NAP), concerned as they are with sin, punishment, and forgiveness, have their focus on the PrepAS.

Jesus' performance in the NAP provokes a negative reaction from scribes, who accuse him of blasphemy in what appears to be his engagement as the AS in a sin-forgiving performance (vv. 6–7). This accusation and Jesus' response (vv. 8–10) effect a *retardation* of the narrative development in the healing miracle story. In order to prove to his accusers that he does indeed, as the "son of man," have the authority *(pouvoir-faire)* to forgive sins on earth, Jesus, returning to the framework of the miracle story, heals the SC. The actual performance is not narrated, but Jesus commands the SC to demonstrate the success of the healing performance. The SC's performance demonstrates, at the same time, the liquidation of the lack in the miracle story, and Jesus' preparedness as active subject in the NP/NAP. In this move there is, however, no return to the previous focus on the InvBNP of the miracle story.

The interlocking of the two programs, miracle story and story of sin, punishment, and forgiveness, comes to its culmination when the SC's demonstration that it is healed functions at the same time as a sanction of the *performance* in the miracle story and the *preparedness* of the active subject (PrepAS) in the story of sin, punishment, and forgiveness. The latter is made explicit in Jesus' command to the SC:

> but *so that you may know* that the Son of Man has authority to forgive sins on earth … (ἵνα δὲ εἰδῆτε ὅτι ἐξουσίαν ἔχει ὁ υἱὸς τοῦ ἀνθρώπου ἀφιέναι ἁμαρτίας ἐπὶ τῆς γῆς …).

The relation between these two NPs can be depicted by means of the following schematic outline:

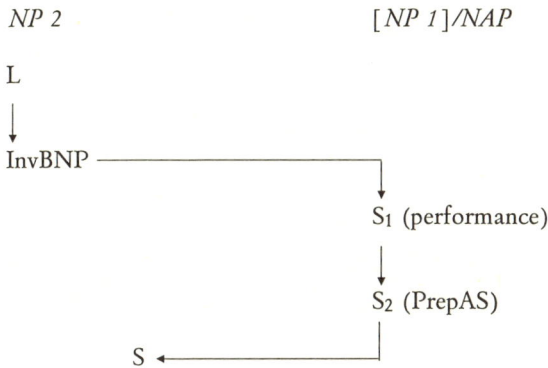

NP 2   [NP 1]/NAP

L

↓

InvBNP ─────────────────────┐
                                             ↓
                                    S₁ (performance)

                                             ↓
                                    S₂ (PrepAS)

                          S ←──────────────┘

The lack of health in the miracle story (NP 2) motivates the InvBNP which prepares Jesus, not immediately for the performance of the healing, but for the sanctioning (S₁) of a performance in an NAP which transforms the SC's need of punishment (due to its conjunction with sins), which resulted in a performance creating the SC's lack of health (NP 1), into a removal of that need by the forgiveness of the SC's sins (disjunction from sins). The performance (forgiveness of sins) is not explicit in the NAP: Jesus merely sanctions the performance. If the narrative ended at that point the focus could have remained on the InvBNP with NP1 functioning as a mere iNP in the miracle story (NP 2), but the negative sanction of Jesus' opponents (S₂) draws NP 1/NAP as a program in its own right into the narrative. The narrative now focuses on the PrepAS in the NAP. The SC picking up its bed and walking (S) functions at the same time as a sanction of the successful *performance* of the miracle story (NP 2), and the *preparedness* of Jesus as active subject in the story of sin, punishment, and forgiveness ([NP 1]/NAP). It is possible, of course, to differentiate the demonstration of the final sanction as an iNP in which Jesus prepares the SC with his command to take up his bed and go home (*devoir-faire*), followed by the commanded performance with the SC as AS, but such a differentiation does not contribute significantly to the investigation of the morphology of the restoration miracle in this narrative.

3.4.3. The miracle story introduces a main NP

Lk 13:10–17 presents a healing miracle story (vv. 10–13) which provokes a discussion on the issue of Sabbath healings in general (vv. 14–17). The local and temporal setting of the healing miracle, in a synagogue and on a Sabbath (v. 19), prepares the conditions for the dispute following the restoration to health. The miracle story itself (vv. 11–13) is *not* described in detail. Jesus, who *teaches* in the synagogue, is not asked to engage in a healing performance. He himself takes the initiative and activates himself intransitively. When *he sees* the SC, a woman who is conjoined with a spirit of infirmity for ten years, Jesus calls her and immediatly heals her from her sickness-demon possession by the laying-on-of-hands. Typically Lukan, the healed SC sanctions not Jesus', but *God's* preparedness for the healing performance (καὶ ἐδόξαζεν τὸν θεόν; v. 13). While this healing miracle story in itself focuses on the PrepBNP=God, the real function of the story is to introduce the following dispute on the general issue of healing on a Sabbath. In fact, it appears as if Jesus by means of the healing miracle intentionally provokes the following dispute. He is *teaching* in the synagogue. His healing performance touches on and devalues the central Jewish *doctrine* of the prohibition to work on the Sabbath. Jesus makes use of the presence of a sick woman to make his point concerning this doctrine. That the woman glorifies *God*, and not Jesus, is significant. In so doing, God is acclaimed as the authority standing not only behind Jesus' miracle preparedness but also behind his criticism of the Sabbath doctrine. That the healing is used by Jesus as an argument in a legal debate is also suggested by the reaction of the ruler of the synagogue: he *answers* (ἀποκριθείς; v. 14), addressing the crowds in the synagogue whom Jesus was instructing, by reiterating the doctrine of Sabbath observation. Since healing is work (ἐργάζεσθαι), it is not permissible to heal on a Sabbath (v. 14). Jesus, however, argues that also observant Jews have to engage in some kind of work on the Sabbath. As an example he refers to the work involved in providing water to oxen or asses, a daily necessity to be undertaken even on a Sabbath (v. 15).

In verse 16, Jesus points back to the incident which provoked the dispute, the healing of the woman. The SC is, in a rhetorically skilled way, juxtaposed with the oxen and asses. Framed as a rhetorical question, Jesus qualifies this woman as a "daughter of Abraham," who, if those animals are allowed to be *loosened from the manger* (λύει ... ἀπὸ τῆς φάτνης) for the purpose of getting water on a Sabbath, will certainly also be allowed to be *loosened from the bond of Satan* (ἔδει λυθῆναι ἀπὸ τοῦ δεσμοῦ τούτου) on the Sabbath. The comparison fulfills its purpose. The opponents of Jesus are silenced and put to shame (κατῃσχύνοντο πάντες οἱ ἀντικείμενοι αὐτῷ; v. 17a), while the people demonstrate that they embrace Jesus' position on the issue of healing on the Sabbath: "the people rejoiced at all the glorious deeds that were done by Jesus" (v. 17b). This positive sanction of Jesus' deeds (πᾶσιν τοῖς ἐνδόξοις τοῖς γινομένοις ὑπ' αὐτοῦ) includes the healing miracle he effected in verses 11–13.

As a pagan example in this category, cf. Epidauros B33:

Thersandros of Halieis with consumption: When he saw no vision in his temple sleep, he was carried back to Halieis on a wagon; one of the sacred serpents, however, was sitting on the wagon and remained for the greater part of the journey coiled around the axle. When they came to Halieis and Thersandros was resting on his bed at home, the serpent descended from the wagon and cured Thersandros.

When the city of Halieis made an inquiry as to what had happened and was at a loss regarding the serpent, whether to return it to Epidauros or to leave it in their territory, the city resolved to send to Delphi for an oracle as to what they should do. The god decided that they should leave the serpent there and put up a sanctuary of Asclepios, make an image of him, and set it up in the temple. When the oracle was announced the city of Halieis erected the sanctuary of Asclepios and followed the rest of the god's commands.

After a failed attempt at the activation of Asclepios at Epidauros, the SC returns home. A sacred snake, the BNP, from the temple at Epidauros accompanies the SC unnoticed. Upon their arrival at the SC's hometown, the snake cures the SC. The main performance, however, is only mentioned in passing. It is not narrated *how* the snake cured the SC. The miracle story itself focuses on the PrepBNP at the phase of preparedness. It describes in detail and at length how the BNP, the snake, *prepares itself* for the healing performance. In the context of the following narrative move, the miracle story appears to become part of an *etiological cult legend*. It accounts for the transfer of the sacred snake from Epidauros to Halieis. In fact, the failed attempt of the SC to activate the healing god at Epidauros appears to have the purpose of providing the pretext for the BNP's transfer to Halieis. The miracle story has, in the larger context of the following NP 2, an introductory function. NP 2 describes the origin of the Asclepios cult at Halieis. The miracle story, now functioning as an iNP, accounts for the presence of the sacred snake at Halieis, and thus for the motivation of the people to send to Delphi for an oracle. The oracle then accounts for the erection of the sanctuary of Asclepios at Halieis. The miracle story itself is not the ultimate purpose of the narrative. Its function is to introduce a distinct NP concerned with an issue other than the liquidation of a lack of health.

As we have seen, Lk 13:10–17 presents a legal debate provoked by a healing miracle performance, demonstrating Jesus' opinion on the issue of Sabbath healings and, at the same time, his preparedness to convince his adversaries in a legal argument. The healing preparedness of Jesus plays only a subordinate role in the narrative. Epidauros B33 has a similar structure. The healing story itself introduces another NP concerned with the establishment of the Asclepios cult at Halieis.

4. The question of acculturation with respect to NT healing narratives

While the preceding analyses treated the Jewish, pagan, and Christian miracle narratives indiscriminately, the investigation which now follows is concerned with the identification of *characteristic features* of each tradition. The morphological analysis (IV.) revealed that there are no differences among these traditions with respect to the *morphology* of healing miracle stories (V. 1.). The freedom of the narrators, regardless of the milieu to which they belong, is restricted to the *choice* of the motifemes to *actualize* and to focus upon, and the selection of allomotifs as fillers of the chosen motifemes. The final outcome of the narrative process, the *performance text*, however, is the result of the creative endeavors of a distinct person. The choice of certain motifs as allomotifs for a specific motifeme and the combination of allomotifs leaves the narrator with an almost unlimited number of possibilities for the realization of the motifeme sequence of the miracle story. In turn, however, distinct culturally determined conventions, what may be referred to as the factor of ecotypification, again restrain narrators in their choice of motifs. The objective of this section is to identify features in the telling of miracle stories *favored* by Jewish, pagan, and Christian milieus. Special attention will be paid to the *types of allomotifs* chosen as fillers for the motifemic slots. It should be clear, however, that due to the geographic closeness of these milieus only certain *tendencies* of ecotypification can be singled out. The task is to identify features characteristic of the distinct milieus in the narration of miraculous healings. After these characteristics have been identified, the question will be posed if the Christian miracle stories reflect a greater proximity to a more Jewish or a more pagan mode of narrating healing miracle stories. As a means of focusing the investigation the question of *acculturation* will be asked with regard to the role of Jesus in miracle stories.

4.1. Characteristic features in Jewish miracle traditions

Characteristic for Jewish literature from the OT to rabbinic times is that *Yahweh* is always the BNP who is able (having the *pouvoir-* and *savoir-faire*) to effect healing.[79] Apparent exceptions to this theologoumenon will be discussed below. This BNP always needs to be *transitively*

---

[79] This has often been observed, for example, Dibelius, *Formgeschichte*, 149; D. Ben-Amos, "Narrative Forms," 87; Schubert, "Wunderberichte," 34; and A. Guttmann, "The Significnce of Miracles for Talmudic Judaism," in *HUCA* 20 (1947), 363–406: "According to Tamudic theology, in its representative utterances, miracles must be deeds of God, even though they may apparently be performed by men" (365).

activated. Yahweh never engages in a miraculous healing performance out of his own motivation. He needs to be activated for this purpose. This may be due to a belief which takes sickness as the result of divine punishment of sin.[80] In healing miracle stories in the OT, especially in the Pentateuch and in some of the traditions of pre-rabbinic Jewish literature, a punishment story immediately precedes the healing story. In these instances[81] the structure of the entire narrative encompassing both NPs is usually identical: a subject commits a sin-in the Pentateuch always an agression against Moses-and is punished by God with sickness, thus becoming an SC for a miracle story. Yahweh is the AS of this punishment NP. The healing NP which follows, antithetical to the preceding one, describes a restoration of the SC to health.[82] The SC or a RSC needs to activate an intermediary subject, a PNP who is able to motivate the BNP, Yahweh, to *reverse* its previous performance. The PNP is bestowed with the special ability to prepare the BNP, Yahweh, through an efficacious *prayer*. The PNP functions as a mediator appealing to the *vouloir-faire* of the transcendent BNP. The BNP never rejects the petition brought forth by the PNP and effects the cure of the SC accordingly. The BNP, Yahweh, is thus simultaneously the AS of the NAP which created the lack of health as well as the AS of the NP of a miraculous healing. Yahweh alone has the power over life and death, health and sickness. This thologoumenon has its foundation in the *monotheistic* faith of Israel as in Dtn 32:39:

See now that I am he; there is no god beside me. I kill and I make alive; I wound and I heal; and no one can deliver from my hand.[83]

These narratives usually focus on the motifeme *preparation of the BNP* with special attention paid to the activity of the PNP preparing the BNP. The healing performance is not depicted in detail. Yahweh appears simply to *decree* healing. Only the success of the unstated main performance is stated.

In Jewish healing miracle stories, the SC has, in general, no direct access to the BNP, Yahweh.[84] An *extraordinary* human being, usually

---

[80] Cf. Joh 9:2; Mk 2:5-7.

[81] Gen 20:1-8; Num 12:1-16; 21:4-9; 1 Kings 13:1-10; 17:17-24; 1QapGen 19:10-20:32; Artapanus, Frg. 3:24-25.

[82] Cf. R.C. Culley, *Studies in the Structure of Hebrew Narrative*, Semeia Supplements (Philadelphia, PA: Fortress Press, 1976), who observes with regard to Num 21:4-9 that "the structure is a blend of a kind of punishment story and a story of Yahweh's miraculous help" (103).

[83] Cf. also 1 Sam 2:6 in the context of Hannah's Prayer which also alludes to the exclusive uniqueness and oneness of Yahweh (v. 2).

[84] For rare exceptions, cf. 2 Kings 20:1-11 and also 1 Sam 1:1-28.

specially chosen for this purpose by the BNP, functions as a *representative* of Yahweh. The representing function of this god-chosen subject is not limited to its role as PNP. The PNP can, at times, also function as a *channel* of the divine power or may even *execute* and directly effect a restoration to health. In these cases, the PNP takes on the special function of a MNP (mediator of numinous power). While the representative of the BNP, as PNP, usually first activates Yahweh, in such cases it mediates, as MNP, the divine power to the SC.[85] This double function of a representative of Yahweh can be depicted in the following schematic way:

SC/RSC → PNP → BNP → MNP → P.

A SC or RSC appeals to a PNP who invokes God, the BNP, who in turn enables a MNP to act as or prepare an AS.

In Num 21:4-9, for example, the SC, the Israelites who have been punished by God with poisonous snakes for their rebellion against Moses and God, invoke Moses by confessing their sins and by other petitions in order that Moses as PNP might pray to Yahweh, and thus appeal to the *vouloir-faire* of the BNP to engage in a NP saving those who have been bitten by snakes. Moses acts accordingly. Yahweh bestows him with a numinous *savoir-faire* enabling him to effect a cure for the SC. He becomes the MNP when, according to the BNP's instructions, he makes a serpent of bronze and puts it on a pole. By means of this construction, he enables the SC through its submission to effect the healing performance, for "whenever a serpent bit someone, that person would look at the serpent of bronze and live" (v. 9). The MNP clearly depends on the BNP: Yahweh bestows it with numinous competence to effect healing.[86] In this way, a PNP becomes the MNP in a NP.

At times, especially when the first part of the schema is not manifest in a narrative, it appears as if the MNP itself were the BNP. Three healing miracle stories in the OT are examples: 1 Sam 16:14-23 describes how David, by playing his harp, is able to expel the demon frightening Saul. It is not indicated how David was bestowed with this extraordinary ability. In 2 Kings 13:20-21, the bones of dead Elisha seem to *incorporate* a miracle effecting power. A dead man thrown into the grave of Elisha,

---

[85] For examples, cf. Num 12:1-16; 21:4-9; 2 Kings 4:18-37; 20:1-11 (here, however, does the SC directly activate God; cf. also Tobit); 1QapGen 19:10-20:32.

[86] This is also presupposed in Sirach 48:1-15, which is concerned with a definition of the relationship between God and *physicians*. The physician is depicted as an instrument of God to effect healing. God created the physician as well as medical herbs. Also the physician, dependent on Yahweh, needs to implore this BNP for a successful healing performance. Cf. also 48:3-5 where the miracles of Elijah are ascribed to the power of the *word of God*: ὁ ἐγείρας νεκρὸν ἐκ θανάτου καὶ ἐξ ᾅδου ἐν λόγῳ ὑψίστου (v. 5; cf. v. 3a).

after touching his bones, revives. In 2 Kings 5:1–19, Elisha, without invoking God for help, bestows the SC Naaman with a numinous *savoir-faire* enabling him to become the AS of his own healing performance. However, in the context of Jewish scripture, it may be presupposed that also in these cases *Yahweh* is ultimately thought to have effected the miraculous performances. This is indicated by 2 Kings 5:15 where the healed Naaman confesses his belief in Israel's monotheism.

The relative self-sufficiency of the healers in Israel's history seems to be emphasized more in Hellenistic Judaism.[87] In Artapanus, Frg. 3:24–25, Moses is able to revive the Egyptian king immediately, apparently without the involvement of Yahweh who, through his *name*, created the lack of life of the SC. Pseudo-Philo, Ant. Biblicae LX 1–3, focuses on the song of David as used in exorcisms. In this case it seems to be the *psalm* itself which bears a numinous power forcing demons out of SCs. The song, which is written out, is not ascribed to Yahweh as its originator. 11QPs[a] XXVII, however, stating that among the many songs David wrote, there were four to be used in exorcisms, explicitly points out that *Yahweh* bestowed David with a creative mind, thus giving Yahweh, not David, ultimate credit for the exorcism power inherent in these songs.

The effectiveness of the recitation of incantations, independent of an *immediate* involvement of Yahweh, is also described in Josephus, Ant. VIII 45–49. The incantations (ἐπῳδαὶ) used by Eleazar to drive out demons, among other means, are ascribed to Solomon who, in turn, was granted a special knowledge concerning the art of driving out demons, in this way especially favored by God (θεοφιλές). In IX 182–183, Josephus recounts 1 Kings 13:20–21 in such a way that Elisha, even after death, still possessed "divine power" (δύναμιν εἶχε θείαν). Elisha, however, is not interpreted as BNP. His astounding and marvelous deeds are seen as clear signs that he was held in honor by God (φανερῶς σπουδασθεὶς ὑπὸ τοῦ θεοῦ), who appears as the ultimate source of Elisha's extraordinary competence.

In post-OT times, thus, especially in Hellenistic Judaism, it appears that the invocation of God was *replaced* by a *direct access* to miracle effecting power. These powers were not *generally* accessible. Only ex-

---

[87] Philo, however, clearly depicts Moses as MNP in miracle stories. Cf. Mos. I 94: after Moses threw his staff on the ground where it turned into a powerful serpent, the Egyptians "now regarded these events not as the works of human cunning or artifices fabricated to deceive (ὡς μηκέτι νομίζειν ἀνθρώπων σοφίσματα καὶ τέχνας εἶναι τὰ γινόμενα πεπλασμένας πρὸς ἀπάτην), but as brought about by some diviner power (δύναμιν θειοτέραν) to which every feat is easy."

traordinary human beings, especially favored by God, were bestowed with a numinous *savoir-faire* and/or *pouvoir-faire*. Different from most OT healing narratives, these MNPs were *permanently* bestowed with healing competence. Consequently, these MNPs could activate their powers whenever they wanted to. This concept of a MNP, detached from the role of a PNP (as in the OT), seems to have flourished among Jews living in a Hellenistic milieu and might represent an adaptation of a Jewish mode of actualizing the structure of healing miracle stories to pagan forms. In this way, the OT ecotype, with Yahweh as BNP and a hero of Israel's history acting as PNP, sometimes also as MNP, underwent a process of acculturation. The result of this process was that the BNP, Yahweh, receded into the background and was barely involved in a miraculous healing, and the former PNPs and MNPs were no longer limited to the function of being petitioning subjects, but appear as substitute BNPs. What has been described here is a *typical but not general tendency* in Jewish traditions between the OT and rabbinic times. Josephus, for example, in recounting healing miracle stories from the OT, still depicts a PNP praying to invoke God as BNP.[88]

In *rabbinic* literature, the role of the MNP, prevalent in Hellenistic times, is abolished. In healing miracle stories, the emphasis rests on the invoking activity of PNPs. With respect to the schema, SC/RSC → PNP → BNP → MNP → P, only the first half is actualized. Yahweh, after having been invoked by an extraordinary PNP through prayer,[89] directly and immediately effects healing. Again, as in the OT, the main performance is not described; only its success is established. Furthermore, while many OT miracle narratives were preceded by a divine punishment story effecting the SC's condition of lack of health, this feature is completely missing in rabbinic literature. It could also be observed that miracle stories in the Jewish tradition are frequently employed as iNPs in the framework of broader narrative developments. Due to the undisputed omnipotence of God in a Jewish milieu, it was not necessary to prove Yahweh's powers by means of miracle healing stories. These stories were, especially in rabbinic literature, often used as arguments in legal debates.

---

[88] Cf. Ant. VIII 325–327.

[89] For an exception, cf. Honi the Circle-drawer who was able to *subject the will of Yahweh* and thus could *force* the BNP into a performance. Cf. the informed article by W. S. Green, "Palestinian Holy Men: Charismatic Leadership and Rabbinic Tradition," in *ANRW* 2,19,2 (1979), 619–47.

4.2. Characteristic features in pagan miracle traditions

In contrast with the Jewish tradition with its emphasis on the role of a *special* PNP, the Greco-Roman milieu almost universally presupposes a *direct access* of the invoking SC or RSC to a transcendent BNP. This is especially characteristic for the inscriptions from Epidauros.[90]

InvBNP is, however, except in the practices associated with the Asclepios cult, often not realized in pagan miracle stories of a Greco-Roman provenance.[91] In these stories, it is typical that a transcendent BNP appears of its own motivation to the SC, RSC, or another subject. The means of communication is often a *dream*.[92] The transcendent BNP might appear directly to the SC and bestow it with a numinous *savoir-faire*, thus preparing it to effect a cure. In other cases, the BNP appears to a RSC or another subject and prepares it as a MNP. So, for example, Diodoros of Sicily, Bibl. Hist. XVII 103:4–8, describes how a snake, carrying a plant in its mouth, appears to king Alexander in a dream and bestows him with numinous *savoir-faire* concerning a secret plant to be used for the healing of the wounded Ptolemy.

The focal point of pagan healing miracle stories is often the main performance by a BNP as AS, or the BNP's bestowal of another subject, at times the SC itself or a MNP, with numinous savoir-faire to act as AS. The main performance, accomplished by the BNP, a MNP, or the SC, is usually described *in detail*. The purpose of these stories is usually to point out the *ability* of the BNP. Especially in the Asclepios tradition at Epidauros *surgery* is emphasized.[93] In later centuries, Asclepios no longer engages directly in the healing performance but gives advice for *cures* and *recipes*.[94]

Non-transcendent BNPs can be identified only sporadically in the pagan environment. The oldest example seems to be Melampous in Apollodoros, Bibliotheca II 2, at the turn of the eras. There is, however, *one* figure who is clearly depicted as immanent BNP *incorporating* numinous powers, the θεῖος ἀνὴρ Apollonios of Tyana in Philostratus' Vita, in the

---

[90] For other examples of direct attempts of SCs or their RSCs at the imploration of a transcendent BNP, cf. Aelian, De nat. animal. XI 32 and 34; Oxyrhynchos 11:1381.

[91] Cf. Insc. Creticae I 17:9, 17–19; Diodoros of Sicily, Bibl. Hist. XVII 103:4–8; Apollodoros, Bibl. III 3; Plutarch, Life of Pericles 13:7–8; Tacitus, Hist. 4:81/Suetonius 7:2–3/Dio, Roman Hist. 65:8; Galen, Sub. Emp. X; Insc. Graecae IV² 1:126; XIV 966a-d; Pausanias, Desc. Graecae X 38:13.

[92] Cf. above IV. 3.2.1.2.1.

[93] Cf. Homer, Iliad 4:192–219.

[94] Cf. Insc. Creticae I 17:17–19 et al., cf. above IV. 3.3.1.

first half of the 3rd century C.E. It is important to note that this is the only pagan immanent BNP to whom *more than one* healing story and other miraculous acts is ascribed.

4.3. Characteristic features in Christian miracle traditions

4.3.1. The Logienquelle Q

There are two miracle narratives transmitted in Q, Mt 8:5–13/Lk 7:1–10, "The Centurion's son,"[95] and Mt 9:32–34/12:22–36/Lk 11:14–23, "The Healing of the Mute Demoniac and the Sources of Jesus' Power." In both cases, the miracle performance itself is only alluded to and retreats into the background of the narrative development. As has been shown above, in Mt 8:5–13/Lk 7:1–10 the *activity of the RSC*=centurion is the focus of the story (InvBNP), indicating his faith and humbleness. In the story of the mute demoniac the miracle healing itself has only an introductory function. In Mt 9:32–34 the focus is on the PrepBNP=Jesus at the phase of the sanction, a positive sanction by the crowds (v. 33b) and a negative one by the Pharisees (v. 34). This sanction is expanded in Mt 12:22–36 and Lk 11:14–23 with Jesus' extensive discussion of the BrepBNP in exorcisms from the same tradition as Mk 3:22–27. In these examples too, the miracle performance plays a subordinate role.

The emphasis on the *Redestoff* in these miracle stories corresponds with the general function of Q, namely to transmit the λόγια of Jesus. It should be noted, furthermore, that these healing miracle stories, especially with respect to their devaluation of the actual miracle performance, have an affinity with OT and Palestinian, Jewish miracle traditions.[96]

4.3.2. The Gospel of Mark

It is impossible to determine a feature characteristic of all healing miracle stories in Mark, except that Jesus is always the BNP. In one case, Mk 3:1–6, the miraculous story is an iNP in a story which has its focus on the liquidation of a lack unrelated to the issue of health. Jesus effects the cure of a man with a useless hand *in order to* make his point in a legal debate concerning the question if it is allowed to do good and to sustain life on a Sabbath. Some miracle narratives in Mark focus on the *activity of invoking subjects*. In those cases (Mk 5:25–34; 7:24–30;

---

[95] For an analysis, cf. above V. 1.2.

[96] Cf. 1QapGen 20, which has its emphasis on the preparation of the PNP, Abram, and not on the main performance. Cf. also the rabbinic traditions which contain miraculous healing (cf. V. 3.4.). Like in the OT, the main performance, if accomplished by the BNP, Yahweh, is never described in detail but simply presupposed.

10:46–52),[97] the *faith* of the SC or the RSC is explicitly sanctioned. Miracle stories like Mk 2:1–12; 3:1–6; 7:24–30; and 10:46–52, none of which focus on Jesus' healing performance, but on the activity (faith) of the invoking subjects, or healing miracle stories used in support of another NP might suggest a Jewish-Palestinian origin. This is especially clear in 2:1–12 where, as in OT miracle stories, the condition of the SC appears to be a punishment by God for sins. The focus in the *miracle* story, apart from its double-function in the context of a superior narrative program, is on the activity of the invoking subjects, as in 7:24–30 and 10:26–52. In 3:1–6 Jesus uses the healing of a SC as an argument in a legal debate. All of these features reveal an OT, rabbinic milieu.

Other miracle stories in Mark, however, clearly stand in a Hellenistic pagan tradition of narrating healing miracles. So, for example, stories with an emphasis on the main performance, demonstrating, often in detail, the power of Jesus as BNP (Mk 1:21–28, 29–31; 5:1–20, 21–24, 35–43; 7:31–37; 8:22–26; 9:14–29).

In Mark, however, a new feature appears. In five of the twelve healing miracle stories narrated by him, Jesus, the BNP, gives instructions following the healing aimed at limiting the spreading of the news about his miraculous power (Mk 1:43–44; 5:19, 43; 7:36; 8:26), a function of the so-called messianic secret. These attempts are in vain. The more Jesus commands not to let anybody know about his healings, the more the healed SCs *proclaim* (κηρύσσειν; cf. 1:45; 5:20) his deeds.[98] It is of particular interest that the healed SCs become the first ones to *proclaim* the power of Jesus manifest in his deeds. They are living demonstrations of his superhuman competence.[99] That this is a concept used by Mark to emphasize the *inevitable* disclosure of the nature of Jesus is also sustained by the fact that the healed SCs are *not punished* by Jesus for their disobedience. In contrast, pagan miracle traditions present the healed SCs minutely executing every command of the divine BNP. This obedience is due to either greatfulness or fear of punishment.[100] The

---

[97] Cf. also 1:40–45; 2:1–12 and 5:21–24, 35–43, where the motif of a special preparedness of the invoking subject (expressions of faith) is also present.

[98] This spreading of the news of Jesus because of his miraculous healings in spite of his prohibitions is also reflected in the summaries of Jesus' healing activity, cf. 1:32–34, 39; 3:7–12; 6:53–56.

[99] Cf. U. Luz, "Das Geheimnismotiv und die markinische Christologie," in *ZNW* 56 (1965), 9–30: "Für Markus ist das Wunder für die Öffentlichkeit bestimmtes Zeugnis; auch wenn Jesus dies nicht will, drängt es in die Verkündigung und hat Erfolg. Das Schweigegebot unterstreicht dann bloß dies Nicht-verborgen-bleiben-können des Wunders" (17).

[100] Cf. for a case where a SC does not keep a contract with the BNP: Epidauros B22, cf. A7. As an example for the awed execution of the BNP's request, cf. Oxyrhynchos 11:1381 and the Apellas Stela.

motif of the BNP's public acclaim against its will appears as a specifically Markan feature of the miracle story. It nevertheless remains in the pagan Hellenistic milieu with its focus on the PrepBNP.

A significant difference between Markan and Jewish-Palestinian exorcism stories is revealed when one compares Mk 1:21-28 and 5:1-20 with 1QapGen 20 and Tobit 6:1-8:3. The Jewish-Palestinian examples do not emphasize the exorcizing act but rather the preparation of the exorcist who is not a BNP. In 1QapGen 20 the *activation* of the PNP, who is also the MNP, Abram (appeal to his *vouloir-faire*) is the focus. Only after a contract is established determining the return of Sarai as condition for Abram's engagement in a healing NP does the PNP invoke God, the transcendent BNP. The healing performance itself is stated only briefly. In the case of Tobit 6:1-8:3, the bestowal of the MNP Tobit with competence (*savoir-faire*) for the miracle healing is described in great detail and at length. He is instructed by the angel Raphael concerning the exorcizing (and healing) effects of distinct body parts of a fish.

Mk 1:21-28 and 5:1-20, in contrast, do not narrate how Jesus, the BNP, was bestowed with competence to engage in the miracle healing. Here the focus is on the PrepBNP (*pouvoir-faire*). His authority as BNP is presupposed and reinforced by the anti-subject's recognition of his power. In accordance with his competence, Jesus is able to subject the will of the demon (*devoir-faire*). The anti-subject's performance as AS is depicted in detail and again attests to the extraordinary abilities of the exorcist as BNP, a motif found in the Hellenistic pagan milieu.[101]

In the Jewish-Palestinian exorcism stories the focus is on the preparedness of either the PNP (Abram) or the MNP (Tobit). These dramatic figures do not *incorporate* numinous exorcizing power. Therefore, the anti-subject's activity, the way it reacts to the exorcist or its main performance-favored foci to point out the authority of a BNP-is not highlighted in these stories. Other motifs are likely to be chosen that make explicit the *conditions* of the activation of the PNP (for example, a contract) or of the bestowal of the MNP with miraculous power.

Mk 7:31-37 and 8:22-26 display an emphasis on the healing *performance* of the BNP, a feature uncommon to Jewish-Palestinian sources. Correspondingly, Matthew omitted these narratives. Two other factors might have contributed to the omission of these Markan stories in Matthew. First, Mark mentions the use of spittle and other means of healing indicating *magical practices*.[102] Secondly, Mark, while concerned with focusing on the PrepBNP = Jesus, shows here no interest in the activity

---

[101] Cf. Lucian, Philops. 16; Philostratus, Vita Apol. 4:20.
[102] Cf. Hull, *Hellenistic Magic*, 76-86.

of the invoking subjects. Therefore, Matthew, with his special interest in the faith of the invoking subject, was given no reference point indicating faith that he could elaborate. While Mk 7:31-37 and 8:22-26 are, in their detailed description of magical practices of Jesus, extreme examples even in Mark, it should be noted that also in Mark Jesus *usually* effects healing by means of a simple touch or a command alone.

4.3.3. The Gospel of Matthew

The studies of H.J. Held[103] and J.M. Hull[104] concerning the miracle stories in Matthew can, in general, be sustained by the present investigation. In his study, Held argues that Matthew *reshaped* the miracle traditions according to his own theological system.[105] This is especially obvious for the traditions taken over from Mark. Matthew generally shortens the description of the lack and other circumstantial specifics concerning the healing performance (cf. Mt 8:28-34; 9:18-26),[106] thus shifting the focus from PrepBNP to the activity of the invoking subject, stressing its faith (cf. Mt 9:18-26; 15:21-28; 17:14-20; 20:29-34). Hull's title for the chapter dealing with the first gospel, "Matthew: The Tradition Purified of Magic,"[107] correctly identifies the direction taken by Matthew's reshaping and refocalizing activity. So, for example, the omissions of Mk 7:31-37 and 8:22-26 were probably motivated because of the proximity to magical practices. Mk 1:23-27 may have been omitted by Matthew because of its strong emphasis on the healing performance of Jesus, on the one hand, and the lack of any reference to the faith of invoking subjects, on the other. It became apparent in this study that Matthew omitted traces of the focus on the PrepBNP = Jesus. Matthew's reshaping activity resulted in a focus on the *faith* of the invoking SCs or RSCs. See, for example, Mt 9:18-26. In both episodes, "Jairus' Daughter" and "The Woman With the Issue of Blood," it is obvious that the references in Mark indicating the severity and aggravation of both circumstances of lack (Mk 5:26, 35, 37) and the details concerning the woman's as well as Jesus' healing performances (Mk 5:29-33, 40b-42) are omitted or radically reduced in Matthew. By so doing Matthew focuses the stories on the motif *faith of the invoking subjects* (filler of the motifemic slot "InvBNP"), which was already present but not elaborated in Mark. In this tendency Matthew's miracle tradition appears to be in close proximity to Q. See especially Mt 8:5-13 par. While in Q the faith of the invoking subject was sanctioned (Mt 8:10=Lk 7:9)

---

[103] "Matthäus als Interpret."
[104] *Hellenistic Magic.*
[105] Cf. Held, "Matthäus als Interpret," 284-287.
[106] Cf. ibid., 286.
[107] *Hellenistic Magic,* 116-141.

it seems certain that Matthew added other motifs which *enhanced* that focus (κύριε in vv. 6 and 8; ἐπίστευσας in v. 13). The specific employment of miracle stories in this gospel, especially the rejection of their usage as a means of demonstrating Jesus' miraculous powers, suggests a Jewish milieu.

4.3.4. The Gospel of Luke

The main features of Luke's healing miracle stories have already been pointed out above.[108] Only the major tendencies of his reshaping and refocalizing traditional miracle stories will be summarized below. Luke does not abstain from mentioning practices which might indicate magic (cf. his version of Mk 5:25–34 in 8:43–48). In addition, like his Markan *Vorlage*, he can give *detailed descriptions* of the methods used by Jesus to effect restorations to health (for example, 4:31–37, 38–39). Most important, however, is Luke's "predilection for adding a reaction of the crowd, usually to praise God."[109] This reshaping has the function of demonstrating that God is the ultimate "source of his power," leading to the people "acknowledging Jesus to be the one whom God has chosen to do his work."[110] In this sense, a relative proximity of Jesus to the OT prophets acting as MNPs can be detected.

In the stories themselves, however, Jesus acts independently from the source of his numinous power, God. He *incorporates* divine healing power in himself. He is a BNP who appears as *super*-prophet. It seems as if Luke tried to combine a pagan mode of his miracle stories with the focus on the PrepBNP with the OT traditions of prophets as MNPs. This resulted in a certain tension inherent in his narratives: while Jesus, in effecting a cure, is depicted as an independent BNP, he is seldom *sanctioned* as the BNP.

A similar tendency could be identified in those Jewish miracle stories which originated in a Hellenistic pagan environment, especially for Josephus.[111] Here, as in Luke, God is not immediately involved in the healing performance but thought to stand behind the substitute BNPs or MNPs as the originator of their miracle powers. Therefore, in Josephus God is sanctioned as the BNP, even though he does not appear *directly* in the healing performances. It should also be noted that Josephus and Luke were *historians*, which might have tempered them from depicting miracle effecting figures as totally independent from God. As

---

[108] Cf. especially IV. 3.2.1.1.

[109] Cf. Achtemeier, "Lucan Perspective," 549–50. For a detailed analysis, cf. above IV. 3.2.1.1.

[110] Idem, 554.

[111] The same might be true also for Artapanus. The authority of Moses is not explicitly derived from God.

historians they may have attempted to avoid the discrediting impression of telling wonder tales of gods wandering on earth. In Luke the people recognize God's concern for *them through* Jesus' miraculous deeds. Jesus' miraculous deeds effect a *renewal of the people's faith in God* and in his involvement in their affairs. So especially in 7:16:

Fear seized all of them; and they glorified God, saying, "A great prophet has risen among us!" and "God has looked favorably on his people!"

While Matthew emphasized the *faith of the individual* as the *precondition* for help, Luke is concerned with the renewed hope and faith of the *collective people* in God as a *consequence* of Jesus' miraculous healings.

4.3.5. The Acts of the Apostles

In Acts too the sanction of a miraculous performance can be in praise of God.[112] However, this motif is not as crucial here as in Luke's gospel since in Acts it is evident that the apostles Peter and Paul *constantly* depend on a transcendent BNP, in contrast with the gospel with its tension between the miraculous deeds of Jesus, who acts as BNP in miracle stories, and the praising of God as the ultimate BNP.[113] In Acts the tendency is for the miraculous restoration to health, rather than effecting praise of God, to motivate witnesses to join the Christian faith-community.[114]

The most typical feature in the miracle stories in Acts is, however, the function of the apostles as PNPs and MNPs, as has been shown above (IV. 3.3.2.). This is understandable, since, with the ascension of Jesus to heaven (Acts 1:11), there is no direct access to a BNP. The apostles function as mediators between the transcendent, divine realm and the innerworldly sphere of the SCs in need of healing. They combine the two roles of PNP and MNP when, first, they invoke God or the resurrected Christ for help, and, secondly, they *channel* the divine power to the SCs. In this respect, Peter and Paul can be compared with the roles played by OT figures, such as, Abraham, Moses, Elijah, and Elisha in miracle narratives of pre-rabbinic Jewish literature. A close parallel outside the OT is 1QapGen 20:28-29, in which Abram effects an exorcism through prayer and the laying-on-of-hands.[115] The apostles also share with the rabbis the motif of *prayer* as the way to invoke and activate the transcendent BNP. The rabbis, however, do not appear as

---

[112] Cf. Acts 3:1-10.

[113] Cf., however, Acts 14:8-18, where the conception of Paul as a BNP is corrected.

[114] Cf. Acts 9:35, 42.

[115] Cf. especially Acts 28:8, where both motifs occur during the healing of a man from fever and diarrhea.

MNPs. In rabbinic literature, Yahweh himself *directly* decrees healing and does not use mediators for the transmission of his divine power. The mediating function of the apostles thus appears in close proximity to Jewish and especially pre-rabbinic modes to narrate miraculous healing stories.

4.3.6. The Gospel of John

The miracles in John are called σημεῖα, signs. This term indicates the function of the miracle stories in the fourth gospel. Jesus' divine nature as one sent by God becomes *epiphanic* through his miraculous deeds which, in their extraordinariness, exceed those narrated in the synoptics.[116] The miracle performances of Jesus signify his divine nature. In John, faith is never a presupposition for Jesus' engagement in a miracle. The emphasis in these stories is on Jesus' revelation in his miraculous performances and, correspondingly, on the *sanction* of his preparedness. Some, especially SCs or RSCs who directly experience the healing power of Jesus, become believers in Jesus.[117] The dominant attitude, however, is disbelief and hostility towards Jesus, leading to the decision to kill him.[118] Jesus' restoration miracles usually introduce a *debate* concerning his preparedness as BNP, but only as a step to recognizing him as the revealer of God. These disputes juxtapose belief and disbelief in him as "son of God" (5:18), "prophet" (9:16-17), or "Son of Man" (9:35). Thus, faith provoked by miracles is also criticized by the author of this gospel because faith in Jesus which does not move beyond him as miracle effecting BNP does not recognize his true identity.[119]

4.3.7. Concluding observations with special reference to the question of Jesus as θεῖος ἀνήρ

The objective at the outset of this chapter was to identify specific features of distinct miracle traditions, especially Jewish and pagan modes of narrating miracle stories. This study has shown that there is a single morphology of healing miracle stories, making the inner-narrative function determinative for the identification of types of miracle stories. It proved useful to investigate first of all on which of the motifemic slots in the structure of a healing miracle narrative the focus rested, and secondly, to compare the *types of allomotifs* to fill the motifemic slots. In his recent study on the "Theios Anēr and the Markan Miracle Traditions," Black-

---

[116] Cf. the list in J. Becker, "Wunder und Christologie. Zum literarkritischen und christologischen Problem der Wunder im Johannesevangelium," in *NTSt* 16 (1970), 130–148, 137, fn. 4.

[117] Cf. 4:53; 9:38; 11:45.

[118] Cf. 5:18; 11:47-53.

[119] Cf. 4:48 versus 53, and 20:29 versus 31.

burn observes that the universal three- or fourfold patterns of the form of miracle stories, proposed and established by Bultmann and Dibelius, and adopted, in variations, by Theißen and Funk, "say nothing, in and of itself, about the dependence of one tradition upon another."[120] This is correct. Almost any narrative would fit these patterns. But with this judgment Blackburn abandons the question of the form, structure, and style of miracle stories altogether, and does not discuss it further. However, from a structural perspective, the consideration of the structure of miracle stories and an assessment of the employed allomotifs, appear crucial for a RGL comparison and investigation of the complex question of acculturation.[121] With respect to the focal-point of a narrative, for example, it was established that a detailed description of the main performance which demonstrates the competence of a BNP as AS could not be found in healing miracle narratives of a Jewish-Palestinian provenance but is clearly a typical feature of a Greco-Roman milieu.

Furthermore, it appears to be typical in a Jewish milieu that ordinary SCs cannot invoke Yahweh directly for a restoration to health. Extraordinary PNPs have the function of mediating the need to the transcendent BNP. This motif is unusual in a Greco-Roman environment in which SCs have immediate access to a healing god. Jewish healing miracle stories often focus on the motifeme InvBNP, which is realized by allomotifs describing the mediation of a PNP and its attempt to activate Yahweh. This motifeme is generally not realized at all in pagan traditions, in which the transcendent healing god, without being transitively activated, frequently gets in contact with a SC or a mediating subject, bestowing it with a numinous savoir-faire.[122] This special competence enables the subject to effect the healing performance.

The differentiation of the functions of the various so-called "miracle-workers" is of fundamental significance for a comparison of Jesus with

---

[120] Blackburn, *Theios Anēr*, 240.

[121] B. Kollmann's review of Blackburn's contribution is to the point: "Mit Sicherheit den größten Widerspruch hervorrufen wird ... Kap. 5 ("Genre", 233–62) ... [denn] hier [wird] auf einen Vergleich der mk Wundergeschichten mit paganen Parallelen unter form- und stilkritischen Gesichtspunkten von vornherein völlig verzichtet" (*ThLZ* 117 [1992], 351–353, 352). The problems begin with the first sentence of the chapter dedicated to "Genre," where Blackburn defines genres as "certain constellations of motifs" (233). "Motifs," however, are not structural elements but belong to a thematic category (cf. the critique of Theißen, *Wundergeschichten*, in Güttgemanns, "Bemerkungen," 20, fn. 12) and, as such, do certainly *not* constitute genres. With respect to the question of genre and structure of miracle stories, Blackburn remains on the level of the *Forschungsstand* represented by Bultmann in the 1920s.

[122] The miracle accounts at Epidauros are exceptions insofar as it is always presupposed, and at times emphasized, that the SCs come to the Asclepios temple at Epidauros and invoke the god of healing for help.

other ancient figures involved in a miraculous restoration to health. Jesus generally functions as BNP like Yahweh, Asclepios, Sarapis, Jupiter, Melampous (according to Diodoros of Sicily) and Apollonios of Tyana. He does not fall in the same category as Moses, Abraham, Elijah, Elisha, Hanina ben Dosa, Vespasian, Alexander, Proclus, Pericles, Peter, Paul, etc. These figures are not BNPs, but PNPs and/or MNPs. This category of PNP/MNP has to be differentiated further: the Jewish and Christian subjects are PNPs as well as MNPs, except for rabbi Hanina ben Dosa who is never a MNP. These figures are *characterized* by their extraordinary ability to invoke God and to mediate his power in the healing performance. Pagan figures typically function as MNPs, not as PNPs. In addition, typically they are singled out to function as MNPs only *once*. The Jewish and Christian PNPs and/or MNPs reappear in various healing miracle stories, while their pagan counterparts exhibit the function of mediating divine power only in a single extraordinary event. It appears that in this respect the healing miracle stories in Acts resemble a *Jewish* mode of narration: whereas in the gospels the SCs and RSCs could find *direct* access to Jesus as BNP, in Acts access to him, or to God, was possible only *through mediation* of the apostles. In a sense, they *replaced* Jesus, but with the difference that they functioned as PNPs or MNPs, not as BNPs.

For the assessment of the function of Jesus in the context of other Jewish and pagan figures effecting miraculous healings, the following additional observations and considerations are relevant. A *great number* of healing miracle stories circulated about Jesus as BNP, as was the case with PNPs and MNPs of the Jewish tradition. In the Greco-Roman environment, too, an accumulation of healing miracles are told about Asclepios, Sarapis, and Apollonios of Tyana, but Vespasian, Proclus, Pericles, and other pagan MNPs are not endowed with a *permanent* healing competence. The healing event is a unique occurrence in their biographies. Jesus of Nazareth and Apollonios of Tyana are the only *immanent* BNPs to whom *numerous* healing miracles narratives are attributed, as well as other stories stressing their superhuman natures. In this regard Jesus can best be compared with Apollonios.[123] Apollonios' Vita, however, was written roughly 150 years after the composition of the gospels.[124]

---

[123] Cf. M. Smith, "Prolegomena to a Discussion of Aretalogies, Divine Men, the Gospels and Jesus," in *JBL* 90 (1971), 174–99, esp. 177–79.

[124] I do not think that the question of the relationship between the gospels and Philostratus' Vita Apollonii is solved yet, even though the important contribution of Petzke, *Traditionen*, seems to represent the general consensus, namely that the Vita Apollonii does *not* depend on the gospels. However, especially Vita Apol. IV 20 and 45 seem promising for a new comparison with Mk 5:1–20 and Lk 7:11–17, respectively. A RGL comparison

In comparing Jesus with other miracle story figures of antiquity it appears that he shared the feature of *immanence* with the Jewish PNPs and/or MNPs, while he had the *quality of a BNP* in common with the *transcendent* pagan BNPs who effected miraculous healing either directly as ASs, or as bestowers of miracle provoking competence to ASs or MNPs. Thus Jesus appears to represent an idealtypical ϑεῖος ἀνήρ: he combines both human (immanent) and divine (transcendent BNP) characteristics. Melampous, according to Diodoros of Sicily in a source *prior* to or *contemporary* with the gospels, is the only other *immanent* BNP who effected miraculous healing. It is important to note, however, that only *one* healing miracle is attributed to Melampous. It is interesting that Diodoros presents Melampous as BNP while he was, in the account of Pherecydes from the fifth century B.C.E., originally a PNP who invoked the transcendent BNP Hera to heal the daughters of Proitos.

Hellenistic Jewish sources point in the same direction: the Greco-Roman world around the turn of the eras showed an increasing interest in extraordinary immanent healing figures who incorporated a divine nature. Josephus represents this trend insofar as he presents Jewish healing figures as substitute BNPs (cf. Ant VIII 45–49; IX 182–83). However, he never fails to mention that Yahweh is the ultimate originator of the extraordinary ability of these subjects.[125]

This development is also reflected in the gospels. Q and the Gospel of Matthew, both of whom have a strong Syrian or Palestinian Jewish background, do not emphasize Jesus' role as BNP in miraculous healings. Mark, combining traditions from a Palestinian as well as from a Greco-Roman milieu, often focuses upon the extraordinary, divine abilities of Jesus. The Markan Jesus, in a Greco-Roman environment, must inevitably have been interpreted as the incorporation of a god.[126]

It appears that Luke/Acts presents a challenge to the impression of Jesus as a god wandering among the people. In many instances, Luke enriches the Jesus tradition with material from the OT. Jesus is compared with the OT prophets, even if he exceeds them. He is seldom praised

---

of these traditions based on structural observations which takes types of employed allomotifs for the question of ecotypification into account, might come to new insights; especially if other exorcism and resuscitation stories of antiquity are also considered and compared.

[125] This tension between a figure who, in miracle stories, *appears* to be acting independently from Yahweh, since invocations are lacking, and the BNP Yahweh who is praised as the one who bestowed a MNP with miracle competence, is also manifest in Luke's depiction of Jesus in miracle stories and is explicitly made an issue in Acts 14:8–18 with respect to Paul.

[126] Cf. Acts 14:8–18, where even Paul and Barnabas are believed to be incorporations of gods.

for his miraculous deeds. All the praise is directed towards God, who uses Jesus (as well as the apostles)[127] as a *means*[128] for the accomplishment of universal salvation.

In John the divinity of Jesus, his *unity* with the divine father is stressed. In this case his ability as a supreme BNP is a mere step to the recognition of him as the unique revealer, son of God. In the Fourth Gospel the boundaries of the miracle story have been transcended.

These multiple interpretations reveal the conflicts accompanying the formation of the Christian church from its outset. Christians from different cultural milieus interpreted the phenomenon of Jesus from their respective perspectives. The image of Jesus was shaped according to culturally predetermined conventions, beliefs, and expectations.[129]

---

[127] Acts 5:12; 19:11.

[128] Acts 2:22.

[129] Cf. the observation of D. Georgi in *Opponents*, 171, "The proclamation of the early Church went different ways in spite of its similar material." P.J. Achtemeier, in his excellent contribution "Gospel Miracle Tradition and Divine Man" (*Interpretation* 26 [1972], 174–197), comes to the same conclusions. The only shortcoming of his investigation is that he interprets the portrayal of the apostles in Acts as exemplifications of a divine-man concept. In analyzing the depiction of Jesus and the apostles in the extracanonical literature from the second century, Achtemeier observes that "traditions about Jesus which we find in our canonical Gospels tended not to be embellished. Perhaps, so one can argue, the Gospels already contained adequate evidence of Jesus as divine man, so that the need for embellishment was obviated. *Yet, surely the same could be said for the apostles in the canonical Acts. But whatever the reason*, the desire to portray Christian figures in divine man terms seems, in the period following the development of the canonical tradition, to have been transferred to the apostles" (196; italics are mine). Achtemeier wonders why the canonical apostolic tradition was embellished with miracle stories while the Jesus tradition was not, since *both* were permeated by the divine-man concept of the Hellenistic world already in the first century C.E. The reason is obvious. The apostles in Acts are clearly *not* depicted as BNPs who would qualify as divine men. They are PNPs and MNPs.

VI. General Conclusion and Prospect

The fundamental question in this investigation was, What is the relationship between the NT, specifically synoptic, healing miracle traditions and those of ancient Jewish or pagan provenance? In order to find an answer I analysed the morphological structure of approximately 150 miracle stories from antiquity, including those of the gospels and Acts.

Syntagmatic analysis provided the means for the RGL comparison. This method made possible a fresh look at the various miracle traditions. It made possible an understanding of the composition of miracle narratives, as well as an unambiguous interpretation of previously dubious motifs by repressing preconceived opinions of the investigator. The distinction between emic and etic levels proved to be especially significant for the RGL comparison because this differentiation allowed an identification of *comparable* units.

The first task was to determine the underlying structure of miracle narratives. It was possible to establish a single morphology from numerous examples of the realization of the distinct narrative elements or motifemic slots of miracle stories. This morphology is represented by the four phases of the Narrative Schema (lack, preparedness, performance, and sanction) and is thus shared by non-miracle narratives. The morphology is determined by a move from a lack (of health) to its liquidation through a (miracle) performance by an active subject specifically prepared for the task. What is distinctive of healing miracle stories is the way certain motifemic slots are filled, that is, the difference of miracle stories from narratives with other themes is to be located on the level of motifs: the initial lack belongs to the category of *health* and a bearer of *numinous power* is involved in the narrative development at the phase of the preparedness and/or performance, either directly or through a mediator.

By means of this morphology it was possible to compare the different motifs or ways in which allomotifs could function as fillers of motifemic slots in different traditions. Through this investigation it became evident that, with regard to the *actualization* of the fundamental structure of the miracle story, the narrators' choice of allomotifs was determined, on the one hand, by their intentions and creativity, and, on the other hand, by cultural restraints. The structure of a miracle story is a transcultural and "universally" uniform phenomenon. Re-telling miracle stories often involves a refocalizing process. By focusing on a particular motifeme, the narrator determines the point of a narrative. It could be shown that miracle stories favor "inner-narrative functions"[1] which emphasize either the competence (preparedness) of the bearer of numinous power or the activity of the invoking subjects. It was possible to establish a classification of miracle stories on the basis of *inner-narrative functions* determining the *focus* of a narrative.

It was also found that miracle stories are frequently employed as instrumental narrative programs in the context of other programs which are concerned with the liquidation of a lack unrelated to health. In those cases, the miracle story takes on an additional function, namely the liquidation of the lack in the dominant program which it serves.

Morphological analysis led to a differentiation of the category "miracle-worker" (Wundertäter), which is significant for religionsgeschichtliche comparison. In order to do justice to the ancient material, it became necessary to distinguish between the ways in which the *petitioner*, the *mediator*, and the *bearer* of numinous power function in the various traditions.

The *petitioner of numinous power* (PNP) is a distinct figure who has the extraordinary ability to invoke and activate a transcendent bearer of numinous power (appeal to its *vouloir-faire*) to engage in a healing performance. In so doing, the petitioner of numinous power mediates a request from a subject of circumstance or its representative(s) to a bearer of numinous power who is not generally accessible. By means of this instrumental narrative program the bearer of numinous power is prepared for the performance. This type of mediator is characteristic of Jewish miracle stories and is also presupposed in Acts with regard to Peter and Paul.

The *bearer of numinous power* (BNP) incorporates an extraordinary "miraculous" competence (*pouvoir-* and *savoir-faire*), enabling it either to be the active subject of a healing performance or to prepare a distinct active subject by bestowing it with numinous competence (*pouvoir-* and/or *savoir-faire*) or motivation (*devoir-faire*). Yahweh is the bearer of numinous power in the Jewish tradition, while Asclepios (and others) has the same function in the pagan milieu.

A *mediator of numinous power* (MNP) channels numinous power from the bearer of numinous power to the subject of circumstance. Different allomotifs can describe the specifics of this mediating activity. A bearer

---

[1] This term refers to the focus of a story, presumably identical with the narrator's intention with regard to the function of a distinct miracle story. "Inner-narrative" is used to delineate this particular investigation from others aimed at the identification of a sociological, what I would call "external," function of miracle stories, their "Sitz im Leben."

of numinous power might endow a subject with a miracle competence in the form of a magical helper for a specific healing purpose. In other cases, the mediating activity can consist of the establishment of a physical contact, predominantly through the laying-on-of-hands, which makes possible the flow of healing power from the transcendent bearer through the mediator of numinous power to the subject of circumstance (cf. pre-rabbinic Jewish miracle traditions and especially Acts). Like petitioners of numinous power, these mediators occur in stories with a transcendent bearer of numinous power who does not come in direct contact with the subjects of circumstance. Mediators of numinous power in Jewish traditions from the OT to pre-rabbinic times and in Acts are usually identical with the petitioner of numinous power. Mediators of numinous power in a pagan milieu are generally restricted to the mediating function. They are not at the same time petitioners of numinous power. Here, the transcendent bearers of numinous power typically come into direct contact with human helpers and bestow them with numinous competence for distinct miracle performances.

After an initial lack was created by a NP, which is not necessarily manifest but always presupposed, the further narrative development in a miracle story depends on the *activation* of the bearer of numinous power. The analysis proved that various allomotifs can fill this motifemic slot, which is always presupposed but not always actualized. If the latter is the case, specific activity on the part of the invoking subjects is necessary. Invoking subjects in Christian miracle stories are often characterized by *faith*. Other allomotifs include *sacrifices* or *promises of payment*. At times, especially in a Jewish milieu, the subject of circumstance (SC) or its representative (RSC) cannot approach the bearer of numinous power, Yahweh, directly. Here, the invoking activity is mediated by a subject who is especially prepared to do so: the petitioner of numinous power (PNP), usually a prophet or rabbi. It was found that the apostles in Acts have an identical function. After the ascension of Jesus into heaven, subjects in need of a restoration to health can no longer invoke Jesus, the bearer of numinous power, directly. Thus, the apostles function as mediators of these invocations, as petitioners of numinous powers.

Once the bearer of numinous power is activated, either by itself or through appeals to its *vouloir-faire*, it either engages directly as active subject in the healing performance or, as a variant on the etic level, prepares another subject, a mediator of numinous power (MNP) for this performance by bestowing it with the necessary *pouvoir-* and/or *savoir-faire*. These subjects function either as active subjects themselves, or as mediators of numinous power, they bestow a distinct subject with preparedness to function as active subject. In the case of exorcisms, the anti-subject which caused the initial lack, through the subjection of its will (*devoir-faire*), and not the bearer or mediator of numinous power, becomes the active subject of the miracle performance. In Mk 1:31 parr, fever functions similarly as a subjected AS. The final phase is the sanction of the success of the miracle performance and/or the preparedness of the bearer or mediator of numinous power. The sanction could be either in the form of a verbal expression or of another action, a performance in an instrumental narrative program (iNP), demonstrating the success of the main miracle performance.

The number of motifemes in miracle stories is, strictly speaking, four, identical with the four phases of the Narrative Schema: the initial lack, preparedness, performance, and sanction. However, distinct types of allomotifs which function as variations of the realization of a motifeme can be identified. For example, the motifeme sanction can be actualized by a *demonstration of the liquidation of a lack*, referring back to the miracle performance, or by a verbal sanction of the *preparedness of the bearer* or the *mediator of numinous power*.

It became clear in the investigation that Jesus was generally conceived of as an *immanent* bearer of numinous power, and that in this regard he could best be compared with Apollonios of Tyana; to both figures were also attributed a great number of healing miracle stories. In fact, the two characteristics (being an *immanent bearer* of numinous power and having *more than one* healing miracle story attributed to it) are shared only by Jesus in the gospels and Apollonios in Philostratus' *Vita*. Since Philostratus' *Vita Apollonii* dates from around 220 C.E., it is evident that the description of Jesus in the gospels is distinct from the other extant contemporary traditions of the first century C.E. insofar as the BNPs of those stories are *transcendent* figures. Indeed, we know of only one other case in the entire miracle story tradition of antiquity before Philostratus' *Vita Apollonii* of an immanent bearer of numinous power, and then only in a singular version of his miracle, Melampous according to Diodoros of Sicily. The *immanent* "miracle workers" of Jewish and pagan miracle stories before or from around the turn of the eras are, with this one exception, PNPs and/or MNPs.

In early Christianity miracle stories provided suitable means for depicting, on the one hand, the authority of the redeemer-figure Jesus, and on the other, the attitudes towards him. The activity exemplifying the preparedness of the invoking subjects is especially prevalent in the synoptic miracle tradition, but stories with the focus on the competence of the bearer of numinous power, describing the activity of Jesus, are not absent.

The motif of the *rejection* of the bearer of numinous power in the gospels, *unique* among ancient healing miracle traditions, serves to demonstrate the *controversy* about Jesus in general and the *stubbornness of his opponents* in particular. Within Christian circles the variety of answers to the question concerning the nature of Jesus' miracle-working power comes to expression in the distinct ways in which the gospel writers reshaped the miracle stories. Mark characteristically, but not exclusively, focuses his miracle stories on the extraordinary preparedness of Jesus as BNP. This form of miracle story, typical of a pagan milieu, is rejected by Matthew, whose interest in the *faith* of the invoking subjects determines his refocalizing activity. Luke, while presenting Jesus as a competent BNP, as Mark does, nevertheless stresses Jesus' subordination to God, to whom all praise is directed. In the actual telling of the miracle story in Luke Jesus appears as the bearer of numinous power, but from the perspective of the sanction he is a mediator of numinous power, revealing the influence of a pagan as well as an OT/Jewish milieu. John, in contrast, presents Jesus as an all powerful BNP in constant unity with, and revealer of, God, his father, with whom he shares numinous power. In this gospel, recognition of Jesus as bearer of numinous power becomes differentiated between those who remain at the level of the miracle-working bearer of numinous power, either positively or negatively sanctioning his miracle competence, and those who recognize that Jesus' demonstration of his numinous power points beyond that power to the revelation of him as the revealer, son of God. In that way the miracle stories in the Fourth Gospel become unique examples of stories that are completely subservient to another revelatory program.

This structural method turned out to be an extremely helpful means for religionsgeschichtliche comparison. Further studies call for a reassessment of all the narrative material of the NT from a structural perspective. A first step should be the comparison of healing or restoration miracle narratives with miracle stories with other themes, such as, relieving people who are starving, imprisoned, or in distress at sea. These narratives probably have an identical structure at the emic level to the one identified in the healing miracle stories analyzed in this thesis. A second step could then be the structural comparison with other narrative genres. The identification of inner-narrative function would be of special importance here. Which other genres favor a functional emphasis on the competence of Jesus or on the activity of people who encounter him (cf., e. g., Lk 19:1–10 with its focus on the activity of Zacchaeus)? A final step would have to widen the scope and take into consideration non-narrative genres. What is, for example, the structural relationship between miracle narratives and *psalms* praising Yahweh for rescue out of a situation marked by a need (cf., e. g., Ps 107; Isa 38:9–20; Tobit 13; 11QPs[a] XXIV [Syriac Psalm III])?

With the method developed in this study it should be possible to identify with a high degree of accuracy the *functions* of the various genres in early Christian literature, and thus come to a better understanding of the Jesus tradition, the task which was formulated clearly for the first time by the *form critics*.

Deutsche Zusammenfassung

von „New Testament Miracle Stories in their Religions-Historical Setting: A Religionsgeschichtliche Comparison from a Structural Perspective" (Werner Kahl, Diss., Emory University, Atlanta/GA 1992)

Diese Studie hat zum Ziel, die Struktur und Funktion der neutestamentlichen Wundertraditionen zu analysieren, indem sie in ihrem religionsgeschichtlichen Kontext gewürdigt werden. Der Schwerpunkt liegt auf den Traditionen, die eine wunderbare Wiederherstellung von Gesundheit oder Leben erzählen. Jüdische, heidnische griechisch-römische und christliche Wundertraditionen aus der Antike werden gleichwertig miteinander verglichen, um Gemeinsamkeiten und spezifische Tendenzen festzustellen.

Eine Übersicht der Forschungsgeschichte macht deutlich, daß in neutestamentlichen Studien ein allgemeiner Mangel an methodologischer Klarheit hinsichtlich des Vergleiches solcher Traditionen besteht (vgl. II.). Die in dieser Untersuchung herangezogene Methode der Analyse und des Vergleiches gründet in den strukturalistischen und semiotischen Arbeiten von V. J. Propp, A. Dundes, A. J. Greimas u. a. (vgl. III.). Für die Analyse und den interkulturellen Vergleich antiker Wundererzählungen empfahl sich dringend die Unterscheidung von strukturalen narrativen Einheiten (Motifeme) und ihren Realisationen (Motife, Allomotife). Diese Unterscheidung garantierte auf der einen Seite, daß nur wirklich vergleichbare narrative Einheiten miteinander verglichen wurden. Auf der anderen Seite machte sie es möglich, die Morphologie der Wiederherstellungswundererzählungen zu identifizieren. Dabei zeigte sich, daß allen untersuchten Wundergeschichten eine einzige morphologische Struktur zugrundeliegt – eine Struktur, die im übrigen alle Erzählungen „komödialen Charakters" (Aristoteles), gleich welchen Themas, gemeinsam haben. Die Morphologie dieses Erzähltyps ist bestimmt durch eine Bewegung von einem *Mangel* (in den hier untersuchten Wundererzählungen: von Gesundheit im weitesten Sinn) zu seiner *Überwindung* durch eine (mirakulöse) *Handlung* eines *aktiven Subjekts,* das für diese Aufgabe besonders *vorbereitet* ist. Nach einer Bestandsaufnahme antiker Heilungs- und Totenerweckungswundergeschichten (vgl. IV. 2.) erfolgt eine detaillierte Analyse der hier verwendeten Motife als Realisationen entsprechender Motifeme (vgl. IV. 3.). Aus strukturaler Perspektive konnte eine Definition der Wiederherstellungswundererzählung unternommen werden: Sie zeichnet sich aus durch eine anfängliche Mangelsituation, die durch die Abwesenheit von Gesundheit oder Leben geprägt ist, und durch die Involvierung eines Trägers numinoser Macht in der Phase der Vorbereitetheit und/oder der Handlung (vgl. V. 1.). In bezug auf die Involvierung der numinosen Sphäre war es möglich, den Begriff „Wundertäter" in die unterschiedlichen Funktionen eines *Trägers,* eines *Bittstellers* und eines *Vermittlers* numinoser Macht zu differenzieren (vgl. IV. 3.2.). Dabei ist es nicht zwingend, daß ein Träger numinoser Macht – der eigentliche Wundertäter – auch das aktive Subjekt der Handlung ist, durch welche unmittelbar die Ausgangssituation in ihr Gegenteil verkehrt wird (vgl. IV. 3.3.). Auf dem Hintergrund dieser Ergebnisse wird dann die Tragfähigkeit strukturaler Analyse für den synoptischen Vergleich aufgezeigt, und zwar anhand eines heidnischen und eines christlichen Beispiels (vgl. V. 2.). Dieser Schritt führt zu einer Kriteriendiskussion in bezug auf die Klassifizierung von Wundererzählungen (vgl. V. 3.1.). Das Kriterium „innernarrative Funktion" ermöglichte die Etablierung zweier unterschiedlicher Typen, mit dem Fokus entweder auf der Vorbereitetheit des Trägers numinoser Macht oder auf der Aktivität um Hilfe flehender Subjekte (vgl. V. 3.2. und 3.3.). Darüber hinaus wurde ersichtlich, daß Wundergeschichten in übergeordnete, nicht-mirakulöse Erzählungen inkorporiert werden können, was in einer Refokussierung der ursprünglichen Wundergeschichte resultieren kann (vgl. V. 3.4.). In bezug auf die Realisation der fundamentalen Struktur der Wundergeschichten zeigte sich, daß die Auswahl von Allomotifen durch die Erzähler zum einen durch eigene Intention und Kreativität und zum anderen durch kulturelle Beschränkungen bestimmt ist (vgl. V. 4.). Der Vergleich eines breiten Spektrums von überlieferten Wundererzählungen aus der Zeit bis zum Ende des ersten Jahrhunderts führte zur Identifizierung von charakteristischen Merkmalen eines jeden Evangelisten in bezug auf die jeweilige Bearbeitung des von ihm übernommenen Wunderstoffes (vgl. V. 4.3.). Die Verschiedenartigkeit, in der sie dieses Material bearbeiteten und umformten, reflektiert die unterschiedlichen theologischen Konzeptionen eines jeden Evangelisten. Außerdem war es möglich, Ökotypen jüdischer und heidnischer griechisch-römischer Milieus auszumachen (vgl. V. 4.1. und 2.). Abschließende Beobachtungen sind dem ϑεῖος-ἀνήρ-Problem gewidmet. Hier wird die Funktion Jesu explizit mit der anderer antiker Wundertäter verglichen (vgl. V. 4.3.7.).

Nachdem sich herausgestellt hat, daß die Kategorie „Wundererzählung" eine zweifelhafte Klassifikation ist, wird in den Schlußfolgerungen eine strukturale Analyse des gesamten narrativen Materials im NT vorgeschlagen (vgl. VI.). Diese an *Funktionen* von Handlungen und Erzähleinheiten orientierte Analyse würde eine Reklassifikation dieses Materials zur Folge haben, die vorschnelle thematische Trennung vermeidet und die Intentionen der Erzähler erhellt.

VII. Bibliography

A. *Editions of Ancient Texts*

Behr, C.A. (ed.), *P. Aelius Aristides. The Complete Works. Vol. II. Orationes XVII–LIII.* Leiden: E.J. Brill, 1981.

Berger, K. (ed.), *Das Buch der Jubiläen.* JSHRZ II/3. Gütersloh: Verlagshaus G. Mohn, 1981.

– and C. Colpe (eds.), *Religionsgeschichtliches Textbuch zum Neuen Testament.* NTD Textreihe, vol. I. Göttingen: Vandenhoeck & Ruprecht, 1987.

Beyer, K. (ed.), *Die aramäischen Texte vom Toten Meer samt den Inschriften aus Palästina, dem Testament Levis aus der Kairoer Genisa, der Fastenrolle und den alten talmudischen Zitaten. Aramaistische Einleitung, Text, Übersetzung, Deutung, Grammatik/Wörterbuch, Deutsch-aramäische Wortliste, Register.* Göttingen: Vandenhoeck & Ruprecht, 1984.

Blunt, A.W.F. (ed.), *Justin Martyr. Apologies.* Cambridge: University Press, 1911.

Brooke, A.E., N. McLean and H.St.J. Thackeray (eds.), *The Old Testament in Greek.* Vol. II/II: 1 & 2 Kings. Cambridge: At the University Press, 1930.

Cary, E. (ed.), *Dio Cassius. Roman History.* LCL. London: W. Heinemann, 1925.

Charlesworth, J.H. (ed.), *The Old Testament Pseudepigrapha.* Vol. I/II. Garden City, NY: Doubleday & Company, Inc., 1983/1985.

Cohn, L., et al. (eds.), *Philo von Alexandria. Die Werke in deutscher Übersetzung.* Vol. I–VII. Berlin: W. de Gruyter & Co., ²1962.

Conybeare, F.C. (ed.), *Philostratus. The Life of Apollonius of Tyana.* Vol. I/II. LCL. London: W. Heinemann, 1912.

Diels, H. (ed.), *Die Fragmente der Vorsokratiker.* Berlin: Weidmannsche, ⁷1954.

Dietzfelbinger, C. (ed.), *Pseudo-Philo: Antiquitates Biblicae.* JSHRZ II/2. Gütersloh: Verlagshaus G. Mohn, 1979.

Dindorf, W. (ed.), *Aristides.* Vol. I. Hildesheim: G. Olms Verlagsbuchhandlung, 1964.

Dittenberger, W. (ed.), *Sylloge Inscriptionum Graecarum.* Leipzig: Hirzel, 1920.

Dupont-Roc, R. and J. Lallot (eds.), *Aristote. La poétique. Le texte grec avec une traduction et des notes de lecture.* Paris: Eadition du Seuil, 1980.

Edelstein, E.J. and L. (eds.), *Asclepius. A Collection and Interpretation of the Testimonies.* Vol. I. New York, NY: Arno Press, 1975 (orig.: 1945).

Elliger, K. and W. Rudolph (eds.), *Biblia Hebraica Stuttgartensia.* Stuttgart: Deutsche Bibelgesellschaft, 1983.

Epstein, I. (ed.), *The Babylonian Talmud.* London: Socino Press, 1935–1948.

Fagles, R. (ed.), *Homer. The Iliad.* New York, NY: Viking Penguin, 1990.

Fiebig, P. (ed.), *Rabbinische Wundergeschichten des neutestamentlichen Zeitalters in vokalisiertem Text.* Kleine Texte für Vorlesungen und Übungen 78. Bonn: A. Marcus und E. Webers Verlag, 1911.

- *Antike Wundertexte zum Studium der Wunder des Neuen Testamentes.* Kleine Texte für Vorlesungen und Übungen 79. Bonn: A. Marcus und E. Webers Verlag, 1911 [= G. Delling, *Antike Wundertexte*, Berlin: W. de Gruyter & Co., ²1960].

Fitzmyer, J.A. and D.J. Harrington (eds.), *A Manual of Palestinian Aramaic Texts (Second Century B. C. – Second Century A. D.).* Rome: Biblical Institute Press, 1978.

Foster, B.O. (ed.), *Livy. From the Founding of the City.* LCL. London: W. Heinemann, 1919.

Frazer, J.G. (ed.), *Apollodorus. The Library.* Vol. I/II. LCL. London: W. Heinemann, 1921.

Greenfell, B.P. and A.S. Hunt (eds.), *The Oxyrhynchus Papyri.* Part XI. London: Oxford University Press, 1915.

Greeven, H. (ed.), *Synopse der drei ersten Evangelien mit Beigabe der johanneischen Parallelstellen.* Tübingen: J.C.B. Mohr (P. Siebeck), ¹³1981.

Guarducci, M. (ed.), *Inscriptiones Creticae.* Roma: Libreria dello Stato, 1935–1942.

Hanson, J.A. (ed.), *Apuleius. Metamorphoses.* Vol. I/II. LCL London: W. Heinemann, 1989.

Harmon, A.M. (ed.), *Lucian. The Lover of Lies.* LCL. London: W. Heinemann, 1921.
- *Lucian. Alexander the False Prophet.* LCL. London: W. Heinemann, 1925.

Herzog ,R. (ed.), *Die Wunderheilungen von Epidauros. Ein Beitrag zur Geschichte der Medizin und der Religion.* Philologus, Supplementband XXII, H. III. Leipzig: Dieterich'sche Verlagsbuchhandlung, 1931.

Holladay, C.R. (ed.), *Fragments from Hellenistic Jewish Authors.* Vol. 1: Historians. SBL Texts and Translations Pseudepigrapha Series. Chico, CA: Scholars Press, 1983.

Jacoby, F. (ed.), *Die Fragmente der griechischen Historiker.* Berlin: Weidmann, 1923–1958.

Jones,W.H.S. (ed.), *Pausanias. Description of Greece. Books VIII–X.* Vol. IV. LCL. London: W. Heinemann, 1935.

Le Bonnieg, H. (ed.), *Arnobe. Contre Les Gentils.* Vol. I. Paris: Société d'édition 'Les belles Lettres,' 1982.

Lohse, E. (ed.), *Die Texte aus Qumran. Hebräisch und Deutsch.* Darmstadt: Wissenschaftliche Buchgesellschaft, ⁴1986.

Luck, G. (ed.), *Arcana Mundi. Magic and the Occult in the Greek and Roman Worlds. A Collection of Ancient Texts, translated, annotated, and introduced.* Baltimore and London: The John Hopkins University Press, 1985.

Maehler, H. (ed.), *Die Lieder des Bakchylides. Erster Teil. Die Siegeslieder; I. Edition des Textes mit Einleitung und Übersetzung.* Leiden: E.J. Brill, 1982.

Martin, F. (ed.), *Narrative Parallels to the New Testament.* SBL Recources for Biblical Study 22. Atlanta: Scholars Press, 1988.

Moore, C.H. (ed.), *Tacitus. History.* LCL. London: W. Heinemann, 1925.

Muehll, P. von der (ed.), *Homeri Odyssea.* Stuttgart: Teubner 1984 (³1962).

Murray, A.T. (ed.), *Homer. The Iliad.* LCL. London: W. Heinemann, 1924–1925.

Nestle, Eb. and Er., K. Aland, et al. (eds.), *Novum Testamentum Graece.* Stuttgart: Deutsche Bibelstiftung, ²⁶1979.

Oldfather, C. H. and C. B. Welles (eds.), *Diodorus of Sicily. Library of History*. LCL. London: W. Heinemann, 1933–1963.

Colson, F. H., G. H. Whitaker and J. W. Earp, (eds.), *Philo*. Vol. I–X. LCL. London: W. Heinemann, 1929–1962.

Perrin, B. (ed.), *Plutarch. Life of Pericles*. LCL. London: W. Heinemann, 1916.

Preisendanz, K. (ed.), *Papyri Graecae Magicae. Die Griechischen Zauberpapyri*. Stuttgart: Verlag B. G. Teubner, ²1974.

Pritchard, J. B. (ed.), *Ancient Near Eastern Texts Relating to the Old Testament*. Princeton, NJ: Princeton University Press, ³1969.

Rahlfs, A. (ed.), *Septuaginta*. Stuttgart: Deutsche Bibelgesellschaft, 1935/1979.

Rogers, B. B. (ed.), *Aristophanes. Plutus, et al*. Vol. III. LCL. London: W. Heinemann, 1924.

Rolfe, J. C. (ed.), *Suetonius. Vespasian*. LCL. London: W. Heinemann, 1914.

Sandys, J. (ed.), *The Odes of Pindar Including the Principal Fragments*. LCL. Cambridge, Massachusetts: Harvard University Press, 1989.

Scholfield, A. F. (ed.), *Aelian. On the Characteristics of Animals*. LCL. London: W. Heinemann, 1959.

Sullivan, J. P., *Petronius. The Satyricon and Seneca. The Apocolocyntosis* (translated with introductions and notes). London: Penguin Books, 1986.

Thackeray, H. St. J., et al. (eds.), *Josephus. Jewish Antiquities. Books I–XX*. Vol. IV–IX. LCL. London: W. Heinemann, 1930–1965.

– *Josephus. The Jewish War. Books I–VII*. Vol. II/III. LCL. London: W. Heinemann, 1926.

Walter, N. (ed.), *Fragmente jüdisch-hellenistischer Historiker*. JSHRZ I,2. Gütersloh: Verlagshaus G. Mohn, 1980.

– *Fragmente jüdisch-hellenistischer Exegeten: Aristobulos, Demetrios, Aristeas*. JSHRZ III,2, 257–99. Gütersloh: Verlagshaus G. Mohn, 1980.

Weber, R. et al. (eds.), *Biblia Sacra. Iuxta Vulgatam Versionem*. Vol. I/II. Stuttgart, Württembergische Bibelanstalten, 1969.

Wettstein, J. (ed.), *Novum Testamentum Graecum*. Vol. I/II. Graz: Akademische Druck- u. Verlagsanstalt, 1962.

Wevers, J. W. (ed.), *Septuaginta. Vetus Testamentum Graecum. Vol. I. Genesis*. Göttingen: Vandenhoeck & Ruprecht, 1974.

– and U. Quast, *Septuaginta. Vetus Testamentum Graecum. Vol. III,1. Numeri*. Göttingen: Vandenhoeck & Ruprecht, 1981.

Zahavy, T. and A. Avery-Peck (eds.), tractate "Berakhot", in J. Neusner, *The Mishna. A New Translation*. New Haven: Yale University Press, 1988.

Ziegler, J. (ed.), *Septuaginta. Vetus Testamentum Graecum. Vol. XIV. Isaias*. Göttingen: Vandenhoeck & Ruprecht, ²1967.

B. *Dictionaries, Concordances, and Grammars*

Bauer, H. and P. Leander, *Kurzgefasste Biblisch-Aramäische Grammatik. Mit Texten und Glossar*. Halle/Saale: Max Niemeyer, 1929.

Bauer, W., *Griechisch-deutsches Wörterbuch zu den Schriften des Neuen Testaments und der frühchristlichen Literatur*. Ed. by K. und B. Aland. Berlin/New York: W. de Gruyter, ⁶1988.

Blass, F., A. Debrunner and F. Rehkopf, *Grammatik des neutestamentlichen Griechisch.* Göttingen: Vandenhoeck & Ruprecht, [16]1984.

Bornemann, E., *Griechische Grammatik.* Frankfurt am Main, et al.: Verlag Moritz Diesterweg, [2]1978.

Gesenius, W., *Hebrew Grammar.* Ed. by E. Kautzsch and A. E. Cowley. Oxford: University Printing House, [2]1910 (= German orig. [28]1909).

- *Hebräisches und Aramäisches Handwörterbuch über das Alte Testament.* Ed. by F. Buhl. Berlin: Springer Verlag, [17]1915. 1. Lieferung, ed. by R. Meyer and H. Donner. Berlin: Springer Verlag, [18]1987.

Hatch, E. and H.A. Redpath, *A Concordance to the Septuagint and the other Greek Versions of the Old Testament (including the apocryphal books).* Vol. I-III. Grand Rapids,Michigan: Baker Book House, 1983.

Institut für Neutestamentliche Textforschung etc., *Konkordanz zum Novum Testamentum Graece von Nestle-Aland, 26. Auflage und zum Greek New Testament, 3rd. edition.* Berlin/New York: W. de Gruyter, [3]1987.

Jastrow, M, *A Dictionary of the Targumim, the Talmud Babli and Yerushalmi, and the Midrashic Literature.* New York: The Judaica Press, 1989.

Jennings, W. and U. Gantillon, *Lexicon to the Syriac New Testament.* Oxford: At the Clarendon Press, 1926 (1962).

Koehler, L., and W. Baumgartner, et al., *Hebräisches und Aramäisches Lexikon zum Alten Testament*, Vol. I-IV. Leiden: E.J. Brill, [3]1967-1990.

Levy, J., *Wörterbuch über die Talmudim und Midraschim.* Vol. I-IV. Berlin/Wien: Benjamin Harz Verlag, 1924.

Liddell, H.G., and R. Scott, *A Greek-English Lexicon.* Vol. I/II. London: Oxford University Press, [9]1940.

Lisowsky, G., *Konkordanz zum Hebräischen Alten Testament.* Stuttgart: Deutsche Bibelgesellschaft, [2]1981.

Margolis, M.L., *Lehrbuch der Aramäischen Sprache des Babylonischen Talmuds. Grammatik, Chrestomatie und Wörterbuch.* München: C.H. Beck'sche Verlagsbuchhandlung, 1910.

Rosenthal, F., *A Grammar of Biblical Aramaic.* Porta Linguarum Orientalium, Neue Serie V. Wiesbaden: Otto Harrassowitz, 1961.

Stowasser, J.M., *Der kleine Stowasser. Lateinisch-deutsches Schulwörterbuch.* München: G. Freytag Verlag, 1979.

C. *Secondary Literature*

Achtemeier, P.J., "Toward the Isolation of Pre-Markan Miracle Catenae," *JBL* 89 (1970), 265-91.

- "The Origin and Function of the Pre-Marcan Miracle Catenae," *JBL* 91 (1972), 198-221.

- "Gospel Miracle Tradition and Divine Man," *Int* 26 (1972), 174-97.

- "The Lucan Perspective on the Miracles of Jesus: A Preliminary Sketch," *JBL* 94 (1975), 547-62.

- "An Imperfect Union: Reflections on Gerd Theissen, *Urchristliche Wundererzählungen*," *Semeia* 11 (1978), 49-68.

Ackroyd, P., "ד, II-V," *ThWAT* 3 (1982), 425–55.

Almqvist, H. *Plutarch und das Neue Testament. Ein Beitrag zum Corpus Hellenisticum Novi Testamenti.* Uppsala: Appelbergs Boktryckeri, 1946.

Alt, A., *"Galiläische Probleme,"* idem, *Kleine Schriften zur Geschichte des Volkes Israel.* Vol. 2. München: C.H. Beck'sche Verlagsbuchhandlung, 1953 (orig. 1937–1940), 363–435.

– "Die Stätten des Wirkens Jesu in Galiläa territorialgeschichtlich betrachtet," idem, *Kleine Schriften.* Vol. 2 (orig. 1949), 436–55.

Annen, F., "Die Dämonenaustreibungen Jesu in den synoptischen Evangelien," *Theol. Berichte* 5 (1976), 107–46.

Aune, D.E., "Magic in early Christianity," *ANRW* 2, 23, 2 (1980), 1507–57.

– *Prophecy in Early Christianity and the Ancient Mediterranean World.* Grand Rapids, Michigan: William B. Eerdmans Publishing Company, 1983.

Bailey, J.L. and L.D. Vander Broek, *Literary Forms in the New Testament. A Handbook.* Louisville, Kentucky: Westminster/John Knox Press, 1992.

Ballard, L.-M., "The Formulation of the Oicotype: A Case Study," *Fabula* 24 (1983), 233–45.

Bammel, E., "John did no Miracle," C.F.G. Moule, (ed.), *Miracles,* 179–202.

Barthes, R., "Introduction à l'analyse structurale des récits," *Communications* 8 (1966), 1–27.

Bartlett, D.L., *"Exorcism Stories in the Gospel of Mark."* Ph.D. diss., Yale University, 1972.

Barton, G.A., "The Origin of the Names of Angels and Demons in the Extra-Canonical Apocalyptic Literature to 100 A.D.," *JBL* 31 (1912), 156–67.

Bauernfeind, O. *Die Worte des Dämonen im Markusevangelium.* Stuttgart: Verlag von W. Kohlhammer, 1927.

Baumgarten, A.I., "Miracles and Halakah in Rabbinic Judaism," *JQR* 73 (1983), 238–53.

Baumgärtel, F., "πνεῦμα, etc. B. Geist im Alten Testament," *ThWNT* 6 (1956), 357–66.

Baur, F.Ch., *Apollonius von Tyana und Christus. Ein Beitrag zur Religionsgeschichte der ersten Jahrhunderte nach Christus.* Hildesheim: Georg Olms Verlagsbuchhandlung, 1966.

Beaugrande, R.-A. de, Dressler, W.V., *Einführung in die Textlinguistik.* Konzepte der Sprach- und Literaturwissenschaft 28. Tübingen: Max Niemeyer Verlag, 1981.

Becker, J., "Wunder und Christologie. Zum literarkritischen und christologischen Problem der Wunder im Johannesevangelium," *NTSt* 16 (1970), 130–48.

Behm, J., *Die Handauflegung im Urchristentum. Nach Verwendung, Herkunft und Bedeutung in religionsgeschichtlichem Zusammenhang untersucht.* Darmstadt: Wissenschaftliche Buchgesellschaft, 1968 (orig. 1911).

Ben-Amos, D., *"Narrative Forms in the Haggadah: Structural Analysis".* Ph.D. diss., Indiana University, 1967.

Beneš, B. "Zur Frage der morphologischen Analyse der Volksprosa. Versuch eines Projektes," *Fabula* 31 (1990), 33–48.

Berger, K., "Die königlichen Messiastraditionen des Neuen Testaments," *NTSt* 20 (1973), 1–44.

- *Exegese des Neuen Testaments. Neue Wege vom Text zur Auslegung.* Heidelberg: Quelle & Meyer, 1977.
- *Formgeschichte des Neuen Testaments.* Heidelberg: Quelle & Meyer, 1984.
- "Hellenistische Gattungen im Neuen Testament," *ANRW* 2,25,2 (1984), 1031–432.

Betz, H. D., *Lukian von Samosata und das Neue Testament. Religionsgeschichtliche und paränetische Parallelen. Ein Beitrag zum Corpus Hellenisticum Novi Testamenti.* Berlin: Akademie-Verlag, 1961.
- "The Early Christian Miracle Story: Some Observations on the Form Critical Problem," *Semeia* 11 (1978), 69–81.
- "Gottmensch II (Griechisch-römische Antike u. Urchristentum)," *RAC* 12 (1983), 234–312.

Betz, O., "The concept of the So-called 'Divine Man' in Mark's Christology," D. E. Aune (ed.), *Studies in New Testament and Early Christian Literature. Essays in Honor of Allen P. Wikgren*, NovTSup 33 (1972). Leiden: E. J. Brill, 1972, 229–40.
- "Das Problem des Wunders bei Flavius Josephus im Vergleich zum Wunderproblem bei den Rabbinen und im Johannesevangelium," O. Betz (ed.), *Josephus-Studien.* FS für O. Michel. Göttingen: Vandenhoeck & Ruprecht, 1974, 23–44.
- and W. Grimm, *Wesen und Wirklichkeit der Wunder Jesu. Heilungen-Rettungen-Zeichen-Aufleuchtungen.* ANTI 2. Frankfurt am Main: Peter Lang GmbH, 1977.
- "Heilung/Heilungen I.," *TRE* 14 (1985), 764–68.

Bieler, L., "Totenerweckung durch Συνανάχρωσις. Ein mittelalterlicher Legendentypus und das Wunder des Elisa," *ARW* 32 (1935), 228–45.
- ΘΕΙΟΣ ΑΝΗΡ. *Das Bild des "göttlichen Menschen" in Spätantike und Frühchristentum.* Vol. I/II. Darmstadt: Wissenschaftliche Buchgesellschaft, 1976.

Bietenhard, H., "ὄνομα etc.," *ThWNT* 5 (1954), 242–283.

Billerbeck, P., (and H. L. Strack), *Kommentar zum Neuen Testament aus Talmud und Midrasch, Vol. 4: Exkurse zu einzelnen Stellen des Neuen Testamentes.* Abhandlungen zur neutestamentlichen Theologie und Archäologie. München: C. H. Beck'sche Verlagsbuchhandlung, 1928.

Bittner, J. B., *Jesu Zeichen im Johannesevangelium. Die Messiaserkenntnis im Johannesevangelium vor ihrem jüdischen Hintergrund.* WUNT 2/26. Tübingen: J. C. B. Mohr (Paul Siebeck), 1987.

Blackburn, B. L., "Miracle Working ΘΕΙΟΙ ΑΝΔΡΕΣ in Hellenism (and Hellenistic Judaism)," D. Wenham and C. Blomberg (eds.), *The Miracles of Jesus.* Gospel Perspectives 6. Sheffield, England 1986, 185–218.
- *Theios Anēr and the Markan Miracle traditions. A critique of the Theios Anēr Concept as an Interpretative Background of the Miracle Traditions Used in Mark.* WUNT 2/40. Tübingen: J. C. B. Mohr (Paul Siebeck), 1991.

Blumenthal, M., *Formen und Motive in den apokryphen Apostelgeschichten.* Leipzig: Hinrichs'sche Buchhandlung, 1933.

Böcher, O, *Dämonenfurcht und Dämonenabwehr. Ein Beitrag zur Vorgeschichte der christlichen Taufe.* BWANT. 5. Folge, Heft 10. Stuttgart, etc: Verlag W. Kohlhammer, 1970.

- *Christus Exorcistica. Dämonismus und Taufe im Neuen Testament.* BWANT. 5. Folge, Heft 16. Stuttgart, etc.: Verlag W. Kohlhammer, 1972.
- *Das Neue Testament und die dämonischen Mächte.* Stuttgarter Bibelstudien 58. Stuttgart: KBW Verlag, 1972.

Boers, H., "Sisyphus and His Rock, Concerning Gerd Theissen, *Urchristliche Wundererzählungen,*" *Semeia* 11 (1978), 1–48.
- *What is New Testament Theology? The Rise of Criticism and the Problem of a Theology of the New Testament.* Guides to Biblical Scholarship, New Testament Series. Philadelphia, PA: Fortress Press, 1979.
- *Neither on This Mountain Nor in Jerusalem. A Study of John 4.* SBL Monograph Series 35. Atlanta,GA: Scholars Press, 1988.

Bokser, M. M., "Wonder-Working and the Rabbinic Tradition: The Case of Hanina ben Dosa," *JStJ* XVI (1985), 42–92.

Bonner, C., "Traces of Thaumaturgic Technique in the Miracles," *HTR* 20 (1927), 171–81.
- "The Technique of Exorcism," *HTR* 36 (1943), 39–49.
- "The Violence of Departing Demons," *HTR* 37 (1944), 334–36.

Bousset, W., *Kyrios Christos. Geschichte des Christusglaubens von den Anfängen des Christentums bis Irenäus.* Göttingen: Vandenhoeck & Ruprecht, 1913. ²1926.

Braun, H., "Zur Terminologie der Acta von der Auferstehung Jesu," *ThLZ* 77 (1952), 533–36.

Bremond, C., "Le message narratif," *Communications* 4 (1964), 4–32.
- "La logique des possibles narratifs," *Communications* 8 (1966), 60–76.
- "Postérité américaine de Propp," *Communications* 11 (1968), 148–64.
- "The Morphology of the French Fairy Tale: The Ethical Modal," H. Jason and D. Segal (eds.), *Patterns in Oral Literature.* The Hague/Chicago: Mouton/Aldine, 1977, 49–76.

Breymayer, R., "Vladimir Jakovlevič Propp (1895–1970) – Leben, Wirken und Bedeutung," *Ling Bibl* 15/16 (1972), 36–66.

Broadhead, E. K., „The Role of *Wundergeschichten* in the Characterization of Jesus in the Gospel of Mark." Ph. D. diss., Southern Baptist Theological Seminary, 1987.

Bultmann, R., *Die Geschichte der synoptischen Tradition.* FRLANT, N. F. 12. Göttingen: Vandenhoeck & Ruprecht, 1921. ⁹1979.
- *Ergänzungsheft.* Göttingen: Vandenhoeck & Ruprecht, 1958. ⁵1979 is prepared by G. Theißen and Ph. Vielhauer.
- *Das Urchristentum im Rahmen der antiken Religionen.* Zürich/Stuttgart: Artemis-Verlag, ²1954.
- and A. Weiser, "πιστεύω, etc.," *ThWNT* 6 (1959), 174–230.
- *The Gospel of John. A Commentary.* Philadelphia, PA: Westminster Press, 1971.

Burkill, T. A., "The Notion of Miracle with Special Reference to St. Mark's Gospel," *ZNW* 50 (1951), 33–48.
- "Mark 3, 7–12 and the Alleged Dualism in the Evangelist's Miracle Material," *JBL* 87 (1968), 409–17.

Busse, O., *Die Wunder des Propheten Jesus. Die Rezeption, Komposition und In-*

terpretation der Wundertratitionen im Evangelium des Lukas. FzB 24. Stuttgart: Katholisches Bibelwerk 1977.

CADIR, "Abraham et Abimelek. Genèse 20," *SB* 4 (1976), 24–38; 5 (1976), 7–28.

– "Récits de Miracles et Récit Évangélique. Remarques de grammaires narratives," *SB* 10 (1978), 27–44.

Calloud, J., *Structural Analysis of Narrative.* Philadelphia: Fortress Press 1976 (French orig. 1973).

–, G. Combet, and J. Delorme, "Essai d'Analyse Sémiotique," Leon-Dufour, X. (ed.), *Les Miracles*, 151–81.

Caquot, A., "גער" *ThWAT* 2 (1977), 51–56.

Carrez, M., "L'Héritage de l'Ancien Testament," Léon-Dufour (ed.), *Les Miracles*, 45–58.

Charlesworth, J. H., *The Pseudepigrapha and Modern Research with a Supplement.* SCST 7. Ann Arbor, Michigan: Edwards Brothers Inc., 1981.

Chu, S. W.-W., "The Healing of the Epileptic Boy in Mark 9:14–29: Its Rhetorical Structure and Theological Implications." Ph. D. diss., Vanderbilt University, 1988.

Clavier, H., "Wunder," *BHH* 3 (1966), 2188–91.

Cochrane, T., "The Concept of Ecotypes in American Folklore," *JFR* 24 (1987), 33–55.

Colby, B. N., "On the Scientific Study of Folktales," *Fabula* 30 (1989), 230–33.

Colpe, C., *Die religionsgeschichtliche Schule. Darstllung und Kritik ihres Bildes vom gnostischen Erlösermythus.* FRLANT, N. F. 60. Göttingen: Vandenhoeck & Ruprecht, 1961.

– "Synkretismus," *Der kleine Pauly 5 (1979), 1648–52.*

Coppens, J., *L'imposition des mains et rites connexes dans le Nouveau Testament et dans l'Église ancienne. Étude de théologie positive.* Paris: J. Gabalda, 1925.

Corrington, G. P., *The "Divine Man." Its Origin and Function in Hellenistic Popular Religion.* American University Studies 7, 17. New York,: Peter Lang 1986.

Courtés, J. "Motif et type dans la tradition folklorique: Problèmes de typologie," *Littérature* 45 (1982), 114–27.

Culley, R. C., *Studies in the Structure of Hebrew Narrative.* Semeia Supplements. Philadelphia, PA: Fortress Press, 1976.

Daube, D., "The Laying on of Hands," idem, *The New Testament and Rabbinic Judaism.* London: The Athlone Press, 1956, 224–49.

Deissmann, A., *Licht vom Osten. Das Neue Testament und die neuentdeckten Texte der hellenistisch-römischen Zeit.* Tübingen: J. C. B. Mohr (P. Siebeck), 1908. 2/31909.

Delling, G., *Jesu Wunder in der Predigt.* Dresden/Leipzig: Verlag C. L. Ungelenk, 1940.

– *"Zur Beurteilung des Wunders durch die Antike," idem, Studien*, 53–71.

– "Das Verständnis des Wunders im Neuen Testament," idem, *Studien*, 146–59.

– "Wunder-Allegorie-Mythus bei Philon von Alexandreia," idem, *Studien*, 72–129.

– "Josephus und das Wunderbare," idem, *Studien*, 130–45.

– "Botschaft und Wunder im Wirken Jesu," H. Ristow and K. Matthiae (eds.),

Der historische Jesus und der kerygmatische Christus. Beiträge zum Christusver-ständnis in Forschung und Verkündigung. Berlin: Evangelische Verlagsanstalt, ³1964, 389-402.

- *Studien zum Neuen Testament und zum hellenistischen Judentum. Gesammelte Aufsätze 1950-1968.* Ed. by F. Hahn, T. Holtz and N. Walter. Göttingen: Vandenhoeck & Ruprecht, 1970.

Delorme, J., "Jésus et l'hémorroisse ou le choc de la rencontre (Marc 5, 25-34)," *SB* 44 (1986), 1-17.

Deselaers, P., *Das Buch Tobit. Studien zu seiner Entstehung, Komposition und Theologie.* OBO 43. Göttingen: Vandenhoeck & Ruprecht, 1982.

Dibelius, M., *Die Formgeschichte des Evangeliums.* Tübingen: J. C. B. Mohr (P. Siebeck), 1919. ²1933. ⁶1971.

- "Stilkritisches zur Apostelgeschichte," H. Schmidt (ed.), *Eucharisterion für H. Gunkel.* FRLANT 19. Göttingen: Vandenhoeck & Ruprecht, 1923, vol. 2, 27-49.

- "Zur Formgeschichte der Evangelien," *ThR* N.F. 1 (1929), 185-216.

- "Wunder: III. Im NT," *RGG* 5 (²1931), 2040-43.

- and P. Fiebig, "Rabbinische und evangelische Erzählungen. Eine Diskussion," *ThB* 11 (1932), 1-12.

Dijk, T. A. van, *Some Aspects of Text Grammars. A Study in Theoretical Linguistics and Poetics.* The Hague: Mouton, 1972.

Dörrie, H., "Marinos (Μαρῖνος)," *Der kleine Pauly* 3 (1979), 1026-27.

Duling, D. C., "Solomon, Exorcism, and the Son of David," *HTR* 68 (1975), 235-52.

Dundes, A., "From Etic to Emic Units in the Structural Study of Folktales," *JAF* 75 (1962), 95-105.

- "Texture, Text, and Context," *SFQ* 28 (1964), 251-65.

- *The Morphology of North American Indian Folktales.* FF Communications 195. Helsinki: Academia Scientiarum Fennica, 1964.

- "Structural Typology in North American Indian Folktales," idem (ed.), *The Study of Folklore.* Eaglewood Cliffs, NJ: Prentice-Hall, Inc., 1965.

- "The Anthropologist and the Comparative Method in Folklore," idem (ed.), *Folklore Matters.* Knoxville, TN: University of Tennessee, 1989, 57-82.

Dupont-Sommer, A., "Exorzismes et Guérisons dans les écrits de Qomran," *SVT* 7 (1960), 246-65.

Edelstein, E. J. and L., *Asclepius. A Collection and Interpretation of the Testimonies.* Vol. II. New York: Arno Press, 1975 (orig.: 1945).

Eißfeldt, O., *Einleitung in das Alte Testament.* Tübingen: J. C. B. Mohr (P. Siebeck), ⁴1977.

Eitrem, S., "La magie comme motif littéraire chez les grecs et les romains," *Symbolae Osloenses* 21 (1941), 39-83.

Esser, D., *"Formgeschichtliche Studien zur hellenistischen und zur frühchristlichen Literatur unter besonderer Berücksichtigung der vita Apollonii des Philostrat und der Evangelien."* Inaugural Dissertation, Bonn, 1969.

Fascher, E., *Die formgeschichtliche Methode. Eine Darstellung und Kritik. Zugleich ein Beitrag zur Geschichte des synoptischen Problems.* BZNW 2. Gießen: A. Töpelmann, 1924.

Fenner, F. *Die Krankheit im Neuen Testament. Eine religions- und medizinge-schichtliche Untersuchung.* Leipzig: J. C. Hinrichs'sche Buchhandlung, 1930.

Fiebig, P., *Aufgaben der neutestamentlichen Forschung in der Gegenwart.* Leipzig: Hinrichs'sche Buchhandlung, 1909.

- *Jüdische Wundergeschichten des neutestamentlichen Zeitalters unter besonderer Be-rücksichtigung ihres Verhältnisses zum Neuen Testament bearbeitet. Ein Beitrag zum Streit um die "Christusmythe."* Tübingen: J. C. B. Mohr [P. Siebeck], 1911.

- "Die Wunder Jesu und die Wunder der Rabbinen," *ZWTh* 54 (1912), 158–79.

- *Der Erzählungsstil der Evangelien im Lichte des rabbinischen Erzählungsstils un-tersucht, zugleich ein Beitrag zum Streit um die "Christusmythe."* Leipzig: Hin-richs'sche Buchhandlung, 1925.

- *Die Umwelt des Neuen Testamentes. Religionsgeschichtliche und geschichtliche Texte, in deutscher Übersetzung und mit Anmerkungen versehen, zum Verständnis des Neuen Testamentes.* Göttingen: Vandenhoeck & Ruprecht, 1926.

- *Rabbinische Formgeschichte und Geschichtlichkeit Jesu.* Leipzig: Hinrichs'sche Buchhandlung, 1931.

- "Wunder: II B. Im Judentum," *RGG* 5 ([2]1931), 2040.

- "Der Erzählungsstil der Evangelien," ΑΓΓΕΛΟΣ. *Archiv für Neutestamentliche Zeitgeschichte und Kulturkunde* 2 (1926), 39–43.

- Book review: "O. Perels, Die Wunderüberlieferung der Synoptiker in ihrem Verhältnis zur Wortüberlieferung," *ThLZ* 23 (1934), 416–18.

Fietz, L., *Strukturalismus. Eine Einführung.* Literaturwissenschaft im Grundstu-dium 15. Tübingen: Gunter Narr Verlag, 1982.

Fitzmyer, J. A., *The Genesis Apocryphon of Qumran Cave I. A Commentary.* Ro-me: Biblical Institute Press, [2]1971.

- *The Gospel According to Luke I-IX. Introduction, Translation, and Notes.* AB 28. New York: Doubleday, 1981.

Flusser, D., "Healing through the Laying-on of Hands in a Dead Sea Scroll," *IEJ* 7 (1957), 107–8.

Fraenkel, D, U. Quast, and J. W. Wevers, "Geleitwort," in idem (eds.), *Studien zur Septuaginta - Robert Hanhart zu Ehren. Aus Anlaß seines 65. Geburtstages* (Göttingen: Vandenhoeck & Ruprecht, 1990), 9–18.

Frankemölle, H., "Exegese und Linguistik - Methodenprobleme neuerer exege-tischer Veröffentlichungen," *ThR* 71 (1975), 1–12.

Fridrichsen, A. J., *Le problème du miracle dans le christianisme primitif.* EHPhR 12. Strasbourg/Paris: Librairie Istra 1925.

Friedrich, G., "δύναμαι," *ExWNT* 1 (1980), 858–60.

- "δύναμις," *ExWNT* 1 (1980), 860–67.

Fuller, R. H., *Interpreting the Miracles.* Philadelphia: Westminster, 1963.

Funk, R. W., "The Form of the NT Healing Miracle Story," *Semeia* 12 (1978), 57–96.

Garrett, S. R., *"Magic and Miracle in Luke-Acts."* Ph. D. diss., Yale University, 1988.

Geller, J. M., "Jesus' Theurgic Powers: Parallels in the Talmud and Incantation Bowls," *JJSt* 28 (1977), 141–55.

Genuyt, F., "La résurrection de Lazare. Evangile de Jean. Analyse sémiotique du chapitre 11," *SB* 44 (1986), 18–37.

George, A., "Miracles dans le monde hellénistique," X. Léon-Dufour (ed.), *Les Miracles*, 95–108.

Georgi, D., *The Opponents of Paul in Second Corinthians*. Philadelphia: Fortress Press, 1986 (tr. from the revised German edition of 1964).

Glöckner, R., *Neutestamentliche Wundergeschichten und das Lob der Wundertaten Gottes in den Psalmen. Studien zur sprachlichen and theologischen Verwandtschaft zwischen neutestamentlichen Wundergeschichten und Psalmen*. Walberberger Studien, Theologische Reihe 13. Mainz: Matthias-Grünewald-Verlag, 1983.

Gnilka, J., *Das Evangelium nach Markus. 1. Teilband Mk 1–8, 26*. EKK 2,1. Zürich/Neukirchen-Vluyn: Benziger Verlag/Neukirchener Verlag, 1978.

Goldin, J., "On Honi the Circle-Maker: A Demanding Prayer," *HTHR* 56 (1963), 233–73.

Goppelt, L., *Theologie des Neuen Testaments*. Ed. by J. Roloff. Göttingen: Vandenhoeck & Ruprecht, ³1985.

Gray, J., *I & II Kings. A Commentary*. OTL. Philadelphia, PA: Westminster Press, 1963.

Green, W. S., "Palestinian Holy Men: Charismatic Leadership and Rabbinic Tradition," *ANRW* 2,19,2 (1979), 619–47.

Greimas, A. J., "Eléments pour une théorie de l'interprétation du récit mythique," *Communications* 8 (1966), 28–59.

- "Elemente einer narrativen Grammatik," H. Blumensath (ed.), *Strukturalismus in der Literaturwissenschaft* (Köln: Kiepenheuer & Witsch, 1972), 47–67.

- *Structural Semantics. An Attempt at a Method*. Lincoln: University of Nebraska Press, 1983 (French orig. 1966).

- *Maupassant. The Semiotics of Text. Practical Exercises*. Amsterdam/Philadelphia: John Benjamins Publ. Comp., 1988 (French orig. 1976).

- and J. Courtés, *semiotique. dictionnaire raisonné de la théorie du langage*. LLC. Paris: Hachette, 1979; ET: *Semiotics and Language. An Analytical Dictionary*. Bloomington, Indiana: University Press, 1982.

Grelot, P., "Les miracles de Jésus et la démonologie Juive," X. Léon-Dufour (ed.), *Les Miracles*, 59–72.

Groß, K., *Menschenhand und Gotteshand in Antike und Christentum*. Ed. by W. Speyer. Stuttgart: Anton Hiersemann Verlag, 1985.

Groupe d'Entrevernes, *Signes et paraboles: sémiotique et texte évangélique*. Paris: Éditions du Seuil, 1977. ET: 1978.

- *Analyse sémiotique des textes. Introduction. Théorie-Pratique*. Lyon: Press Universitaires, 1979.

Grundmann, W., article "δύναμαι, δύναμις," in *ThWNT* 2 (1935), 286–318.

Güttgemanns, E., *Offene Fragen zur Formgeschichte des Evangeliums. Eine methodologische Skizze der Grundlagenproblematik der Form- und Redaktionsgeschichte*. BEvTh 54. München: Chr. Kaiser Verlag, 1970.

- "Einleitende Bemerkungen zur strukturalen Erzählforschung," *LingBibl* 23/24 (1973), 2–47.

- "Narrative Analyse synoptischer Texte," *LingBibl* 25/26 (1973), 50–72.

- "Fundamentals of a Grammar of Oral Literature," H. Jason and D. Segal (eds.), *Patterns in Oral Literature*, 77–97.

- "Strukturale Erzählforschung und Ideologie," *LingBibl* 53 (1983), 9–44

Guttmann, A., "The Significance of Miracles for Talmudic Judaism," *HUCA* 20 (1947), 363–406.

Gutwenger, E., "Die Machterweise Jesu in formgeschichtlicher Sicht," *ZKTh* 89 (1967), 176–90.

Habicht, C., *Die Inschriften des Asklepieions*. Vol. 8,3. Berlin: De Gruyter, 1969.

Haenchen, E., *Die Apostelgeschichte*. Kritisch-exegetischer Kommentar zum Neuen Testament, Abt. 3. Göttingen: Vandenhoeck & Ruprecht, ⁵1965.

Hahn, F., *Christologische Hoheitstitel*. FRLANT 83. Göttingen: Vandenhoeck & Ruprecht, ³1966.

Hanhart, R., *Text und Textgeschichte des Buches Tobit*. MSU 27. Göttingen: Vandenhoeck & Ruprecht, 1984.

Hanson, A.T., "Handauflegung I. Altes Testament/Judentum/Neues Testament/Religionsgeschichtlich," *TRE* 14 (1985), 415–22.

Harnisch, W., *Die Gleichniserzählungen Jesu. Eine hermeneutische Einführung*. Göttingen: Vandenhoeck & Ruprecht, ²1990.

Hegermann, H., "σοφία," *ExWNT* 3 (1983), 616–24.

– "σοφός," in *ExWNT* 3 (1983), 624–26.

Heinemann, I., "Die Kontroverse über das Wunder im Judentum der hellenistischen Zeit," A. Schreiber (ed.), *Jubilee Volume in Honour of Prof. Bernhard Heller*. Budapest 1941, 170–91.

Heitmüller, W., *"Im Namen Jesu." Eine sprach- und religionsgeschichtliche Untersuchung zum Neuen Testament, speziell zur altchristlichen Taufe*. Göttingen: Vandenhoeck & Ruprecht, 1903.

Held, H.J., "Matthäus als Interpret der Wundergeschichten," G. Bornkamm, G. Barth and H.J. Held, *Überlieferung und Auslegung im Matthäusevangelium*. WMANT 1. Neukirchen: Neukirchener Verlag, 1960, 155–287.

Hempel, J., "Religionsgeschichtliche Schule," ³*RGG* 5 (1961), 991–94.

Hengel, M. and R., "Die Heilungen Jesu und medizinisches Denken," A. Suhl (ed.), *Der Wunderbegriff im Neuen Testament*. Wege der Forschung 295. Darmstadt: Wissenschaftliche Buchgesellschaft, 1980, 338–73 (orig. 1959).

Hengel, M., *Judentum und Hellenismus. Studien zu ihrer Begegnung unter besonderer Berücksichtigung Palästinas bis zur Mitte des 2. Jh. v. Chr.* WUNT 10. Tübingen: Mohr (P. Siebeck), 1969.

Henrichs, A., "Vespasian's Visit to Alexandria," *ZPE* 3 (1968), 51–80.

Holladay, C.R., *Theios Aner in Hellenistic-Judaism: A Critique of the Use of This Category in New Testament Christology*. Atlanta: Scholars Press, 1977.

Honko, L., "Traditional Barriers and Adaption of Tradition," *Ethnologia Scandinavia: A Journal for Nordic Ethnology* (1973), 32–49.

– "The Formation of Ecotypes," N. Burkaloff and C. Lindahl, (eds.), *Folklore on Two Continents: Essays in Honor of Lindahl Dégh*. Bloomington: Trickster Press, 1980, 280–85.

Hornig, G., *Die Anfänge der historisch-kritischen Theologie. Johann Salomo Semlers Schriftverständnis und seine Stellung zu Luther*. Göttingen: Vandenhoeck & Ruprecht, 1961.

Horst, P.W. van der, *Aelius Aristides and the New Testament*, Leiden, 1980.

– Book review: "Mills, M.E.: Human Agents of Cosmic Power in Hellenistic Judaism and the Synoptic Tradition," *ThLZ* 116 (1991), 431–32.

Hruby, K., "Perspectives rabbinique sur le miracle," X. Léon-Dufour (ed.), *Les Miracles*, 73–94.

Hull, J. M., *Hellenistic Magic and the Synoptic Tradition*. Naperville, IL: Alec R. Allenson Inc., 1974.

Iber, G., "Zur Formgeschichte der Evangelien," *ThR* N. F. 24 (1956/57), 283–338.

Jason, H., "The Problem of 'Tale Role' and 'Character' in Propp's Work," idem, D. Segal (ed.), *Patterns in Oral Literature*. The Hague/Paris: Mouton & Co., 1977, appendix I, 313–20.

- and A. Kempinski, "How old are Folktales?," *Fabula* 22 (1981), 1–27.
- "Genre in Folk Literature: Reflections on Some Questions and Problems," *Fabula* 27 (1986), 167–94.

Jeremias, J., *Neutestamentliche Theologie. Erster Teil: Die Verkündigung Jesu.* Gütersloh: Verlagshaus Gerd Mohn, 1971, ⁴1988.

Jirku, A. *Die Dämonen und ihre Abwehr im Alten Testament*. Leipzig: A. Deichert'sche Verlagsbuchhandlung, 1912.

Jobling, D., *The Sense of Biblical Narrative: Three Structural Analyses in the Old Testament*. JSOTSS 7. Sheffield, England: JSOT Press, 1978.
- *The Sense of Biblical Narrative II: Structural Analysis in the Hebrew Bible*. JSOTSS 39. Sheffield, England: JSOT Press, 1986.

Johnson, L. T., *The Writings of the New Testament. An Interpretation*. Philadelphia: Fortress Press, ³1988.

Jüttner, G., "Heilmittel," *RAC* 14 (1988), 249–74.

Kanda, S. H., "*The Form and Function of the Petrine and Pauline Miracle Stories in the Acts of the Apostles.*" Ph. D. diss., Claremont Graduate School, 1974.

Käsemann, E., "Wunder IV. Im NT," *RGG* 6 (³1962), 1835–37.

Kazmierski, C. R., "Evangelist and Leper: A Socio-Cultural Study of Mark 1.40–45," *NTSt* 38 (1992), 37–50.

Kee, H. C., "The Terminology of Mark's Exorcism Stories," *NTSt* 14 (1967), 232–46.
- *Miracle in the Early Christian World. A Study in Sociohistorical Method*. New Haven, CN: Yale University Press, 1983.
- *Medicine, Miracle and Magic in New Testament Times*. Cambridge/London: Cambridge University Press, 1986.

Kerényi, K., *Der göttliche Arzt. Studien über Asklepios und seine Kultstätten*. Darmstadt: Wissenschaftliche Buchgesellschaft, ²1956.

Kertelge, K., *Die Wunder Jesu im Markusevangelium. Eine redaktionsgeschichtliche Untersuchung*. STANT 23. München: Kösel-Verlag, 1970.
- "*Die Wunder Jesu in der neueren Exegese*," *Theol. Berichte* 5 (1976), 71–105.

Kilian, R., "Die Totenauferweckungen Elias und Elisas – eine Motivwanderung?," *BZ* 10 (1966), 44–56.

Kirchschläger, W., "Exorzismus in Qumran?," *Kairos* 18 (1976), 135–53.

Kleinknecht, H., F. Baumgärtel, W. Bieder, E. Sjöberg and E. Schweizer, "πνεῦμα, etc.," in *ThWNT* 6 (1959), 330–453.

Klostermann, E., *Die Synoptiker*. HNT 2,1. Tübingen: J. C. B. Mohr, 1919.

Koch, D.-A., *Die Bedeutung der Wundererzählungen für die Christologie des Markusevangeliums*. BZNW 42. Berlin: de Gruyter, 1975.

Koehler, L., *Das formgeschichtliche Problem des Neuen Testaments.* Tübingen: J. C. B. Mohr (Paul Siebeck), 1927.

Kolenkow, A. B., "Relationships between Miracle and Prophecy in the Greco-Roman World and Early Christianity," *ANRW* 2, 23, 2 (1980), 1471–1506.

Kollesch, J., "Medizin," *Der kleine Pauly* 5 (1997), 1624–28.

Kollmann, B., *"Jesu Schweigegebote an die Dämonen,"* *ZNW* 82 (1991), 267–73.

- Book review of "Blackburn, *Theios Anēr*," ThLZ 117 (1992), 351–53.

Korol, D., "Handauflegung II (ikonographisch)," *RAC* 13 (1986), 493–519.

Kosmala, H., "גבר etc.," *ThWAT 1 (1973), 901–919.*

Köster, H., "Formgeschichte/Formkritik II. Neues Testament," *TRE* 11 (1983), 286–99.

Kötting, B., "Epidauros," *RAC* 5 (1961), 531–36.

Kratz, R., *Rettungswunder. Motiv-, traditions- und formkritische Aufarbeitung einer Gattung.* Europäische Hochschulschriften XXIII, 123. Frankfurt am Main: Verlag Peter Lang, 1979.

Kremers, H., "Die Ethik der galiläischen Chassidim und die Ethik Jesu," K. Ebert (ed.), *Alltagswelt und Ethik.* Wuppertal: Peter Hammer Verlag, 1988, 143–56.

Krüger, H. P., "Aramäisch II. Im Neuen Testament," *TRE* 3 (1978), 602–9.

Kreyenbuhl, J., "Ursprung und Stammbaum eines biblischen Wunders," *ZNW* 16 (1909), 265–76.

Kudlien, F., "Anatomie," *Der kleine Pauly* 1 (1979), 335–36.

- "Asklepiades," *Der kleine Pauly* 1 (1979), 117.

- "Chirurgie," *Der kleine Pauly* 1 (1979), 1150.

- "Herophilos I," *Der kleine Pauly* 2 (1979), 1109–10.

- "Erasistratos," *Der kleine Pauly* 2 (1979), 343–44.

- "Heilkunde," *RAC* 14 (1988), 223–49.

Kümmel, W. G., *Das Neue Testament. Geschichte der Erforschung seiner Probleme.* Freiburg/München: Verlag Karl Alber, 1958.

- *"Jesusforschung seit 1965. IV. Bergpredigt - Gleichnisse - Wunderberichte (mit Nachträgen),"* *ThR* 43 (1978), 105–61.

Leeper, E. A., *"Exorcism in Early Christianity."* Ph. D. diss., Duke University, 1991.

Légasse, S., "L'historien en quête de l'évènement," Léon-Dufour (ed.), *Les Miracles*, 109–45.

Leipoldt, J., "Wunder und Zauber im Urchristentum," *ZKG* 54 (1935), 1–11.

Léon-Dufour, X., "Structure et Fonction du Récit de Miracle," idem (ed.), *Les Miracles*, 289–353.

- (ed.), *Les Miracles de Jésus selon le Nouveau Testament.* Paris: Éditions du Seuil, 1977.

Lévi-Strauss, C., "Structure and Form: Reflexions on a Work by Vladimir Propp," V. Propp, *Theory and History*, 167–88.

Lindars, B., "Elijah, Elisha and the Gospel Miracles," C. F. D. Moule (ed.), *Miracles*, 63–79.

- "Rebuking the Spirit. A New Analysis of the Lazarus Story of John 11," *NTSt* 38 (1992), 89–104.

Lindner, M. and M. Pfister, "Structuralism in Germany: A Survey of Recent Developments," *Structuralist Review* 2 (1980), 88–119.

Löffler, I., *Die Melampodie*. Beiträge zur klassischen Philologie 7. Meinsenheim am Glau: A. Hain, 1963. (1963).

Lohmeyer, E., *Galiläa und Jerusalem*. Göttingen: Vandenhoeck & Ruprecht, 1936.

Lohse, E., "χείϱ, etc.," *ThWNT* 9 (1973), 413-27.

Long, B.O., "The Social Setting for Prophetic Miracle Stories," *Semeia* 3 (1975), 46-63.

– *1 Kings with an Introduction to Historical Literature*. FOTL 9. Grand Rapids, Michigan: William B. Eerdmans, 1984.

– *2 Kings*. FOTL 10. Grand Rapids, Michigan: William B. Eerdmans, 1991.

Loos, H. van der, *The Miracles of Jesus*. SNT 9. Leiden: E.J. Brill, 1965.

Luck, G., *Arcana Mundi. Magic and Occult in the Greek and Roman Worlds*. Baltimore: The John Hopkins University Press, 1985.

Lührmann, D., "Rudolf Bultmann and the History of Religion School," T.W. Jennings (ed.), *Text and Logos. The Humanistic Interpretation of the New Testament*. FS H. Boers. Scholars Press Homage Series. Atlanta, GA: Scholars Press, 1990, 3-14.

Luz, U., "Das Geheimnismotiv und die markinische Christologie," *ZNW* 56 (1965), 9-30.

– *Das Evangelium nach Matthäus (Mt 8-17)*. EKK I/2. Zürich: Benziger Verlag, 1990.

Maehler, H., *Die Lieder des Bakchylides. Erster Teil. Die Siegeslieder. II. Kommentar*. Leiden: E.J. Brill, 1982.

Maier, J., "Geister (Dämonen): B. III. b. Frühes u. hellenistisches Judentum," *RAC* 9 (1976), 626-40.

Maisch, I., *Die Heilung des Gelähmten: Eine exegetisch-traditionsgeschichtliche Untersuchung zu Mk 2, 1-12*. SBS 52. Stuttgart: Katholisches Bibelwerk 1971.

McCasland, S.v., "The Asclepius Cult in Palestine," *JBL* 58 (1939), 221-27.

– "Religious Healing in First Century Palestine," T.J. McNeill et al. (ed.), *Environmental Factors in Christian History*. Chicago, IL: University of Chicago Press, 1939, 18-34.

McGinley, L.J., *Form-Criticism of the Synoptic Healing Narratives. A Study in the Theories of Martin Dibelius and Rudolf Bultmann*. Woodstock, Maryland: Woodstock College Press, 1944.

Meyer, E., "Epidauros," *Der kleine Pauly* 2 (1979), 303-5.

Meyer, R., "Das Gebet des Nabonid. Eine in den Qumran-Handschriften wiederentdeckte Weisheitserzählung," W. Bernhardt (ed.), *Zur Geschichte und Theologie des Judentums in hellenistisch-römischer Zeit. Ausgewählte Abhandlungen von Rudolf Meyer*. Neukirchen: Neukirchener Verlag, 1991, 71-129.

Mills, M.E., *Human Agents of Cosmic Power in Hellenistic Judaism and the Synoptic Tradition*. JSNTSS 41. Sheffield, England: JSOT Press, 1990.

Milne, P.J., *Vladimir Propp and the Study of Structure in Hebrew Biblical Narrative*. Bible and Literature Series 13. Sheffield, England: Academic Press, 1988.

Milot, L., "Guérison d'une femme infirme un jour de Sabbat (Luc 13, 10-17). L'importance d'une comparaison," *SB* 39 (1985), 23-33.

Moule, C.F.D. (ed.), *Miracles. Cambridge Studies in their Philosophy and History*. London: A.R. Mowbray & Co. LTD, 1965.

- "Excursus 2. The Classification of Miracle Stories," idem (ed.), *Miracles*, 239–43.
Müller, H.P., "Die Wurzeln עִיק, יָעַק und עוק," *VT* 21 (1971), 561.
Müller, K., *Das Judentum in der religionsgeschichtlichen Arbeit am Neuen Testament. Eine kritische Rückschau auf die Entwicklung einer Methodik bis zu den Qumranfunden.* Judentum und Umwelt 6. Frankfurt/Bern: Peter Lang, 1983.
- "Die religionsgeschichtliche Methode. Erwägungen zu ihrem Verständnis und zur Praxis ihrer Vollzüge an neutestamentlichen Texten," *BZ* NF 29 (1985), 161–92.
Nehrbass, R., *Sprache und Stil der Iamata von Epidauros. Eine sprachwissenschaftliche Untersuchung. Philologus, Suppl. XXVII 4.* Leipzig: Dieterich'sche Verlagsbuchhandlung, 1935.
Neirynck, F., "The Miracle Stories in the Acts of the Apostles. An Introduction," F.v. Segbroeck (ed.), *Evangelica. Gospel Studies – Études D'Évangile. Collected Essays.* Leuwen: University Press, 1982, 835–80.
Neusner, J., "The Use of the Later Rabbinic Evidence for the Study of First-Century Pharisaism," W.S. Green (ed.), *Approaches to Ancient Judaism: Theory and Practice.* Brown Judaic Studies 1. Missoula, Montana: Scholars Press, 1979, 215–28.
- "Current Events in the Study of Rabbinic Sources," idem, *Invitation to the Talmud. A Teaching Book.* New York: Harper & Row, [2]1984, 329–50.
Noy, D., "The Jewish Versions of the 'Animal Languages' Folktale (AT 670). A Typological-Structural Study," J. Heinemann and D. Noy (eds.), Studies in Aggadah and Folk-Literature. Jerusalem: At the Magnes Press, 1971, 171–208.
Oepke, A., Art. "ἰάομαι etc.," *ThWNT* 3 (1938), 194–215.
Osswaldt, E., "Beobachtungen zur Erzählung von Abrahams Aufenthalt in Ägypten im 'Genesis-Apocryphon'," *ZAW* 72 (1969), 7–25.
Patte, D., *What is Structural Exegesis?* Guides to Biblical Scholarship. New Testament Series. Minneapolis, Philadelphia: Fortress Press, 1976.
- *The Gospel According to Matthew: A Structural Commentary on Matthew's Faith.* Philadelphia, PA: Fortress Press, 1987.
- *Structural Exegesis for New Testament Critics.* Minneapolis/Philadelphia: Fortress Press, 1990.
- *The Religious Dimensions of Biblical Texts. Greimas's Structural Semiotics and Biblical Exegesis.* SBL Semeia Studies. Atlanta: Scholars Press 1990.
Peek, W., "Fünf Wundergeschichten aus dem Asklepion von Epidauros," *Abhandlungen der Sächsischen Akademie der Wissenschaften zu Leipzig. Phil.-hist. Klasse,* Vol. 56,3. Berlin: Akademie-Verlag, 1964.
Perels, O., *Die Wunderüberlieferung der Synoptiker in ihrem Verhältnis zur Wortüberlieferung.* Stuttgart: Kohlhammer, 1934.
Pesch, R., *Der Besessene von Gerasa. Entstehung und Überlieferung einer Wundergeschichte.* SBS 56. Stuttgart: Katholisches Bibelwerk, 1972.
- *Das Markusevangelium.* Vol. 1 and 2. HThKNT 2. Freiburg: Herder, 1976-1977.
- and R. Kratz, *So liest man synoptisch. Anleitung und Kommentar zum Studium der synoptischen Evangelien,* Vol. II: "Exorzismen-Heilungen-Totenerweckungen," Vol. III: "Rettungswunder-Geschenkwunder-Normenwunder-Fernheilungen." Frankfurt am Main: Josef Knecht, 1976.

Peterson, E., EIS ΘΕΟΣ. Epigraphische, formgeschichtliche und religionsge-schichtliche Untersuchungen. FRLANT N.F. 24. Göttingen: Vandenhoeck & Ruprecht, 1926.

Petzke, G., *Die Traditionen über Apollonius von Tyana und das Neue Testament.* Studia ad corpus Hellenisticum Novi Testamenti 1. Leiden: E.J. Brill, 1970.

– "Historizität und Bedeutsamkeit von Wundergeschichten. Möglichkeiten und Grenzen des religionsgeschichtlichen Vergleiches," H.D. Betz and L. Schott-roff (eds.), *Neues Testament und christliche Existenz.* FS H. Braun. Tübingen: J.C.B. Mohr (P. Siebeck), 1973, 367–85.

– "Die historische Frage nach den Wundertaten Jesu dargestellt am Beispiel des Exorzismus Mark. IX. 14–29 par," *NTS* 22 (1975/76), 180–204.

– *Das Sondergut des Evangeliums nach Lukas.* Zürcher Werkkommentare zur Bibel. Zürich: Theologischer Verlag, 1990.

Pike, K.L., *Language in Relation to a Unified Theory of Human Behavior. Vol. I-III. The Hague/Paris: Mouton & Co,* ²1967 (orig. 1954–1960).

Pfister, F., "Epode," *PW* Suppl. 4 (1924), 323–44.

Preisendanz, K., "Aberglaube," *Der kleine Pauly* 1 (1975), 8–12.

Preisigke, F., "Die Gotteskraft der frühchristlichen Zeit," *Der Wunderbegriff im Neuen Testament.* Darmstadt: Wissenschaftliche Buchgesellschaft, 1980 (re-print of the original from 1922), 210–47.

Pritchard, J.B., "Motifs of Old Testament Miracles," Crozer Quarterly 27 (1950), 97–109.

Propp, V., *The Morphology of the Folktale.* Austin/London: University of Texas, ⁵1975.

– "The Principles of Classifying Folklore Genres," A. Liberman (ed.), *Theory and History of Folklore.* Minneapolis, MN: The University of Minnesota Press, 1984, 39–47 (orig. 1964).

Puech, E., "11QPsApª: Un rituel d'éxorcismes. Essai de reconstruction," *RevQ* 55 (1990), 377–403.

"Récits de miracles et récit évangelique. Remarques de grammaires narrative," *S&B* 10 (1979) [without a reference to the author], 27–44.

Rehm, M., *Das erste Buch der Könige. Ein Kommentar.* Würzburg: Echter Verlag 1979.

– *Das zweite Buch der Könige. Ein Kommentar.* Würzburg: Echter Verlag 1982.

Reitzenstein, R., *Hellenistische Wundererzählungen.* Stuttgart: B.G. Teubner, 1906.

Rengstorf, K.H., *Die Anfänge der Auseinandersetzung zwischen Christusglaube und Asklepios-frömmigkeit.* Schriften der Gesellschaft zur Förderung der West-fälischen Landesuniversität zu Münster 30. Münster: Aschendorff, 1953.

– "σημεῖον, etc.," *ThWNT* 7 (1964), 199–268.

Richter, W., *Exegese als Literaturwissenschaft. Entwurf einer alttestamentlichen Li-teraturtheorie und Methodologie.* Göttingen: Vandenhoeck & Ruprecht, 1971.

Ringgren, H., "נוּן,"in *ThWAT* 5 (1086), 318–22.

Robbins, V., "The Healing of Blind Bartimaeus (10: 46–52) in the Marcan Theo-logy," *JBL* 92 (1973), 224–43.

Roloff, J., *Das Kerygma und der irdische Jesus. Historische Motive in den Jesus-Erzählungen der Evangelien.* Göttingen: Vandenhoeck & Ruprecht, 1970.

Ruiz-Montero, C., "The Structural Pattern of Ancient Greek Romances and the Morphology of the Folktale by V. Propp," *Fabula* 22 (1981), 183–213.

Rüttimann, R.J., *"Asclepius and Jesus: The Form, Character and Status of the Asclepius Cult in the second-century CE and its influence on Early Christianity."* Th.D. diss., Harvard University, 1986.

Sabourin, L., "Hellenistic and Rabbinic 'Miracles'," *BThB* 2 (1972), 281–307.

Sandmel, S., "Parallelomania," *JBL* 81 (1962), 1–13.

Schenke, L. *Die Wundererzählungen des Markusevangeliums.* SBB 33. Stuttgart: Katholisches Bibelwerk, 1974.

Schille, G., *Die urchristliche Wundertradition. Ein Beitrag zur Frage nach dem irdischen Jesus.* Arbeiten zur Theologie I, 29. Stuttgart: Calwer Verlag, 1967.

– Book review: "G. Theißen, Urchristliche Wundergeschichten," *ThLZ* 100 (1975), 430–33.

– "Zur Relation von Linguistik und Formgeschichte," *ThLZ* 115 (1990), 87–93.

Schlatter, A., *Das Wunder in der Synagoge. Gütersloh: Bertelsmann, 1912.*

Schmidt, K.L., *Der Rahmen der Geschichte Jesu. Literarkritische Untersuchungen zur ältesten Jesusüberlieferung.* Berlin: Trowitzsch & Sohn, 1919.

Schmithals, W., "Kritik der Formkritik," *ZThK* 77 (1980), 149–85.

– *Wunder und Glaube. Eine Auslegung von Markus 4, 35–6,6a.* Biblische Studien 59. Neukirchen-Vluyn: Neukirchener Verlag, 1970.

Scholtissek, K., *Die Vollmacht Jesu. Traditions- und redaktionsgeschichtliche Analysen zu einem Leitmotiv markinischer Christologie.* Neutestamentliche Abhandlungen, N.F. 25. Münster: Aschendorffsche Verlagsbuchhandlung, 1992.

Schottroff, W., "Gottmensch I (Alter Orient u. Judentum)," *RAC* 12 (1983), 155–234.

Schubert, K., "Wunderberichte und ihr Kerygma in der rabbinischen Tradition," *Kairos* 24 (1982), 31–37.

Seybold, K., *Das Gebet des Kranken im Alten Testament. Untersuchungen zur Bestimmung und Zuordnung der Krankheits- und Heilungspsalmen.* BWANT 5. Folge 19. Stuttgart: Verlag W. Kohlhammer, 1973.

– and U. Müller, *Sickness & Healing.* Biblical Encounters Series. Nashville,TN: Abingdon, 1981 (German orig. 1978).

Smith, M., "A Comparison of Early Christian and Early Rabbinic Tradition," *JBL* 82 (1963), 169–76.

– "Prolegomena to a Discussion of Aretalogies, Divine Men, the Gospels and Jesus," *JBL* 90 (1971), 174–99.

– *Jesus the Magician.* San Francisco: Harper & Row, 1978.

Stipp, H.-J., *Elischa – Propheten – Gottesmänner. Die Kompositionsgeschichte des Elischazyklus und verwandter Texte, rekonstruiert auf der Basis von Text- und Literarkritik zu 1 Kön 20.22 und 2 Kön 2–7.* St. Ottilien: EOS Verlag, 1987.

Strack, H.L., *Introduction to the Talmud and the Midrash.* Philadelphia, PA: The Jewish Publication Society Press, 1931.

Strauss, D.Fr., *Das Leben Jesu, kritisch bearbeitet*, Vol. I/II. Tübingen: Verlag C.F. Osiander, 1835/1836.

Strecker, G. and U. Schnelle, Einführung in die neutestamentliche Exegese. Göttingen: Vandenhoeck & Ruprecht, 1983.

Suhl, A. (ed.), *Der Wunderbegriff im Neuen Testament.* Darmstadt: Wissenschaftliche Buchgesellschaft, 1980.

Sydow, C.W. von, "Geography and Folk-Tale Oicotypes," in L. Bødker (ed.),

C. W. von Sydow, Selected Papers on Folklore. Copenhagen: Rosenkilde and Bagger, 1948, 44–59.

- "Popular Prose Traditions and Their Classification," in ibid., 127–45.

Taylor, V., The Transformation of the Gospel Tradition. Eight Lectures. London: MacMillian and Co., 1933. ²1935.

Theißen, G., Urchristliche Wundergeschichten. Ein Beitrag zur formgeschichtlichen Erforschung der synoptischen Evangelien. Gütersloh: Verlagshaus G. Mohn, 1974. ⁵1987.

- "Lokal- und Sozialkolorit in der Geschichte von der syrophönizischen Frau (Mk 7, 24–30)," ZNW 75 (1984), 202–25.

Tiede, D. L., The Charismatic Figure as Miracle Worker. SBLDS 1. Missoula, Montana: Society of Biblical Literature, 1972.

Thiel, H. van, Der Eselsroman. I. Untersuchungen. München: C. H. Beck'sche Verlagsbuchhandlung, 1971.

Thraede, K., "Exorzismus," RAC 7 (1969), 44–117.

Todorov, T., "Les catégories du récit littéraire," Communications 8 (1966), 125–51.

Trummer, P., Die blutende Frau. Wunderheilungen im Neuen Testament. Freiburg: Herder, 1991.

Turiot, C., "La Guérison de Naaman. Analyse du Texte de 2 Rois 5, Versets 1 ag 27," SB 16 (1979), 8–32.

Vermes, G., Jesus the Jew. A Historian's Reading of the Gospels. New York: Macmillian, 1973.

- "Hanina ben Dosa," idem, Post-Biblical Jewish Studies. Leiden: E.J. Brill, 1975, 178–214.

Vielhauer, Ph., Geschichte der urchristlichen Literatur. Berlin: de Gruyter, 1978.

Vogel, C., "Handauflegung I (liturgisch)," RAC 13 (1986), 482–493.

Wachsmuth, D., "Wunderglaube, -täter," in Der kleine Pauly 5 (1975), 1395–98.

Wegner, U., Der Hauptmann von Kafernaum (Mt 7, 28a; 8, 5–10. 13 par Lk 7, 1–10). Ein Beitrag zur Q-Forschung. WUNT 2. Reihe, 14. Tübingen: J. C. B. Mohr (P. Siebeck), 1985.

Weimar, P., "Formen frühjüdischer Literatur," J. Maier and J. Schreiner (eds.), Literatur und Religion des Frühjudentums. Würzburg: Echter Verlag, 1973, 123–62.

Weinreich, O., Antike Heilungswunder. Untersuchungen zum Wunderglauben der Griechen und Römer. GVV. Giessen: Verlag A. Töpelmann, 1909.

- "Gebet und Wunder. Zwei Abhandlungen zur Religions- und Literaturge-schichte," TBA, 5. Heft (1929), 169–464, reprinted in idem, Religionsgeschicht-liche Studien. Darmstadt: Wissenschaftliche Buchgesellschaft, 1968, 1–298.

- "Zum Wundertypus der συναναχρωσις," ARW 32 (1935), 246–64.

Wendland, P., Die hellenistisch-römische Kultur in ihren Beziehungen zu Judentum und Christentum. HNT I/2. Tübingen: J. C. B. Mohr (Paul Siebeck), 2/31912.

- Die urchristlichen Literaturformen. HNT I/3. Tübingen: J. C. B. Mohr (Paul Siebeck), 2/31912.

Wenham, D. and C. Blomberg (eds.), The Miracles of Jesus. Gospel Perspectives 5. Sheffield, England: JSOT Press, 1986.

Westermann, C., "Sinn und Grenze religionsgeschichtlicher Parallelen," ThLZ 60 (1965), 489–96.

Wiefel, W., *Das Evangelium nach Lukas*. ThHkNT 3. Berlin: Evangelische Verlagsanstalt, 1987.

Winkler, J. J., *Auctor & Actor: A Narratological Reading of Apuleius's The Golden Ass*. Berkley/Los Angeles, CA: University of California Press, 1985.

Wire, A. C., "The Structure of the Gospel Miracle Stories and their Tellers," *Semeia* 11 (1976), 83–113.

Wounde, A. S. van der, "שׁם," *ThWNT* 2 (1976), 935–63.

Würthwein, E., *Die Bücher der Könige. 1. Kön. 17–2. Kön. 25*. ATD 11, 2. Göttingen: Vandenhoeck & Ruprecht, 1984.

Zan, Y., "The Scientific Motivation for the Structural Analysis of Folktales," *Fabula* 30 (1989), 205–29.

Zeller, D., "Wunder und Bekenntnis. Zum Sitz im Leben urchristlicher Wundergeschichten," *BZ* 25 (1981), 204–22.

Zintzen, C., "Mantik, Mantis," *Der kleine Pauly* 3 (1975), 968–976.

- "Zauberei (μαγεία), Zauberer (μάγος)," *Der kleine Pauly* 5 (1975), 1460–72.

- "Geister (Dämonen): B. III. c. Hellenistische u. kaiserliche Philosophie," *RAC* 9 (1976), 640–668.

Zmiejewski, J., "δυνατός," *ExWNT* 1 (1980), 868–71.

Forschungen zur Religion und Literatur des Alten und Neuen Testaments

Herausgegeben von Wolfgang Schrage und Rudolf Smend. Eine Auswahl:

Vandenhoeck
& Ruprecht